Encounter, Engagement, and Exchange: How Native Populations of the Americas Transformed the World

SALALM Secretariat
Latin American Library
Tulane University

Encounter, Engagement, and Exchange: How Native Populations of the Americas Transformed the World

Papers of the Fifty-Third Annual Meeting of the
SEMINAR ON THE ACQUISITION OF
LATIN AMERICAN LIBRARY MATERIALS

New Orleans, Louisiana
May 30-June 3, 2008

John B. Wright
Editor

SALALM Secretariat
Latin American Library
Tulane University

ISBN: 0-917617-84-3

Contents

Early and Late Encounters

Indigenous Languages, Books, and Writing

Interpreters, Translators, and Collectors

Documenting Indigenous and Human Rights

Indigenous Influences in the Arts

Library Professional Development

Library Encounters, Engagements, and Exchanges

Preface

The fifty-third Seminar on the Acquisition of Latin American Library Materials (SALALM) met May 30-June 3, 2008 to discuss how the native populations of the Americas transformed the world. Speakers and panelists presented papers examining 1) the encounter of cultures as New World inhabitants came into contact with Old World explorers and adventurers, 2) how these people and cultures engaged each other as they sought to understand or exploit each other, and 3) the exchanges that occurred as a result of the collision of cultures. I hope the reader of these papers will immediately recognize the similarity these themes have with the role we play as librarians. The library represents a new world to many of our patrons. Housed inside its walls is documentary evidence of ideas expressed by people—many of which may seem very foreign to the library user. We provide services to help the library user engage these resources as they encounter the library's holdings. The time spent with our resources allows the library user to exchange ideas with their creators and come away a different person.

While planning the conference program, it was important to me to bring all members of SALALM together daily for a general session. This was my desire so that we could encounter, engage and exchange ideas as a group. Our first such event was the keynote address delivered by Dr. Alfred W. Crosby, Professor Emeritus of History at the University of Texas at Austin, who intrigued conference attendees with a look at the first Americans. Like his book, *The Columbian Exchange*, Crosby's address started the conference off helping us all examine specific issues associated with the results of the New World/Old World confrontation and gain a large perspective for understanding the significance of this meeting of cultures. The second day of the conference program began with an address delivered in a general session in which Frances Karttunen, a Nahuatl expert and author of *Between Worlds: Interpreters, Guides, and Survivors*, explored in broad ways the significant roles played by historical interpreters in helping both the New World and Old World regard one another. The last day of the conference included a general session in which Dan Peters, an author of historical novels on each of the major pre-Columbian civilizations (*The Luck of Huemac*, *Tikal*, and *The Incas*), shared his experience with writing these novels and how the library was a source of information used to get his portrayals right. Each of these speakers helped set the tone for the three main themes of the conference and provided an opportunity for those in attendance to view the large vistas associated with these themes.

The rest of the conference consisted of twenty-four panels in which specifics of encounter, engagement and exchange could be discovered and discussed in more detail. The topics presented in each panel were varied and far-ranging. I believe all readers of these papers will find something of interest to investigate further. A major reason for this variety was the participation of local scholars and faculty associated with the host institution along with SALALM members. Tulane University and The Stone Center for Latin American Studies, along with the libraries to support each institution, has attracted noteworthy scholars who are each doing wonderful things to make indigenous civilizations in the Americas more understood. While all the conference presentations were definitely diverse, the majority centered on a concept that illustrates how indigenous peoples have had a transformative impact on the world. Panels discussed assumptions first formed as these civilizations encountered each other, then how these assumptions entered into the engagement experienced among each culture, discipline, etc. Finally, we see included in the panel presentations discussions of how ideas and disciplines are exchanged and how this exchange enriches all. In addition to these panels, which could be called theme panels, other panels were organized in which our attentions were focused on specific issues related to librarianship—collecting, organizing, teaching, preserving, etc.—as colleagues shared services they offer and how things are done at their own institutions and highlighted specific collections held in their institutions. But even in these panel presentations, we see evidence that, like the interpreters and guides who assisted in the encounter, engagement and exchange, we librarians stand at the nexus of the world of scholarship and the world of the researcher. We provide services that facilitate access of the researcher to the recorded world of the scholar.

This conference helped me appreciate even more the extent of the native civilizations of the Americas and their influence on the rest of the world. I know that I probably still hold a romantic view of these peoples and their cultures; however, participating in this conference helped me develop a more balanced perception and understanding of these people. I believe my hopes for this conference were realized. I believe that each person came away from the conference realizing that the important work we do as book dealers, publishers, and librarians matters. All the acquiring, distributing, publishing, collecting, referencing, teaching, organizing, and preserving of Latin American materials is important not because we are doing it, but because the work we do allows all who access these materials the opportunity to know and understand the peoples who created them. Each of us also came away from the conference with a clearer vision of how we can assist our patrons most by getting out of their way and letting them experience these wonderful cultures as they interact with these marvelous materials themselves.

John B. Wright

Acknowledgements

Hortensia Calvo must be thanked first and foremost. Not only did Hortensia, as the Executive Secretary of SALALM, keep me informed and on task, but she also served as the Chair of the Local Arrangements Committee. That is amazing! She coordinated the Host Institution reception held in the Latin American Library and even arranged for an exhibit of the Codex Tulane, which certainly was a highlight of our conference experience. Hortensia also organized the details for the excellent and very well-appointed *Librero*'s reception held at the Louis XVI Restaurant. The Hotel Monteleone in New Orlean's French Quarter was delightful and had wonderful facilities to make our conference very comfortable and memorable. Everything was fantastic. Hortensia's professional friendship with faculty colleagues at Tulane was of utmost importance. Many of our conference presenters were Tulane faculty members. Their scholarship and insights into indigenous studies and how they are documented added greatly to our conference theme. The willingness of these Tulane colleagues to participate in our conference is directly related to the professional relationship Hortensia has developed with them. Having the conference in New Orleans was a delight. It gave us all an opportunity to see an important American city and how it has dealt with a long history of encounter, engagement and exchange, as well as coping and rebuilding after the horrible devastation experienced as a result of Hurricane Katrina in 2005.

I must also extend my gratitude to Carol Ávila of the SALALM Secretariat who helped process all the conference registration and was such help at the conference. Many thanks must go to the following individuals from the Latin American Library at Tulane University: Erika Anguiano, David Dressing, María Dolores Espinosa, Sean Knowlton and Verónica Sánchez. Others from Tulane University need to be thanked as well: Richard Conway, Amy Guilbeau, Mirzam Handal, Paige Hoffman, Cindy Martínez, Rosary Pérez, Alejandra Sánchez and Aurora Vega. I also express gratitude to the Latin American Library, the Howard-Tilton Memorial Library, and the Stone Center for Latin American Studies of Tulane University, as well as the Harold B. Lee Library of Brigham Young University for their sponsorship of this conference. I thank the sponsors of our opening Book Exhibit Reception: America Reads Spanish, Gale-Cengage Learning and ProQuest. Attendees at the conference are always appreciative of the *Libreros* for the reception they provide and the opportunity that gives us to share time together. I want to thank them for offering us a great time again this year. Of special note, I must thank the following *Libreros* who were special sponsors of our evening at the Louis XVI Restaurant: Casalini Libri, Blackwell North America, Inc., Howard Karno Books, Inc., Librería García Cambeiro, and Libros Latinos.

I also thank the many SALALM members who participated in this conference. Some got involved early by submitting program proposals, others prepared and presented interesting papers, others assisted with the flow of the conference by serving as moderators for individual panels, and others served as rapporteurs, helping us to get summaries prepared for the *SALALM Newsletter* and make digital recordings of each session. Roberto Delgadillo, SALALM's Rapporteur General, deserves many thanks for coordinating these recording responsibilities.

Special thanks go to the professional and attentive staff of the Hotel Monteleone who provided comfortable conference rooms and lodging accommodations. Being situated in an historic hotel, in the historic French Quarter lent a sense of history to the conference.

I express gratitude also to Orchid Mazurkiewicz who, in her role as Chair of SALALM's Editorial Board, has assisted greatly in getting these papers ready for publication. Thanks also to Mark Grover who continues to be a great mentor to me. Sincere gratitude and love also goes to my wife Mary and our children who are a constant source of encouragement, strength and support.

John B. Wright

Keynote Address

1. The First Americans
Alfred W. Crosby

The inadequacy of the image of the American Indian imprinted on my psyche as a boy by American popular culture of the 1930s and 1940s—i.e., the golden age of Hopalong Cassidy, Tom Mix, the Lone Ranger and...Tonto?—is an image of naked savages galloping around and around a covered wagon, screaming bloody murder and waving tomahawks. Its full inadequacy did not come home to me until I grew up and saw for the first time a photo of the enormous mound that pre-Columbian Indians had raised at Cahokia at East Saint Louis, Missouri.

I could ignore the pyramids of Mexico and Peru. They were a long ways off and way down there on the map, south of even New Orleans, wherever that was. (I'm a Yankee.) But this mound—thirty meters high, sixteen acres at the base, with traces of related structures all around it—was in the real America.

Cahokia certainly was not built by a gang of bloodthirsty maniacs, but by a large population of well-organized people. Maybe I had heard speculation that the eastern Mediterranean Phoenicians had crossed the Atlantic, marched a thousand miles inland to Missouri and built Cahokia. Likely? Unlikely? I started reading around, and this morning I want to tell you some of what I have learned.

To start with, let me nominate the American Indians as the greatest of all pioneers. I am interested in the category of pioneers because I am not a political, economic, or military historian, but a bio-historian: the impact of organisms newly arrived in a given area on the resident biota and vice versa can be significant, even spectacular.

To check out American Indians as involved in trans-oceanic, trans-continental biological transfers requires that we go back to the very beginning of our species. We humans, all of us, are African in our origins. Our species first appeared in Africa 150,000–200,000 BP. There were not many of us, and so we—their descendants—are genetically very closely related, more so than the members of most species. Our DNA indicates that we are all, so to speak, cousins.

We were great trekkers. By fifty thousand years ago, we had trekked as far as marsupial Australia but had not reached the New World. By 40,000 BP, the prototypes of American Indians were in central Asia learning how to exist in a cold climate—a requirement for getting to the Americas because the way into the New World led through Siberia and Alaska.

The dating of human arrival to the New World is hard to fix because of two blockages. In the coldest millennia the oceans were lower than they are now. The Bering Strait was dry land, and getting from Siberia to Alaska was possible on foot, but one could get no deeper into North America than Alaska because continental glaciers occupied Alaska and NW Canada.

When the climate warmed, passages through the glaciers or along the ocean shore opened. But the oceans rose, leaving the Bering Strait under water. Even so, Native Americans persisted, and were living in America by no less than 14,000 BP at the latest and probably further back than that.

Whenever their ancestors got here, the uniformity of the DNA of today's American Indians suggests that Native Americans are descendants of only a few thousand Asians. (The Inuit came much more recently and did not mix much with the locals.)

Roughly (very roughly) ten thousand years before the present, the ice advanced again. The low country connecting Siberia and Alaska flooded, isolating the American Indians by themselves with two continents, North and South America, to play with.

They became the greatest pioneers, the greatest frontiersmen of all. Columbus, Captain Cook, Lewis and Clark, etc., were latecomers. American Indians preceded Christopher Columbus by millennia.

Pioneers are often very ecologically influential. They sometimes fail because they are—in body and accompanying micro-life, equipment and custom—not adapted to their new homes. Nor, for that matter, are the members of the ecosystems of their new homes adapted to them. The ancestors of the American Indians changed the ecosystems of regions of the New World profoundly.

The first Indians arrived without domesticated animals except probably for the dog—an Asian creature. They would domesticate some American animals—guinea pigs, llamas, maybe some fowl but nothing as important as the Old World's horses, cattle, sheep, goats, pigs, etc. Why? Perhaps because the New World had few sufficiently adaptable candidates. (We'll return to this again.)

They also arrived without crop plants for two irrefutable reasons. One, the latitudes of Siberia where they hailed from were too far north for farmers. Two, the advance of the ice cut them off from the first developments of farming in southwest Asia before the development of agriculture. They were hunters and gatherers, and had to invent agriculture all by themselves.

Eventually the Indians domesticated a number of plants and a few animals and increased into dense populations in the tropics—i.e., they had independent farming revolutions, and the organisms they domesticated were native to the New World.

The Indians, members of an Old World species, added themselves to the American biota, but did little else to mix the biotas of the Old and New Worlds.

But they may have played an important role in the reduction of the American biota. In the Upper Paleolithic—very roughly ten- to eleven-thousand years ago—no less than half of all the world's species of land mammalian megafauna (animals with adult weights of over 44 kilo/100 pounds) disappeared—mammoths, mastodons, giant sloths, giant bison, giant this, giant that went extinct. As Alfred Russell Wallace, Darwin's great contemporary, recorded, "We live in a zoologically impoverished world, from which all the hugest, and fiercest, and strongest forms have recently disappeared."

Why? Climate changes certainly played a role; this was an age of the advance and retreat of continental glaciers. But megafauna had survived such advances and retreats before, so there must have been some additional factor or factors. Among others, my favorite paleo-geoscientist, Paul S. Martin of the University of Arizona, suggests *Homo sapiens* hunters as the decisive factor—the straw that broke the camel's back—though the energy they commanded to direct at the animals was only as much as human muscles could store.

Some dismiss this theory as absurd. How could scrawny bipeds—human beings—kill millions of huge animals? But consider that big animals have very low birth rates: one doesn't have to kill them all at once, but simply jack their death rate up a bit higher than their birth rate for two or three or four centuries. Consider that human hunters had excellent projectile equipment: spears, *atlatl*, and later the bow and arrow. Consider that the megafauna had no previous experience with death by the thrown projectiles. They didn't know enough to attack or be frightened of little bipeds scampering in the bush. Consider that human elimination of megafauna has happened several times recently, i.e., in the Post-Paleolithic era. In Madagascar and New Zealand, the arrival of human beings within the last two millennia was followed soon after by the disappearance of the most mega of the local megafauna, giant birds three meters high and weighing two hundred and more kilograms. Consider also how human whalers of the age of sail used to kill their immense prey by paddling up to them and sticking them with what were, relative to the size of the whales, knitting needles. Whales did not know, and many still do not, how dangerous people can be. Indeed, we still do not know how ecologically damaging scrawny bipeds can be.

Oh well, who can say what knocked off so many megafauna ten millennia back? But let us not forget the American Indians' hunting prowess and control of fire, i.e., their ability to alter whole landscapes and ecosystems.

Their contribution as practical botanists was unquestionably immense. In domesticating certain American plants, they changed the course of human history. There are scores—probably hundreds—of Amerindian food crops. The most important are maize, beans of many kinds, white potato, sweet potato, manioc (cassava, tapioca), squashes, pumpkin, papaya, guava, avocado, pineapple, tomato, chile peppers, cacao. Of these, the most important for the past few centuries and for today in terms of tonnage produced and devoured per year are maize, white potato, and manioc. I will talk about maize, because of its primary importance.

John Lawson, in South Carolina early in the 17th century, may have been right when he called maize "the most useful grain in the world." It was and is an amazingly generous plant, even without plows or the domesticated animals to pull them. In the tropics its greatest rival among the grains for productivity is rice, but unlike wetland rice, maize does not necessarily require an infrastructure of reservoirs, dikes, and paddies. The Indians cultivated maize with no more than the digging stick, without help from domesticated animals, and with or without irrigation.

Maize kernels can be dried and stored safely for very long periods. Maize makes good beer and good whiskey (though not the latter for the pre-Columbian Indians, who did not distill before 1492). William Cobbett, an early 19th-century agricultural expert and publicist, called maize "the greatest blessing God ever gave to man." American Indians did better than that; they often made maize into a god.

Maize is the most adaptable of all our major crops. The others clearly have limits. Rice likes the wet tropics. Wheat likes the temperate climate and does poorly in sustained hot weather and unvarying day length. Maize cares not for seasons, insofar as you mean short-day seasons and long-day seasons. When Europeans first arrived in North America, the Indians were raising maize on the banks of the St. Lawrence, in the rain forests of Tabasco, in the arid southwest of the present United States, right on the equator in Ecuador, and far to the south. Within the Thirteen Colonies alone there were two general categories of strains: a southern kind cultivated in the South and Middle Colonies that grew to eight feet and took a half year to ripen, and a New England and Canadian kind that rarely exceeded three or four feet in height and matured in a quarter year.

Maize, however, is not a perfect food. Depend on it too exclusively and you will suffer from severe malnutrition and even a potentially fatal disease, pellagra, as have millions in our South and peasants all over the Old World from Spain to Indonesia. Amerindians have rarely suffered so, even if restricted to a vegetarian diet, because they included in their diet other foods, particularly beans, that supplied what maize did not. And they prepared maize for consumption in a way that rendered it more broadly nourishing than did people who adopted the crop later. The technique is called *nixtamalization*, a word derived from the Nahuatl, the language of the Aztecs, among others. The Indians first soaked maize grains and then cooked them with lime or wood ashes. That made them much easier to grind but, more important, it transformed this food so as to make available much more of its nutritional value. Millions upon millions of Old World peoples, Euro- and African Americans, specifically poor share-croppers in our Southeast, have suffered and even died on corn diets, but not Amerindians.

Euro-Americans brought little to compensate Amerindians for the gift of maize, but one important item was the wheel. For centuries, Amerindian women had spent much of every day grinding maize on the *metate*, the oblong grinding stone, rocking back and forth, back and forth. You can see the effects in the distortions of the skeletons of pre-Columbian Amerindian women. The Europeans brought the wheel for carts and wagons—and for mills— enormously improving the lives of Indian women (provided, of course, that they survived contact with the invaders at all).

They ground maize on the *metate* a thousand years ago, and they take it to the village mill today for the purpose of making it into meal to make into tortillas. Today's variety of tortillas is narrow compared to what it once was. The sixteenth century's fray Bernadino de Sahagún (or, to be more accurate, his Mexica informants) tells us that in the market:

> The food seller sells tortillas which are thick, thickest, thick over all, extremely thick; he sells thin ones: thin tortillas, stretched-out tortillas with shelled beans, cooked and shelled beans, with shelled beans mashed, tortillas with meat and grains of maize, folded with chile, ashen tortillas, washed tortillas. He sells folded tortillas, thick tortillas, coarse tortillas. He sells tortillas with turkey eggs, tortillas made with honey, pressed ones, glove-shaped tortillas, plain tortillas, assorted ones, braised ones, sweet tortillas, amaranth-seed tortillas, squash tortillas, green maize tortillas, brick-shaped tortillas, tuna cactus tortillas; broken, crumbled, old tortillas; cold tortillas, toasted ones, dried tortillas, stinking tortillas.

Europeans came to British North America with their breads and with their preconceptions of what bread is, i.e., something made from grain that has risen—something leavened and rather fluffy compared, for instance, to tortillas. This is currently changing, with the freshening of Latino immigration and the diversification of American tastes.

I have saved for last what is probably the most important element in the story of the American Indians and their collision with the imperialists from the Old World: infectious disease. By 1492, the populations of the advanced societies of the Old and New Worlds were similar in significant ways: thin in the north and thick in the warmer regions.

We do not have precise statistics for the more densely populated regions in the Americas, but obviously you do not build anything like the monuments at Cahokia, much less Tenochtitlan (Mexico City) and Machu Picchu, unless you can draw on the labor and skills of thousands. We have our most reliable estimates from the Mexican regions because the Spanish got there before the demographic collapse, wrote about what they saw in letters and reports, and made estimates of population size for—shall we say?—taxation purposes. Its largest cities were bigger than any of Spain's and probably all of Western Europe's except for London, Paris, and Rome. The population of Mexico was something like twenty-million, to cite a conservative estimate. (Europe's, west of Russia, was between sixty- and seventy-million.)

Both the Mexican and the Native American population of many regions of the New World were dense enough to provide fuel for epidemics of infectious diseases; and the populations were immunologically vulnerable. The Mexicans, for instance, had no herds of livestock with which to exchange and cultivate infectious diseases, like smallpox, which the Europeans had passed back and forth with their cattle and other barnyard animals for at least a thousand years. I theorize that the natives of Mexico had no herds of livestock because the natives had been instrumental in eliminating those species back when the proto-Indian hunters from the Old World spread across the New World.

Let us focus on one disease: smallpox. It probably first afflicted native people of the Americas around 1520, when it swept from Espanola through the Greater Antilles to the mainland. Hernán Cortés and his forces carried it from the coast to Tenochtitlan, where it proved to be his most potent ally. From Mesoamerica it spread to Peru and no one knows how much further. In a letter dated 10 January, 1519, the Hieronymite fathers wrote on Española: "When the Indios were leaving the mines to return to their villages, in December of the past year, it pleased our Lord to send upon them a pestilence of smallpox that is not yet ceasing and of which have died and are at present dying almost one third of the afore-mentioned Indios."

There are similar reports from all over the future Spanish empire in the sixteenth and seventeenth centuries. While there is no record of smallpox in what is now the United States and Canada in the sixteenth century, the first recorded smallpox epidemic the United States was in Plymouth, Boston, and that vicinity in the early 1630s. Smallpox detonated there among the Algonquins of Massachusetts: "Whole towns of them were swept away, in some not so much as one soul escaping destruction."

William Bradford of Plymouth Plantation provides a few more details of just how hard the nearby Algonquins were hit and just how death rates could soar to such heights in these epidemics. Some of the victims, he wrote:

> fell down so generally of this disease as they were in the end not able to help one another, nor to make a fire nor fetch a little water to drink, nor any to bury the dead. But would strive as long as they could, and when they could procure no other means to make fire, they would burn the wooden trays and dishes they ate their meat from, and their very bows and arrows. And some would crawl out on all fours to get a little water, and sometimes die by the way and not be able to get in again.

The disease raged through New England westward into the St. Lawrence-Great Lakes region and beyond. Smallpox whipsawed back and forth through New York and the surrounding areas in the 1630s and 1640s, reducing the populations of the Huron and Iroquois confederations by an estimated fifty percent. After this, smallpox never seemed to stay away for more than two or three decades at a time. The Jesuit and Mennonite missionaries, the traders from Montreal and Charleston—they all had the same appalling story to tell about smallpox and the indigenes. They said that in 1738 it destroyed half the Cherokee; in 1759, nearly half the Catawbas; in the first years of the nineteenth century, two-thirds of the Omahas and perhaps half the entire population between the Missouri River and New Mexico; in 1837–38, nearly every last one of the Mandans and perhaps half the people of the high plains.

The disease spread far beyond the European frontier, often to people who had barely heard of the invaders. Smallpox probably reached the Puget Sound area on the North West Pacific coast in 1782 or 1783—a part of the world then as distant from the main centers of human population as any place on earth. When the explorer George Vancouver sailed into the Sound in 1793, he found Amerindians with pockmarked faces, and human bones scattered along the beach at Port Discovery–skulls, limbs, ribs, backbone—so many as to produce the impression that this was "a general cemetery for the whole of the surrounding country." He judged that "at no very remote period this country had been far more populous than at present." It was an assessment he could have accurately extended to the entire continent.

What imported disease meant for the Amerindians is neatly expressed in a legend of the Kiowa of the southern plains of the U.S., who suffered at least three—and probably four—epidemics of smallpox in the nineteenth century. Saynday, the mythic hero of the tribe, comes upon a stranger dressed in a black suit and a tall hat like a missionary. The stranger speaks first:

Who are you?

I'm Saynday. I'm the Kiowa's Old Uncle Saynday. I'm the one who's always coming along. Who are you?

I'm smallpox.

Where do you come from and what do you do and why are you here?

I come from far away, across the Eastern Ocean. I am one with the white men—they are my people as the Kiowa are yours. Sometimes I travel ahead of them, and sometimes I lurk behind. But I am always their companion and you will find me in their camps and in the houses.

What do you do?

I bring death. My breath causes children to wither like young plants in the spring snow. I bring destruction. No matter how beautiful a woman is, once she has looked at me she becomes as ugly as death. And to men I bring not death alone, but the destruction of their children, the blighting of their wives. The strongest warriors go down before me. No people who have looked at me will ever be the same.

The white invaders took a sunnier view of imported disease. John Winthrop, first governor of the Massachusetts Bay Colony—a Puritan and a lawyer—noted on May 22, 1634, "For the natives, they are near all dead of smallpox, so as the Lord hath cleared our title to what we possess."

Note: My piece, "The First Americans" has not aged gracefully in all its features. In particular, recent findings from DNA have sharpened the picture of early human migration. Readers seeking résumés of fresher interpretations might want to consult Heather Pringle's cover article of the same title in the November 2011 issue of *Scientific American*.

Scientific and Demographic Encounters

2. New Data for the Existence of Plantain Cultivation in Coastal Brazil before 1492

William Balée

Introduction

Genetic evidence places the origins of all cultivated *Musa* (bananas and plantains) in Malaysia. The cultivated bananas and plantains are all believed to be derived from the crossing of two species, *Musa balbisiana* Colla and *Musa acuminata* Colla[1], which produced diploid AB hybrids and triploid hybrids, all of which depend on vegetative reproduction or parthenocarpy, and not sexual reproduction, given female sterility. Most writers and scholars take for granted Spanish colonial history, which holds that in 1516 a Spanish priest introduced the plantain into Hispaniola, and assume that no members of the domesticated *Musa* hybrids (all classified in *Musa x paradisica*[2]) existed in the New World before that[3]. Considerable circumstantial evidence[4], however, exists for one member of the *Musa* genus—the plantain, or "cooking banana,"—being present in the New World before Columbus. Some of this circumstantial evidence is decidedly linguistic in nature, but to date has not been subjected to linguistic analysis per se. Some of these data concern non-Tupian, northwestern South American languages. My focus here will be eastern South America for the most part, and Tupí-Guaraní languages. Chroniclers of the mid-16th century noted the existence of Tupinamá Indians cultivating plantains in coastal Brazil[5]. These plants were called *pacoba*, or a very similar term, but the term is phonemically best rendered as /pakoßa/, since the beta, not the b, is the actual phoneme in this word position in the old Tupinambá language, as it was in the even older Proto-Tupí-Guaraní.[6]

Tupí-Guaraní Languages and the Order Zingiberales

In an earlier study of 625 plant names in five Tupí-Guaraní languages, it was determined that names for non-domesticated plants were, in comparison to names for domesticated and semi-domesticated plants, more labile.[7] The linguistic reason for this instability is related to a distinction between literal and metaphorical plant names. It was noted that literal "plant words are those which contain a literal plant morpheme...literal plant morphemes are here defined as those which have as their sole reference a specific plant."[8] In contrast, a metaphorical plant name is usually transparent morphologically, consisting of parts that refer to things other than plants, and it does not contain a literal plant morpheme that actually refers to the plant so named. In English, poison oak is not a kind of oak (a literal plant morpheme), so it is metaphorical; dogwood is also a metaphorical plant name because neither dog nor wood refer to specific plants.[9] Such marked terms as dogwood or poison oak are older, for obvious reasons, than their constituent morphemes. In the parsing of names of Tupí-Guaraní terms that appear in Tables I through VII, 'L' refers to literal plant morpheme.

One way of understanding the origins of terms for plantain in Tupí-Guaraní languages would be to examine the names of various terms in different yet closely related taxa. The family of the plantain (and the banana, for that matter) is Musaceae. Musaceae is one of eight families in the Order Zingiberales, the others being Cannaceae, Costaceae, Heliconiaceae, Lowiaceae, Marantaceae, Strelitziaceae, and Zingiberaceae.[10] The Order is considered to be "well characterized and sharply defined; its limits have occasioned no controversy."[11] All of these families save one, Lowiaceae, are found in tropical South America. Many of the specific and generic taxa in these families are named by Tupí-Guaraní terms that I and others have collected, either with or without the botanical referents, in the course of long-term fieldwork.[12] The question to be addressed here from the perspective of linguistic evidence in the Tupí-Guaraní family of languages is whether the botanical family Musaceae, which consists of only two genera, *Musa* and *Ensete*, the latter exclusive to northern Africa, existed at all in South America, specifically coastal Brazil, before the arrival of Columbus.

The lexicographer Silveira Bueno refers to the plantain as an introduction to Brazil in colonial times, not as a native plant.[13] He further points out that the Tupí-Guaraní term for plantain (*pacoba*) originally applied to another plant with a fruit similar to that of plantain, and that at the time of the introduction of banana, the term was expanded in range of meaning to include the plantain. It is not clear what plant he meant; possibly he was referring to *pacová*, which is phonetically very similar, and which he defines as an unidentified member of the Zingiberaceae family.[14] Another lexicographer, Holanda Ferreira, suggests *Renealmia alpinia* (Rottb.) Maas (formerly *R. exaltata*) to be the identity of this plant.[15] *R. alpinia* is found in Amazonia as well as the Atlantic Coastal Forest. *R. alpinia* seems problematic, however, as an original referent of the term *pakova*, *pakoßa*, *pakoß* or any similar, unmarked term. The three attestations of *R. alpinia* in Table VII do not incorporate any *pako*-like term, and these are from three different subgroups of Tupí-Guaraní (Tembé, Araweté, and Ka'apor). It is the case that two of them do incorporate a base term for sugar cane (Tembé and Araweté). Indeed, zingiberaceous plants, perhaps *Renealmia* in particular, seem to be much more likely to be modeled on sugar cane than on musaceous cultivars. In Língua Geral Amazônica, from subgroup 2, which is likely descended from Tupinambá, the term for such plants appears to be *cana-rána* or "other sugar cane."[16] Had the original term for *Renealmia alpinia* been *pacová*, then the marking, if anything, should have rendered the term something like *pacová-rana*, not *cana-rána*. Therefore, it is unlikely that *Renealmia alpinia* was originally named in Tupinambá with an *unmarked* *pako*-like term, if it incorporated a *pako*-like term at all.

When one examines the botanical nomenclature, this seems to be indeed the case. Systematist Maas noted, "*Renealmia alpinia* is a species which can hardly be confused with any other."[17] In his list of synonyms, and names preceding synonyms for the plant, one finds *Paco Seroca*. This is a Tupí-Guaraní marked term, meaning "rotten plantain" or "hunger plantain" (see below). M. Adanson included a genus he called *le Pacoseroca* in his family "*Les Gingembres*" which also included *Costus*, *Curcuma*, *Zingiber*, *Alpinia*, and *Maranta*, which are all names, of course, that would be associated with the Order Zingiberales.[18] In his great botanical treatise, Adanson describes a genus called *Pacoseroca* (a marked term) as what appears to be *R. alpinia*, or "paniculate flowers with the raceme outside the leaves" (my translation).[19] This means that in the 1700s, if not much earlier, *pako* was the plantain, and the name for *Renealmia alpinia* was modeled on it, not the reverse. There is no evidence of a marking reversal having occurred, which I discuss further, below.

Key Aspects of the Linguistic Evidence

I propose to examine plantain words and names for taxa related to the plantain specifically from firsthand data in several languages in four of the eight subgroups of the Tupí-Guarani family; these are groups 4, 5, 6, and 8.[20] The data are from my own collections among the Araweté, Assurini do Xingu, Guajá, Ka'apor, and Tembé, except where otherwise noted, during the 1980s and 1990s; the data from Parintintin are from La Vera Betts[21] and those from the Wayãpi are from Françoise Grenand[22] and Pierre Grenand.[23] The most complete datasets are from the Ka'apor and Wayãpi, owing to extensive, long-term, and comprehensive collections of plants and plant names among them, by myself and Françoise and Pierre Grenand, respectively.

The names for plants in Tables I through VII are spread across the Order Zingiberales found in the Amazon region, with the exception of known introductions, such as the dessert bananas (in the Musaceae, introduced from West Africa) and turmeric and ginger (both in the Zingiberaceae, introductions from Southeast Asia). I am also excluding the only member of the Cannaceae family present in the region, *Canna indica* L., a domesticated shrub, for which data, in the present sample, are extant only in Wayãpi (*palakalu'a*, a borrowing from a Cariban language[24]) and Ka'apor *awaí* "rattlesnake,"[25] a metaphorical name unrelated to many other kinds of terms found among traditional domesticates as well as other members of the Zingiberales. Cannaceae and Marantaceae appear to form a clade separate from a Zingiberaceae/Costaceae

clade within the Zingiberales,[26] and for the most part it is the Zingiberaceae/
Costaceae clade that is more relevant to discussion of plantain and related terms
in Tupí-Guaraní languages, in addition to Heliconiaceae and Strelitziaceae.

Table I: Generic terms in three subgroups of Tupí-Guaraní
for Costus spp. (Costaceae)

Subgroups, Languages, and Terms

	#4	#5	#8		
Species					
	Tembé	Araweté	Guajá	Ka'apor	Wayãpi
Costus arabicus L.	taza-ran 'cocco-other'; syn. **kana-ran** 'sugar cane-other'	--	ka'i-kəmə-'ï 'capuchin monkey-?-stem'	tayahu-pako-ro 'white-lipped peccary-plantain-leaf'	kapiyuwa-asikalu[1] 'capybara-sugar cane'
Costus scaber R.&P.		--	ka'a-tamkï 'herb-?	ãyaŋ-rãkwãi 'demon-penis'	kapiyã'ï-pilã[2] 'capybara food-red'
Costus spiralis (Jacq.) Roscoe	--	kaní-əhə 'sugar cane-big'			kapiyã'ï-ɛ'ɛ[3] 'capybara food-authentic'

1. Grenand 1989: 220
2. Grenand 1989: 220
3. Grenand 1989: 220

A certain amount of name-modeling, always metaphorical as to its
analysis and classification, is found among non-domesticated Zingiberales
plants across the various languages in the study. Names can be modeled on
analogy for domesticated plants, as with *taza-ran* "cocoyam (*Xanthosoma
sagittifolium* [L.] Schott)-other" and *kana-ran* "sugar cane-other" which are
synonyms in Tembé for *Costus arabicus* L. (in the Costaceae) (Table I). The
first is modeled on cocoyam (a native tropical South American domesticate
closely related to taro) and the other is modeled on sugar cane, a domesticate
long ago introduced from Southeast Asia. The underlying principle is the
same for Araweté *kaní-əhə* "sugar cane-big" in reference to the closely related
Costus spiralis (Jacq.) Roscoe (Table I). The morpheme *-ran* in Tembé is

cognate with *-lā* in Wayãpi[27], *-rī* in Araweté, *-rána* in Assurini do Xingu, -ran in other languages. This postposed term means "false" or "other" (that is, in the sense of other than authentic or prototypical) and it is frequently applied to plant names formed by analogy on cultivated models. Typically, these are traditionally non-domesticated plants.[28]

Table II. Generic terms in three subgroups of Tupí-Guaraní for Heliconia spp. (Heliconiaceae)

Subgroups, Languages, and Terms

	#4	#5		#8		
Species						
	Tembé	Araweté	Assurini	Guajá	Ka'apor	Wayãpi
Heliconia spp.	**paku-ran-'ïw** 'plantain-other-stem'	**padidi** L	**pariri** L	**kwači-ka'a** coati-herb	**ayahu-pako-ro** 'white-lipped peccary-plantain-leaf'	**palili** L

PTG: *pariri

In other words, names for traditional (native) domesticates do not as a rule incorporate the morpheme meaning "false" or "other" or "other than authentic." Names for Zingiberales plants that incorporate this morpheme include the Tembé examples above as well as Tembé *paku-ran-'ïw* "plantain-false-stem" for *Heliconia* spp. and Tembé *paku-ran* "plantain-false" for the wild banana, or bananeira brava, *Phenakospermum guyannense* (L.C. Rich) Endl. (Strelitziaceae) (Tables II, VI). In other orders of plants (such as Cucurbitales and Convolvulales), a similar pattern is seen in Ka'apor: *kawasu-ran*, or "bottle gourd-other," is not a bottle gourd (*Lagenaria siceraria* L.) but a cucurbitaceous vine of the forest and *yïtïk-ran*, or "sweet potato," is not a sweet potato (*Ipomoea batatas* L.) but rather a morning glory vine of old swiddens, and so on.[29] These are sometimes called unproductive primary lexemes because the head (or base) terms do not refer to actual generic categories.[30] They are, of course, metaphorical terms as well.[31]

Analogies Based on Domesticated Plant Names

Pierre Grenand had earlier perceptively noted a cognitive barrier between cultivated and non-cultivated plants in Wayãpi.[32] Other terms and metaphorical constructions apart from the use of *-ran* equally imply that a plant is non-domesticated. When a plant is not a member of the class of which its generic name is indicative, then as a rule of thumb one is considering a plant in a state of non-domestication. Just as *paku-ran* is not a banana or plantain in Tembé plant classification, in Ka'apor, *tayahu-pako-ro*—literally, "white-lipped peccary's banana leaf"—is neither a banana nor plantain, and refers instead to the non-domesticated *Costus arabicus* L. (Table I). Although not a member of the Zingiberales, it should be noted that orchids, which are called "sloth-plantain" (*a' ï hu-pako*), are also not classified as plantains in Ka'apor ethnobotany.[33] The term is an unproductive primary lexeme (the base term *pako*, which normally means plantain, is not in this usage referring to a plantain, hence the unproductivity of the entire name, or lexeme). However, it is also the case that orchids, like all Zingiberales plants, are monocotyledons, and hence members of the same class of flowering plants as plantains. Sloths eat the leaves of this orchid, according to Ka'apor informants. Usually, unproductive primary lexemes containing animal constituents do refer to plants that are ecologically associated with the animal denoted in the attributive.[34] In contrast, at least in the Ka'apor language, animal attributives incorporated into folk specific names for cultivated plants are virtually never associated ecologically with the domesticate in question.[35] In any case, in relation to the present data, this orchidaceous example is the only case of a family outside the Order Zingiberales in which a *pako* term is in use.

   Costus spp. in the Wayãpi language are referred to generically as "capybara food."[36] Pierre Grenand further noted, in regard to *C. arabicus* (the Wayãpi name which means "capybara's sugar cane" [Table I]) specifically that "It is eaten by *capivaras*" (italics in original).[37][38] In further regard to non-domesticated plants named by analogy for domesticated plants, by far most of the models are traditional domesticates, not introductions post-1492. The exceptions to this pattern are the various modelings on sugar cane (supra), originally from Indonesia: Tembé *kana-ran* "sugar cane-other" for *Costus arabicus* L. and *Renealmia alpinia*, Araweté *kaní-əhə* "sugar cane-big" for *C. spiralis* (Jacq.) Roscoe and *R. alpinia*, Guajá *akana-hu* "sugar cane-big" for *Calathea* spp. (Marantaceae), and Ka'apor *kurupi-kã* "forest sprite-sugar cane" for *R. alpinia* (Tables I, II, VII). *Ischnosiphon* of the Marantaceae, an important genus in native basketry, does not seem to be related to any plantain terms—see Table IV—and it would likely not be models for any possible original Tupí-Guaraní term for plantain. Morphologically this makes sense, all else being equal and keeping the exception of the "sloth's plantain"-orchid in mind, since Marantaceae along with Cannaceae seem to form a separate clade within the Order.[39]

Table III: Generic terms in three subgroups of Tupí-Guaraní
for Calathea spp. (Marantaceae)

Subgroups, Languages, and Terms

	#4	#5	#8		
Species					
	Tembé	Araweté	Guajá	Ka'apor	Wayãpi
Calathea spp.	**ka'a-põ**	**tuwa-čiŋo**	**akana-hu**	**suruwi-ka'a**	**tapana**
			ka-a-tai'ï		**walapisis-ipilã**
			ka'a-hu		**tatulem**
			akaru-hu-ruwi		**ulu-ka'a**
			pariri		**iñamu-ka'a**
					pulupululi-sili
					ulu-sili

Sugar cane was introduced by the first white colonists in Brazil,[40] and borrowing of the term came about from the principle of need: these languages obviously did not have a word for it before.[41] Instead of coining a new one, they needed to borrow an existing one from the contact language—Portuguese in this case. What one can attest is an abbreviated number of non-domesticated plants modeled on sugar cane. In contrast, *pakoβa* and its cognates by inspection are greatly disseminated and have considerable internal differentiation.

It is plausible that the Portuguese term for sugar cane was borrowed rapidly by a variety of closely related Tupí-Guaraní languages not only because it was an introduction, but also because of the historical-ecological importance of sugar cane in the 16th-century crown colony of Brazil, and because Indians speaking these languages were initially enslaved in the plantation economy, and referred to by their masters as "escravos da terra," before their labor became gradually replaced by Africans.[42] The borrowing of names for plants of extraordinary economic importance, even native plants that already had native names, such as cacao, where change in the historical ecology of local societies and local landscapes occurred in the early to mid-eighteenth century, has been documented for the lower Amazon region.[43] It would be relatively easy to rename and model the new names of economically unimportant non-domesticates such as zingiberaceous herbs like *Renealmia* spp. on sugar cane, a plant of such profound economic importance that it was involved in the transport ultimately of millions of people in the tragedy of the Middle Passage.

Table IV. Generic terms in three subgroups of Tupí-Guaraní
for *Ishnosiphon* spp. (Marantaceae)

Subgroups, Languages, and Terms

	#4	#5	#8		
Species					
	Tembé	Araweté	Guajá	Ka'apor	Wayãpi
Ischnosi-phon spp.	**uru-wïw-wa-'i** 'wood quail-stem-fruit-small'	**uru-'i** 'wood quail-little'	**arïwï** 'surubim'	**arumã** L	**ulu** 'wood quail'

PTG ***uru**

In the Ka'apor language, the only other name for any traditional domesticate modeled by analogy on an introduced plant is *kase-ran* "coffee-other" (the referent is a small, common tree of fallow forests, *Casearia javitensis* H.B.K.).[44] Tupí-Guaraní languages lacked *f*, so intervocalic *f* in this Ka'apor plant name was replaced by *s* in the borrowing from Portuguese of *café*.[45] Of course, coffee (*Coffea arabica* L.) is an introduced plant of economic importance comparable, at some point in time (especially the late 19th and early 20th centuries) to sugar and cacao. Coffee was introduced into Brazil, perhaps from India, sometime toward the end of the 17th century; it became an important crop in the lower Amazon region for a time after about 1727.[46] Cacao also became important in the lower Amazon economy around that time, even more important than coffee, and arguably an introduced term for it was borrowed by the Ka'apor language from the Creole language known as Língua Geral Amazônica (LGA).[47] So it is enough for a crop to have been of historical-ecological importance within only the last three hundred years to envision a name-change for it, due to borrowing from a donor language. It is similarly not difficult to fathom the historical ecology underpinnings behind why the name for a relatively unimportant non-domesticate (in this case, *C. javitensis*, which is edible only to fewer than three game species and has no other uses to the Ka'apor) would have changed and become modeled on the loanword for an introduced domesticate, coffee.[48]

Where Did *Pakoβa* Come From?

At last we come to the question: is *pakoβa* a term for a native plant, whether musaceous or not, or is it a term, like the terms for sugar cane and coffee, that was borrowed from a language originating on a continent other than South America? If it is a term for a native plant, did it refer to a pre-Columbian cultivar of plantain? Or did it refer to another plant, another member of the Zingiberales? The data are suggestive of its existence in the Brazilian Amazon long before the eighteenth century, given the presumable age of the different subgroups in the sample. Table V shows six plantain terms in four subgroups of Tupí-Guaraní languages. Arguably the reconstruction is *pakoß* and most likely this same term also for the fruit since:

a)
*ß/V_# > v in #6
*ß/V_# > ø in all others

b) and less significantly:
*o/C_# > /u/ (in Guajá and Tembé)
> /ɔ/ (in Wayãpi)

and

c) majority rules in deleting the glottal stop found intervocalically in the Parintintin term. We are confronted with another possible problem, however, in light of the Araweté term for the plantain, *padidi* (Table V). This Araweté term is also used to refer to *Heliconia* spp. (Table II). Indeed, the Proto-Tupí-Guaraní (PTG) term for *Heliconia* spp. based on the data from Table II can be reconstructed as *pariri* by the following logic:

a) *r > l in Wayãpi
b) *r /V_V > d (or ð—the voiced dental non-sibilant fricative) [Eduardo Viveiros de Castro, e-mail message to author, May 26, 2008]
c) the other terms in the sample of Table II are several disjunctive metaphorical terms, based on modeling by analogy on the plantain (as in Ka'apor and Tembé) or some other metaphorical construction using a life-form term (as in Guajá) and therefore could not be original constructs.

Araweté could be in the second stage of a marking reversal (Witkowski and Brown 1983), wherein plantains have been recently introduced, were modeled by analogy on the term for *Heliconia* spp., and have at this point become so familiar that they are equal, in a sense, to the familiarity of *Heliconia*, and therefore have the same term. Given the importance of plantain vis-à-vis *Heliconia* spp. in an economic sense, a reasonable outcome in the future would be for *Heliconia* spp. to become marked (by something like -rĩ "other," as in *padidi-rĩ*) and for the plantain to continue to be attested in unmarked form, as *padidi*. Evidence from Araweté, however, is the most challenging of all the internal linguistic evidence to the proposition that *pako* or *pakoßa* are Proto-Tupí-Guaraní terms for the plantain and its fruit.

Table V. Generic terms in four subgroups of Tupí-Guaraní
for the plantain (Musaceae)

Subgroups, Languages, and Terms

	#4	#5	#6	#8		
	Tembé	Araweté	Parintintin	Guajá	Ka'apor	Wayãpi
Species						
Musa x paradi-siaca (plantain)	paku	padidi[1]	pa'akov-ete[2]	paku	pako	pakɔ -ï[3]
	L	L	L-authentic	L	L	L-stem

1. Viveiros de Castro 1992:327
2. Betts 1981:233
3. Grenand 1989: 330

PTG: ***pakoß**

Reasons:

- because in Tembé and Guajá, $*o$ /C_# $> u$

- because in Parintintin, $*ß \rightarrow v$

- because in Wayãpi $*o \rightarrow ɔ$

- majority rules in deleting the glottal stop found in Parintintin from the reconstruction because Araweté is the only language here to equate the plantain lexically with *Heliconia* spp.

The Araweté term for the neotropical wild "banana," or bananeira brava, a native plant (*Phenakospermum guyannense* [Rich.] Miq.) that looks very much like a large banana plant (as does its relative from Madagascar, the traveler's tree—*Ravenala madagascariensis* Gmel., seen pantropically as an ornamental) in the Strelitziaceae, is *pakõa*, which term appears cognate by an inspection as an unmarked, generic term. If that is the case, pako-like terms in the other languages for plantain could be the result of a marking reversal. In other words, *pakoßa* may indeed be the Proto-Tupí-Guaraní term for *P. guyannense*. In this scenario, *P. guyannense* would be now marked (as in Tembé, Ka'apor, and Wayãpi—Table VI) and the plantain would have lost its marking. One problem with this argument, however, is that the plantain did not lose marking in Araweté. The original term for wild banana would not have been **pariri* for none of the other languages use that. Rather, what seems to have happened is Araweté lost cultivation of the plantain and its original name for some time, then regained these, and with that reacquisition betokened the plantain with a root term for a pre-existing plant of the forest, which by definition they had not lost, *Heliconia* spp. They had also not lost, by definition, the bananeira brava, *pakõa*, but arguably dropped its modifier (that is, its marking) because there was nothing else closely related, or musaceous enough, to contrast it with. A much more serious problem with the entire argument of whether the *pako* words that refer to plantain today once referred to the bananeira brava, before the white man, is that *there evidently was no bananeira brava in the lands first colonized by the Portuguese, and inhabited by the Tupinambá and Guaraní, namely, the Atlantic Coastal Forest.*

Table VI. Generic terms in four subgroups of Tupí-Guaraní
for *Phenakospermum guyannense* (Rich.) Endl. ex Miq.
(Strelitziaceae), also known as wild banana, bananeira brava, and sororoca

Subgroups, Languages, and Terms

	#4	#5	#6	#8		
	Tembé	Araweté	Parintintin	Guajá	Ka'apor	Wayãpi
Species						
Phenako-spermum	**paku-ran**	**pakõa**[1]	**pa'akov**[2]	**yawar-ka'a-hu**	**pako-sororo**	**pakɔ-tala**[3]
guyan-nense	L-other	L	L	jaguar-herb-big	L-hunger	L-*Conna-rus* spp.

1. Viveiros de Castro 1992:327
2. Betts 1981:231
3. Grenand 1989: 331

PTG: ***pakoβ***-'mark'

Reasons:

See Table V.

Also, because majority rules: although in languages from two subgroups (Araweté and Parintintin, of groups 5 and 6, respectively) the plant is unmarked, it is marked in all four languages represented in two other subgroups (Tembé of group 4, Guajá, Ka'apor, and Wayãpi of group 8).

The wild banana or bananeira brava (*P. guyannense*) does not occur in the online catalog of vascular plant species of eastern Brazil of the International Plant Science Center: C.V. Starr Virtual Herbarium of the New York Botanical Garden (2008) which lists 208 plant families with a total of thousands of genera and species. Included in these families are members of the Zingiberales, such as Cannaceae, Costaceae, Heliconiaceae, Marantaceae, and Zingiberaceae. Strelitziaceae, however, the family of *P. guyannense*, is not listed at all. Thomas et al. (2008) in several years of collecting at the Una Biological Reserve near Ilhéus, Bahia, a remaining Atlantic Coastal Forest considered to be very rich in vascular plant species, and incidentally very near to where Pedro Álvares Cabral first made landfall in 1500 and claimed Brazil for the Portuguese crown, do not report a single example of *P. guyannense* on their extensive preliminary checklist of the flora, though several taxa in the Heliconiaceae and Marantaceae are reported. Out of 850,000 individual collections reported thus far online, fewer than 14 specimens of *P. guyannense* are reported, by Scott Mori in French Guiana and myself in eastern Amazonian Brazil (International Plant Science Center 2008).

Table VII. Generic terms in three subgroups of Tupí-Guaraní for
Renealmia spp. (Zingiberaceae)

Subgroups, Languages, and Terms

Species	#4	#5	#8		
	Tembé	Araweté	Guajá	Ka'apor	Wayãpi
Rebnealmia alpina (Rottb.)	kana-ran 'sugar cane-other'	kani-əhə 'sugar cane-other'	---	kurupi-kã 'forest sprite - sugar cane'	---
Renealmia floribunda K. Sch.	---	---	ka'a-kačə 'herb-dark'	kurupi-pïïm 'forest sprite - tobacco'	kulimakɔ-ul[1] 'L-dark'

1. Grenand 1989: 331; Grenand (1989:241) indicates that kulimakɔ is the generic term for Renealmia spp. It seems possible that the original Tupi-Guarani term from these limited data for Renealmia spp. would have been a term that contained the non-morphemic element *kur-, if only because the original term could not have contained the morpheme for sugar cane which is a borrowing from Port. 'cana'; that is, unless, of course the retention of kur is not a shared innovation in Ka'apor and Wayãpi, which arguably split apart only within about the last 250 years (Balée 2003).

The term *pa'akov-ete* "plantain-true" in Parintintin is suggestive also of a possible marking reversal, but the arguments in favor of that are similarly inconclusive. Finally, in Table V, it should be noted that Guajá, a language of hunter-gatherers, retained a cognate term for plantain (*paku*) though they have not cultivated it in hundreds of years. They lost agriculture due to various effects of European conquest, but they did not lose all terms for all cultivated plants.[49] They also did not lose names for "wild" plants, such as *P. guyannense*, for which is attested the highly metaphorical term *yawarka'ahu* ("the jaguar's big herb"); I collected *P. guyannense* among the Guajá (on voucher series #3350), the herbarium specimen of which is viewable online at *http://sweetgum.nybg.org/vh/specimen_list.php*. The term for *bananeira brava* is likewise in the other two languages in the sample of subgroup 8, Ka'apor *pako-sororo* "L-hunger" and Wayãpi *pakɔ-tala* "L-a wild forest vine" as well as in the one language from subgroup 4, Tembé *paku-ran* "L-other" (Table VI). Given the widespread markings of the wild banana, and the differences among the markings, these do not look liked shared innovations. I will provisionally consider the PTG term of *P. guyannense* to have been *pako* with some kind of marking. In this regard, my argument is strengthened by the fact that the word for plantain in LGA, spoken in the early 20th century in the Central Amazon River area, near the town of Tefé, Brazil, was *pakoa*, whereas one of the words for a non-domesticated banana is *pacoua sororoca* (translated as *banana rota, retalhada*—that is "broken banana," which I would have translated as "hunger plantain") for a similar word in Ka'apor.[50] Another non-domesticated zingiberaceous plant is referred to as *pacoa ayua*, meaning "rotten plantain."[51] LGA is in subgroup 3, along with Tupinambá, an extinct language; however, it is not included in the analysis in the tables because there is evidence of some loanwords in Ka'apor from LGA.[52]

Linguistically, I am arguing that *pakoβa*-like terms for musaceous (or even strelitziaceous or heliconiaceous) plants are native Proto-Tupí-Guaraní terms, but some suggestions have been made to the contrary, arguing for an African origin. The evidence for such a position is either quite weak or nonexistent, however, both historically and linguistically. It is worth noting that Léry referred to *paco-aire* as distinguished from *paco* the fruit; the editor of this edition of Léry's 1578 work, in a footnote, proposes that bananas (that is, plantains) were only "recently introduced into Brazil" (footnote c, p. 105). Léry, however, who is one of the earliest and most astute chroniclers of Brazil, made no mention of the plant having been introduced. He wrote that it was the "savages" who employed the word *paco* for the fruit, not the Frenchmen, who referred to this fruit as a fig.[53] Léry's compatriot, Andre Thevet, had preceded him in southern Brazil by about two years, and though he remained for much less time, he too reported on a "tree...that the savages call Paquoere" (my translation).[54] The plant was most likely musaceous: "*C'est arbre ne porte iamais fruit qu'une fois*" (the tree [i.e., stem] bears fruit only once [my translation] which is true of the individual suckers or clones of the plantain). He compared the fruit, as best he could, to something he knew from France: cucumbers.[55] Léry further noted that the plantain is one of the finest fruits "of the land of Brazil," not of some other land.[56] Léry knew of the Portuguese bringing sugar cane to various other colonies of theirs, and he knew that oranges and lemons (that is, *Citrus* spp.) were introduced in America,[57] so why would he not know that the plantain was introduced also, if that were the case?

Writing in 1587 at the latest, Soares de Sousa, another astute observer of 16th century Brazil, informs us of the *pacoba* as "uma fruta natural desta terra" (a native fruit of this land, my translation) and gives an incisive description of how the plant is harvested and propagated.[58] Many of the local Tupí-Guaraní people by this time, also, were "escravos da terra" (slaves of the land), the ironic human analogue to their own musaceous domesticate.[59] At this early point in time, if *pacoba* had been introduced into Brazil only after 1516, one would have to be considering a maximum time period for its dissemination as such of only 71 years. That time span seems insufficient for the plantain to gain a foothold, let alone to be found to have been widespread throughout the Neotropics, *shortly after* 1516, in spite of difficulties of cultivation and propagation intrinsic to the biology of the plant.[60] Soares de Sousa had elicited information from the local people about displacements of populations in the past due to indigenous warfare shortly before and after the arrival of the Portuguese.[61] He relied on the detailed memory of "very elderly" informants of events that dated back long before his arrival in Brazil ca. 1569, and even before the arrival of the first Portuguese.[62] The events recounted are of displacements of three different ethnic groups due to warfare, and the accounts are told from "generation to generation."[63] Soares de Sousa writes of the introduction into Brazil of sugar cane, orange trees, lime trees, fig trees, grapefruit, coconut, tamarind trees, ginger, rice, and other cultigens, but not of plantain.[64] The obvious question is why, unless he and his indigenous informants were right — the plantain already was, before the Portuguese at least, a "fruta natural desta terra," that is, a pre-Cabraline native fruit of Brazil. According to the scholar and firsthand observer of Brazil, Pero Magalhães de Gandavo, who knew the Brazilian littoral well, though it is hard to pinpoint exactly whereabouts he writes sometimes, "Também ha huma fruita que lhe chamão Bananas, e pela lingua dos indios Pacovas" ("Also there is a fruit that they call bananas, and in the indigenous language pacovas," my translation).[65] Gandavo was writing before 1573, so within the time frame of Léry and Soares de Sousa. With such a long memory, Tupian societies such as the Wayãpi (and no doubt many other indigenous societies) can record significant information orally, back about two hundred years or so, though accuracy seems to stop around three hundred years ago from a modern perspective.[66 67] This means that had the Portuguese or Spanish brought plantains into Brazil sometime after 1500 (the presumable date of Cabraline discovery), the indigenes and their successive descendants should have been able to relate that information to Léry and Soares de Sousa, who arrived only about 55-70 years later, and who were generally so capable of rendering such details of introductions into their indispensable works. What is linguistically most intriguing from the Brazilian data is that people not only knew how to cultivate, harvest, and propagate the plantain from one end of the Brazilian coast to the other by 1587, the year of submission of Soares de Sousa's treatise, but they had also divided it up into a number of folk species: *pacoba* itself (evidently the prototype), *pacobuçu* (pacoba grande, i.e., large plantain), *pacobamirim* (pacoba pequena, i.e., small plantain), and another reddish plantain for which he does not give us a name but which is evidently distinguished with one from the rest.[68] If plantain had been a one-time introduction into America (in 1516 or later), the differentiation of *pacoba* into varieties is interesting because "new varieties [of the plantain] are rare."[69]

These varieties are distinguished from *bananas*, which Soares de Sousa had noted were preferred over the *pacoba* by the African slaves of Bahia.[70] Soares de Sousa more specifically indicated that the term *banana* as well as the banana plants themselves came over to Brazil from São Tomé, an island in the Gulf of Guinea that had become a major port of the Portuguese since 1484.[71] São Tomé is referred to by de Alencastro as a "laboratório tropical," where the Luso-Brazilian South Atlantic slave trade would have been initially prepared, thanks to a ruling of the Portuguese crown in 1519.[72] That ruling provided for methods of selection, embarkation, alimentation, transport, branding, treatment, and training of captive Africans for the era of modern chattel slavery in the South Atlantic.[73]

If São Tomé was a principal port from where both bananas and slaves came to Bahia, where did the plantain come from, if it were introduced after 1516? São Tomé had been uninhabited before 1484.[74] In fact, bananas were introduced into São Tomé by the Portuguese, and bananas were introduced into West-Central Africa in general only *after* the arrival of the Europeans in the fifteenth century;[75] they apparently came from East Africa or India, via maritime not terrestrial routes, at least in part because of problems with geographical barriers on the continent itself.[76] If bananas were introduced to São Tomé, as were African slaves from the mainland, the next logical question to ask is whether any plantain cultivar was brought to São Tomé from the nearby mainland, either by the Portuguese or the slaves, before 1516. Simmonds suggested that *pacova* was "perhaps of African origin," though he gives no citation for that;[77] an older lexigraphic source indicated that the word *pacova* came from the Kingdom of Congo and from Angola.[78] Kongo Bantu was spoken in the Kingdom of Congo (which included a part of present-day Angola), and according to Vansina, the terms for triploid plantain (AAB) across a vast area of the Congo River basin, both east and west of the river itself, were in the 16th century kɔnde, kɔndɔ, and kɔ.[79] The plantain was introduced into Africa before 3000 kya.[80] *Ensete gillettii* (Musaceae), which is indigenous to Africa, is reconstructed in Benue-Congo languages as **kom*. The name for plantain in Bantu was originally modeled on the *kom* root, and widespread Bantu reflex terms include the ones above as well as *kondo* and *kombo*.[81] Rossel reports *konde* as the Bantu generic term for plantain in the Congo River basin, the East Ituri River basin, in the countries of the Democratic Republic of the Congo, Gabon, and Cameroon.[82]

In interior Mozambique, which Rossel considers a "marginal" *Musa* area, two
Bantu languages of the Shona subgroup had forms for the plantain which are
phonetically similar to *pakoβa*: Ndau *ma-kova* and Naranga *mu-hova*.[83] The
Portuguese had subjected coastal Mozambique to their control by the early
sixteenth century. It is plausible the terms were borrowed by the Portuguese
and taken to Brazil with the plantain. If so, however, it seems unlikely that
Tupí-Guaraní languages as well as Portuguese which have canonical /m/ in
initial position would replace that with /p/. Rossell suggests *koba* and terms
like it as independent generics for plantain in certain Bantu languages, and
she points out that many *Musa* terms in Africa (as elsewhere) are borrowed.[84]
It seems these terms, if anything, were borrowed *from* Portuguese, not *by*
Portuguese.

If the Spanish had brought the plantain to Hispaniola only once, one
would expect the Spanish term to have diffused throughout Hispanic America.
Smole has offered considerable counterevidence on this point.[85] He rightly
points out there was some confusion between usage of plátano (European
plane tree) with plantain. On the other hand, he was mistaken on one point
regarding *pako*-like usages. Smole wrote: "Throughout an enormous area...
the name pacova for the musaceous plantain became firmly established early in
the colonial period. No such word was used in Spanish America or the Iberian
Peninsula."[86] Antonio Ruiz de Montoya, however, whose 1640 dictionary of the
Old Guaraní language spoken in the Spanish-speaking Jesuit missions of what
is now northern Argentina, extreme southern Brazil, and eastern Paraguay,
records the following terms: for *platano arbol*: *pacobaĭ*; for *plátano el fruto*
(the fruit): *pacobá*; for *plátano la hoja* (the leaf): *pacoba ró*; and *plátano la
hoja* (the leaf) *o cascara del arbol* (or bark of the tree): *pacoba rĭbapé*.[87] Old
Guaraní, which is now extinct, is classified in subgroup 1 of Tupí-Guaraní.[88]
Why did the Guaraní of this subtropical region (the area of Atlantic Coastal
Forest, subtype Paraná Forest, today seen, for example, in Misiones Province,
Argentina), where plantains and bananas grow well, if they did not have the
plantain originally, not borrow the Spanish term for it? Why was their term
evidently similar to or the same as Tupinambá? One should not forget that
these Guaraní speaking people were enemies both of the Brazilians and of the
Tupinambá. The best argument is that they already had the plantain, before the
Spanish and the Portuguese arrived.

Finally, the one generic term closest to the Tupí-Guaraní terms discussed
for a plantain in Africa, remarkably, is found on São Tomé, and that term is
pakoba.[89] That leads to a probable conclusion concerning the directionality of
borrowing, based on the weight of the evidence thus far considered.

Proposed Directionality of Borrowing

Proto-Tupí-Guarani *pakoβ →Tupinambá pakoβa →Portuguese pakoba →
São Tomé pakoba

What happened is not that plantains were absent in Brazil and eastern South America before the Europeans. At least one variety was present, and it was ultimately exported, possibly returned to Africa, rather than the other way around. Whereas the point of embarkation of the first plantains to South America cannot be ascertained, the data herewith further strengthen the hypothesis that human beings from somewhere other than South America brought the plantain to Brazil before the Europeans arrived.

Acknowledgements

I would like to thank Anne Bradburn, Hortensia Calvo, Stéphen Rostain, and Eduardo Viveiros de Castro for helpful advice and assistance in preparing this paper.

NOTES

1. Blench, Roger. "Bananas and Plantains in Africa: Reinterpreting the Linguistic Evidence." The sixth World Archaeological Congress. Dublin, Ireland. June 29-July 5, 2008. See also, Rossel, Gerda. *Taxonomic-Linguistic Study of Plantain in Africa.* Leiden, the Netherlands: Research School CNWS, School of Asian, African and Amerindian Studies, 1998: 11. See also, Simmonds, N.W. *The Evolution of the Bananas.* New York: John Wiley and Sons, 1962, and, Simmonds, N.W. *Bananas.* New York: Longman, 1966.

2. Watts, Donald, ed. *Elsevier's Dictionary of Plant Names and Their Origin.* Amsterdam: Elsevier Science, B.V., 2000. Cited in Smole, William J. "Plantains (Musa) Cultivation in Pre-Columbian America: An Overview of the Circumstantial Evidence." *Pre-Columbiana* 2(4): 272.

3. For example, Métraux, Alfred. "The Tupinambá." In *Handbook of South American Indians*, volume 3. Ed. by Julian Steward. *Bureau of American Ethnology*, Bulletin 143. Washington, DC: US Government Printing Office, 1948. P. 99. See also Simmonds, N.W. *Bananas.* 2nd ed. New York: Longman, 1966.

4. Heyerdahl, Thor. *Early Man and the Ocean: A Search for the Beginnings of Navigation and Seaborne Civilizations.* Garden City, New York: Doubleday, 1979: 78-80. See also Smole, William J. "*Musa* cultivation in pre-Columbian South America." *Geosciences and Man* 21 (1980): 47-50; and Smole, William. "Plantains (*Musa*) Cultivation in Pre-Columbian America: An Overview of the Circumstantial Evidence." *Pre-Columbiana* 2(4) (2002): 269-296.

5. Balée, William, and Denny Moore. "Similarity and variation in plant names in five Tupi-Guarani languages (Eastern Amazonia)." *Bulletin of the Florida Museum of Natural History, Biological Sciences*, 35(4) (1991):217. See also, Léry, Jean de. *History of a Voyage to the Land of Brazil.* Trans. Janet Whatley. Los Angeles: University of California Press, 1990: 105. See also, Lisboa, Cristóvão. *História dos animais e árvores do Maranhão.* Lisbon: Publicações do Arquivo Histórico Ultramarino e Centro de Estudos Históricos Ultramarinos, 1967: 122. See also, Smole, William J. "*Musa* Cultivation in Pre-Columbian South America." *Geosciences and Man* 21 (1980):47-50, and Smole, William J. "Plantains (*Musa*) Cultivation in Pre-Columbian America: An overview of the Circumstantial Evidence." *Pre-Columbiana* 2(4) (2002):269-296. See also, Soares de Sousa, Gabriel. *Tratado descritivo do Brasil em 1587.* Brasiliana, vol. 117. 4th

ed. São Paulo: Editora Nacional, 1987: 188-189. See also, Vasconcellos Simão de. *Chronica da Companhia de Jesu no Etado do Brasil*. Lisbon: A.J. Fernandes Lopes, 1865: 136.

6.   Personal communication with Aryon D. Rodrigues, 1990.

7.   Balée, William, and Denny Moore. "Similarity and Variation in Plant Names in Five Tupi-Guarani Languages (Eastern Amazonia)." *Bulletin of the Florida Museum of Natural History, Biological Sciences*, 35(4) (1991):209-62.

8.   Ibid.: 231.

9.   Ibid.

10.   Cronquist, Arthur. *The Evolution and Classification of Flowering Plants*. 2nd Edition. Bronx: New York Botanical Garden, 1988: 488, cf. Rossel, Gerda. *Taxonomic-Linguistic Study of Plantain in Africa*. Leiden, the Netherlands: Research School CNWS, School of Asian, African and Amerindian Studies, 1998: 17.

11.   Cronquist, Arthur. *The Evolution and Classification of Flowering Plants*. 2nd Edition. Bronx: New York Botanical Garden, 1988: 488.

12.   Balée, William. *Footprints of the Forest: Ka'apor Ethnobotany—The Historical Ecology of Plant Utilization by an Amazonian People*. New York: Columbia University Press, 1994. See also, Betts, La Vera. *Dicionário parintintin-português, português-parintintin*. Brasília: Summer Institute of Linguistics, 1981. See also, Grenand, Françoise. *Dictionnaire Wayãpi-Français: Lexique Français-Wayãpi (Guyane Française)*. Paris: Peeters/Société d'Études Linguistiques et Anthropologiques de France (SELAF) (Langues et Sociétés d'Amérique traditionelle 1), 1989. See also, Viveiros de Castro, Eduardo. *From the Enemy's Point of View: Humanity and Divinity in an Amazonian Society*. Trans. Catherine V. Howard. Chicago: University of Chicago Press, 1992.

13.   Bueno, Francisco da Silveira, *Vocabulário tupi-guarani-português*. São Paulo: Brasilivros Editora, 1987: 577. Cited in Smole, William J. "Plantains (*Musa*) Cultivation in Pre-Columbian America: An Overview of the Circumstantial Evidence." *Pre-Columbiana* 2(4) (2002): 286.

14.   Ibid.: 242

15.   Holanda Ferreira, Aurélio Buarque de. *Novo Dicionário da Língua Portuguesa*. Rio de Janeiro: Nova Fronteira, n.d.:1015.

16.   Stradelli, Ermano. "Vocabularios da Lingua geral portuguez-nheêngatú e nheêngatu-portuguez, precedidos de um esboço de grammatica nheênga-umbuê-sáua mirî e seguidos de contos em lingua geral nheêngatú poranduua." *Revista do Instituto Histórico e Geographico Brasileiro*, Tomo 104, Vol. 158 (1929):394.

17.   Maas, P.J.M. *Renealmia (Zingiberaceae-Zingiberoides) Coistoideae (addisions) Zingiberaceae)*. *Flora Neotropica, Monograph 18*. Bronx: New York Botanical Garden, 1977: 35.

18.   Adanson, M. *Familles des Plantes*. 2 vols. Paris: Chez Vincent, Imprimeur-Libraire de Mgr de Compte de Provence, 1763: 61.

19.   Ibid.: 67.

20.   Jensen, Cheryl. *Tupí-Guaraní*. *The Amazonian Languages*, ed. R.M.W. Dixon and Alexandra Y. Aikhenvald. Cambridge: Cambridge University Press, 1999: 125-63. See also, Rodrigues, Aryon Dall'Igna, and Ana Suelly Arruda Câmara Cabral. "Revendo a classificação interna da família tupí-guaraní." *Línguas indígenas brasileiras: fonologia, gramática e história*, ed. Ana Suelly Arruda Câmara Cabral and Aryon Dall'Igna Rodrigues. Atas do I Encontro Internacional do Grupo de Trabalho sobre Línguas Indígenas ANPOLL. Belém, Pará: EDUFPA, 2002: 327-37.

21.   Betts, La Vera. *Dicionário parintintin-português, português-parintintin*. Brasília: Summer Institute of Linguistics, 1981.

22.   Grenand, Françoise. *Dictionnaire Wayãpi-Français: Lexique Français-Wayãpi (Guyane Française)*. Paris: Peeters/Société d'Études Linguistiques et Anthropologiques de France (SELAF), 1989. (Langues et Sociétés d'Amérique traditionelle 1).

23. Grenand, Pierre. *Introduction a L'Étude de L'Univers Wayãpi: Ethnoécologie des Indiens du Haut-Oyapock (Guyane française)*. Langues et Civilisations à Tradition Orale 40. Paris: Société d'Études Linguistiques et Anthropologiques de France (SELAF), 1980.

24. Grenand, Françoise. *Dictionnaire Wayãpi-Français: Lexique Français-Wayãpi (Guyane Française)*. Paris: Peeters/Société d'Études Linguistiques et Anthropologiques de France (SELAF), 1989. (Langues et Sociétés d'Amérique traditionelle 1): 333.

25. cf. Balée, William. "Nomenclatural patterns in Ka'apor ethnobotany." *Journal of Ethnobiology* 9(1) (1989): 1-24.

26. Stevenson, Dennis Wm. and Janice Wassemer Stevenson. "Zingiberaceae (Ginger family)". *Flowering Plants of the Neotropics*, ed. Nathan Smith, et al. Princeton, New Jersey: Princeton University Press, 2004: 494-5.

27. "lã: L'espèce végétale est ici nommée par rapport à une autre avec laquelle il ne faut pas la confondre: en général, la fausse, par rapport à l'autre, ne présente pas d'utilité pour l'homme." See Grenand, Pierre. *Introduction a L'Étude de L'Univers Wayãpi: Ethnoécologie des Indiens du Haut-Oyapock (Guyane française)*. Langues et Civilisations à Tradition Orale 40. Paris: Société d'Études Linguistiques et Anthropologiques de France (SELAF), 1980: 38.

28. Balée, William. "Nomenclatural Patterns in Ka'apor Ethnobotany." *Journal of Ethnobiology* 9(1) (1989): 19. See also, Grenand, Pierre. *Introduction a L'Étude de L'Univers Wayãpi: Ethnoécologie des Indiens du Haut-Oyapock (Guyane française)*. Langues et Civilisations à Tradition Orale 40. Paris: Société d'Études Linguistiques et Anthropologiques de France (SELAF), 1980: 38.; cf. Berlin, Brent, Dennis E Breedlove, Peter H. Raven. *Principles of Tzeltal Plant Classification*. New York: Academic Press, 1974: 38.

29. Balée, William. "Nomenclatural Patterns in Ka'apor Ethnobotany." *Journal of Ethnobiology* 9(1) (1989):18, Table 6.

30. Balée, William. *Footprints of the Forest: Ka'apor Ethnobotany—The Historical Ecology of Plant Utilization by an Amazonian People*. New York: Columbia University Press, 1994. See also, Berlin, Brent, Dennis E Breedlove, Peter H. Raven. *Principles of Tzeltal Plant Classification*. New York: Academic Press, 1974.

31. Balée, William, and Denny Moore. "Similarity and variation in plant names in five Tupi-Guarani languages (Eastern Amazonia)." *Bulletin of the Florida Museum of Natural History, Biological Sciences*, 35(4) (1991): 209-62.

32. Grenand, Pierre. *Introduction a L'Étude de L'Univers Wayãpi: Ethnoécologie des Indiens du Haut-Oyapock (Guyane française)*. Langues et Civilisations à Tradition Orale 40. Paris: Société d'Études Linguistiques et Anthropologiques de France (SELAF), 1980: 43.

33. Balée, William. "Nomenclatural patterns in Ka'apor ethnobotany." *Journal of Ethnobiology* 9(1) (1989): 21.

34. Ibid. See also, Balée, William. *Footprints of the Forest: Ka'apor Ethnobotany—The Historical Ecology of Plant Utilization by an Amazonian People*. New York: Columbia University Press, 1994

35. Ibid.

36. Grenand, Françoise. *Dictionnaire Wayãpi-Français: Lexique Français-Wayãpi (Guyane Française)*. Paris: Peeters/Société d'Études Linguistiques et Anthropologiques de France (SELAF), 1989 (Langues et Sociétés d'Amérique traditionelle 1): 220.

37. Grenand, Pierre. *Introduction a L'Étude de L'Univers Wayãpi: Ethnoécologie des Indiens du Haut-Oyapock (Guyane française)*. Langues et Civilisations à Tradition Orale 40. Paris: Société d'Études Linguistiques et Anthropologiques de France (SELAF), 1980: 276.

38. Elle est mangé par les *capivaras*.

39. See Stevenson, Dennis Wm. and Janice Wassemer Stevenson. "Zingiberaceae (Ginger family)." *Flowering Plants of the Neotropics*, ed. Nathan Smith et al. Princeton, New Jersey: Princeton University Press, 2004: 494-5.

40. See de Alencastro, Luiz Felipe. *O trato dos viventes: Formação do Brasil no Atlântico Sul, séculos XVI e XVII*. São Paulo: Companhia das Letras, 2000. See also, Métraux, Alfred. "The Tupinambá." *Handbook of South American Indians*, volume 3, ed. Julian Steward, 95-133. *Bureau of American Ethnology*, Bulletin 143. Washington, DC: US Government Printing Office, 1948: 99.

41. Campbell, Lyle. *Historical Linguistics: An Introduction*. Cambridge: The MIT Press, 1999: 9.

42. de Alencastro, Luiz Felipe. *O trato dos viventes: Formação do Brasil no Atlântico Sul, séculos XVI e XVII*. São Paulo: Companhia das Letras, 2000: 117-27.

43. Balée, William. "Historical-ecological influences on the word for cacao in Ka'apor." *Anthropological Linguistics* 45(3) (2003): 259-80.

44. Balée, William. "Nomenclatural patterns in Ka'apor ethnobotany." *Journal of Ethnobiology* 9(1) (1989): 18, Table 6.

45. cf. Campbell, Lyle. *Historical Linguistics: An Introduction*. Cambridge: The MIT Press, 1999: 61.

46. Dean, Warren. *With Broadax and Firebrand: The Destruction of the Brazilian Atlantic Forest*. Los Angeles: University of California Press, 1995: 179.

47. Balée, William. "Historical-ecological influences on the word for cacao in Ka'apor." *Anthropological Linguistics* 45(3) (2003): 259-80.

48. Balée, William. *Footprints of the Forest: Ka'apor Ethnobotany—The Historical Ecology of Plant Utilization by an Amazonian People*. New York: Columbia University Press, 1994: 288.

49. Ibid. See also Cormier, Loretta A. *Kinship with Monkeys: The Guajá Foragers of Eastern Amazonia*. New York: Columbia University Press, 2003.

50. Stradelli, Ermano. "Vocabularios da Lingua geral portuguez-nheêngatú e nheêngatu-portuguez, precedidos de um esboço de grammatica nheênga-umbuê-sáua mirî e seguidos de contos em lingua geral nheêngatú poranduua." *Revista do Instituto Histórico e Geographico Brasileiro*, Tomo 104, Vol. 158 (1929): 583.

51. Ibid.: 85, 583.

52. Balée, William. "Historical-ecological influences on the word for cacao in Ka'apor." *Anthropological Linguistics* 45(3) (2003): 259-80.

53. Léry, Jean de. *History of a Voyage to the Land of Brazil*. Trans. Janet Whatley. Los Angeles: University of California Press, 1990: 105.

54. Thevet, Andre. 1982 [orig. 1558]. *Les singularités de la France Antarctique autrement nommée Amerique*. Facsimile of 1558 original edition. Paris: Le Temps, 1982.

55. Ibid.: 62

56. Léry, Jean de. *History of a Voyage to the Land of Brazil*. Trans. Janet Whatley. Los Angeles: University of California Press, 1990: 106.

57. Ibid.: 106-7.

58. Soares de Sousa, Gabriel. *Tratado descritivo do Brasil em 1587. Brasiliana*, vol. 117. 4th ed. São Paulo: Editora Nacional, 1987: 188.

59. de Alencastro, Luiz Felipe. *O trato dos viventes: Formação do Brasil no Atlântico Sul, séculos XVI e XVII*. São Paulo: Companhia das Letras, 2000: 117-27.

60. Blench, Roger. "Bananas and plantains in Africa; Reinterpreting the linguistic evidence." Sixth World Archaeological Congress, Dublin, Ireland, June 29-July 5, 2008. See also, Heyerdahl, Thor. *Early Man and the Ocean: A Search for the Beginnings of Navigation and Seaborne Civilizations*. Garden City, New York: Doubleday, 1979. See also, Sauer, Carl Ortwin. "Cultivated Plants of South and Central America." *Handbook of South American Indians*, volume 6: 487-543. *Bureau of American Ethnology*, Bulletin 145. Washington, DC: US Government Printing Office, 1950. See also, Smole, William J. "Plantains (*Musa*) Cultivation in Pre-Columbian America: An Overview of the Circumstantial Evidence." *Pre-Columbiana* 2(4) (2002): 284.

61. Balée, William. "Complexity and Causality in Tupinambá Warfare." *Latin American Indigenous Warfare and Ritual Violence*, ed. Richad J. Chacon and Rubén G. Mendoza. Tucson: University of Arizona Press, 2007: 184-5.

62. Soares de Sousa, Gabriel. *Tratado descritivo do Brasil em 1587. Brasiliana*, vol. 117. 4th ed. São Paulo: Editora Nacional, 1987: 299-300.

63. Ibid: 300.

64. Ibid: 165-9.

65. Gandavo, Pero de Magalhães. *Historia da Província Santa Cruz, Tratado da Terra do Brasil*. São Paulo: Obelisco, 1964: 86.

66. Grenand, Pierre. *Ainsi parlaient nos ancêtres: Essai d'éthnohistoire "Wayãpi."* Travaux et Documents de L'Office de la Recherche Scientifique et Technique Outre-Mer (ORSTOM). Paris: ORSTOM, 1982: 153.

67. "De la culture vécue au XVIIe siècle, les Wayãpi ne retiennent que des fragments cristallisé surtout àtravers les chants et les mythes."

68. Soares de Sousa, Gabriel. *Tratado descritivo do Brasil em 1587. Brasiliana*, vol. 117. 4th ed. São Paulo: Editora Nacional, 1987: 188-9.

69. Smole, William J. "Plantains (*Musa*) Cultivation in Pre-Columbian America: An Overview of the Circumstantial Evidence." *Pre-Columbiana* 2(4) (2002): 284.

70. Soares de Sousa, Gabriel. *Tratado descritivo do Brasil em 1587. Brasiliana*, vol. 117. 4th ed. São Paulo: Editora Nacional, 1987: 189.

71. Ibid.

72. de Alencastro, Luiz Felipe. *O trato dos viventes: Formação do Brasil no Atlântico Sul, séculos XVI e XVII*. São Paulo: Companhia das Letras, 2000: 63.

73. Ibid: 65. See also, Vansina, Jan. *Paths in the Rainforests: Toward a History of Political Tradition in Equatorial Africa*. Madison, WI: University of Wisconsin Press, 1990: 200.

74. cf. Ibid.

75. Blench, Roger. "Bananas and plantains in Africa; Reinterpreting the linguistic evidence." Sixth World Archaeological Congress. Dublin, Ireland. June 29-July 5, 2008. See also, Rossel, Gerda. *Taxonomic-Linguistic Study of Plantain in Africa*. Leiden, the Netherlands: Research School CNWS, School of Asian, African and Amerindian Studies, 1998: 95.

76. Ibid.

77. Simmons, N. W. Bananas. 2nd ed. New York: Longman, 1966: 56; quoted in Smole, William J. "Plantains (Musa) Cultivation in Pre-Columbian America: An Overview of the Circumstantial Evidence." *Pre-Columbiana* 2(4) (2202): 285.

78. Friederici, Georg. *Caráter da descoberta e conquista da América pelos europeus*. Trans. Guttorm Hansen. Rio de Janeiro: Ministério da Educação e Cultura, Instituto Nacional do Livro, 1967: 134; cited in Smole, William J. "Plantains (*Musa*) Cultivation in Pre-Columbian America: An Overview of the Circumstantial Evidence." *Pre-Columbiana* 2(4) (2202): 285.

79. Vansina, Jan. *Paths in the Rainforests: Toward a History of Political Tradition in Equatorial Africa*. Madison, WI: University of Wisconsin Press, 1990: 289.

80. Blench, Roger. "Bananas and plantains in Africa; Reinterpreting the linguistic evidence." Sixth World Archaeological Congress. Dublin, Ireland. June 29-July 5, 2008; cf. Rossel, Gerda. *Taxonomic-Linguistic Study of Plantain in Africa*. Leiden, the Netherlands: Research School CNWS, School of Asian, African and Amerindian Studies, 1998.

81. Ibid.

82. Rossel, Gerda. *Taxonomic-Linguistic Study of Plantain in Africa*. Leiden, the Netherlands: Research School CNWS, School of Asian, African and Amerindian Studies, 1998: 210.

83. Ibid: 97, 113.

84. Ibid: 112.

85. Smole, William J. "*Musa* Cultivation in Pre-Columbian South America." *Geosciences and Man* 21 (1980): 47-50. See also, Smole, William J. "Plantains (*Musa*) Cultivation in Pre-Columbian America: An Overview of the Circumstantial Evidence." *Pre-Columbiana* 2(4) (2002): 269-296.

86. Smole, William J. "Plantains (*Musa*) Cultivation in Pre-Columbian America: An Overview of the Circumstantial Evidence." *Pre-Columbiana* 2(4) (2002): 281.

87. Ruiz de Montoya, Antonio. *Arte y Vocabulario de la lengua Guarani*. Facsimile ed. Madrid: Ediciones de Cultura Hispánica ACEI, UNESCO, 1994: 142.

88. Jensen, Cheryl. "Tupí-Guaraní." *The Amazonian Languages*, ed. R.M.W. Dixon and Alexandra Y. Aikhenvald. Cambridge: Cambridge University Press, 1999: 125-63.

89. Rossel, Gerda. *Taxonomic-Linguistic Study of Plantain in Africa*. Leiden, the Netherlands: Research School CNWS, School of Asian, African and Amerindian Studies, 1998: 211-12.

BIBLIOGRAPHY

Adanson, M. *Familles des Plantes*. 2 vols. Paris: Chez Vincent, Imprimeur-Libraire de Mgr de Compte de Provence. 1763.

Balée, William. "Nomenclatural patterns in Ka'apor ethnobotany." *Journal of Ethnobiology* 9, no. 1 (1989):1-24.

------. *Footprints of the Forest: Ka'apor Ethnobotany—The Historical Ecology of Plant Utilization by an Amazonian People*. New York: Columbia University Press, 1994.

------. "Historical-ecological influences on the word for cacao in Ka'apor." *Anthropological Linguistics* 45, no. 3 (2003): 259-80.

------. "Complexity and causality in Tupinambá warfare," in *Latin American Indigenous Warfare and Ritual Violence*, ed. Richad J. Chacon and Rubén G. Mendoza, 180-97. Tucson: University of Arizona Press, 2007.

Balée, William, and Denny Moore. "Similarity and variation in plant names in five Tupi-Guarani languages (Eastern Amazonia)." *Bulletin of the Florida Museum of Natural History, Biological Sciences*, 35, no. 4(1991): 209-62.

Berlin, Brent, Dennis E Breedlove, Peter H. Raven. *Principles of Tzeltal Plant Classification*. New York: Academic Press, 1974.

Betts, La Vera. *Dictionário parintintin-português, português-parintintin*. Brasília: Summer Institute of Linguistics, 1981.

Blench, Roger. "Bananas and plantains in Africa; Reinterpreting the linguistic evidence." Sixth World Archaeological Congress. Dublin, Ireland. June 29-July 5, 2008.

Bueno, Francisco da Silveira. *Vocabulário tupi-guarani-português*. São Paulo: Brasilivros Editora, 1987.

de Alencastro, Luiz Felipe. *O trato dos viventes: Formação do Brasil no Atlântico Sul, séculos XVI e XVII*. São Paulo: Companhia das Letras, 2000.

Campbell, Lyle. *Historical Linguistics: An Introduction*. Cambridge: The MIT Press, 1999.

Cormier, Loretta A. *Kinship with Monkeys: The Guajá Foragers of Eastern Amazonia*. New York: Columbia University Press, 2003.

Cronquist, Arthur. *The Evolution and Classification of Flowering Plants*. 2nd Edition. Bronx: New York Botanical Garden, 1988.

Dean, Warren. *With Broadax and Firebrand: The Destruction of the Brazilian Atlantic Forest*. Los Angeles: University of California Press, 1995.

Friederici, Georg. *Caráter da descoberta e conquista da América pelos europeus*. Trans. Guttorm Hansen. Rio de Janeiro: Ministério da Educação e Cultura, Instituto Nacional do Livro, 1967.

Gandavo, Pero de Magalhães. *Historia da Província Santa Cruz, Tratado da Terra do Brasil* (1576). São Paulo: Obelisco, 1964.

Grenand, Françoise. *Dictionnaire Wayãpi-Français: Lexique Français-Wayãpi (Guyane Française)*. Paris: Peeters/Société d'Études Linguistiques et Anthropologiques de France (SELAF) (Langues et Sociétés d'Amérique traditionelle 1). n.d.

Grenand, Pierre. *Introduction a L'Étude de L'Univers Wayãpi: Ethnoécologie des Indiens du Haut-Oyapock (Guyane française)*. Langues et Civilisations à Tradition Orale 40. Paris: Société d'Études Linguistiques et Anthropologiques de France (SELAF), 1980.

------. *Ainsi parlaient nos ancêtres: Essai d'éthnohistoire "Wayãpi."* Travaux et Documents de L'Office de la Recherche Scientifique et Technique Outre-Mer (ORSTOM). Paris: ORSTOM, 1982.

Heyerdahl, Thor. *Early Man and the Ocean: A Search for the Beginnings of Navigation and Seaborne Civilizations*. Garden City, New York: Doubleday, 1979.

Holanda Ferreira, Aurélio Buarque de. *Novo Dicionário da Língua Portuguesa*. Rio de Janeiro: Nova Fronteira. n.d.

International Plant Science Center. "The C.V. Starr Virtual Herbarium of the New York Botanical Garden." 2008. http:www//sciweb.nybg.org/Science2/hcol.sebc/seb-checklist.asp.

Jensen, Cheryl. 1999. Tupí-Guaraní. In The Amazonian Languages, ed. R.M.W. Dixon and Alexandra Y. Aikhenvald, 125-63. Cambridge: Cambridge University Press.

Jett, Stephen C. 2002. Archaeological hints of pre-Columbian plantains in the Americas. Pre-Columbiana 2(4):314-16.

Léry, Jean de. *History of a Voyage to the Land of Brazil*. Trans. Janet Whatley. Los Angeles: University of California Press, 1990.

Lisboa, Cristóvão. *História dos animais e árvores do Maranhão*. Lisbon: Publicações do Arquivo Histórico Ultramarino e Centrl de Estudos Históricos Ultramarinos, 1967.

Maas, P.J.M. *Renealmia (Zingiberaceae-Zingiberoides) Coistoideae (addisions) Zingiberaceae). Flora Neotropica, Monograph 18*. Bronx: New York Botanical Garden, 1977.

Métraux, Alfred. "The Tupinambá," in *Handbook of South American Indians*, volume 3, ed. Julian Steward, 95-133. Bureau of American Ethnology, Bulletin 143. Washington, DC: US Government Printing Office, 1948.

Rodrigues, Aryon Dall'Igna, and Ana Suelly Arruda Câmara Cabral. "Revendo a classificação interna da família tupí-guaraní," in *Línguas indígenas brasileiras: fonologia, gramática e história*, ed. Ana Suelly Arruda Câmara Cabral and Aryon

Dall'Igna Rodrigues, 327-37. Atas do I Encontro Internacional do Grupo de Trabalho sobre Línguas Indígenas ANPOLL. Belém, Pará: EDUFPA, 2002.

Ruiz de Montoya, Antonio. *Arte y Vocabulario de la lengua Guarani.* Facsimile ed. Madrid: Ediciones de Cultura Hispánica ACEI, UNESCO, 1994.

Rossel, Gerda. *Taxonomic-Linguistic Study of Plantain in Africa.* Leiden, the Netherlands: Research School CNWS, School of Asian, African and Amerindian Studies, 1998.

Sauer, Carl Ortwin. "Cultivated Plants of South and Central America. Métraux," in *Handbook of South American Indians*, volume 6, p. 487-543. Bureau of American Ethnology, Bulletin 145. Washington, DC: US Government Printing Office, 1950.

Simmonds, N.W. *The Evolution of the Bananas.* New York: John Wiley and Sons, 1962.

------. *Bananas.* 2nd ed. New York: Longman, 1966.

Smole, William J. "*Musa* cultivation in pre-Columbian South America." *Geosciences and Man* 21 (1980): 47-50.

------. "Plantains (*Musa*) cultivation in Pre-Columbian America: An overview of the circumstantial evidence." *Pre-Columbiana* 2, no. 4 (2002): 269-296.

Soares de Sousa, Gabriel. Tratado descritivo do Brasil em 1587. Brasiliana, vol. 117. 4th ed. São Paulo: Editora Nacional. 1987.

Stevenson, Dennis Wm. and Janice Wassemer Stevenson. "Zingiberaceae (Ginger family)," in *Flowering Plants of the Neotropics*, ed. Nathan Smith et al., 494-5. Princeton, New Jersey: Princeton University Press, 2004.

Stradelli, Ermano. "Vocabularios da Lingua geral portuguez-nheêngatú e nheêngatu-portuguez, precedidos de um esboço de grammatica nheêga-umbuê-sáua mirî e seguidos de contos em lingua geral nheêngatú poranduua." *Revista do Instituto Histórico e Geographico Brasileiro*, Tomo 104, Vol. 158 (1929): 11-768.

Thevet, Andre. *Les singularités de la France Antarctique autrement nommée Amerique.* Facsimile of 1558 original edition. Paris: Le Temps, 1982.

Thomas, William Wayt, André M. de Carvalho, André Amorim, Judith Garrison. "Preliminary checklist of the flora of the Una Biological Reserve." 2008. http://www.nybg.org/bsci/res/una.html.

Vansina, Jan. *Paths in the Rainforests: Toward a History of Political Tradition in Equatorial Africa.* Madison, WI: University of Wisconsin Press, 1990.

Vasconcellos Simão de. *Chronica da Companhia de Jesu no Etado do Brasil.* Lisbon: A.J. Fernandes Lopes, 1865.

Viveiros de Castro, Eduardo. *From the Enemy's Point of View: Humanity and Divinity in an Amazonian Society.* Trans. Catherine V. Howard. Chicago: University of Chicago Press, 1992.

Witkowski SR and Cecil H. Brown. "Marking-reversals and cultural importance." *Language* 59 (1983): 69-82.

Watts, Donald, ed. *Elsevier's Dictionary of Plant Names and Their Origin.* Amsterdam: Elsevier Science, B.V, 2000.

3. The "Berkeley School" and the Great Mesoamerican Demographic Debate: *Un homenaje*

Peter Stern

How many people lived in America, or "The Americas," or the pre-Hispanic Caribbean, or pre-Conquest Mexico are all questions which have engendered a great deal of controversy in the last half-century. As one scholar put it, "estimation of population size at contact is not a trivial issue. Rather, knowledge of the size of native population at the time of contact engenders a better understanding of the magnitude...of population decline throughout the Americas after 1492."[1] Such numbers have also bolstered the "case," conducted sometimes in academia, but more often in popular discourse, of the magnitude of the "crime" committed, willfully or unknowingly, by the Europeans against the indigenous inhabitants of the New World.

Woodrow Borah, one of the central figures of what the French annales historians called "*L'ecole Berkeley*," pointed out that matters of European conscience, reparations for historical and material wrongs to native peoples, exaltation of European culture and even the search for *indigenismo* as national identity rode on such population estimates.[2]

The literature on Amerindian demographics is immense, and in my brief essay I shall not attempt to list it. I will review the history of this question, highlighting the central contribution of the "Berkeley School": Lesley Byrd Simpson, Sherburne Cook, Carl Sauer, and Woodrow Borah. Four scholars from Spanish, history, geography, and physiology, all teaching at the University of California, who represent a remarkable cross-disciplinary collaboration long before such partnerships became common in academia. (I exclude anthropologist Alfred Kroeber from membership in *l'ecole*, although his work on Native American population was seminal, because he worked in an earlier time period, and not in collaboration with the School members.)

It was Pierre Chanu, author of more than 50 books, including the classic *Séville et l'Atlantique, 1504-1650*, who identified "the Berkeley School of Hispanic American History," with a focus on colonial economy and Indian demography. He included Borah, Simpson, Cook, as well as Sauer, James Parsons, Robert West, Homer Aschmann, and B. Le Roy Gordon as key members. Sauer has often been referred to as the "father of cultural geography."[3]

I shall briefly describe the early careers of the four members of *L'ecole Berkeley*, and then outline the methods and definitions, all disputed, of counting or calculating which delineate the parameters of the debate.

The most senior of the quartet was Carl Ortwin Sauer, born in Missouri in 1889. After earning his doctorate from Chicago in 1915 in geography ("The Geography of the Ozark Highland of Missouri") Sauer taught in Ann Arbor, before coming to Berkeley in 1923. When he arrived, the department consisted of two doctorate-less instructors. He literally built the department in his thirty years as chair. Soon after arriving on the West Coast, Sauer discovered the Baja Peninsula, as a "conveniently accessible area in which little scientific work had been done." He started taking students into Baja, and later into Mexico, exploring aboriginal and colonial populations, cultivated plants, and the carrying capacity of the land.

Amazingly, it was *after* his retirement that he wrote a quartet of memorable books on the historical geography of the Americas: *The Early Spanish Main, Northern Mists, Sixteenth-Century North America: The Land and People As Seen by Europeans*, and *Seventeenth Century North America*.[4]

Leslie Byrd Simpson was also born in Missouri, in 1891, although he grew up in Los Angeles. After enrolling at UC Berkeley, at a time when ROTC was compulsory, he became a pilot and flew bombers in World War I. After the war ended he worked, attended school, and taught in California until he joined UC Berkeley's Spanish department as an associate, teaching while working on his doctorate, which he finished in 1928. The fact that his doctoral thesis was in history, rather than language or literature ("The Development of the Theory of Forced Native Labor in the Spanish Colonies With Particular Regard to Española and New Spain") may have retarded his progress within the department. Promotion came very slowly to Simpson. He began his life's work, the study of Spanish colonial society through its administrative control of Mexico's Indians, always utilizing Spanish colonial records.

Sherburne Friend Cook was born in Springfield, Massachusetts in 1896. As a linguist, he studied in Germany, then served in the American Expeditionary Force in France during The Great War. Returning to Harvard, he completed a doctorate in 1925 in anatomy and physiology ("The Toxicity of the Heavy Metals in Relation to Respiration"). Cook then did further studies in Cambridge, England, and Berlin, before going to Berkeley in 1928 as a professor in cell biology. He began the Berkeley School's prodigious output with an article entitled "Diseases of the Indians of Lower California in the Eighteenth Century," published in 1935.[5]

The last member of the Berkeley quartet (and the only one I had the privilege to know personally) was Woodrow Borah. Born in rural Mississippi in 1912, he was reared in Los Angeles, and attended graduate school in Berkeley in the 1930s. In both his 1985 *HAHR* interview[6] and in personal reminiscences to me, he painted a vivid picture of attending Cal during the Depression, when the university's superb library and its athletic facilities represented a kind of paradise to a lean and hungry generation. He finished in 1940, with a dissertation entitled "Silk Raising in Colonial Mexico." Herbert Eugene Bolton, the elder dean of Mexican studies, warned Borah—as he put it to me, "in a kindly fashion"—that as a Jew he would have trouble obtaining a university position; indeed, when Borah taught at Princeton after finishing his Ph.D., it was as an instructor. They made it clear to him, he told me more than thirty years later, that it was a temporary post. Borah served in the OSS (in Washington) during the war, and returned to Berkeley in 1948 to teach in its Department of Speech, where he remained for fourteen years before being offered the Shepherd Chair in History. He was only the second Jew to become a professor in its History Department.[7]

Having outlined, albeit briefly, the origins and early careers of the members of the Berkeley School, I shall move to their body of relevant work. Cook got the ball rolling early in his career examining Native Americans in Baja California. His first article on the subject was published in the journal *California and Western Medicine*. His next essay was published in a periodical which became the "house organ" of the Berkeley School, *Ibero-Americana*. Number one of this irregular series appeared in 1932, with the introduction "The series IBERO-AMERICANA, is to form a collection of studies in Latin American cultures, native and transplanted, pre-European, colonial, and modern. Physical and racial backgrounds have a place in the collection, but it is anticipated that the studies will be in the main contributions to culture history." The editors were Herbert E. Bolton, A.L. Kroeber, and C.O. Sauer.[8] The first number was entitled "Aztatlán: Prehistoric Mexican Frontier on the Pacific Coast," by Carl Sauer and Donald Brand. The second was a comparative ethnology of Northern Mexico before 1750, the third a classic: "The Road to Cíbola," also by Sauer. "Cíbola" is classic Sauer: an examination of early Spanish *entradas* into Western Mexico, with careful attention to both the Spanish text and corresponding geographical details.

Ibero-Americana was published between 1932 and 1977. All of the members of "the School" published seminal work in it. Years before he produced his classic study *The Encomienda in New Spain*, Lesley Simpson published "Studies in the Administration of the Indians in New Spain," as number 7 of *Ibero-Americana*, in 1934. Borah turned his doctoral thesis into "Silk Raising in Colonial Mexico," *Ibero-Americana* number 20, in 1943.

What of the native depopulation? The question comes down to population data, which can only be calculated for the pre-European Americas. Historians and scientists have used *ethnohistorical sources, archaeological data, physical anthropological data, ecological evidence,* and *demographic data,* when it is available. Populations must be counted across time and space, and without hard statistical data, other, creative methods must be employed.

In what one scholar calls the *ethnohistorical methods*, one may employ *subpopulation projections*, in which information about a subpopulation of a larger group is simply multiplied out to the larger unit. *Subareal projections* parallel the subpopulation method, in which calculations for a small area are then multiplied to achieve a larger total. These methods are, of course, open to questioning based on the accuracy of the initial data.

Ecological projection is based on more indirect information: e.g., projections of average village or household size, using subpopulation or subareal methods to gain a "total" number. Another popular method is *carrying-capacity projection*, where environmental and technological calculations establish how many people *could have been supported* in a particular geographical area. This technique is highly problematic, not only from the basic objection that people who *could* have been supported does not necessarily translate into people who *were* supported. In addition, assumptions made about ecological conditions, including patterns for rainfall, soil, plant and animal food in the past may not be valid for present conditions.

Finally, *depopulation projections* include epidemiological projections and mathematical and statistical formulas, where known populations are projected back in time to establish earlier population figures.[9] To sum up, as another anthropologist listed them, the data sources are narrative accounts, mission and municipal records, archaeological documentation, and human remains. All these sources, he noted, "have strengths and weaknesses, but each have the potential for providing important perspectives on contact-period population biology, including areas such as demographic reconstruction, dietary history, health status, and activity patterns."[10]

Biologists, anthropologists, geographers and historians have been arguing for a few centuries about "the evidence" and its validity or lack thereof. The "low" baseline school is generally accepted to be represented by James Mooney, whose *The Aboriginal Population of America North of Mexico*, published in 1928, proposed a total North American (i.e., the U.S. and Canada) population of only 1.5 million inhabitants; Kroeber later reduced that to 900,000.[11] Kroeber had calculated that the arable land in Mexico for beans and maize production would allow for a population of 10 million persons, although he reduced that *for antiquity* by four-fifths. In contrast, a French scholar calculated a population for Mexico in 1492 of 4.5 million.[12]

In 1948, Cook and Simpson teamed up to produce *Ibero-Americana* no. 31, "The Population of Central Mexico in the Sixteenth Century." The duo used unpublished materials from Spanish archives, including *suma de visitas*, *relaciones de tasaciones*, tribute *relaciones*, *relaciones geográficas*, and various *cartas* and other reports written by ecclesiastics. Here we see the element of documentary reliability coming into play. Many of the critics of the Berkeley School have based their critiques on the supposed unreliability and exaggeration of contemporary observers, both civil and religious. Since Cook and Borah later used depopulation projections in their work in the 1960s, the accuracy of the colonial data becomes crucial.

Cook and Simpson's meticulous documentation for the time period between 1540 and 1570 allow them to propose a central Mexican population of 3,234,385 persons, excluding Nueva Galicia. Since they believed that the *suma* estimates were too low, they adjusted the figure to 4.2 million (4,204,700, to be exact).[13] They believed that their estimates for 1565 to be reasonably accurate, and the soundest that could be had for 16th-century Mexico. However, it was important to obtain some notion of the magnitude of the decline of the population during the hundred years following the conquest. This, they admitted, could be achieved only in broad outline, since "with the information now available or ever likely to be uncovered it is impossible to determine annual or even decennial fluctuations of a minor or local sort."[14]

Simpson and Cook took into account such factors as supposed average family size, infant and adult mortality, military estimates of warriors correlated to total adult population, and urban density estimates. Their four data points for the sixteenth century show a smooth curve downwards.[15]

Sherburne Cook published on his own an *Ibero-Americana* volume the next year, 1949, entitled "Soil Erosion and Population in Central Mexico" (number 34), which, running contrary to a generalized notion of the pre-contact Americas as a paradise, proposed that central Mexico was actually poised on the brink of ecological catastrophe when the Spaniards arrived.

Ibero-Americana's numbers 43, 44, and 45 contain central elements of the School's demographic work. All written by Sherburne Cook and Woodrow Borah, numbers 43-45 are as follows: "The Population of Central Mexico in 1548: An Analysis of the *Suma de visitas de pueblas*" (1960), "The Indian Population of Central Mexico, 1531-1610" (1960), and "The Aboriginal Population of Central Mexico on the Eve of the Spanish Conquest" (1963). The last of these raised the first of several "red flags" to other historians, for it proposed the highest population estimate ever made for pre-Conquest Mexico.

Cook and Borah, in the introduction to the first 1960 work, put their finger on one of the most controversial aspects of their work:

> The publication of the Cook-Simpson estimates, with their radically high values for the earlier decade of the sixteenth century and their postulation of a catastrophic loss in numbers during the sixteenth century, led to animated debate among scholars. Even though Cook and Simpson attributed the depopulation primarily to the introduction of Old World diseases, over which the Spaniards could have had little or no control, a number of scholars were disturbed at what they feared would become substantial reinforcement of the so-called "black legend" of Spanish oppression the New World natives.[16]

Many others flatly refused to accept such high population estimates, some from chauvinism (one French scholar admitted to Borah that he couldn't believe that pre-Columbian Mexico had a higher population than *la belle France*) while others found it difficult to believe that the pre-Hispanic population was higher than that of contemporary Mexico.[17]

Cook and Borah used the *sumas de visitas*; literally, the household counts carried out by Spanish civil authorities which were translated into tribute counts for settled areas. Over the course of eighty years, they traced a precipitous decline in Indian numbers.

It was in their last *Ibero-Americana*, number 45, "The Aboriginal Population of Central Mexico on the Eve of the Spanish Conquest" that Cook and Borah made their most famous (or infamous) proposal: that the pre-Conquest population of Central Mexico was 25.2 million people. The first section of their study, entitled "The Problem," recapitulated the evidentiary problems involved in people-counting, as well as historical prejudices which informed the debate.

Eighteenth-century historians tended to dismiss as exaggerations statements about the size of Indian armies, and stories of vast cities. "Indians were known to be brutish savages still using crude implements of bone and stone, incapable of the organization and marshalling of resources necessary for building cities or maintaining imperial institutions." Allowance, wrote William Robertson for one, must be made for the "warm imaginations of Spanish writers."[18] Francisco Clavijero, writing centuries later, vigorously defended the contemporary statements of Spanish conquistadors, missionaries, and government functionaries, pointing out that such authorities, acting from different motivations and points of view, would hardly have conspired or colluded to exaggerate the historical record.

After a careful description of tribute collection records, Cook and Borah calculated an average family size of 4.5 persons in tribute-collecting areas of Mexico, and a corresponding population of over 25 million. Even allowing for smaller families, they ended their study by stating that "the evidence nevertheless clearly supports the conclusion that central Mexico had a very dense aboriginal population when Cortés landed on the Gulf Coast, and that, in general, early Spanish statements and accounts are in accord with fiscal evidence."[19]

The Berkeley School's work culminated a decade later in the publication of Cook and Borah's Essays in *Population History: Mexico and the Caribbean*, the first volume of which was published by the University of California Press in 1971. The eighteen essays which make up the three volumes cover a wide range of topics, including explorations of the pre-Columbian Mesoamerican diet and royal revenue collection in New Spain, but which also contained the second of the prominent "red flags" which enraged certain critics: extremely high population estimates for pre-contact Hispaniola, as well as for Mexico. Friar Bartolomé de Las Casas had estimated a population of 3 to 4 million or even more, but his interest in magnifying the extent of depopulation owing to Spanish cruelty and depredation made his figures suspect.

Borah and Cook begin by reviewing previous population estimates, starting with that of one of their most prominent critics, Ángel Rosenblat, a Venezuelan linguist, essayist, and historian. As early as 1935, Rosenblat wrote a series of pieces entitled "El desarrollo de la población indígena de América," which he followed up with several books, *La población indígena de América desde 1492*, and *La población indígena y el mestizaje de América*, the first published in 1945, and the second in 1954.

Rosenblat, wrote Cook and Borah, "really listed items rather than attempting the massive critical examination of sources customary in medieval and ancient European studies." His estimate was 100,000 persons living on the island at the time of Columbus' arrival.

Cook and Borah quote contemporary statements from Columbus and Las Casas which indicate that the new land was a densely-populated island. The *repartimiento* of 1514 (the Spaniards exported their labor institutions, which proved so destructive to the natives) indicated some 22,000 surviving males, a figure which Rosenblat accepted. Some discussion on the percentage of children over and under 14 years of age, as well as the category of *naborias de casa* as well as *indios de servicio* follows, but Cook-Borah also quote Las Casas (3 million), fourteen Dominican friars (2 million souls), Peter Martyr (1.2 million), and a *Licenciado* Zuazo, an *oidor* in the *audiencia* of Santo Domingo (1.13 million), etc.

A controversial aspect of the Cook-Borah Hispaniola estimate is that they doubled the 1496 population count, on the grounds that the Spanish only controlled half of the island, and that "the half still free from Spanish control had not as yet been subjected to the adverse effect of direct physical contact with the invaders."[20] They estimate "conservatively" that there were 2.26 million potential tributaries on the entire island.[21] By the end of the chapter, they had reached an estimated population count of 7 to 8 million, pointing out that the inhabitants of the Caribbean islands could cultivate manioc, which had higher yields than maize, and better agricultural conditions than drought-prone Mexico.[22]

Discussing probable causes, Cook and Borah referred to Sauer and attributed not disease, but rather harsh systems of labor exploitation and the disruption of native social and economic organization in destruction of the indigenous population.[23]

Rosenblat counter-attacked against the Cook-Borah thesis in his 1967 essay on the population of Hispaniola in 1492, which was translated for William Denevan's *The Native Population of the Americas in 1492*, a seminal work with essays on the whole population estimate question, and chapters on native numbers in the Caribbean, Mesoamerica, and South America, including the Andes, Argentina, and Brazil, as well as North America. Here Woodrow Borah and Ángel Rosenblat "squared off" against each other—in print, of course.

Rosenblat opened with a scarcely-veiled attack on Cook and Borah: "All historiographical work carries with it the proclivities of its authors...[it is] common for the scholar to slant facts and even figures in order to reach preconceived conclusions. There is no more malleable material than statistics."[24]

He continues to give historical analogies, such as the number of Persians invading Greece under Xerxes, as proof that historical exaggeration is a norm, not an aberration, before comparing Las Casas, Fernando de Oviedo, and a modern historian, Charles Verlinden, to re-affirm his estimation of 100,000. Along the way, he takes a swipe at Carl Sauer for supposedly idealizing native agriculture, health, and nutritional values before using the term "hyperbolic calculations" to condemn high counters, or the entire Berkeley School.[25]

Borah's essay in the same volume, "The Historical Demography of Aboriginal and Colonial America: An Attempt at Perspective," is not an answer to Rosenblat's criticisms, but rather an overview of the questions involved in people-counting and its attendant guesswork. Borah reviews the numbers given by contemporaries and scholars over the course of centuries, and the techniques being used in population "guesstimates." His concluding statement was "Whatever the problems of evidence and analysis, careful regional studies are being carried out in increasing volume. Our great need now is to search out the evidence, test it with care, and let it lead us where it will."[26]

Another scholar who took vigorous aim at Cook and Borah is David Henige. In an *HAHR* article from 1978, "On the Contact Population of Hispaniola: History as Higher Mathematics," Henige questioned their methods, their conclusions, and even their "questionable" translations of original source material. "Cook and Borah," he wrote, "have, I think, given evidence in the essay under review how very difficult it is to subordinate theory to evidence." He did, however, concede "But if one cannot agree with their methods or their conclusions, one may still be grateful to them for prompting us to ask questions about just what historians are, or ought to be."[27]

Henige returned to the attack in *Numbers From Nowhere: The American Indian Population Contact Debate*, published by the University of Oklahoma Press in 1998. The title itself was provocative, suggesting figures pulled out of thin air, and Henige devotes a significant portion of his book attacking the Berkeley School. His very chapter titles are provocative: "Do Numbers Lie?"; "Higher Numbers, Higher Ground"; "Damning the Torpedoes"; "Giving Disease a Bad Name"; "Rashomon the Chronicler"; "Contact Does Not Equal Contagion"; "I Came, I Saw, I Counted"; "The Jury Will Disregard"; "Epidemic Hyperbole," etc. In "Damning the Torpedoes," he takes dead aim at Cook-Borah.

However, Noble David Cook, in a book review in *The Journal of Interdisciplinary History*, more or less eviscerates Henige's claim that he is a lone voice crying in the wilderness. Henige's thesis is that the "high counters" were successful in establishing a new historical paradigm in spite of questions about their quantitative methods. But Henige, who accuses his critics of using sources selectively, does the same himself, according to Cook.[28]

Henige's most questionable charge is that Cook and Borah's work was not subject to rigorous review. In footnote 131, page 331 of *Numbers From Nowhere*, he writes: "There is reason to suspect that Cook and Borah did not benefit from criticism at the front end of the process, either. The volumes on Mexico were all published in *Ibero-Americana*, a series under their control, while the University of California Press—a house organ—published their other works."[29] If Henige has "reason to suspect" this, he does not provide evidence of it in a book of 532 pages. As someone who has had the privilege of working with Woodrow Wilson Borah over the course of a decade, I can state categorically that if any scholar possessed a sense of academic integrity, it was Borah.

Henige wonders why Woodrow Borah, who by the 1980s was the only living member of the Berkeley School, has not defended his thesis, as he is puzzled by what he calls the silence of most of the rest of the high counters. Borah, saddened and diminished (as he acknowledged to me) by the deaths of the friends with whom he had worked so closely for so many years, chose to shift his attention and energy elsewhere in the last decades of his life, finishing the superb *Justice by Insurance: The General Indian Court of Colonial Mexico and the Legal Aides of the Half-Real* in 1983.

But the debate was carried on by others: R. A. Zambardino critiqued Henige's *HAHR* article the same year in the same journal. While he accepted Henige's doubts about the "extraordinary" figure of 8 million for Hispaniola, he accuses Henige of hyperbole when he throws cold water on all such demographic work: "He seems to imply that his rejection of the Borah and Cook estimates extends to the rest of the New World, and, after an attack on the abuse of mathematical methods and the inhumanity of logarithms, he concludes with a deeply pessimistic note with the assertion that at present it would be futile to attempt population estimates for the early period of Spanish rule."[30] Hispaniola, he continues, is only a sideline of Cook and Borah, and "their work on central Mexico differs by orders of magnitude, both in quantity and quality, from their brief and late study of Hispaniola. The abandonment of their Hispaniola estimate cannot be extended in an unqualified way to their other works."[31] Henige then responded to Zambardino in a subsequent number of the *HAHR*, and no doubt tenure was happily earned by one and all.

The Berkeley School, as I have noted, had its heyday in the decades before and after the Second World War. Sherburne Cook passed away in 1974, Carl Sauer in 1975, and Lesley Byrd Simpson in 1984. Woodrow Borah soldiered on, finally succumbing in 1999. What I find remarkable about *L'ecole* is the sense of intellectual community among scholars of such disparate disciplines. Simpson was a committee member for Borah's oral examinations; they later served together on such committees decades afterwards. Carl Sauer, though not particularly involved in the "numbers debate," brought a geographical context to the study of the conquest of the New World, the conditions of the places involved, or, in his own words "to learn what the Spaniards found of nature and culture at their coming and what they did in accepting, adapting, and replacing prior conditions."[32]

His advice (to geographers, and by extension to all scholars) was to physically hunker down, test the air and soil, and get a feel for the terrain. He provided the geographical context for examining more than colonial manuscripts. Simpson absorbed this advice; he begins his classic *Many Mexicos* with a description of Mexico's unforgiving geography, as well as its dependence on one primary food-crop (maize) for its sustenance. Simpson's meticulous use of primary materials helped define archival investigation for colonial Mexico. Woodrow Borah continued this example, plunging into regional, municipal, parish, or other records to uncover data from the past, urging his students to "take it gently" and develop *siztfleish*. He wrote twenty-two books and articles with Sherburne Friend Cook, a physiologist who provided much of the scientific context within which to place the archival data.

To conclude, let me quote Arnold Bauer in his obituary for Borah in the *Hispanic American Historical Review*:

> Had l'ecole Berkeley, as the French called it, stuck to the relatively solid ground of archival research, their work would undoubtedly have been widely regarded as both original and fundamental. What has provoked most critical attention to it was their statistical projection of the demographic curve backward to suggest truly spectacular population figures at the time of European contact. These estimates, ranging as high as 25 million people and more for central Mexico alone, made their way into polemical tracts and popular texts, but have come in for keen criticism by specialists in the field. Whatever the final resolution of this debate, Borah and Cook's monumental work provided the point of departure for serious demographic history in the Americas and the standard against which present research is measured.[33]

Postscript: This paper was presented at SALALM LIII in May, 2008. During the question and answer period at the panel, the question was asked, how do the Borah-Cook numbers appear today, some half a century after their formulation? Has anyone come up with a better methodology, and does the high number still stand in Mexican historiography?

In 2008, Massimo Livi Bacci's *Conquest: The Destruction of the American Indios* was published in English translation. In this work, Bacci "attempt[s] a synthesis of the numeric data, an evaluation of the human resources which the voyage of Columbus put at risk. It is a technical argument, though one with many ideological and historic implications...we can say that the estimates of the so-called low counters from the first half of the twentieth century have been replaced by those of the 'high counters' in the second half."[34]

The difference between the low and high estimates (for all of America) range from under 10 million to over 100 million. Those for Central Mexico range from a low of 3.2 (Kroeber) to a high of 25.2 (Cook-Borah). The median value of 13 million is just that, Bacci states. After a careful and extensive review of both epidemiological and tribute-calculations. Bacci writes that criticisms of the "ingenious and composite estimates of Borah and Cook are well-founded,"[35] but still states that "we know little about the Mexican population between contact and 1568." Bacci believes that *reliable* information about the native population is limited, but that the total population in 1568 was not far from 3 million, and had suffered a sustained decline of around 2 percent per year for the three decades following conquest, due to the disastrous impact of war, smallpox, and exploitation of the natives after the fall of Tenochtitlan.[36] He concludes

> Much remains to be understood about the demographic history of Mexico during the first century of the Conquest. Given a population reduced to less than 1.3 million at the end of the century, it is conceivable that, over a stretch of eighty years, the pre-Conquest population was halved three times, so an initial figure of ten million seems plausible.[37]

This then, in 2008, is the latest, but almost certainly not final, word on the Great Debate. But in the end, it is not the numbers, but the historical process of examination and analysis which matters most. Woodrow Borah remarked to me that neither he nor Cook ever expected their calculations to stand as definitive or absolute. What mattered most to them, as members of *L'ecole Berkeley*, was that the questions be posed, and the answers sought, wherever the trail might lead.

NOTES

1.   Clark S. Larsen, "In the Wake of Columbus: Native Population Biology in Postcontact Americas." *Yearbook of Physical Anthropology*, 37 (1994), p.

2.   Woodrow Borah, "The Historical Demography of Aboriginal and Colonial America: An Attempt at Perspective," in *The Native Population of the Americas in 1492*. Edited by William M. Denevan. Madison: The University of Wisconsin Press, 1976: 19-20.

3.   William M. Denevan, "Carl Sauer and Native American Population Size." *The Geographical Review*, v.86, no.3 (July 1996): footnote 3, p.393.

4.   Woodrow W. Borah, John Leighly, James J. Parsons. Lesley B. Simpson, University of California: In Memorium, May 1977. Calisphere, http://content.edlib.org/xtf/view?docId=hb119 9n68c&brand=calispere.

5.   Hardin B. Jones, Robert F. Hizer, Nello Pace. University of California: Sherburne F. Cook: In Memorium, May 1977. Calisphere, http://content.edlib.org/xtf/view?docId=hb1199n68 c&brand=calispere.

6.   Woodrow Borah, James W. Wilkie, and Rebecca Horn. "An Interview With Woodrow Borah." *Hispanic American Historical Review*, v.65, no.3 (August 1985): 401-441.

7.   Gunther Barth, Margaret Chowning, Tulio Halperín-Donghi, Eric Van Young. Woodrow Borah: In Memorium, 2000. Calisphere.

8.   Carl Sauer and Donald Brand. "Aztatlán." *Ibero-Americana*, 1 (Berkeley: University of California Press, 1932): frontispiece.

9.   Russell Thornton. *American Indian Holocaust and Survival: A Population History Since 1492*. Norman: University of Oklahoma Press, 1987: 21-22.

10. Clark Spencer Larsen. "In the Wake of Columbus: Native Population Biology in the Postcontact Americas." *Yearbook of Physical Anthropology*. (Yearbook series—Supplement …to the American Journal of Physical Anthropology), v.37: S19 (1994): 110.

11. Russell Thornton. "Population: PreContact to the Present." *Encyclopedia of North American Indians*. Edited by Frederick E. Hoxie. Boston: Houghton Mifflin Company, 1996: 500.

12. A. L. Kroeber, *Cultural and Natural Areas of Native North America* (Berkeley, 1939): 150-151; Paul Rivet, in Meillet and Cohen, *Les Langues du Monde* (Paris, 1924): 599-602; both cited in George Kubler, "Population Movements in Mexico 1520-1600." *The Hispanic American Historical Review*, Vol. 22, No. 4, (November 1942): 607, footnote 9.

13. Sherburne F. Cook and Lesley Byrd Simpson, "The Population of Central Mexico in the Sixteenth Century." *Ibero-Americana*, no.31 (1948): 16.

14. Ibid: 17.

15. Ibid: 46.

16. Sherburne F. Cook and Woodrow Borah. "The Indian Population of Central Mexico, 1531-1610." *Ibero-Americana*, no.44 (1960): 1.

17. Ibid.

18. Ibid: 1-2.

19. Ibid: 88.

20. Sherburne F. Cook and Woodrow Borah. "The Aboriginal Population of Hispaniola," in *Essays in Population History: Mexico and the Caribbean*. Berkeley: University of California Press, v.1 (1971): 396.

21. Ibid.

22. Ibid: 408-409.

23. Ibid: 409.

24. Angel Rosenblat. "The Population of Hispaniola at the Time of Columbus," in *The Native Population of the Americas in 1492*. Edited by William Denevan. Madison: University of Wisconsin Press, 1976: 43.

25. Ibid: 62-63.

26. Woodrow Borah, "The Aboriginal Demography of Aboriginal and Colonial America: An Attempt at Perspective," in *Denevan, The Native Population of the Americas in 1492*,32.

27. David Henige. "On the Contact Population of Hispaniola: History as Higher Mathematics." *The Hispanic American Historical Review*, Vol. 58, No. 2 (May 1978): 236.

28. David Noble Cook. "Book Review: Numbers From Nowhere: The American Indian Contact Population Debate." *The Journal of Interdisciplinary History*, v.30, no.3 (1999): 516-520.

29. David Henige. *Numbers From Nowhere: The American Indian Contact Population Debate*. Norman: University of Oklahoma Press, 1998: 331.

30. R. A. Zambardino. "Critique of David Henige's 'On the Contact Population of Hispaniola: History as Higher Mathematics.' " *Hispanic American Historical Review*, Vol. 58, No. 4 (Nov 1978): 701

31. Ibid.

32. Carl Sauer. *The Early Spanish Main*. Berkeley: University of California Press, 1966, p.v; as quoted in. Denevan, op. cit., p.392.

33. Arnold J. Bauer. "Obituary: Woodrow W. Borah (1912-1999)." *Hispanic American Historical Review* v. 80, no.3 (2000): 565-567.

34. Massimo Livi Bacci. *Conquest: the Destruction of the American Indios*. Malden, MA: Polity, 2008: 4-5.

35. Ibid: 131.

36. Ibid.

37. Ibid: 154.

4. El papel de la expedición botánica dirigida por José Celestino Mutis en el desarrollo de las bibliotecas especializadas en Colombia

Ketty Rodríguez Casillas

Propósito

El propósito de este trabajo es establecer un marco conceptual que facilite la investigación del papel de la Expedición Botánica dirigida por Celestino Mutis en el desarrollo de la biblioteca especializada en Colombia y proveer una bibliografía que ayude realizar la investigación. Se identificaron fuentes bibliográficas, o colecciones que pueden ser útiles para la investigación. El marco conceptual que se desarrolló es amplio y dinámico y para ello se utilizó una metodología cualitativa. Se realizó una búsqueda de la literatura utilizando los siguientes temas combinados de diferentes formas: José Celestino Mutis, la expedición botánica de Nueva Granada, el Iluminismo de la segunda mitad del siglo dieciocho en Nueva Granada, la Inquisición en América, el mercado del libro, la censura, las bibliotecas y/o colecciones personales o privadas y los aspectos internacionales del desarrollo de las bibliotecas especializadas

Al intentar abordar el tema, afloraron las siguientes preguntas: (1) ¿Cómo desarrollar un marco conceptual para este estudio cuando el personaje que dirige la Expedición Botánica fue tan polifacético, controversial y complejo? (2) ¿Cómo abordar la literatura sobre la Expedición Botánica en Nueva Granada en la segunda mitad del siglo dieciocho y el papel de Mutis, siendo esta tan abundante? (3) ¿Cómo identificar literatura sobre Mutis, como bibliógrafo, cuando parece ser la faceta menos estudiada? El marco conceptual tiene en cuenta estas preguntas.

Hipótesis

Se arguye que siendo la Expedición Botánica una actividad de gran importancia para la Corona Española, ésta tenía que estar dotada de un jugoso presupuesto. Como la actividad principal de la expedición era la investigación, ésta tenía que estar sustentada por una colección de libros especializados en botánica y otras fuentes de referencia (una biblioteca por pequeña que fuera que permitiera alcanzar los objetivos de la Expedición). Se propone que el origen de la biblioteca especializada en Colombia muy bien pudiera ser aquella colección que Mutis tuvo que tener para apoyar la investigación de la Expedición Botánica.

Metodología

Se utilizó la metodología cualitativa para analizar las posibles variables y poder entender el impacto de un evento. Para el desarrollo del marco conceptual que nos permita investigar el papel de la Expedición Botánica dirigida por José Celestino Mutis y el desarrollo de la biblioteca especializada como institución en Colombia, se partió desde la misma definición de biblioteca especializada. Esta definición indica que la biblioteca especializada surge como necesidad de una institución u organización y que su función es ayudar a que esa institución alcance sus objetivos.[1] Se planteó como premisa que para alcanzar los objetivos de la Expedición Botánica en Nueva Granada dirigida por Mutis, era necesario una colección de libros. Mutis era un hombre de ciencias, influenciado por el movimiento ilustrado, y valoraba todo lo que avanzara el conocimiento científico y el pensamiento crítico. Para el desarrollo del marco conceptual se realizó un repaso de la literatura en siete áreas consideradas importantes para el desarrollo de la investigación propuesta. Estas son (1) el movimiento Ilustrado del siglo dieciocho en Nueva Granada; (2) trasfondo histórico sobre el desarrollo de la biblioteca especializada desde la perspectiva internacional; (3) identificar qué propósito tenía la Corona en las Expediciones Científicas; (4) cuál era el propósito de la Expedición Botánica de Nueva Granada (Colombia); (5) José Celestino Mutis como personaje, como bibliógrafo y educador; (6) la influencia de la Inquisición y la censura en relación con los libros en América, las bibliotecas, el mercado del libro y con Mutis; (7) el papel de las bibliotecas privadas.

Premisas del estudio

1. Se consideró que la Real Expedición Botánica de Nueva Granada necesitaba una biblioteca especializada.

2. El siglo dieciocho presentó grandes transformaciones: la Revolución Industrial en el plano económico; la ascensión de la burguesía en el plano social; y en el campo político la Revolución Francesa y la independencia de Estados Unidos.[2] Como resultado de estos cambios surgió una nueva filosofía de vida y nuevas ideas donde la aplicación de la ciencia al quehacer diario cobró importancia. Esta nueva filosofía se conoció como el Iluminismo Ilustración.

3. La Inquisición y la censura jugaron un papel importante en el desarrollo de la ciencia, la educación, la cultura en general y especialmente en el mundo del libro el cual está relacionado con las bibliotecas.

4. Las universidades eran administradas casi totalmente por el clero y predominaba la filosofía escolástica.[3]

5. Las primeras manifestaciones ilustradas en el ámbito cultural educativo de los estudios superiores en Colombia se iniciaron con Mutis en 1762.[4]

La Ilustración en el siglo dieciocho

La Ilustración empezó a penetrar en España en la primera mitad del siglo dieciocho y fue apoyada por las Sociedades Económicas de Amigos del País, pero tuvo oposición de algunos sectores de la Iglesia y de la nobleza tradicional. En el aspecto económico, la Iglesia poseía grandes propiedades y en el educativo monopolizaba casi totalmente la enseñanza promoviendo una educación clásica y escolástica, cada vez más desacreditada, que defendía la Inquisición.[5] En las colonias de América se replicaban las mismas estructuras políticas, sociales y culturales de España.

En Nueva Granada surge el movimiento Ilustrado durante los reinados de Carlos III (1759-1788) y Carlos IV (1788-1808) que coinciden con el movimiento político preliminar de la independencia de las colonias americanas. Mutis recibió las corrientes de la Ilustración en Cádiz y Madrid.[6] La Ilustración llega a Nueva Granada a través de funcionarios públicos, del clero ilustrado, de miembros de las expediciones científicas, de libros, viajeros o visitantes y de criollos que se desplazaron a Europa.[7]

La biblioteca especializada en Colombia

Las bases para que naciera la biblioteca especializada se dan con el movimiento Ilustrado que llegó a Nueva Granada y que se distingue por un profundo respeto por el conocimiento de la ciencia y la tecnología. Es el desarrollo del conocimiento, la ciencia, la tecnología y la educación lo que promueve el surgimiento de la era industrial. Casi todos los países muestran un desarrollo similar de la biblioteca especializada, la cual aparece con el surgimiento de la industrialización o cuando el país consigue su independencia después de la colonización. En los países industrializados el gran auge de las bibliotecas especializadas fue después de la Segunda Guerra Mundial.[8] La biblioteca especializada es un fenómeno del siglo diecinueve que surge por la creciente industrialización.

Es necesario definir el término biblioteca especializada que ha causado mucha confusión en el ámbito internacional por el problema asociado con la definición de términos afines tales como: documentación, ciencia de la información, bibliotecología especializada y por la falta de estándares.[9][10] Las bibliotecas en general deben su existencia a una organización o institución principal (conocida en inglés como "parent institution"). En ese sentido las metas y objetivos de las bibliotecas están determinadas por las de la institución principal. En el caso de la biblioteca especializada este hecho es transparente.

Se puede definir la biblioteca especializada "como un departamento o facilidad responsable por la adquisición, indización y distribución (diseminación) de conocimiento directamente relacionado con el trabajo de una organización especializada o un grupo especial de usuarios".[11] Quizás las características que más definen a las "bibliotecas especializadas" no tengan que ver tanto, con lo que hacen sino con "cómo lo hacen". Las bibliotecas especializadas se caracterizan por la anticipación a la demanda y el servicio activo y rápido. La biblioteca puede ser especializada por el tipo de tema cubierto, su origen geográfico o localización de materiales y clientes, o por el tipo de servicio ofrecido de acuerdo a los requerimientos de sus clientes. En este estudio se parte precisamente de la definición del término biblioteca especializada que indica que "ésta sirve a una organización especial o a un grupo especial de usuarios". También se identificó el propósito y los resultados de la Expedición Botánica de Nueva Granada, como organización y el papel de su director, José Celestino Mutis como unidad de estudio.

Propósito de la Corona con las Expediciones Científicas

Al concluir la Guerra de los Siete Años (1756-1763), en la cual Gran Bretaña derrotó a España y Francia, se inició una lucha por parte de Gran Bretaña, Rusia y Francia en contra de la hegemonía de las rutas marítimas de España en América. Carlos III lanzó un programa político con el propósito de recuperar el control de las colonias americanas. El programa del Carlos III era producto del movimiento Ilustrado. El mismo pretendía convertir a España en un imperio colonial. "Algunos políticos sostenían que si la colonias eran el mayor problema de la monarquía podían ser también el remedio".[12] Para ello se intentó modernizar las viejas estructuras con el fin de estrechar los lazos con los territorios americanos y explotar así intensamente los recursos fiscales, naturales y políticos. De esta manera la introducción de nuevas disciplinas como astronomía, química o botánica en los virreinatos es consistente con el nuevo plan político de la corona también conocido como el reformismo Borbón.

Propósito de la Expedición Botánica de Nueva Granada (Colombia)

La Expedición Botánica de Nueva Granada (Colombia) dirigida por José Celestino Mutis se oficializó con la real cédula del 1ro de noviembre de 1783. Los objetivos de la expedición eran "colección, descripción, clasificación, nomenclatura y dibujo de las plantas—el reino vegetal, sino también en los demás productos de otros dos reinos, animal y mineral, incluyendo observaciones astronómicas y geográficas".[13] El libro de Frías Núñez *Tras el Dorado vegetal: José Celestino Mutis y la Real Expedición Botánica del Nuevo Reino de Granada (1783-1808)*, describe a Mutis como personaje y su trabajo como Director de la Expedición Botánica. Además analiza con objetividad situaciones controversiales sobre Mutis. Si se considera la infraestructura y nivel de desarrollo de Colombia y del mundo para esa época, la tarea para alcanzar los objetivos de la Expedición Botánica era monumental. Por tanto, la creación de la biblioteca especializada es una herramienta indispensable para ayudar a alcanzar dichos objetivos. Al morir Mutis en 1808, la obra sobre *La Flora Granadina* comprendía "5,393 dibujos, 2, 945 de ellos a color con sus respectivas descripciones en latín que no habían sido publicadas".[14] Tal vez dado el hecho de que no haya prueba contundente de que dicha obra existió, el título de la obra varia cuando en diferentes escritos se hace referencia a la misma. Así se le ha llamado, entre otros, *La Flora Granadina*, *La Flora* y *La Flora de Bogotá*.

Sinforoso Mutis, sobrino de Mutis, estaba sistematizando las descripciones de *La Flora* cuando estalló la Guerra de Independencia de Colombia. En 1816, por mandato expreso del Rey, el General Morillo confiscó *La Flora Granadina* e inventarió parte, en 104 baúles que remitió a Madrid. En este proceso se extraviaron casi todas las descripciones de Mutis y otros valiosos documentos, entre ellos 15 cajas correspondientes a los minerales. Sólo quedaron 48 cajas que contenían el herbario.[15]

Cerca de 150 años permaneció *La Flora* en cajas en el Jardín Botánico de Madrid. En el siglo veinte, por medio de un convenio cultural entre los gobiernos de Colombia y España se comenzó a difundir la obra. En 1930, Ellsworth Payne Killip, conservador del Smithsonian Institution trabajó en el Jardín Botánico de Madrid desempacando el herbario de Mutis y afirmó que los manuscritos de *La Flora* no existieron y que ello explicaba la demora de Mutis en entregar el trabajo para su publicación. Refiriéndose al trabajo de *La Flora* dice Killip "el trabajo pictórico de la Expedición Botánica ha quedado resaltado y admirado a lo largo de los últimos doscientos años, pero los manuscritos correspondientes a La Flora han sido objeto de cuestionamiento, dudándose, incluso de su existencia".[16] El herbario de Mutis y el conjunto de láminas han sido recogidos en detalle en el trabajo de Paloma Blanco Fernández de Celaya (1992).

José Celestino Mutis—El personaje

José Celestino Mutis nació en Cádiz, España, en 1732. Recibió el grado de bachiller en medicina en Sevilla y continuó su educación en Madrid de 1757 a 1760. Se marchó a América en 1760 como médico del Virrey de Nueva Granada (Colombia), el Marqués Pedro Mesía de la Cerda.[17] En 1772 fue ordenado sacerdote. En 1782 fue nombrado director de la Real Expedición Botánica de Nueva Granada.[18] Vivió en Colombia 48 años y murió en Bogotá, en 1808.

Un rápido vistazo de la abundante literatura sobre Celestino Mutis revela lo multifacético, complejo y controversial de este personaje. Se muestra a Mutis con intereses que van desde la medicina, minería, astronomía, matemáticas, física, química, religión, educación, botánica, humanismo, y bibliografía que lo impulsan a su gran actividad gestora.

Muchos investigadores de Colombia consideran a Mutis como punto de partida del desarrollo científico, cultural y emancipador de ese país.[19] Como gestor científico es incuestionable su formación en medicina y sus aplicaciones de ésta a la botánica y su labor como director de la Real Expedición Botánica que le dio renombre más allá del mundo científico hispanoparlante.[20][21][22]

La actividad gestora de Mutis se evidencia en el área empresarial por su interés en la explotación de las minas de Montuosa (Pamplona) y las minas de Real del Sapo (Ibagué). También jugó un papel importante en la comercialización de la quina, el té de Bogotá y la canela. Igualmente tuvo una participación decisiva en la construcción del Observatorio Astronómico en Bogotá.[23]

Mutis es considerado un protoprócer de la cultura colombiana.[24] En el área educativa fundó la primera escuela científica de medicina e instituyó la enseñanza de las matemáticas y química, así como su aportación indirecta en cuatro planes de estudios universitarios.[25] Mutis promovió el desarrollo de las Sociedades Económicas de Amigos del País las cuales desaparecieron luego de la guerra de Independencia en1808. Las Sociedades Económicas estimulaban tertulias que resultaron beneficiosas en la gestación del movimiento de Independencia.[26] Como administrador, Mutis fue considerado práctico y símbolo del reformismo Borbón.[27]

Por otro lado, Mutis ha recibido serias críticas. Para acercarse al personaje desde la perspectiva de sus críticos, Lafuente recomienda la obra de Javier Puerto, *La ilusión quebrada: Botánica, sanidad y ciencia en la España ilustrada*, como fuente de referencia indispensable, e indica que la obra de José Antonio Amaya, *Celestino Mutis y la Expedición Botánica*, hace un esfuerzo por presentar una imagen balanceada de los éxitos y fracasos de Mutis. También recomienda la obra de Raúl Rodríguez Nozal, *Plantas americanas para la España ilustrada: Génesis, desarrollo y ocaso del proyecto español de expediciones botánicas*.

Francisco José Caldas, integrante de la Expedición Botánica de Nueva Granada, fue uno de los principales críticos de Mutis a la muerte del sabio en 1808. En referencia a *La Flora de Bogotá* Caldas dice "Ya preveo el asombro que va a causar a la nación y al mundo sabio los manuscritos de Mutis. ¿Quién puede creer que un hombre lleno de virtudes, de conocimientos, de sosiego y de comodidades, haya dejado unos vacios tan inmensos y difíciles de llenar?".[28] Sin embargo, Frías Núñez hace constar que Mutis se había olvidado de Caldas en su testamento personal. También añade que quizás esa era la razón por la cual Mutis iba alargando la entrega de los textos porque quizás no los tenía conformados en su totalidad. Respecto a la conservación o no de dicho manuscrito Frías Núñez concluye que aún hoy no se puede decir de forma tajante la existencia real de dicho trabajo. Pérez Arbeláez, científico colombiano, y un ardiente defensor de la obra de Mutis cita al ilustre botánico colombiano José Jerónimo Triana, indicando que éste adopta una actitud antimutisiana al referirse a la historia de la quina.

El interés de Mutis fue sobre todo la ciencia, principalmente la investigación botánica. Tanto amaba la ciencia que por ello se hizo sacerdote. El criterio que tienen los biógrafos de Mutis sobre su posición religiosa es que algunos lo consideraban un católico convencido mientras que otros creen que se ordenó sacerdote en 1772 porque "creyó encontrar en aquel estado mayor facilidad para consagrase a la ciencia" o más bien para ponerse a salvo de las sospechas de la Inquisición.[29] Es importante explorar más los motivos de Mutis para hacerse sacerdote así como su "pleito científico y personal" con Hipólito Ruiz, encargado de la expedición Botánica de Perú.[30]

Mutis ¿Bibliógrafo?

Desde 1783 hasta el 1790 Mutis vivió en Mariquita, ciudad situada al pie de los Andes de Quindío, cerca del Río Magdalena en Colombia. Existen varias referencias a la biblioteca de Mutis que indican que su casa también se utilizaba como Centro de Operaciones Científicas. Una descripción bastante detallada describe la distribución de la casa como sigue: "Otro de los departamentos estaba ocupado por la oficina de pintura y los demás se hallaban destinados al citado herbario y a la biblioteca".[31] Refiriéndose a la biblioteca, Schumacher indica: "Mutis dedicó gran parte de sus ingresos a la ampliación de su biblioteca. Como ahora debía ordenar y trabajar en sus colecciones a fin de describir y sistematizar sus tesoros, hizo que, con este fin, desde Europa se le enviase considerable cantidad de publicaciones, creando así una fuente de información importante para las ciencias naturales, ciertamente un milagro para los Andes Sudamericanos".[32]

Mutis como bibliógrafo ha sido poco estudiado. Las cartas de Mutis son una fuente valiosa para estudiar su faceta de bibliógrafo. En ellas se recoge su comunicación relacionada con la compra de libros, incluso listas completas de libros adquiridos y otros detalles que arrojan luz sobre el mercado del libro frente a la censura de la época. Igualmente arrojan luz sobre el carácter de Mutis. De gran utilidad fue la consulta del *Archivo epistolar del sabio naturalista José Celestino Mutis* de Guillermo Hernández de Alba. En una carta que Mutis escribió a Martínez de Sobral en 1789, le indicaba: "He disipado sin previsión mía el caudal que iba adquiriendo, por hallarme imposibilitado de volver a Europa, y pegado mi corazón a mi excelente biblioteca y gabinete".[33] Es necesario señalar la importancia y aprecio que siempre Mutis adjudicó a los libros en su vida, evidenciado por la inversión de sus ingresos para adquirir libros y mejorar sus colecciones y por su admiración y respeto por la ciencias y las tecnologías.

Mutis conocía el mercado de los libros ya que su padre Julián Mutis era librero de oficio en Cádiz.[34] Al estudiar a Mutis en la faceta de bibliógrafo se le debe explorar como educador por la tangencia directa con el tema. El libro *Mutis educador de la élite neogranadina* de Soto Arango estudia a Mutis como educador dentro del contexto histórico de su época, proyectando su impacto en el futuro del país. Se describe en detalle la gestión educativa de Mutis y otras organizaciones y/o instituciones que ayudaron a formar la primera generación de científicos colombianos, incluyendo las bibliotecas, asociaciones y el papel de la Iglesia Católica. También se ofrece una descripción de las universidades de esa época, las cuales eran administradas casi totalmente por el clero y en donde predominaba la filosofía escolástica, desacreditada por su apoyo a la Inquisición. Tenían acceso a la universidad los españoles y un pequeño grupo de criollos. Se reconoce la influencia de las bibliotecas en el desarrollo del pensamiento y quehacer ilustrado. "A pesar de la censura llegaron a formarse nutridas bibliotecas en Santafé. Las bibliotecas privadas o personales juegan un papel importante en la formación de muchos criollos y en el desarrollo de las bibliotecas en Colombia. Se puede destacar la de los Jesuitas, que fue la base de la Biblioteca Pública que fundó el fiscal Moreno durante el gobierno del Virrey Manuel Guirior, origen de la actual Biblioteca Nacional de Colombia".[35]

En alusión a la formación de Francisco José Caldas, integrante de la Expedición Botánica de Mutis,[36] indica que Caldas usó la biblioteca personal de su patrón José Félix Restrepo, en Popayán y posiblemente la de Antonio Nariño. Se conoce que entre las bibliotecas privadas importantes de la época se encontraban la de Mutis, Camilo Torres, Antonio Nariño y la de José Félix Restrepo en Popayán.[37][38]

El tema de las bibliotecas privadas o particulares y su influencia en el desarrollo de las bibliotecas en general en América Latina debe ser explorado con profundidad ya que tal vez pueda aportar a entender el desarrollo de las bibliotecas especializadas. Otros temas que podrían aportar a entender el desarrollo de la biblioteca especializada serían la identificación y análisis del contenido de la colección de la Biblioteca de Mutis, y el de otras colecciones privadas e inclusive los fondos de la actual Biblioteca.

Nacional de Colombia. Para estudiar estos temas se identificaron las siguientes artículos: Ruiz Martínez, "Bibliotecas neogranadinas durante la Ilustración;" Hall, "Hambre de libros: La república de las letras en la América moderna y homem;" "Grandes bibliotecas particulares." Además también se identificó el libro de Hampe Martínez, *Bibliotecas privadas en el mundo colonial: La difusión de los libros e ideas en el virreinato de Perú, siglos XVI y XVII.*

Para explorar el contenido y evaluación de la Biblioteca de Mutis, se recomienda consultar a Jaime Mejía Duque, *Libros comprados por Mutis y el Archivo epistolar del sabio naturalista José Celestino Mutis*, de Guillermo Hernández de Alba. Esta obra sobre el archivo epistolar del sabio consiste de dos tomos y representa una fuente sin igual por ser material primario y por la riqueza de temas y descripciones y porque ayuda a ubicar cronológicamente el evento o suceso. Un atisbo en cuanto a la riqueza del contenido de la Biblioteca de Mutis, se percibe por la comparación que hace el erudito Alemán Alexander Von Humboldt según la siguiente descripción: "Humboldt se asombró de la espléndida biblioteca del botánico español que comparó con la famosa de Joseph Banks, en Londres".[39] Otras fuentes importantes lo son Ovalle Mora *El fondo de José Celestino Mutis de la Biblioteca Nacional de Colombia* y el *Catálogo del fondo documental José Celestino Mutis del Real Jardín Botánico*, publicado conjuntamente por el Real Jardín Botánico de Madrid y el Instituto de Cultura Hispánica de Colombia en 1996.

Por el impacto directo que tiene la censura en el pensamiento crítico y en las bibliotecas es importante estudiar a Mutis y la Inquisición. En el contexto histórico, el siglo dieciocho es el siglo del Iluminismo, donde se reconoce la importancia de las ciencias y las tecnologías en el saber y se está desarrollando un cambio de mentalidad. La Iglesia Católica con la Inquisición trata de prevenir o bloquear toda idea nueva que se aparte del dogma y de su apego a todo lo tradicional. Mutis no está ajeno a esa realidad y se da cuenta de lo difícil de emprender una carrera de investigación en las ciencias en dicho contexto, por ello se ordenó sacerdote en 1772. Refiriéndose a cómo operaba la Inquisición, se indica: "Their families, or spies, were particularly active in seaports and coastal cities, on guard against the importation of heresy by persons or books".[40]

A raíz de las nuevas propuestas de estudio de Mutis que fueron apoyadas por el fiscal Francisco Moreno y Escandón y aprobadas en 1774, los Dominicos se declaran en contra del plan porque veían en ellas una lesión directa a sus intereses de monopolio educativo y suscitan una polémica que llega al tribunal inquisitorial, pero Mutis salió airoso.[41] Desde el punto de vista actual no cabe duda de que Mutis tuvo la razón en dicha disputa. No obstante, sabemos que la Inquisición era implacable y que en casi todos los casos los acusados resultaban culpables.[42] Por lo tanto, es interesante que aunque Mutis tenía la razón saliera airoso de dicha contienda. Surge la interrogante de las variables que entraron en juego en la decisión a favor de Mutis entre estas el hecho de que Mutis era sacerdote y era respaldado por la estructura política de Nueva Granada (el Virrey e inclusive el fiscal quizás tuvieron gran influencia en el veredicto). La obra de Bragado describe la función del Juez de Imprentas y manifiesta la arbitrariedad e ineficacia en la evaluación de los manuscritos. Se dice que sólo los Jesuitas se atrevían a desafiar a la Inquisición.[43] Otras obras relevantes al tema lo son los artículos "Mutis y la Inquisición," de Gonzalo Hernández de Alba; "Inquisición y censura de libros en el siglo XVIII: A propósito de tres autores franciscanos," de Sánchez Gil; "Inquisición y prensa periódica en la segunda mitad del siglo XVIII," de Larriba y el libro *Reclamos y representaciones: Variaciones sobre la política en el nuevo reino de Granada 1770-1815*, de Margarita Garrido. Otra perspectiva que menciona Soto Arango quizás de valor en este tema es que la desaparición de los periódicos no se debió a la censura sino más bien a falta de recursos económicos.

Al reexaminar a Mutis como bibliógrafo basándonos en las fuentes y circunstancias expuestas y partiendo de la literatura consultada, encontramos a un Mutis que a veces es contradictorio. Por un lado Mutis era un hombre ilustrado, defensor de la ciencia y de la verdad, gestor de grandes proyectos e ideas innovadoras pero, sin embargo, se percibe cierto recelo de su parte a compartir ese conocimiento. ¿Porqué Mutis no publicaba sus investigaciones a medida que las iba completando como hizo Hipólito Ruiz, encargado de la expedición Botánica de Perú? ¿Acaso Mutis temía que alguien tomara ventaja y avanzara más que él en ciertas áreas? Las razones que se dan para "el pleito científico y personal" de Mutis con Hipólito Ruiz no son del todo convincentes por lo que es necesario investigar más este aspecto. José Antonio Amaya en *Celestino Mutis y la Expedición Botánica*, hace un esfuerzo por presentar una imagen balanceada de los éxitos y fracasos de Mutis, sin embargo indica que Mutis tenía "ambición por riquezas", que era "autoritario" y que se desempeñaba como un "diseminador e ideólogo de la ciencia, más bien que un científico sistemático".[44] Frías Núñez incluye un capítulo titulado "La publicación de los trabajos" donde describe con detalles los problemas y controversia sobre La flora de Bogotá y otras publicaciones.

NOTAS

1.   John Van Halm, The Development of Special Libraries as an International Phenomenon. New York: Special Library Association, 1978.

2.   Diana Soto Arango, Mutis: educador de la élite neogranadina. Bogotá: Rudecolombia Universidad Pedagógica y Tecnológica de Colombia, 2005.

3.   Ibid.

4.   Ibid.

5.   Ibid.

6.   Marcelo Frías Núñez, Tras el Dorado vegetal: José Celestino Mutis y la Real Expedición Botánica del Nuevo Reino de Granada (1783-1808), Sección Histórica V Centenario del Descubrimiento, 18, Sevilla: Diputación Provincial de Sevilla, 1994.

7.   Soto Arango, Mutis.

8.   Van Halm, The Development of Special Libraries.

9.   Tefko Saracevic, Introduction to Information Science, New York: R. R. Bowker, 1970.

10.   Van Halm, The Development of Special Libraries.

11.   Ibid.

12.   Antonio Lafuente, "Enlightenment in an Imperial Context: Local Science in the Late-Eighteenth Hispanic World," Osiris, 15. (2000): p. 158.

13.   Frías Núñez, Tras el Dorado vegetal, 58.

14.   José Celestino Mutis, Mutis y la Expedición Botánica (Documentos). Bogotá, Colombia: El Ancora Editores, 1983, 8.

15.   Ibid., 33.

16.   Frías Núñez, Tras el Dorado vegetal, 289.

17. C. C. Gillispie, Dictionary of Scientific Biography. Ed. CC. Gillispie 15. Supl. 1, New York: Charles Scribner's Sons, 1978.

18. Mutis, Mutis y la Expedición Botánica.

19. Frías Núñez, Tras el Dorado vegetal.

20. Max Olaya Restrepo, "El pensamiento médico del doctor José Celestino Mutis". Boletín Cultural y Bibliográfico, 11 (1968): 119.

21.

22. Frías Núñez, Tras el Dorado vegetal.

23. Federico Gredilla, Biografía de José Celestino Mutis con relación de su viaje y estudios practicados en el Nuevo Reino de Granada, Junta para la Ampliación de Estudios e Investigaciones Científicas. Madrid, 1911.

24.

25. Frías Núñez, Tras el Dorado vegetal.

26. Olaya Restrepo, "El pensamiento médico".

27. Soto Arango, Mutis.

28. Ibid.

29. Lafuente, "Enlightenment in an Imperial Context".

30. Frías Núñez, Tras el Dorado vegetal, 292.

31. Soto Arango, Mutis, 17.

32. Olaya Restrepo, "El pensamiento Médico".

33. Frías Núñez, Tras el Dorado vegetal, 111.

34. Herman Shumacher, Mutis un forjador de la cultura, Bogotá: ECOPETROL, 1984: p. 105.

35. Frías Núñez, Tras el Dorado vegetal, 299.

36. Ibid.

37. Soto Arango, Mutis, 144.

38. Thomas F. Glick, "Science and Independence in Latin America (with Special Reference to New Granada". The Hispanic American Historical Review 71.2 (1991 May): 307-334.

39. Soto Arango, Mutis.

40. Glick, "Science and Independence", 307-334.

41. Frías Núñez, Tras e Dorado vegetal, 137.

42. Abraham. A. Newman, "Medina Historian of the Inquisition". In José Toribio Medina: Humanist of the Americas an Appraisal, Ed. Maury A. Bromsen. Washington, D.C.: Pan American Union General Secretariat, n.d., p. 82.

43. Soto Arango, Mutis.

44. Javier Bragado Lorenzo & Ceferino Caro López, "La Censura Gubernativa en el Siglo XVIII". Hispania 64/2.217 (2004): 571-600.

45. Newman, "Medina Historian of the Inquisition".

46. José Antonio Amaya, Celestino Mutis y la Expedición Botánica, Madrid: Ediciones Debate/Itaca, 1986, p. 37, 42, 66.

BIBLIOGRAFÍA

Amaya, José Antonio. Celestino Mutis y la Expedición Botánica, Madrid: Ediciones Debate/Itaca, 1986.

Bohórquez Casallas, I. A. La evolución educativa en Colombia. Bogotá: Cultural Colombiana, 1957.

Bragado Lorenzo, Javier. & Caro López, Ceferino. "La Censura Gubernativa en el Siglo XVIII". Hispania 64/2.217 (2004):571-600.

Frías Núñez, Marcelo. Tras el Dorado vegetal: José Celestino Mutis y la Real Expedición Botánica del Nuevo Reino de Granada (1783-1808), Sección Histórica V Centenario del Descubrimiento, 18, Sevilla: Diputación Provincial de Sevilla, 1994.

Garrido, Margarita. Reclamos y representaciones: Variaciones sobre la política en el Nuevo Reino de Granada 1770-1815. Santafé de Bogotá: Banco de la República. 1993.

Gillispie, C. C. Dictionary of Scientific Biography. Ed. CC. Gillispie 15. Supl.1, New York: Charles Scribner's Sons, 1978.

Glick, Thomas F. "Science and Independence in Latin America (with Special Reference to New Granada". The Hispanic American Historical Review 71.2 (1991 May): 307-334.

Gómez Guerrero, Alejandro. "Mutis–Bibliógrafo". Boletín de la Real Sociedad Bascongonda de Amigos del País. 54.1 (1998): 243-253

Gredilla, Federico. Biografía de José Celestino Mutis con relación de su viaje y estudios practicados en el Nuevo Reino de Granada, Junta para la Ampliación de Estudios e Investigaciones Científicas. Madrid, 1911.

Hall, David. D. "Hambre de libros: La república de las letras en la América moderna". Cultura Escrita & Sociedad 2 (2006): 108-127.

Halm, John. Van. The Development of Special Libraries as an International Phenomenon. New York: Special Library Association, 1978.

Hampe Martínez, Teodoro. Bibliotecas privadas en el mundo colonial: La difusión de los libros e ideas en el virreinato de Perú, siglos XVI y XVII, Frankfort: Vervuert. 1996.

Hernández de Alba, Guillermo. Archivo epistolar del sabio naturalista José Celestino Mutis. Tomo 1. Bogotá: Imprenta Nacional, 1949

Hernández de Alba, Gonzalo. "La medicina tradicional en la Expedición Botánica del Nuevo Reino de Granda". Quipu 1.3 (1984 septiembre-diciembre):335-348.

Hernández de Alba, Gonzalo. "Mutis y la Inquisición". Correo de los Andes 33 (1985 agosto-septiembre): 50-53.

"History of Science in Latin America" The Cambridge Encyclopedia of Latin America and the Caribbean, 2nd ed. Cambridge University Press, 1992. Pp. 451-459.

Homem, Homero. "Grandes bibliotecas particulares", Revista de Cultura Brasileña 32 (1971 diciembre): 111-119.

Lafuente, Antonio. "Enlightenment in an Imperial Context: Local Science in the Late-Eighteenth Hispanic World", Osiris, 15 (2000): 155-173.

Larriba, Elisabel. "Inquisición y prensa periódica en la segunda mitad del siglo XVIII" Cuadernos de Ilustración y Romanticismo 13 (2005): 77-92.

Mejía Duque, Jaime. Libros comprados por Mutis, Bolívar 10.48 (1957 octubre): 521-524.

Mutis, José Celestino. Mutis y la Expedición Botánica (Documentos). Bogotá, Colombia: El Ancora Editores, 1983.

Neu, J. Current Bibliography of the History of Science and its Cultural Influences. Isis 82 (1991): 1-271.

Newman, Abraham. A. "Medina Historian of the Inquisition". In José Toribio Medina: Humanist of the Americas an Appraisal, Ed. Maury A. Bromsen. Washington, D.C.: Pan American Union General Secretariat, n.d.: 79-95.

Olaya Restrepo, Max. "El Pensamiento Médico del Doctor José Celestino Mutis". Boletín Cultural y Bibliográfico 11 (1968): 57-120

Ovalle Mora, J. H. "El fondo de José Celestino Mutis de la Biblioteca Nacional de Colombia", Boletín de Historia y Antigüedades, 93.833 (2006): 359-374.

Puerto, Javier. La ilusión quebrada: Botánica, sanidad y ciencia en la España Ilustrada. Barcelona: El Serbal/CSIC, 1988.

Pérez Arbeláez, E. José Celestino Mutis y la Real Expedición Botánica del Nuevo Reino de Granada. Bogotá: Ediciones Tercer Mundo, S.A, 1967.

Consejo Superior de Investigaciones Científicas, Real Jardín Botánico e Instituto de Cultura Hispánica de Colombia. Catálogo del fondo documental José Celestino Mutis del Real Jardín Botánico. Madrid: Real Jardín Botánico, 1996.

Rodríguez Nozal, Raúl. Plantas americanas para la España Ilustrada: Génesis, desarrollo y ocaso del Proyecto Español de Expediciones Botánicas. Madrid: Editorial Complutense, 2000.

Ruiz Martínez, E. "Bibliotecas neogranadinas durante la Ilustración". Senderos, 5.25/26 (1993):587-612.

Sánchez Gil, Víctor. "Inquisición y censura de libros en el siglo XVIII: A propósito de tres autores franciscanos". Archivo Iberoamericano 39.155-156 (1979): 439-465.

Saracevic, Tefko. Introduction to Information Science, New York: R. R. Bowker, 1970.

Shumacher, Herman. Mutis un forjador de la cultura. Bogotá: ECOPETROL, 1984.

Soto Arango, Diana. Mutis: educador de la élite neogranadina. Bogotá: Rudecolombia Universidad Pedagógica y Tecnológica de Colombia, 2005.

Thompson, Lawrence. S. "Bookbinding in the Americas". Interamerican Review of Bibliography 12.3 (1962):253-268.

Communicative Encounters
in Colonial Mexico

5. The Atrio Cross and the Communication of Catholic Doctrine in Colonial Mexico
Derek Burdette

The Spanish friars who set off to indoctrinate the native population of central Mexico in the years following the conquest were faced with the task of communicating to the indigenous community the doctrine of the church in both a compelling and understandable fashion. The visual arts provided the friars with a way to do just that. The arts circumvented many of the problems associated with language-based communication by using visual referents to communicate and reinforce key concepts. One of the best examples of this can be seen in the atrio crosses that were erected within patios fronting early colonial churches. These crosses, adorned with symbols of the Christ's Passion, known as the *arma Christi*, were able to communicate to the indigenous population the narrative of Christ's passion in a fashion that was easily understood. In addition, the crosses played an important part in the dramatic recreation of the Mass of Saint Gregory, which illuminated the doctrine of transubstantiation and reinforced the significance of the Eucharist.

The Passion, the Eucharist, and Popular Devotion

The narrative of Christ's passion played a central role in early-modern Catholicism in both Europe and the Americas. By the twelfth century, Europe's religious landscape was dotted with relics of the passion that had been carried west after the fall of Constantinople.[1] The ascendance of the Franciscan order, led by Saint Francis the *alter Christus*, ensured that the theme of Christ's passion played an increasingly predominant role in late-medieval religious culture.[2][3] This shift toward a more Christocentric devotion was felt within the institutional church as well, and in 1215 the Fourth Lateran Council established the doctrine of Transubstantiation, which declared that the host was miraculously transformed into the body of Christ during mass.[4] William Christian notes that by the sixteenth century, Spanish denunciations of heretical behavior had shifted from those focused on the Virgin Mary to those dealing with Christ and the Eucharist.[5] Christ's Passion, and the liturgical celebration of it, had come to dominate Spanish religious culture.

This uniquely passion-oriented devotion made its way to the Americas with the first wave of mendicants, led by a Franciscan majority. These friars were in charge of indoctrinating the native community, which meant teaching them the significance of both Christ's passion and the symbolically complex act of the Holy Communion.[6] The importance of doing so became clear in 1537, when Pope Paul III afforded the native community the right to participate in the holy sacraments.[7] No longer an abstract question of doctrine, the significance of the Eucharist was now a matter of practice. In light of this development, I believe that the mendicants were quick to develop a strategy for ensuring that the significance of the act remained true to Spanish intentions, turning to the legend of the Mass of Saint Gregory.

The Mass of Saint Gregory

Although based on the life of the sixth-century Pope known as Gregory the Great, the legend of the Mass of Saint Gregory did not fully develop until the early modern period.[8] The story appears to have emerged from a related narrative known as the legend of the doubting matron, which was recorded as early as the seventh century. Jacobus de Voragine, in his thirteenth-century work *The Golden Legend*, records a version of the story that focuses on the disbelief, and eventual conversion, of the woman responsible for baking the altar breads for Saint Gregory. One Sunday, in response to Saint Gregory's assertion that the very bread she had baked had been transformed into the body of Christ, the woman laughed in disbelief. In response, Gregory prayed, and the host was transformed into Christ's finger before the entire congregation.[9]

The twelfth-century manuscript illumination entitled *St. Gregory and the Doubting Matron* makes clear the miraculous transformation of the bread into the body of Christ by depicting the host, held by Saint Gregory, alongside Christ's finger, which rests atop the chalice. The legend and the illustration reduce the complex doctrine of transubstantiation to a simple equation between the finger and the Eucharist, answering the doubts of the baker and viewer alike.

By the fifteenth century, Saint Gregory himself had replaced the woman in the role of the doubtful onlooker and his doubt was met with a much grander apparition. Christ himself appeared on the altar. An engraving by the Flemish artist Israel van Meckenem from the turn of the sixteenth century illustrated this shift in the legend, depicting Christ as the "man of sorrows" surrounded by the elements of his passion. Those elements, seen arrayed above the figure of Jesus, are known as the *arma Christi*, or the arms of Christ.[10] Individually, they represent the various episodes in the passion narrative. Collectively, they form both a coat of arms that represents the majesty of Christ, and the weapon with which he defeated the devil—a play on the word *arma*, which means both weapon and heraldry.[11] Beneath the altar, Saint Gregory and his assistants kneel, their belief in the Eucharist reaffirmed by the apparition of Christ's suffering body. Crowds of onlookers gather on each side of the altar. They too find their faith reaffirmed by the events. The combination of these elements made the legend well suited to the evangelization efforts of the friars in New Spain, as they address both the importance of the passion and reaffirm the complex significance of the Eucharist.

The Legend in Mexico

Several New Spanish artworks created during the early colonial period demonstrate the impact that the legend had on the visual discourse of evangelization. *The Mass of Saint Gregory*, executed in 1539 by native artisans at the School of San José de los Naturales, employs the traditional indigenous technique of featherwork to render a distinctly American reproduction of the legend.[12] A comparison of this work with the print of the same subject executed by Meckenem reveals the degree to which the native artist drew upon European prototypes during the creative process.[13] The intricacies of the gothic interior are replaced with a brilliant field of blue, dotted with the *arma Christi* that have moved from the contained field inscribed in the altar to the occupy the whole of the picture plane.

Similar renderings of the legend cropped up in more permanent mediums in the sixteenth century, including a number of murals located within monastic churches. Extant examples at the churches of Tepeapulco and San Gabriel in Cholula, exemplify this tradition and demonstrate the popularity of the narrative among the religious community.[14] A mural in the church of San Gregorio in Tlayacapan presents an incomplete rendering of the Mass of Saint Gregory, leaving un-figured both the body of Christ and that of Saint Gregory himself.[15] Mariano Monterrosa posits that a sculptural Christ, housed within the grave-like niche located directly in front of the mural, complemented the two dimensional elements of the narrative.[16] I suggest that the friar stationed at the church took the place of Saint Gregory during mass, conflating the colonial reality with that of the legend. By using both static and performative elements, the friars were able to involve the native population in a dramatic recreation of the legend. This recreation would have made clear the doctrine of transubstantiation in a fashion that was both compelling and easily understood by the laity. I believe that a similar significance can be appreciated in the numerous atrio crosses, adorned with the *arma Christi* and placed at the center of the patios built to accommodate outdoor masses.

The Atrio Cross

The tradition of erecting large-scale wooden crosses at the center of the monastic complex began as a means to visually stake claim over the territory. By the late 1530s, the large wooden crosses gave way to smaller stone versions adorned with the *arma Christi*. Two examples of peninsular crosses from the early sixteenth century demonstrate the way that the arms of Christ had previously been applied to a cruciform design, providing perhaps the most convincing and most often overlooked inspirations for the Mexican examples.[17] Although executed in a different medium, the Spanish prototypes share a great deal in common with the New Spanish atrio crosses, including the subject matter and general composition. Strikingly similar in both style and content, the crosses from Catalunya and Daroca both combine a number of anthropomorphic elements, including the face of Christ represented on Veronica's veil and the crucified hands and feet of Jesus, with a number of inanimate components of the *arma Christi*. As a result, these crosses not only represent Christ crucified, but also visually refer to the entire passion narrative. Drawing on this tradition, the friars of New Spain were able to modify the Conquest-era act of erecting crosses as symbols of socio-religious domination to address the educational concerns of evangelization.

By drawing heavily upon the native artistic tradition, the artist responsible for the works ensured that the crosses not only addressed the issues of Catholic doctrine, but that they did so in a way that facilitated cross-cultural communication. Three similar atrio crosses from central Mexico provide insight into the way that the Catholic doctrine was given form in accordance with an autochthonous aesthetic. Located at Tepeyac, Atzacoalco and Huichapan, it is believed that these three crosses were executed by a single native artist, possibly from the school of mechanical arts at San José de los Naturales.[18]

The cross at Tepeyac, likely executed in 1556, clearly illustrates the impact of the native artistic tradition on the creative process.[19] Although the elements rendered are in keeping with the European tradition, their style and execution recalls more clearly the pre-Columbian past. Take for example the depiction of the three nails that adorn the extremes of the crossbar and the middle portion of the cross's base. At the tip of each nail explodes a collection of teardrop-shaped elements, which we know to be blood. Constantino Reyes Valerio, in his work concerning the syncretic qualities of early colonial sculpture, notes that this depiction of blood, seen also on the crosses at Atzacoalco and Huichapan, recalls the native symbol for *Chalchiuhatl*, or precious water.[20] A comparison of the blood from the atrio cross with several depictions of the symbol for *Chalchiuhatl* as they appear in central Mexican manuscripts makes the similarity clear. Reyes Valerio posits that the native artists, either on their own or in conjunction with priests, chose to depict the blood of Christ in visual terms consistent with the conceptual significance it carried in theological discourse—as the lifeblood of man. This allowed the message of Christ's sacrifice to be translated into visual terms comprehensible to a newly indoctrinated native population. Thus, the European content was adapted to the native worldview and expressed in accordance with native tradition.

Several scholars have theorized that the native influence extended beyond the use of individual elements to the broader style of the stonework.[21] John McAndrews and Elizabeth Wilder Weismann both comment on the pre-Columbian appearance of the stonework. Weismann notes specifically that the crosses often include distinctly two-layered relief, such as that seen in the cross at Tepeapulco. The relief is undercut and given an inflated quality that lends the flat surface a sense of volume, similar to pre-contact sculpture.[22] Others, including Manuel Toussaint, have emphasized the resemblance between the style of imagery depicted on crosses and that seen within the Mexican manuscript tradition, focusing particularly on the arrangement of the symbols within space.[23] Indeed, when viewed in light of the native tradition of filling the picture plane with an array of evenly placed symbols, exemplified in the tributary section of the Codex Mendoza, crosses such as that from Tlaxcala seem to reflect an indigenous aesthetic. This style would have had an impact on the efficacy of the cross as a mechanism for spreading the doctrine, as the iconography of the cross would have been easily read by the native population conditioned to record narratives through the use of logographs. As a result, the crosses emerged as important venues for the communication of the Passion narrative to the indigenous community.

The Cross and the Performance of the Mass of Saint Gregory

But how did the cross, adorned with the *arma Christi*, and located at the center of the atrio relate to the mass of Saint Gregory? The connection was, I believe, a complex and impermanent one that can only be fully appreciated by looking at the larger liturgical and performative landscape of the atrio complex.

It is important to bear in mind that the atrio was more than simply a meeting place for the native population. The friars, prohibited by law from administering mass more than once a day and required to do so within an enclosed space, used the atrios to stage large-scale services that were unheard of in Europe.[24] Open-air chapels were constructed that faced the open patio, providing the friars a limited enclosure for the altar. During mass, thousands of native worshipers gathered in the atrio, converting the space into an outdoor sanctuary. At the center stood the cross, towering above the crowds of devotees.

As the atmosphere of the atrio changed to accommodate the mass, the significance of the cross changed along with it. Scholars such as Jaime Lara have overlooked the importance of this dynamic ritual landscape when examining the atrio crosses and are left to conclude that "in no Mexican atrial cross does there appear the body of Christ, or Pope Gregory, or the unbelieving witnesses—elements that are never omitted from the Mass iconography."[25] In fact, these elements of the narrative would have been present during mass, although not carved in stone. The actors and rituals that surrounded the stone cross would have completed the iconography of the mass of Saint Gregory.

The cross, although slightly outside of the traditional canon of two-dimensional depictions of the subject, represented both the *arma Christi* and the body of Christ. The arms of Christ would have been positioned *on* the cross instead of around it, reflecting the demands of the medium. The crosses at Acolman, Tepeyac, and Tlaxcala, among many others, go as far as to render the crucified body of Christ himself, anthropomorphizing the cross through the addition of the sudarium or Veronica's veil. The cross at Tepeyac, to choose one among many, depicts both the chalice and the host directly beneath the blood of Christ at the foot of the sculpture. This inclusion of the Eucharist pairs the earthly body of Christ with his body in the form of the holy sacrament, making Christ dually present.

The friar administering mass within the open chapel would have performed the role of Saint Gregory, just as was the case within the church of San Gregorio in Tlayacapan. The friars would have fit the role, adorned in the regalia of the church and privileged to administer the sacrament of the Eucharist. In many cases, their position at the altar would have been in line with the atrio cross, which were often positioned in front of the open chapel.[26] As for the unbelieving witnesses, there would undoubtedly have been many. The native audience members were left to cast themselves as the doubting onlookers, edified by the evidence and strengthened in their devotion.

Together, the cross, the friar, and the native audience reproduced the Mass of Saint Gregory. Long after the performance of the mass had been completed, the cross, still bearing the message it sought to reinforce, would have remained for all to see.

Conclusion

I believe that the performed mass in the atrio would have provided the Spanish with a mechanism through which the native population could be educated and their faith in the Eucharist reconfirmed. Building upon the legend, popularized through a number of artistic avenues, the friars could blend visual communication with performed liturgy to involve and educate the indigenous community. The atrio crosses stood at the center of this campaign, both literally and conceptually. They functioned as permanent reminders of Christ's Passion and the doctrine of transubstantiation. Their style made them ideal venues for this kind of communication, as the native aesthetic ensured that the catholic doctrine was represented in an understandable fashion. Today, the crosses stand as reminders of both the performed and the permanent communications that dominated religious discourse in colonial central Mexico.

NOTES

1.   Gertrud Schiller, *Iconography of Christian Art*, trans. Janet Seligman (Greenwich: New York Graphic Society Ltd., 1971), 189. Santiago Sebastián, Mariano Monterrosa, José Antonio Terán, Iconografía del arte del siglo XVI en México (Zacatecas: Universidad Autónoma de Zacatecas, 1995), 31.

2.   For Saint Francis see: Sebastian, Monterrosa, and Terán, 32.

3.   Michael Heinlen, "An Image of a Mass of St. Gregory and Devotion to the Holy Blood at Weingarten Abbey," *Gesta*, 37, no. 1 (1998): 59.

4.   Heinlen, 59.

5. William Christian, *Local Religion in Sixteenth-Century Spain* (Princeton: Princeton University Press, 1981), 190.

6. The issue of Christ's death was one that was alternatively stressed and glossed over in accordance with the fears of the mendicants. The potential for the act to be construed as a form of human sacrifice led some to downplay the crucifixion and instead focus on less problematic aspects of Catholic doctrine. Sebastián, Monterrosa, and Terán, 45.

7. Claire Farago, "*Mass of Saint Gregory*, School of San José de los Naturales," (Cat. 1) from *Painting a New World: Mexican Art and Life 1521-1821*, ed. Pierce, Donna, Rogelio Ruiz Gomar, and Clara Bargellini (Denver: University of Texas Press, 2004), 98.

8. For more see: Christine Gottler, "Is Seeing Believing? The Use of Evidence in Representations of the Miraculous Mass of Saint Gregory," *Germanic Review* 76, no. 2 (2001): 124-5.

9. Jacobus de Voragine, *The Golden Legend* (Princeton: Princeton University Press, 1993), 179-80. For an earlier account of the legend see Bertram Colgrave, *The Earliest Life of Gregory the Great* (Lawrence: The University of Kansas Press, 1968), 105-109. This version comes from an anonymous account of Saint Gregory's life dating to the seventh century and greatly resembles the version recorded by Voragine five centuries later.

10. For more on the individual elements see Sebastián, Motnerrosa, and Terán, 27-38. For more on the *arma Christi* as a group, see Schiller, 184-197.

11. Emile Male, *Religious Art in France: The Late Middle Ages*, trans. Marthiel Mathews (Princeton: Princeton University Press, 1986), 104, Schiller 184, 192.

12. For more on this work in particular see Farago, 98-102.

13. Farago, 98-102.

14. For more information on the murals see Sonia Perez Carrillo, "Aproximación a la iconografía de la misa de San Gregorio en America," *Cuadernos de arte colonial* 42 (1988): 101.

15. Monterossa, "una misa," 15.

16. Monterrosa, "una misa," 15.

17. Several other scholars have speculated as to the origins of the atrio cross, however, I believe that Elisa García Barragan has definitively shown that these examples, among others like them, are indeed the main source of inspiration for the colonial works. See Elisa García Barragan, "Precedentes de las cruces atriales de la Nueva España," *Traza y Baza* 7 (1978): 130-132.

18. Elena Isabel E. de Gerlero, "Atrial Cross," (Cat. 115) from *Mexico: Splendors of Thirty Centuries* (New York: The Metropolitan Museum of Art, 1990), 250-252.

19. Gerlero, "Atrial Cross," 250.

20. Constantino Reyes-Valerio, *Arte Indocristiano* (Cordoba, Mexico: Instituto Nacional de Antropología e Historia, 1978), 276.

21. The crosses have long been considered examples of what Moreno Villa in his influential work on Mexican Sculpture referred to as Tequitqui, a style of work that combined the native aesthetic with Spanish content. José Moreno Villa, *La escultura colonial mexicana* (México: Fondo de Cultura Económica, 1942), 16-18.

22. Elizabeth Wilder Weismann, *Mexico in Sculpture* (Cambridge: Harvard University Press, 1950), 11.

23. Manuel Toussaint, *Pintura Colonial en México* (México: Impresora Universitaria, 1965), 26.

24. John McAndrews, *Open Air Churches 16th-Century Mexico* (Cambridge: Harvard University Press, 1965), 205.

25. Jaime Lara, *City, Temple, Stage* (Notre Dame: University of Notre Dame, 2004), 161.

26. Lara, 173.

BIBLIOGRAPHY

Binski, Paul. *Medieval Death: Ritual and Representation*. Ithaca: Cornell University Press, 1996.

Boone, Elizabeth. "Pictorial Documents and Visual Thinking in Postconquest Mexico." *Native Traditions in the Postconquest World*. Edited by Elizabeth Hill Boone and Tom Cummins. Washington, D.C.: Dumbarton Oaks, 1998: 149-199.

Colgrave, Bertram. *The Earliest Life of Gregory the Great*. Lawrence: The University of Kansas Press, 1968.

Duverger, Christian. *Agua y fuego: Arte sacro indígena de México en el siglo XVI*. México: Landucci Editores, 2003.

Edgerton, Samuel. *Theaters of Conversion: Religious Architecture and Indian Artisans in Colonial Mexico*. Albuquerque: University of New Mexico, 2001.

Farago, Claire. "Mass of Saint Gregory, School of San José de los Naturales," (Cat. 1). From *Painting a New World: Mexican Art and Life 1521-1821*. Eds., Donna Pierce, Rogelio Ruiz Gomar and Clara Bargellini. Denver: University of Texas Press, 2004.

García Granados, Rafael. "Reminiscencias idolátricas en monumentos coloniales." *Anales del Instituto de Investigaciones Estéticas* 5 (1940): 54-55.

García Barragan, Elisa. "Precedentes de las cruces atriales de la Nueva España." *Traza y Baza* 7 (1978): 130-132.

Gerlero, Elena Isabel E. de. "Mass of Saint Gregory, School of San José de los Naturales," (Cat. 1). From *Painting a New World: Mexican Art and Life 1521-1821*. Eds., Donna Pierce, Rogelio Ruiz Gomar and Clara Bargellini. Denver: University of Texas Press, 2004.

------. "Atrial Cross," (Cat. 115). From *Mexico: Splendors of Thirty Centuries*. New York: The Metropolitan Museum of Art, 1990.

------. "Gremial of Archbishop Juan de Zumárraga," (Cat. 118). *From Mexico: Splendors of Thirty Centuries*. New York: The Metropolitan Museum of Art, 1990.

Gerlero, Elena Isabel E. de and Maríta Martínez del Río del Redo, "The Mass of Saint Gregory." From *Mexico: Splendors of Thirty Centuries*. New York: The Metropolitan Museum of Art, 1990.

Gottler, Christine. "Is Seeing Believing? The Use of Evidence in Representations of the Miraculous Mass of Saint Gregory." *Germanic Review* 76, no. 2 (2001): 120-143.

Heinlen, Michael. "An Image of a Mass of St. Gregory and Devotion to the Holy Blood at Weingarten Abbey." *Gesta* 37, no. 1 (1998): 55-62.

Kubler, George. *Mexican Architecture of the Sixteenth Century*. New Haven: Yale University Press, 1948.

Lara, Jaime. *City, Temple, Stage*. Notre Dame: University of Notre Dame, 2004.

Male, Emile. *Religious Art in France: The Late Middle Ages*. Translated by Marthiel Mathews. Princeton: Princeton University Press, 1986.

McAndrews, John. *Open Air Churches of 16th-Century Mexico*. Cambridge: Harvard University Press, 1965.

Monterrosa, Mariano, "¿Una misa de San Gregorio en Tlayacapan?" *Boletín* 42 (1970): 1-3.

Moreno Villa, José. *La escultura colonial Mexicana*. México: Fondo de Cultura Económica, 1942.

Perez Carrillo, Sonia. "Aproximación a la iconografía de la misa de San Gregorio en América." *Cuadernos de arte colonial* 42 (1988): 91-106.

Reyes-Valerio, Constantino. *Arte Indocristiano*. Cordoba, Mexico: Instituto Nacional de Antropología e Historia, 1978.

Richards, Jeffrey. *Consul of God: The Life and Times of Gregory the Great*. London: Routledge & Kegan Paul Ltd., 1980.

Sebastián, Santiago, Mariano Monterrosa, and José Antonion Terán, Eds. *Iconographía del Arte del Siglo XVI en Mexico*. Zacatecas: Universidad Autónoma de Zacatecas, 1995.

Schiller, Gertrud. *Iconography of Christian Art*. Translated by Janet Seligman. Greenwich: New York Graphic Society Ltd., 1971.

Toussaint, Manuel. *Pintura colonial en México*. México: Impresora Universitaria, 1965.

Voragine, Jacobus. *The Golden Legend of Jacobus de Voragine*. Translated from Latin by Granger Ryan and Helmut Ripperger. New York: Longmans, Green and Col, Inc., 1941.

Wilder Weismann, Elizabeth. *Mexico in Sculpture*. Cambridge: Harvard University Press, 1950.

6. Colonial Literacy in Yucatec Maya: An Authentic Indigenous Voice, or Regional Interethnic Lingua Franca?
Mark Lentz

Like many of the regions inhabited by large native populations in Mesoamerica, Yucatan's scribal tradition continued in a drastically altered form, but mostly uninterruptedly. In the early stages of the new form of writing, with the gradual transition made from hieroglyphic, logosyllabic indigenous writing to the form of Maya written in the Latin alphabet, only a few Maya elites and the Franciscan proselytizers used the language. Yucatan's Franciscans, in the interests of conversion, wrote grammars, dictionaries, and indigenous-language religious instruction materials and trained indigenous writers who set down their own language in a new orthography, replacing pre-Columbian writing systems with the Roman alphabet. These friars and the literate Maya elite first trained by the Franciscans in this new writing system initially were the only producers of Maya documents. However, during the course of the colonial period, a wider variety of Yucatecans learned to read or write in the province's indigenous language. Like those who were literate in Maya, oral fluency usually conformed to the prevailing colonial concept of a divided Latin American society: on one hand, a republic of Spaniards (*república de españoles*), and on the other a republic of the natives (*república de los indios*), one speaking the language of the colonizers, the other speaking the native language. By the end of the colonial period, the language moved beyond the blurred boundaries of these two no longer distinct sectors of society. This paper examines evidence of a more widespread use of the Maya language across racial lines by the end of the eighteenth century.

In Yucatan, the Franciscans' role was paramount in preserving the scribal tradition of the Yucatecan Maya in its transition to a Roman alphabet. Diego de Landa, rightfully vilified for burning nearly all Maya codices, also deserves grudging credit for writing down the only existing—if flawed—translation between syllabic glyphs and the European alphabet. Franciscans created detailed grammars and dictionaries, still important to historians and anthropologists translating recently discovered Maya documents.

Mayas soon adopted the writing and used it for legal purposes, not only for the religious purposes intended by the friars. The oldest known document, the Crónica de Maní, is held at Tulane, and dated 1557. Maya writing continued relatively uninterruptedly until the 1870s, and a revitalized form of the written language is used today. Most Mayas continued to speak their native language, with the exception of Mérida's large, independent indio ladino population, many of the capital's criados, and some of the urban-based Maya elites.

Issues of landownership and abusive treatment by priests, *encomenderos*, or individuals who held rights to native labor from the Conquest period, and local Spanish officials motivated most of the colonial writings by Mayas. For most of the sixteenth century, after the completion of the conquest of Yucatan, and into the seventeenth century, Franciscans were almost the only Spaniards who had constant contact with the Mayas and the leaders in studies of the Maya language. Among the leading scholars of the time were fray Juan Coronel, who published a grammar, confession manual, series of sermons, Christian doctrine, and brief vocabulary in 1620. Tulane University, the Library of Congress, Brigham Young University and the Tozzer Library of the Peabody Museum of Harvard University are among the few repositories for the Photostat copies of this document.

After about 1650, Franciscans in Yucatan lost ground in the province as secular clergyman—those who did not belong to a religious order—began to take over parishes. But Yucatan's Mayas continued to speak and write in their native language into the nineteenth century. As the Franciscans lost control over a growing number of parishes, secular clergymen were forced to learn the native language. Members of religious orders such as the Jesuits also had a small number of their clergymen learn the language. According to Gerard Decorme, the French historian of the Jesuits in the Spanish Americas, the Aragonese Francisco Javier Gómez, the "gran apóstol de los Mayas," traveled from town to town preaching to the Maya in their own language. Starting at a distinct disadvantage from the Creole priests who heard Maya from birth, Gómez spent a full year in a Maya village cut off from other Spanish speakers to learn the language.[1]

Still, Franciscans continued to produce the most rigorous studies of the Maya language and most of the devotional and liturgical literature written in Maya. But evidence suggests that in everyday speech, the language gained ground and that most Yucatecans, even those of European descent, spoke at least rudimentary Maya. In a prologue to a 1746 *Arte de la Lengua Maya*, the Franciscan who updated and compiled the work of his Franciscan predecessors defended the need for an updated version. "Why," he asked, was another Maya grammar needed "if nearly everyone speaks, or knows how to speak this language?"[2] He also wrote later in the same prologue that although many spoke the language, few fully understood the structure and meaning of Maya well.[3]

During the eighteenth century, the Maya population began to recover, paralleling a growth in the European and mixed-descent population. This demographic upswing brought people from different backgrounds into contact with each other and led to the growth of Yucatan's mixed-race and African-descent population. In traditional models of Yucatecan society, these mixed-race and African groups served as the front line of Hispanization.[4] This statement is certainly too sweeping and not entirely accurate.

A description from 1795 of a small pueblo in Yucatan refutes this perception of Mayas and Afro-Yucatecans as junior partners of the European colonial project. Captain don Mateo de Cárdenas, a battle-tested and highly regarded veteran who previously served as a graduated captain of the elite grenadiers unit of the Spanish militia, arrived in Chikindzonot with orders to undertake a sweeping reform of the pueblo, resolving issues such as disputes over tribute and the supposed intransigence and disrespect for lay authorities on the part of the local priest.[5]

After arriving, Capitan Cárdenas described Chikindzonot in the following way:

> The pueblo of Chikindzonot, has always been composed of Indians, and some fifty vecinos (non-Maya residents), mostly mulattos, as rustic and pusillanimous as the Indians, whose language they speak exclusively; They are not accustomed to travel to other parts of the province, and they pass a miserable life from the scarce yield of their small plots of corn, which they work with their own hands.[6]

Cárdenas' description is overwhelmingly negative, but between the lines he describes a phenomenon not completely well-understood. Not all individuals in the countryside living like Mayas were ethnically indigenous. The fifty or so Afro-Yucatecans living in Chikindzonot belonged much more fully to a Maya world than a Spanish one, living among them, speaking their language, and practicing the same subsistence agricultural practices.

A teleological trajectory of Westernization has prevailed as a model for intercultural interaction not only for Yucatan but for many colonial societies. In this paradigm, European colonizers gradually overwhelm indigenous societies, which pass into slow, inexorable decline. The loss of language often figures prominently as a marker of cultural degeneration.

A reading of official Spanish documents from the time shows a concerted effort to make Castilian the language of the entire empire, a project that gained momentum in the eighteenth century. In 1770, Carlos III of Spain ordered that all educators and religious instructors of Indians teach only in Castilian in order to unite the provinces around a single spoken language.[7] Twenty-odd years later, the bishop of Mérida sought to open a school for elite Mayas for them to learn Castilian, an obviously incomplete goal.[8]

Orders from above need to be contrasted with documentary evidence on the ground confirming or qualifying the effectiveness of high-level decrees. In this case, documents from everyday life in Yucatan reveal that the native language remained prevalent in Yucatan even among many non-Mayas. To deal with Maya language petitions, land sales, wills, and other legal documents that were admissible in Spanish courts, the colonial government created the position of interpreter. The 1591 royal decree that established this post mandated the existence of three official translators, one based in Campeche and two in Mérida.

The presence of interpreters in court cases underscores the degree to which Yucatan's Mayas continued to use their own language. In a protracted trial that followed the aftermath of the assassination of Yucatan's governor in 1792, prosecutors questioned nearly four hundred Mayas, both for futile early leads and to later disprove the alibi of the prime suspect. Only two of them, the Mérida-based brother and sister Maria and Luis Ventura, testified in Spanish.[9] Both were urban-based. Maria served as a servant in the house of an elite Spaniard, don Pedro Rafael Pastrana, and Luis lived in front of the sacristy of the Cathedral in Mérida. Further from the city, Maya prevailed.

Yucatan's Mayas also held onto their language in both its written and spoken form, making the language not just a "major medium of resistance," as Robert M. Hill II described an analogous situation in colonial Guatemala, but in fact the lingua franca of the countryside.[10] Besides the Maya population, a vast majority of the mixed-race and black population also spoke Maya in the countryside. Chikindzonot, the small rural community described above, gives a case study of the language use patterns in late eighteenth-century Yucatan. It served as a pivotal point in an assassination trial that followed in the wake of the 1792 murder of Yucatan's governor. The accused assassin, a man with powerful connections to the Church, stated that he could not have been in Mérida on the night of the murder since he was in Chikindzonot.

A few of the mostly Afro-descent non-Mayas of Chikindzonot are distinguishable by their different occupations such as the shoemaker Felipe Gómez, or the tailor Laureano Rivero, and Sergeant Manuel Rajon, the militia officer.[11] All are identifiable by their Spanish surnames, and all but three of the forty-seven male witnesses with Spanish surnames testified in Maya.[12] Three could sign their names.[13] Otherwise, all of Chikindzonot's castas were indistinguishable in lifestyle and language from the pueblo's Maya majority, with many mentioning tending their milpas as a pretext for not giving specific testimony.[14]

Some witnesses who needed interpreters to testify were either surprisingly close or even part of the Spanish government at low levels. A sergeant of the local militia of Chikindzonot, Manuel Rajon, needed an interpreter on both of the occasions he testified, since he spoke Maya fluently and little Spanish.[15] He was not the only military man who served the crown but spoke no Spanish. In an earlier round of interrogations, a soldier with the Infantry Battalion of Castile of Campeche, Santiago Briseño ("awkward in the Spanish language") required the services of don Estevan de Castro, one of the two interpreter generals at the time, to translate his testimony from Maya to Spanish.[16] Tomasa

Santos, the widow of the *juez español* don Pedro Gutiérrez testified in Yucatec Maya, as did her daughter.[17]

The number of interpreters also suggests an expansion of the knowledge of Maya during the eighteenth century. In all, eighteen interpreters—sixteen in addition to the two official interpreters general of Mérida—translated during the course of the trial that followed in the wake of the assassination of the governor. Several interpreters came from military backgrounds, such as Mariano Ancona, who served as a corporal in the white Spanish militia; Eugenio Cano, who served as a corporal in the white militia before serving as one of the nominally Spanish officers overseeing the pardo militia; don Manuel Alcala, a first lieutenant with the "milicias urbanas" of Calotmul; and don Manuel de Aguilar, a lieutenant with the Infantry Battalion of Castile.[18] At least two of the impromptu interpreters served in low-level governmental posts. Ancona served as the *juez español* of neighboring Tihosuco.[19] Only don Vicente de Ávila and don Esteban de Castro made their living exclusively from their work as interpreters.[20] In terms of elite status, a majority of the interpreters were addressed officially with the honorific "don." A few of the interpreters, especially those who were based in the rural sphere, did not, such as Eugenio Cano, the juez español of Chikindzonot Mariano Ancona, Simeon Caro, Diego Santana, and Juan Gervasio Silva of Cancabdzonot.[21] Apparently, all were natives of Yucatan, the one commonality.[22]

Historians have only recently begun to incorporate Maya language texts in studies of a province in which the indigenous language prevailed as the lingua franca. The latest innovation used by scholars is to examine Maya language texts not as a way of opening a window onto an authentic, undisturbed native culture, but to view these documents as a medium of intercultural exchange. Two forthcoming dissertations take similar approaches. Mark Christensen's work on literature designed to aid in proselytizing examines Maya-Christian dialogue in Maya texts. At the University of Arizona, Ryan Kashanipour's doctoral project highlights the similarities and exchanges between medicinal practices and beliefs on the part of Yucatan's Maya and non-native populations. The final section of this work focuses on everyday interactions of a small business nature and at the local government level.

Effective local government at the pueblo level, whether by Spaniards or Mayas, required an extensive knowledge of Maya. Don Pedro Gutiérrez, the juez español, or leading Spanish governmental official of Chikindzonot who died of dysentery in prison, had his belongings and personal effects inventoried after his death. He had five Maya-language documents in his possession, three from Mayas and two written by non-Mayas, one by Eulogio Tomas and the other a government decree translated into Maya by one of the two interpreters general.[23] His widow, Tomasa Santos, spoke only Maya, making it even more probable that the *juez español* was bilingual in reading and speaking.[24]

His direct overseer, the subdelegado don Pedro Rafael Pastrana, also had a variety of untranslated Maya documents in his possession at the time of his arrest, suggesting that he also conducted routine business in the native lingua franca. The inventory of his confiscated papers included a total of forty-four "papers of Indians."[25] Only one of these Maya-language documents found its way into the volume of correspondence related to the case. The subdelegado, who valued Maya documents much less than a modern historian, turned over the certification of the Mayas of Sacalaca and used it to write a personal letter of his own.[26]

These local Spanish authorities based around Chikindzonot were not the only ones fluent and sometimes literate in Maya in the eastern and largely Maya-speaking half of the province. Of the three largest settlements in colonial Yucatan—Campeche, Mérida, and Valladolid—the port city of Campeche, exposed to outside influences that arrived with ships and cargo, appeared most European while Valladolid retained the character of pre-Columbian Zaci, the town upon whose ruins conquering Spaniards built their new villa. Tihosuco and Chikindzonot, the focus of Dr. Guillén's investigations, fell under the domain of Valladolid. Here, during the time of the Gálvez assassination, don Francisco Muñoz, lieutenant of the governor of Valladolid, the highest authority figure in this area, wrote fluently in Maya. Rather than rely on an interpreter to pass on the orders to the towns within his area of control, including the villages of Chemax, Ebtun, Xocen, Chichimila, Tixcacal Cupul, Tekom, Dzitnup, Kaua, Piste, Xocenpich, Dzitaas, Tunkas, Baca, Tinum, Uayma, and Popola, Muñoz translated several documents himself. The same man who was held responsible for distributing criados to allies without accounting for their baptism also had the advantage of fluency and literacy in Maya to aid him as an intermediary. Between 1785 and 1789, during the terms of don José Merino y Ceballos and don Lucas de Gálvez, don Manuel faithfully reproduced in Maya various orders from Mérida for the Maya-speaking majority surrounding Valladolid.[27]

Priests, Power, and Maya Literacy in the Eighteenth Century

As mentioned above, priests continued to produce prayer books, gospels, confessionals, and linguistic studies in Maya during the eighteenth century. Yet not all of the priests' efforts went into conversion. Priests also used their linguistic expertise for political ends.

The most dramatic example of how this literacy played out is in the priest don Manuel Correa's fraudulent production of a certification by the Maya elites of Chikindzonot, attesting to the murder suspect's presence in the pueblo during the time of the governor's assassination. Father Correa's nephew don José Maria Rodríguez, one of the very few Spanish residents of Chikindzonot, dictated the certification that vouched for the suspect's presence to one of the literate assistants of the Church, the *teniente de coro*. Father Correa insisted that the *teniente de coro* write it because the scribe, a member of the secular Maya administration, did not have good handwriting.[28] According to the witness, the *cacique*, or the leading native elite of the pueblo, resisted. However, after the priest pressured him and offered the members of the *cabildo* each a bit of aguardiente, they relented.[29]

Two of Father Correa's successors, don Domingo de Cárdenas and don Jacinto Rubio, were also literate in Maya and equally intransigent in thwarting the efforts of the subdelegado and the *juez español* to impose royal control and conduct an investigation with witnesses uninfluenced by outsiders. Their ability to write in Maya allowed them to communicate discreetly through messages secretly passed to leading men of the pueblo. Father Rubio defied an order to limit the number of assistants who owed him tribute in labor, sending two messages in Maya to the cacique, don Nicolas Catzim of Ekpetz, contradicting Captain Cárdenas' orders regarding the services of two Mayas who were exempted from tribute in labor.[30] The priest of nearby Ekpetz was even more intimidating and much more to the point about the assassination. He concluded a brief letter in Maya that concluded none too subtly that he was observing the cacique as to whether or not he was telling the truth! It was one of the clearest examples of an attempt to sway testimony in the entire murder trial.[31]

Conclusion

Unlike predicted trajectories that forecast a gradual, constant loss of native culture in colonial settings, Yucatan's Mayas determinedly held onto their language until the end of the colonial period and beyond. Yet Maya documents produced during the late colonial period cannot only be considered in terms of cultural resistance or preservation, but also as an idiom common to Yucatan, especially outside the walls of the cities. Mixed-race and African-descent populations, rather than act as the vanguards of Hispanic culture, often took on the language, subsistence lifestyle, and even husbands and wives from the Maya majority. Instead of maintaining isolation from the Maya countryside, many Spanish-descent individuals adapted to this persistence of the native language by developing a high level of fluency and literacy. Moving away from the original goal of proselytizing the population, this expertise in the native language served as an important tool for political power for these intermediaries by the end of the colonial period.

NOTES

1.   Decorme, *La obra de los jesuitas mexicanos*, vol. 1, 269.

2.   Beltrán, *Arte de el idioma maya*, "Prologo al Lector." "...*Pero para qué es este arte, si ya casi todos hablan, o saben hablar esta Lengua?*" (s/n).

3.   Beltrán, *Arte de el idioma maya*, "Prologo al Lector."

4.   Robert Patch, *Maya and Spaniard* (Stanford: Stanford University Press, 1993).

5.   AGS, Secretaría del Despacho de Guerra, 7296, No. 12, f. 5.

6. AGN, Criminal 335, Exp. 2, f. 195.

7. Tulane University Latin American Library Archives, Manuscript Collection, Chiapas Collection (no. 33), II "Printed Ephemera," Box 5, Folder 2, Real Cedula, 16 April 1770. In this Real Cedula that affirmed previous orders, mandated: "a fin de que se instruya a los Inidos en los dogmas de nuestra Religion en Castellano, y se les enseñe a leer y escribir en este Idioma, que se debe estender, y hacer unico, y universal en los mismos Dominos, por ser el proprio de los Monarcas, y Conquistadores, para facilitar la administracion, y paso spiritual a los naturals, y que estos puedan ser entendidos de los Supriors, tomen amor a la Nacion Conquistadora, destierren la Idolatría, se civilizen para el trato, y Comercio; y con mucha diversidad de Lenguas no se confundean los hombres, como en la Torre de Babél."

8. The attempts of the bishop of Mérida to found a school for the education of young Maya children in Castilian was just one more of the mostly failed efforts to create a Castilian-speaking majority during the colonial period. The letter cited in Chapter 1 found in Carrillo y Ancona, Crescencio, *El Obispado de Yucatán: Historia de su Fundación y de sus Obispos..., t. II* (Mérida: R. Caballero, 1895), 945-6, deals with the controversy over this proposed school's fundings.

9. AGI, Mexico 3036, No. 119, ff. 16-18.

10. Robert M. Hill, II, *Colonial Cakchiquels: Highland Maya Adaptation to Spanish Rule, 1600-1700* (Fort Worth: Harcourt Brace Jovanovich, 1992), 127.

11. AGN, Criminal 332, ff. 6, 10, and 32-33.

12. AGN, Criminal 332, ff. 32-33, 102-103. The casta men are distinguished from the Mayas not only by their surnames but by their identification as "vecinos."

13. One of the men who signed his name and spoke Spanish actually went by two names, Pablo Flota and Fabian Flota. He stated that he went by Pablo Flota for the sake of his Maya neighbors who found it easier to pronounce "Pab" rather than "Fab." (AGN, Criminal 332, f. 143.)

14. AGN, Criminal 332, ff. 3-33, 102-103.

15. AGN, Criminal 335, Exp. 2, f. 183. His wife, Meregilda Zetina also required an interpreter. (AGN, Criminal 332, f. 214.)

16. AGI, Mexico 2029, No. 2, ff. 15-17.

17. AGN, Criminal 332, f. 237.

18. AGS, Secretaría del Despacho de Guerra, 7299, No. 3, ff. 41 and 49; AGS, Secretaría del Despacho de Guerra, 7207, No. 41, f. 220; AGS, Secretaría del Despacho de Guerra, 7206, No. 29, f. 191; The interpreter identified as don Bernardino Medina may have been the same person as the Captain of the Battalion of Castile, don Agustín Bernardino de Medina. (AGS, Secretaría del Despacho de Guerra, 7299, No. 2, f. 5).

19. AGN, Criminal 335, Exp. 2, ff. 197-197v.

20. The two both translated and signed as "interprete general" during the 1792 interrogations of Luis Lara. (AGI, Mexico 3036, No. 120, Testimonio No. 1, f. 71.). (AGEY, Ramo Colonial, Sección AGEY, Ramo Colonial, Sección Ayuntamientos, vol. 1, exp. 3, f. 1.)

21. AGN, Criminal 332; AGN, Criminal 316; Criminal 302, No. 6, ff. 6-7; Criminal 317.

22. AGS, Secretaría del Despacho de Guerra, 7207, No. 19, Sub-no. 5, f. 93 lists Aguilar as a native of Campeche.

23. AGN, Criminal 316, Cuad. 48, f. 3v.

24. AGN, Criminal 332, f. 237.

25. AGN, Criminal 332, 1a, Exp. 2, ff. 22-28.

26. AGN, Criminal 322, 1a, Exp. 2, ff. 52-52v.

27. "Documentos varios de lengua maya, 1571-1869," Ayer Manuscript Collection, Newberry Library, ff. 71-84.

28. AGN, Criminal 317, f. 192v.

29. AGN, Criminal 317, f. 192v-194, 199v.

30. AGN, Criminal 335, Exp. 2, Cuad. 49, f. 222-229v.

31. AGN, Criminal 335, Exp. 2, Cuad 59, f. 254-54v.

7. The Art of Economic Manuscripts: Nahuatl Writing in Land and Tribute Documents from Central Mexico, 1540-1640

Richard Conway

On February 12, 1686, a Nahua lady named doña Josepha Cortés Cerón y Alvarado appeared before a Mexico City court.[1] As the illegitimate daughter of the last dynastic ruler of Xochimilco, a prominent lakeside city located to the south of the vice regal capital, doña Josepha could trace her ancestry back to Aztec royalty.[2] While illegitimate status jeopardized her inheritance of the family estate and claims to noble title, doña Josepha was able to present a hefty bundle of papers in support of her lawsuit. Her family's estate records, which are today housed in Mexico City's Archivo General de la Nación, include a wide variety of materials, among them a rare and unusually rich corpus of Nahuatl-language documentation in alphabetic and pictorial forms.[3] These sources reveal that the family commanded considerable wealth in the form of land and urban residences. Doña Josepha stood to lose a small fortune if her lawsuit failed.[4]

Doña Josepha had to surmount two hurdles in her lawsuit. Beyond the question of her uncertain status, she also had to demonstrate the family's legitimate ownership of property. In this second matter, the pictorial Nahuatl records, complemented by notarial sources, likely served as compelling evidence in her favor. The pictorial sources consisted of cadastral records, or diagrams and maps of land and property. These cadastral records contain glyphs and other pictorial conventions, which formed an integral part of Nahua ways of producing written records, a tradition that extended back to Pre-Columbian times. The use of pictorial sources in litigation testifies to their continued relevance in society. Their presence in legal records, moreover, now affords us with an opportunity to observe remarkable continuity in Nahua writing traditions even as they underwent change through exposure to Spanish influences like alphabetic script.

This resilience in the use of Nahuatl writing contrasts with the conclusions of some early art historians. John Glass and Donald Robertson wrote of the abrupt demise of Native manuscript art. Glass argued that manuscript painting "quickly degenerated or came to an abrupt halt,"[5] while Robertson similarly wrote of "the speed with which exotic civilizations crumbled under the impact of European culture."[6] More recent scholarship, exemplified by the work of Elizabeth Boone, has revealed that indigenous writing systems did not swiftly collapse after the arrival of the Spaniards. Spaniards recognized Nahua pictorials as writing traditions and, accordingly, Boone notes, "indigenous pictorials easily entered and adjusted to the postconquest situation." Boone has demonstrated that "the indigenous tradition of manuscript painting and pictorial documentation continued strongly for three generations after the conquest, until almost 1600."[7] The Xochimilco materials, among other pictorial sources from the Valley of Mexico, demonstrate that Boone's observation can be extended even further. Half of the pictorial documents in doña Josepha's case date from 1600 and after.[8] The inclusion of pictorial records in her case suggests that even at such a late date they still retained some communicative relevance, if only to suggest their authenticity as manifestations of earlier writing traditions. How then did pictorial Nahuatl survive so long into the colonial period?

Part of the answer lies in the Spaniards' acceptance of pictorial documents as evidence in courts. This legal validity followed from Spaniards' early recognition of Nahua records as an authentic form of writing.[9] Pictorial documents had originated in bureaucratic traditions of the Aztec imperial state. Scribes known as *tlacuiloque* ("painters of books") had been a well-established presence in Nahua society prior to the arrival of Spaniards.[10] The long-standing writing tradition likely supported those continuing to find work as notaries after the conquest, as was the case of Mateo Ceverino de Arellano of Xochimilco who contributed to the *Florentine Codex*, compiled by the Franciscan friar Bernardino de Sahagún.[11] Legal recognition of Nahuatl sources, moreover, followed from Spaniards' interest in obtaining information about the fledgling colony.[12] As early as 1523, the Spanish monarch requested information from Nahuas about tribute in order to determine potential crown income.[13] The *Codex Mendoza* exemplifies the utility of Nahua record keeping practices for Spaniards, commissioned as it was by Charles V in 1541 for information on the former Aztec Empire. The codex combined an ethnographic chronicle of everyday life with an historical account and, importantly, extensive tribute data.[14]

Beyond those records generated expressly for use in court or at the behest of Spaniards, Nahuas kept their own community records. In the contexts of the expansion of the Aztec imperial state and then Spanish rule, providing documentary evidence of land ownership proved crucial to Nahuas. In writing about Spanish usurpation of territory in the colonial era, the historian Charles Gibson remarked upon the tradition of Nahuas to assiduously guard their lands, fully cognizant of the dangers of alienation, which had been a "standard feature of Indian life" since the late Aztec period.[15]

Accordingly, formal procedures arose for determining ownership of land. In the colonial period, these procedures acted as an extension and revision of pre-existing Nahua traditions.[16] Like Spanish cartographers and surveyors, Nahuas used scribes who, in the words of the chronicler Fernando de Alva Ixtlilxochitl, specialized in "paintings of districts, boundaries and borders of cities, provinces, towns and villages as well as the parceling out and distribution of land."[17] The resulting records typically contained common elements: information about the location and ownership of land; details of the size of the holdings; and, in some instances, field shapes, soil composition, and types of crops cultivated. This information was conveyed in cadastral records through glyphs and, as the colonial period wore on, through alphabetic script.

Beyond the practical benefits of producing pictorial manuscripts, matters of cultural preference also account for the longevity in the use of older writing conventions. Elizabeth Boone employs the term "visual thinking" to refer to the way Nahuas graphically conveyed information. Rather than entirely adopting alphabetic script, she maintains that Nahuas continued to generate documents in pictorial form. This glyphic language did not intend to communicate speech, as did European alphabetic scripts, but rather preserved meaning "visually and within its own pictorial conventions...the images themselves encode, structure, and present knowledge graphically. As with a musical score or mathematical notation, one can read a pictorial document without constructing a verbal narrative."[18]

Doña Josepha's cadastral records exhibit many of the characteristics of visual thinking Boone describes. Cadastral records form part of what art historians call economic or practical manuscripts, which also include censuses, tribute records, inventories of possessions, and genealogies.[19] In the cadastral sources, lands were commonly presented in ordered, regular shapes together with prominent geographical features.[20] Plans of property often resemble what today might be considered blueprints of houses. The records provided order and structure to representatives of space through geometric forms. Such representations relied upon measurements and, as a result, pictorial manuscripts frequently contain glyphs for numbers and measurements.

The very comprehensibility of glyphs by Nahuas and Spaniards may explain their enduring presence in pictorial sources. Scholars have uncovered the meaning of many of them.[21] Glyphs provide a wealth of data, ranging from measurements to what art historian Barbara Williams describes as sociological information, which consists of glyphs depicting people, either as householders in censuses or as owners of land.[22] Glyphs referring to people express differences according to gender and age through such communicative devices as hairstyles and the inclusion of torsos.[23] Other artistic embellishments add further details: wrinkles identify a person as elderly, tears indicate that a person is a widower, and hairstyles show marital status.[24] Other common features of the pictorial system found in colonial era records include footprints, glyphs for houses and rulers' palaces, toponyms, soils, and, most commonly, measurements.

Nahuas had used standardized measurements and formal systems for counting prior to the arrival of Spaniards. They made frequent use of measurements, as attested by their expression in cadastral records, wills and the dictionaries of Franciscan friars like Alonso de Molina.[25] The standard unit of measuring land was the *quahuitl*, meaning tree, wood, stick or staff.[26] Quahuitl units were equivalent in length to approximately 2.5 meters, although this varied according to region. This unit could be divided into fractions, shown by glyphs for arrows (*cenmitl*), hearts (*cenyollotli*), and hands (*cenmatl*). Hearts represented the distance from the chest to the hand while the hand glyphs referred to the distance from the elbow to the hand, as Barbara Williams has shown.[27] Other glyphs representing quantities but not linear measurements appear in tribute as well as cadastral records. Several receipts of payment for tribute delivered by Cuitlahuac, a town located to the east of Xochimilco, display numerous numerical glyphs that also appear in the Xochimilco records and the *Codex Mendoza*.[28] Some of these glyphs represent numbers disconnected from quantified units, analogous to the dot counters found in a variety of codices (with each dot representing a single unit). The glyph resembling a banner (which looks like a flag, termed *pantli* in Nahuatl) refers to a full count in the vigesimal system (i.e. twenty). This other counting system was independent of measured units and thus found application in different types of sources. There was thus a widespread use of numerical longevity in their use.

Because glyphs appeared across the gamut of Nahua pictorial sources — in divinatory codices, maps, and economic manuscripts like tribute and census registers as well as cadastral records — notaries would have had occasion to use them with some measure of frequency. Scribes would also have been familiar with producing different types of documents that shared the same glyphs. Several pictorial manuscripts demonstrate the simultaneous use of different documentary genres, as with the *Codex Mendoza*. From Xochimilco, we have two documents that demonstrate not only the blending of writing traditions in a single record but also the use of measurement glyphs and other stylistic conventions associated with cadastral records. The property listing of Petronile Francisca and Constantino de San Felipe functions like a tribute register with clothes and other belongings being presented along with glyphs connoting measurements (note the inclusion of a banner glyph). The document also includes a house plan as well as parcels of land (the rectangles on the right-hand side). The genealogy of Miguel Damían also incorporates elements from different documentary genres. While lacking measurement glyphs — presumably of little relevance here — this genealogy includes footprints and glyphs representing people and toponyms.

Over time, though, the pictorial aspects of cadastral records did not remain unchanged. Pictorial writing underwent a trend towards decline during the colonial period, with varying rates of obsolescence in the use of glyphs. Some glyphs, for instance of measurements, lasted well into the seventeenth century, demonstrating that some ways of representing landscape found expression for longer than others. Charting the usage of glyphs thus provides a sense of the ways in which Nahuas adjusted to Spanish artistic and writing conventions. Some Spanish influences were manifested in additional features including brush strokes, the use of watercolor, inclusion of crosses, and, perhaps most notably, alphabetic script. Alphabetic writing, however, as James Lockhart contends, remained largely superfluous in these records, occasionally translating the visual vocabulary employed by Nahuas into cursive form but often presenting alternative information instead.[29] By annotating records in alphabetic Nahuatl, Native scribes were employing an alternative means of communication. Some cadastral records also included Spanish annotations, revealing that Spanish officials consulted and modified them.

Table 1 demonstrates that in a sample of twenty-five pictorial records from Xochimilco and Mexico City, the overall presence of glyphs diminished over time. Whereas measurements appear in a majority of the sources, the incidence of glyphs representing other information, for instance of a sociological nature, was generally lower; they never appear in more than half of the pictorial sources examined.

Table 1: Comparison of the incidence of glyphs representing measurements and other information in cadastral records submitted in lawsuits, 1540-1616[31]

Date	Number of sources in sample	Number containing measurement glyphs	Percentage with measurements	Number with other glyphs	Percentage with other glyphs
1540s-50s	2	2	100	1	50
1560s	4	4	100	2	50
1570s	8	6	75	3	37.5
1580s	6	6	100	0	0
1590s-1610s	5	3	60	1	20

After the 1560s, the use of sociological glyphs diminishes considerably, presumably reflecting changes in their perceived necessity. During the second half of the sixteenth century, sociological glyphs become increasingly superfluous, perhaps because their information was readily apparent in a legal context.[32] Furthermore, the inclusion of alphabetic script may explain the declining use of certain pictorial conventions. Sociological glyphs identifying the owner of a piece of land would be redundant given that lawsuits involved the very people who claimed ownership, particularly if the records were produced expressly for use in court. By contrast, it might be inferred that numerical glyphs signifying amounts and measurements retained their communicative value for longer.[33]

Overall, visual markers for measurements remained an integral part of economic manuscripts until the first decades of the seventeenth century, suggesting that they retained their communicative currency longer than sociological glyphs, although not without some degree of decline. Their enduring presence attests to a lasting need for their inclusion. Indeed, Nahuatl measurements remained in common use for much of the colonial era. In a 1737 will from Xochimilco, testator Antonio Juan referred to land in quahuitl units.[34] The vocabulary of measurements remained intact even though Spaniards employed comparable ways of recording distances and spatial relationships, common ones being known as *brazas* and *varas*. Resilience in the use of measurement glyphs may have been bound up with parallels between Nahua and Spanish methods of recording measurements. Indeed, both the terms quahuitl and its Spanish equivalent vara referred to a staff of office as well as a unit of measure, attesting to linguistic similarities and, perhaps by extension, some degree of comprehensibility.[35] While the arrival of Spaniards in Mexico involved an encounter across cultural differences, the worlds of record keeping and measurements may not have proved mutually unintelligible.[36]

Doña Josepha Cortés Cerón y Alvarado's papers reveal changes in the use of glyphs and Nahua visual thinking. Changes during the sixteenth century involved a varied decline between dimension and sociological glyphs, the latter finding less frequent expression and faster obsolescence. The utility of glyphic language to convey important information in legal settings accounts, in part, for varying rates of decline. Glyphs for measurements, as a readily comprehensible and succinct form of expression, retained a communicative currency longer than sociological glyphs. Their inclusion in economic manuscripts continued at least until the second decade of the seventeenth century. Nahua traditions of recording measurements were not entirely dissimilar to their Spanish equivalents. Pictorial records remind us not only of the manifest importance of land in colonial society but also that cross-cultural exchanges could operate on a variety of levels and exhibit remarkable complexity. Notwithstanding the complexity in Native writing systems, pictorial manuscripts of land, tribute, and other matters met and fulfilled a variety of needs for both Nahuas and Spaniards. Their very utility helped pictorial records secure a continuing place in colonial society, as shown in their inclusion in legal proceedings. While pictorial records long remained important for Nahua audiences—as shown in their presence in doña Josepha's lawsuit—so these rich sources also facilitated the incorporation of Native society and economy into a new, Spanish colonial society.

NOTES

1.   Archivo General de la Nación, Mexico City (henceforth referred to as AGN), Ramo Vínculos y Mayorazgos, vol. 279, expediente I. AGN Ramo Indios, vol. 29, exp. 249, f. 201-202 v.

See also the analysis of these papers by S.L. Cline, "A Cacicazgo in the Seventeenth Century: The Case of Xochimilco," in H. R. Harvey, ed., *Land and Politics in the Valley of Mexico: A Two-Thousand Year Perspective* (Albuquerque: University of New Mexico Press, 1991), especially page 265.

2.   The Cerón y Alvarado family could trace its genealogy back to Acamapichtli, the forebear of the Aztec Emperor Montezuma Xocoyotzin. Charles Gibson, *The Aztecs Under Spanish Rule: A History of the Indians of the Valley of Mexico, 1519-1810* (Stanford: Stanford University Press, 1964), 157.

3.   The papers also include the legal proceedings as well as wills, other notarial records, certificates attesting to noble status, and a genealogy. For comments on the rarity of these records see Gibson, *The Aztecs Under Spanish Rule*, 157.

4.   Many of the family's lands still generated considerable income. Just a few years before lodging her suit, for instance, doña Josepha's father, don Martín Cortés Cerón y Alvarado had established a variety of expensive pious works and bequests that, following his death, would be paid from the proceeds of valuable parcels of land scattered extensively throughout his patrimony. It was comparatively rare for the indigenous nobility, in the middle of the seventeenth century, to establish such pious works as chantries. See the "informe sobre el testmento de Martín Zeron de Alvarado," Biblioteca Nacional de Antropología e Historia de México (hereafter referred to as INAH). Fondo Franciscano, vol. 48, fs. 19-19v.

5.   John B. Glass, "A Survey of Native Middle American Pictorial Manuscripts," in Howard F. Cline, ed., *The Handbook of Middle American Indians: Guide to Ethnohistorical Sources*, part three, vol. 14 (Austin: University of Texas Press, 1975), 4.

6.   Donald Robertson, *Mexican Manuscript Painting of the Early Colonial Period: The Metropolitan Schools* (Norman: The University of Oklahoma Press, 1994 [first published in 1959]), 1.

7.   Elizabeth Hill Boone, "Pictorial Documents and Visual Thinking in Postconquest Mexico," in E. Boone and T. Cummins, eds., *Native Traditions in the Postconquest World* (Washington, D.C.: Dumbarton Oaks, 1998), 159, 149.

8.   A particularly rich document for the Mexico City district of San Juan Tepetitlan, which dates from 1644, contains glyphs redolent of the writing traditions of the sixteenth century. AGN Ramo Tierras, vol. 101, exp. 2, f. 24.

9.   See Elizabeth Hill Boone, "Introduction: Writing and Recording Knowledge," in Boone and Walter D. Mignolo, eds., *Writing without Words: Alternative Literacies in Mesoamerica and the Andes* (Durham: Duke University Press, 1994), 3-26.

10.   Historian James Lockhart has noted that scribes typically kept such records as "religious and divinatory manuals, historical annals, censuses, land cadastrals, and tribute lists, in a form as much pictorial as glyphic." James Lockhart, *The Nahuas After the Conquest: A Social and Cultural History of the Indians of Central Mexico, Sixteenth Through Eighteenth Centuries* (Stanford: Stanford University Press, 1992), 40.

11.   *The Florentine Codex* was an early equivalent of an encyclopedia about Nahua life and knowledge. See Lockhart, *Nahuas After the Conquest*, 472.

12.   Thus a Xochimilcan named Juan Badianus, for instance, wrote the *Badianus de la Cruz Herbal*, a codex that in its use of both Nahuatl and Latin demonstrates extraordinary manifestations of cultural mixing. John B. Glass and Donald Robertson, "A Census of Native Middle American Pictorial Manuscripts," in Howard Cline, ed., *Handbook of Middle American Indians: Guide to Ethnohistorical Sources*, vol. 14 (Austin: University of Texas Press, 1974), 115. See also Charles Gibson, *The Aztecs Under Spanish Rule: A History of the Indians of the Valley of Mexico, 1519-1810* (Stanford: Stanford University Press, 1964), 300.

13.   See Boone, "Pictorial Documents and Visual Thinking in Postconquest Mexico," 156.

14.   See Frances F. Berdan and Patricia Rieff Anawalt, *The Essential Codex Mendoza* (Berkeley and Los Angeles: University of California Press, 1997).

15. Gibson, *The Aztecs Under Spanish Rule*, 271.

16. Xochimilco records show that once indigenous rulers submitted petitions for adjudication, the viceroy would then order the presiding Spanish magistrate to survey lands under dispute. On the appointed day, the magistrate met with indigenous officials, an interpreter, and witnesses who inspected the lands in dispute. Community members were notified of the date of the survey, usually when assembled for church services or other community events. These surveys could involve the continued mediation of *tlalhuehuetque* (or "land-elders"). These figures were charged with verifying land ownership and, to this end, may have maintained and consulted with community land registers. AGN Ramo Tierras, vol. 1525, exp. 5, fs. 3-6. See also Gibson, *The Aztecs Under Spanish Rule*, 262, and Lockhart, *The Nahuas After the Conquest*, 143-144.

17. Scribes may have copied these community records for court. If not, a scribe recorded the land's measurements and topographical features after the completion of the inspection. Cited in Richard L. Kagan, *Urban Images of the Hispanic World, 1493-1793* (New Haven: Yale University Press, 2000), 48. Spanish chroniclers, including Alonso de Zorita and fray Juan de Torquemada mentioned Nahua records of land in ways that indicate familiarity with them. Ibid, 48-49.

18. Boone, "Pictorial Documents and Visual Thinking in Postconquest Mexico," 158.

19. Glass categorized colonial era documents as economic; Boone calls them practical documents, referring to their utilitarian value, "to explain their social and administrative niches and the documentary needs they served." Boone, "Pictorial Documents and Visual Thinking in Postconquest Mexico," 150; Glass, "A Survey of Native Middle American Pictorial Manuscripts," 36-37. Cadastral and pictorial tribute records have received comparatively little attention from art historians more attracted to the artistic sophistication of more famous cartographic histories and divinatory codices. These latter pictorial manuscripts manifested greater complexity than did the cadastral records, promoting interest in Mesoamerican mathematics, astronomical and calendrical systems. Few scholars have extended their studies of colonial pictorial manuscripts to cover spatial concepts and systems of measurements. An exception includes the scholarship of Herbert R. Harvey and Barbara J. Williams, "Aztec Arithmetic: Positional Notation and Area Calculation." *Science*, 210 (1980): 499-505, and Herbert R. Harvey and Barbara J. Williams, *The Codice De Santa Maria Asuncion: Facsimile and Commentary: Households and Lands in Sixteenth-Century Tepetlaoztoc* (Salt Lake City: University of Utah Press, 1997).

20. Additional information in these records is presented according to color. Color indicates different patterns of land tenure, for instance, lands associated with nobles, royal palaces, and commoners' lands. These conventions appear in some of doña Josepha's documents from Xochimilco.

21. Howard F. Cline, "The Oztoticpac Lands Map of Texcoco, 1540," *Quarterly Journal of the Library of Congress*, 23 (1966): 77-115; Barbara J. Williams, "Pictorial Representations of Soils in the Valley of Mexico: Evidence from the Codex Vegara," *Geoscience and Man*, 21 (1980): 51-62; Williams, "The Lands and Political Organization of a Rural Tlaxilacalli in Tepetlaoztoc, c. A.D. 1540," in Harvey, ed., *Land and Politics in the Valley of Mexico, 187-208*; Williams, "Mexican Pictorial Cadastral Registers: An Analysis of the Códice de Santa María Asunción and the Codex Vergera," in H. R. Harvey and Hans Prem, eds., *Explorations in Ethnohistory* (Albuquerque: University of New Mexico Press, 1984), 103-125; Barbara J. Williams and H. R. Harvey, eds. *The Códice de Santa Maria Asunción: Facsimile and Commentary: Households and Lands in Sixteenth-Century Tepetlaoztoc* (Salt Lake City: University of Utah Press, 1997); Williams and Harvey, "Content, Provenience, and Significance of the Codex Vergara and the Codice de Santa Maria Asuncion," *American Antiquity*, Vol. 53, No. 2. (Apr., 1988), pp. 337-351; H. R. Harvey, "Aspects of Land Tenure in Ancient Mexico," in Harvey and Prem, eds., *Explorations in Ethnohistory*, 83-102; Harvey, "The Oztoticpac Lands Map: A Reexamination," in Harvey, ed., *Land and Politics in the Valley of Mexico*, 163-186, and Jerome A. Offner, "Household Organization in the Texcocan Heartland: The Evidence in the Codex Vergara," in Harvey and Prem, eds., *Explorations in Ethnohistory*, 127-146.

22. Williams, "Mexican Pictorial Cadastral Registers," 105.

23. Williams and Harvey, *The Códice de Santa Maria Asunción*, 21.

24. Of the glyphic language used, the historian H. R. Harvey and Williams remark that "the pictorial system expresses the demographic variable of age and sex of individuals, a person's civil and tribute status, size of nuclear families and households, and household social and economic organization." Ibid, 22.

25. Fray Alonso de Molina, *Vocabulario en Lengua Castellana y Mexicana y Mexicana y Castellana*, ed. Miguel León-Portilla (México: Editorial Porrúa, 2001). See also S. L. Cline and Miguel León-Portilla, eds., *The Testaments of Culhuacan* (Los Angeles: UCLA Latin American Center Publications, 1984).

26. See Frances Karttunen, *An Analytical Dictionary of Nahuatl* (Austin: University of Texas Press, 1983), 58.

27. Williams, "Mexican Pictorial Cadastral Registers," 107.

28. For the Cuitlahuac "cartas d epago," or receipts of payment, see Newberry Library, Chicago, Ayer Collection, Ms. 1476 A I-VIII.

29. Lockhart, *The Nahuas After the Conquest*, 143.

30. Excluding footprints.

31. These sources have been selected because they constitute a part of a broader set of legal and administrative records that provide context and background. They also have reliable dates. Materials for Xochimilco come from AGN Ramo Vínculos y Mayorazgos, vol. 279, exp. 1, fas. 36, 78, 116, 36v, and 53; AGN Ramo Tierras, vol. 1525, exp. 5, f. 3; Ibid., vol. 2753, exp. 11, f. 2; "Property of Petronila Francisca and Constantino de San Felipe," *Handbook of Middle American Indians*, vol. 14, no page number given but the originals are located at the Newberry Library, Chicago, Ayer Collection, Ms. 1901, and the "Document relating to the descendants of Don Miguel Dámian," *Handbook of Middle American Indians*, vol. 14, no page number given, Newberry Library, Chicago, Ayer collection, Ms. 1900. The Mexico City materials for this sample, while housed in the AGN, come from Luis Reyes García, Eustaquio Celestino Solís, Armando Valencia Ríos, Constantino Medina Lima, and Gregorio Guerrero Díaz, eds. Documentos nauas de la Ciudad de Mexico del siglo XVI (México: CIESAS y Archivo General de la Nación, 1996), 90, 112, 122, 126, 145, 163, 174, 179, 186, 206, 249, 262, 280, 286, 290, and 298.

32. Whereas art historians have demonstrated that pictorial evidence in *lienzos* and cartographic histories conferred authority and legitimacy upon local elites, such was not the case in pictorial records presented in court. No correlation between elites involved in the legal cases, who could have afforded added details and embellishments, and the incidence of glyphs can be detected. See in particular chapters five, six, and nine in Elizabeth Hill Boone, *Stories in Red and Black: Pictorial Histories of the Aztecs and Mixtecs* (Austin: University of Texas Press, 2000), 87-161, 238-250; Dana Liebsohn, "Primers for Memory: Cartographic Histories and Nahua Identity," in Elizabeth Hill Boone and Walter Mignolo, eds., *Writing Without Words: Alternative Literacies in Mesoamerica and the Andes* (Durham: Duke University Press, 1994), 161-187.

33. John Glass, for instance, wrote, "There is little doubt that the manuscript and writing systems of Central Mexico continued to develop under European influence at least until the last quarter of the 16th century." Glass, "A Survey of Native Middle American Pictorial Manuscripts," 4. The varying rates and extent of decline in this visual language may be explained by the utility of such information in legal settings. Two documentary forms can be discerned among the cadastral records. Community records represent patterns of record keeping designed for the needs of local residents. Community sources, while sometimes admitted as evidence in legal cases, were not expressly manufactured for that purpose and, as such, display more information and manifest a wider array of glyphic images than do the pictorial records generated under the auspices of Spanish courts. One such community record (of cadastral and tribute information) known as the *Códice de Santa Maria Asunción* contains information about many people in one place, thereby requiring a greater variety and number of glyphs. The comparatively elaborate nature of the *Códice de Santa Maria Asunción* stems, in part, from the variety of information it contains; communities would

have consulted this codex for information about land holding, tribute, and demography. Legal records, by contrast, were produced specifically for the requirements of the court. Accordingly, a large number of them from Mexico City evince a consistent style and comparative simplicity vis-à-vis community versions of cadastral records. Notwithstanding these differences, legal and community documents shared the same essential visual language. When glyphs for people, places, and measurements appear in these two documentary forms, they do not change appreciably in style or meaning. Rather, what differentiates them is the extent of their inclusion or exclusion. Glyphs connoting fractions are exhibited with less frequency in court documents, presumably because relatively small measurements were of less relevance when questions about the very ownership of that land were at stake. The Xochimilco documents presented by doña Josepha suggest a kind of intermediary origin between community and legal records. They were produced for the family's use, albeit not necessarily for posterity's sake but rather for practical use, for instance, in a legal context (as an integral part of documentation that proved ownership of land and property). They were also tailored to suit the requirements of the court, thus explaining the extensive alphabetic notation in Nahuatl and Spanish. See Williams and Harvey, *The Códice de Santa Maria Asunción* and Williams and Harvey, "Content, Provenience, and Significance of the Codex Vergara and the Codice de Santa Maria Asuncion," 337-351.

34. AGN Ramo Civil, vol. 1230, exp. 7, f. 2-2v. Nahuas did come to adopt Spanish loanwords, and with them measuring systems, as shown in the testament of don Nicolas de Silva from 1736 in which he bequeathed to relatives "a piece of land at Tlillan where a fanega of grain can be sown." Excerpted in James Lockhart, *Nahuatl as Written: Lessons in Older Written Nahuatl, with Copious Examples and Texts* (Stanford: Stanford University Press and UCLA Latin American Center Publications, 2001), 137.

35. Gibson, *The Aztecs Under Spanish Rule*, 605, 600. Some measurements, for instance *leguas* (leagues) remained vague and inexact, much as Nahua equivalents based on the human body did. With similar ambiguity, the Spanish term *fanega* translated to the amount of "tilled ground as was necessary to sow" a certain amount of wheat using a weight also known as a *fanega*. See David Vassberg's definition of the Spanish term fanega in his glossary. See David E. Vassberg, *Land and Society in Golden Age Castile* (New York: Cambridge University Press, 1984), xvi. Also, see Roland Chardon, "The Elusive Spanish League: A Problem of Measurement in Sixteenth-Century New Spain," *The Hispanic American Historical Review*, Vol. 60, No. 2. (May, 1980), pp. 294-302.

36. Which is not to suggest that cross-cultural communication was not without its misunderstandings: Gibson notes that confusion could arise in attempts by Nahuas to comprehend measurements in Spanish terms (and vice-versa). He writes, "Measurements were vigesimal and often vague ('400 braças o mas y sea de 800 braças'), and varas and brazas were confused." Gibson, *The Aztecs Under Spanish Rule*, 266.

Early and Late Encounters

8. French Colonial Perspectives of Indigenous Latin America from the William J. Haggerty Collection of French Colonial History

Martha Daisy Kelehan

Every library has its hidden collections, collections that should receive more attention. At Binghamton University, one of our hidden gems is the William J. Haggerty Collection of French Colonial History.[1] This collection of some 20,000 books, pamphlets, and journals was originally the library of the private colonialist society, the Union Coloniale Française. By reading one small corner of the Haggerty Collection, focused on the depictions of indigenous Latin America, one can begin to see how French colonial lobbyists of the late nineteenth and early twentieth century developed their argument for the moral necessity of French high imperialism, the so-called *mission civilatrice*.

Binghamton acquired the Haggerty Collection in 1984 from SUNY-New Paltz, where it had been since 1966. The library of the Union Coloniale opened in 1894, just a year after the creation of the society by businessmen from Marseilles and Bordeaux with economic interests in colonies. The Union Coloniale, as an advocate for colonial endeavors, collected a wide variety of materials on France's colonies, with particular emphasis on its Africa and Asian colonies.[2] The materials range from economic and commercial data, to travelogues, to lush publications on colonial exhibitions, to scientific articles from gentlemen's geographic and anthropological societies. While individual titles in the collection tend not to be particularly rare or valuable, taken as a whole, the Haggerty Collection is an excellent resource for the study of this period of French history, and is believed to be one of the strongest collections of this kind outside of Aix-en-Provence, home to the official archives of the Union Coloniale.

The French colonialist societies were hugely influential in morphing the idea of French nationalism into French imperialism during the Third Republic, 1870-1940. Focusing national energies on France's civilizing role abroad seemed a good way to distract from France's humiliating loss of territory in continental Europe during the Franco-Prussian War. The colonies were positioned as a place to revitalize France. They could provide new trading partners, new investment opportunities, and raw materials to maintain France's status as a "world power." Colonialism was couched rather as a natural extension of social Darwinism, and the imperialist propaganda produced and collected by the colonialist societies deliberately emphasized the political, economic, cultural, and racial superiority of the French, supplying a moral justification for empire.

While France's late-nineteenth-century colonies in the Americas were few (certainly the heyday of French Atlantic empire passed with the loss of Canada, Haiti, and the sale of the Louisiana territories), there remained a fascination with indigenous life and culture. Colonialist publications tend to portray indigenous Latin Americans as falling on the extreme ends of a spectrum, as either "noble savages" or as cannibals. As one can see from the Haggerty Collection, the inhabitants of the colonies were routinely portrayed as inefficient stewards of their countries' natural resources in such a way as to give French colonizers the moral right, even the responsibility to exploit the resources to the fullest potential.

One discovery from the collection is the fictional adventure story *A travers la Foret Vierge, Aventures extraordinaires de deux jeunes francais au Bresil*.[3] This book from 1907 is something of an anomaly for the Haggerty Collection, which has very little fiction. In the book, two young Frenchmen (the heroes, *naturellement*) decide to go to Brazil after they discover a hidden manuscript by Jean de Lery in a copy of Hans Staden's book that details the location of a treasure trove of diamonds buried in an Indian grave. Upon arrival in Brazil, the heroes seek out their friend Carlos's plantation to get their bearings before setting out treasure hunting. While at the plantation, Carlos's little sister Carlotta is kidnapped by a band of Indians and stolen into the jungle. Our heroes, with Carlos (and five of the strongest slaves on the plantation), mount a rescue mission, but they are captured and sold to a group of cannibals. Thanks to the smart decision to swipe a Guaraní dictionary from Carlos's library, one of the heroes is able to pick up enough of the language to impersonate the tribe's shaman at a key moment, creating a necessary distraction, which allows our party to escape the cannibals. After 100 pages of additional hijinks—including a mummy and some grave desecration à la Indiana Jones—the heroes end up with two huge perfect diamonds worth a million francs.

What is interesting is how our heroes are written to feel perfectly entitled to rob the graves and claim the diamonds as their own. They have not even the slightest twinge of conscience about their actions in Brazil. The various indigenous groups in the book are little more than caricatures. They are depicted as naïve, living so close to nature that they think diamonds are nothing more than *"pierres transparentes,"* or they are unnatural cannibals or malicious kidnappers, in which case they do not deserve the diamonds.[4] It is a neat justification for the plundering of the Americas and a tidy bit of colonialist propaganda aimed at young readers. Thus, the exotic Americas are shown to be the perfect setting for this adventure story complete with lost manuscripts, jungles, diamonds, plantation heiresses, and of course, cannibals.

Even in non-fiction, the Caribs, the Americas' first cannibals, hold a particular fascination for the French. Consider the following two books from the Haggerty Collection, both published after World War II. The first is from 1948, part of the series La Joie de Connaitre L'Adventure Humaine by Henry de Lalung, entitled *Les Caraïbes, un peuple étrange aujourd'hui disparu.*[5] The second book is a pamphlet by the very prolific author[6] and library director of the Geographic Society, Henri Froidevaux. The pamphlet, from 1953, is entitled *Une civilisation primitive disparue, les Caraïbes de la Guadeloupe vers 1650.*[7] In the pamphlet, the French anthropologist Jean Baptiste Delawarde[8] reports that by the 1950s, there are only 400-500 Dominican Caribs left on reservations.[9] There is little discussion of how this came to be, but rather the emphasis that one often finds in writings about indigenous Latin America is on how populations have "*disparu*" and how the Americas are empty lands, full of virgin forests, ready for colonization. Rather than characterizing the lack of indigenous populations in the Americas as genocide, the language of "*disparu*," seen in both titles, suggests a demographic mystery, not a crime. The emphasis on this presence as an absence allows the Caribbean to be seen as a blank slate, while absolving European consciences of any blame.

Of course, this trope of indigenous peoples as a presence/absence is not limited to the Caribbean. In a 1906 travelogue to be discussed in more detail later, Gaston Donnet poses the question "*Comment peupler le Brésil?*" then goes on to answer: "*Cette question de peuplement est une très grosse question. L'Amérique du Sud est vide.*"[10] Empty. Ready to colonize. Ready to repurpose. Ready for French entrepreneurs. In the first decade of the twentieth century, there seemed to be considerable concern that the French were lagging behind other colonial and neo-colonial powers in establishing economic relations in the Americas.

In a work from the turn of the century, not long after the U.S. redrew the maps in the Caribbean post-1898, by Auguste Plane, entitled *À travers l'Amérique équatoriale: Le Pérou*, the author cannot resist chiding French businessmen for not taking better advantage of the available economic opportunities.[11] He writes in the introduction:

> *Le commerce français est en infériorité de plus en plus marquée dans le mouvement commercial des républiques sud-américaines, malgré la parenté de race et de language qui facililte les relations. Au Pérou en particulier, les Américains du Nord et les Anglais font 75 pour 100 des échanges; ils ont construit et monopolisé les grandes voies de communication et obtenu d'importantes concessions minières et agricoles. Ce pays, grâce à ses richesses naturelles et à la salubrité de son climat, est destiné à un avenir prochain très brilliant.*[12]

There seems to be anxiety that France is behind the neo-colonial times with regards to the Americas, with its natural riches and brilliant future.

Indigenous Latin Americans were also used to put forward various "scientific" theories about race and culture, a debate that was prominent in the development of anthropology as a discipline, and certainly used to justify the civilizing mission of French imperialism. In Gaston Donnet's *De l'Amazone au Pacifique par la Pampa et les Andes* from 1906, the travelogue is basically a place to expound on his beliefs of the inferiority of non-European races. In chapter 5, "Indigenes et Bresilienes," he compares indigenous Brazilians to dogs in an extended, offensive metaphor.[13]

Later, he includes the story of the "beautiful Mrs. K," which he heard from a friend, basically hearsay, to describe the dominance of nature over nurture.

> *Une jeune fille acauan avait été élevée, dans un collège de la capitale, avec le plus grand soin. Elle était brevetée, diplômée en toutes espèces de parchemins et jouait du Beethoven sur un piano à queue. Un ingéniuer allemand l'aimait et l'épousa. Ils vécurent ensemble cinq ou six ans, à l'européenne, dans une grande ville. Elle avait ses jours de réception, de bals et de concerts. On disait: «la belle madame K...»; ses toilettes étaient célèbres. L'ingénieur mourut; elle le pleura convenablement huit mois. Puis, elle vendit son piano à queue, ferma son salon, changea sa robe à traîne contre un pagne de cotonnade, et la «belle madame K» s'en alla, dans le Matto Gross, rejoindre ses frères et ses soeurs qui se couvrent le corps de bouses de vache pour se préserver du diable. Et le plus curieux, c'est que ce cas d'atavisme n'est point le seul; on le retrouve pareil chez deux aborigènes austrailiens gradués de Cambridge, qui retournent sur les bords de la Murray, dès qu'ils ont atteint leur majorité.[14]*

That these individuals preferred to live where they were born is evidence to Donnet of the shared nature of primitive people, where indigenous Americans are no different from Aborigines. Implicit in this story is the idea of a hierarchy of peoples, where for Donnet, it seems clear, the pinnacle of mankind is surely represented by grand pianos and reception days.

In one of the densest books in the collection, *Anthropologie Bolivienne*, one sees further attempts to use the latest "scientific" methods to understand the differences among the races.[15] This three-volume work from 1908 was written by Arthur Chervin, based on notes from the "Mission Scientifique" of G. de Crequi Montfort and E. Senechal de la Grange to Bolivia in 1903-1904. The book represents the cutting-edge research of the time being done using anthropometry, craniology, and metric photography. Although originally scheduled to be part of the mission, Chervin was not able to accompany them to Bolivia. Since he could not be there in person to take the measurements himself, he devised a strict method of photographing his subjects following

Bertillon, the French inventor of anthropometry. There is a chapter in the book dedicated to how Chevrin directed his proxies in Bolivia to assemble the camera in order to have the subjects exactly the same distance away. He then took measurements from the photographs to compile tables upon tables of data. He used this data, coupled with ethnographic information collected through a series of questions posed in Bolivia, to draw his conclusions about the various indigenous populations across Bolivia, without having set foot in the country.

Anthropologie Bolivienne was an important book, as evidenced by the number of reviews it received in anthropological journals outside France. In a review in the journal *Man*, published by the Royal Anthropological Institute of Great Britain and Ireland from 1909, they summarize Chervin's chief demographic conclusions remarking on 1) the importance of the mestizo community with regards to the economic and political governance of Bolivia, and 2) arguing that the sparseness of the Bolivian population is "totally inadequate for making the most of the agricultural and mineral wealth of the country."[16] This piece of information is very suggestive. The message, here, is that Bolivia is ripe for development for those able to meet the interests of the small mestizo populations running the country. And on the off-chance a French businessman might have to deal with the indigenous populations, he would be prepared having read the introduction where Chervin explains how to tell the city-dwelling Quechuas from the Aymara, by their dress, gait, and the shape of their face.[17] Despite the obvious flaws with his "research methods," the book is full of photographs from all over Bolivia, with wonderfully detailed notes on costume and customs, the music and history, the cities and villages, of the many people living in Bolivia at this time.

That is not to say that everyone believed in a biological conception of race. This period was marked by a vigorous debate on these ideas. Binghamton also has a first edition copy of the Haitian anthropologist and educator Antenor Firmin's *De l'égalité des races humaines (Anthropologie positive)*.[18] Written in response to Gobineau's racist *L'inégalité des races*, Firmin's book from 1885 decisively refutes the idea of a hierarchy of races, rather declaring the essential equality of all people. His book also incorporates critiques of craniology and anthropometry, and is considered to be one of the earliest proponents of a social theory of race.

In addition to providing people as subjects for study, the Americas were a place for the French to "discover" new plants and animals, to experiment with new agricultural practices, to unearth pre-Colombian antiquities, and to make advances in public health, geography, archaeology, and engineering. Some of the most interesting works from the collection breathlessly declare to be the first photographs of certain Patagonian peaks,[19] describe the mushrooms of Guadeloupe,[20] and detail the various depths at which to dig the Panama Canal.[21] Let us consider one last book. Produced by the Ministry of War, Arms, and the Colonies in 1920, *Les bois de la Guyane française et du Brésil* makes explicit the important role that the colonies play in providing raw materials.[22] While the book does contain considerable botanical information, the authors admit to focusing their attentions on those woods that would likely provide the most use in rebuilding post-war France. In describing Guyana's geography, the authors use the language of colonial propaganda:

> *Notre vielle colonie de la Guyane Francaise forme une contrée complète-*
> *ment vierge, encore peu connue, et presque completèment déserte. Ce*
> *vaste territoire de 8.7000 kilomètres carrés, limité par les fleuves Maroni*
> *et Oyapock, les monts Tumuc-Humac et l'Océan Atlantique, est entière-*
> *ment et uniformément couvert par la forêt.*[23]

A little later they continue: "*A l'interiéur, dans la forêt, il n'y a guère qu'un population nomade, composée de mineurs et de balatistes, à laquelle il faut ajouter quelques tribus noires ou indiennes.*"[24] In emphasizing how little known and how sparsely populated the country is, the authors seem to suggest that no one would care, or even notice, if they sent in the whole French army to start chopping down trees.

After that brief introduction, the book is laid out like an encyclopedia with entries for individual species. Given the authors' emphasis on useful woods, it is probably not surprising that the first thing mentioned for each tree is its commercial name. But also included are the scientific and vernacular names, a botanical description, the texture and density of the wood, principal and presumed uses, and perhaps most interestingly, the "*usages indigenes*" or local uses. While researchers most often use the Haggerty Collection in order to study colonialism, one can learn quite a bit about the history of science.

The publications collected by the private colonialist society, the Union Coloniale Française, paint a portrait of the Americas as lands of opportunity for French scientists and entrepreneurs, and lands full of potential for exotic adventures. French authors used indigenous Latin Americans to illustrate certain points as part of a larger argument in favor of French imperialism. As is often the case when looking at books written about the "Other," one learns far more about the French authors than about the individual indigenous people that the books purport to be about. These few books highlighted here form a small part of the much larger William J. Haggerty Collection of French Colonial History, just as the Americas represent only a small part of France's *mission civilatrice* of the late nineteenth and early twentieth centuries.

NOTES

1.   For a collection-level description of the Haggerty Collection, see http://library. binghamton.edu/specialcollections/haggerty.html.

2.   The library also provided reference service for the public. According to Henri Brunschwig's study of the Union Coloniale, the library responded to some 563 queries for

information in 1903. Henri Brunschwig, *French Colonialism 1871-1914 Myths and Realities* (London: Pall Mall Press, 1966), 123.

3. Charles Guyon and Rene Guyon, *A travers la forêt vierge, Aventures extraordinaires de deux jeunes français au Brésil*. Paris: Gédalge, 1907.

4. Guyon, 60.

5. Henri De Lalung, *Les Caraïbes, un peuple étrange aujourd'hui disparu*. Paris: Bourrelier, 1948.

6. The Haggerty collection has some 57 books by Froidevaux, dating from 1893-1953.

7. Henri Froidevaux, *Une civilisation primitive disparue, les Caraïbes de la Guadeloupe vers 1650*. Paris: Impr. nationale, 1953.

8. The Haggerty has three books by Delawarde; two on Martinique's Amerindian antiquities and one on peasants in 17th century Martinique.

9. Froidevaux, 107.

10. Gaston Donnet, *De l'Amazone au Pacifique par la Pampa et les Andes* (Paris: C. Delagrave, 1906), 53.

11. Auguste Plane, *À travers l'Amérique équatoriale: Le Pérou*. Paris: Plon-Nourrit et Cie., 1903.

12. Plane, i.

13. Donnet, 59.

14. Donnet, 63.

15. Arthur Chervin, *Anthropologie bolivienne*. Paris: Imprimerie nationale, 1907-1908.

16. A. C. H., "Review of *Anthropologie Bolivienne*." *Man* 9 (1909): 123. Available from http://www.jstor.org/stable/2840655.

17. Chervin, xxxi-xxxii.

18. Joseph-Anténor Firmin, *De l'égalité des races humaines (Anthropologie positive)*. Paris: F. Pichon, 1885.

19. L. Gallois, *Les Andes de Patagonie*. Paris: A. Colin, 1901.

20. N. Patouillard, Champignons de la Guadeloupe. France: Société mycologique de France, 1899.

21. A. Dumas, *Projet d'achèvement du canal de Panama*. Paris: E. Bernard, 1891.

22. France, "Les bois de la Guyane française et du Brésil." v. 5 of *Mission d'études forestières envoyée dans les colonies françaises par les Ministères de la guerre, de l'armement et des colonies*. Paris: É. Larose, 1920.

23. France, 3.

24. France, 3.

BIBLIOGRAPHY

A. C. H. "Review of *Anthropologie Bolivienne*." *Man* 9 (1909): 123-125. http://www. jstor.org/stable/2840655.

Binghamton University Libraries. "William J. Haggerty Collection of French Colonial History." http://library.lib.binghamton.edu/special/haggerty.html. Accessed June 27, 2008.

Brunschwig, Henri. *French Colonialism 1871-1914 Myths and Realities*. London: Pall Mall Press, 1966.

Chervin, Arthur. *Anthropologie bolivienne*. Paris: Imprimerie nationale, 1907-1908.

De Lalung, Henri. *Les Caraïbes, un peuple étrange aujourd'hui disparu*. Paris: Bourrelier, 1948.

Donnet, Gaston. *De l'Amazone au Pacifique par la Pampa et les Andes*. Paris: C. Delagrave, 1906.

Dumas, A. *Projet d'achèvement du canal de Panama*. Paris: E. Bernard, 1891.

Firmin, Joseph-Anténor. *De l'égalité des races humaines (Anthropologie positive)*. Paris: F. Pichon, 1885.

France. "Les bois de la Guyane française et du Brésil." v. 5 of *Mission d'études forestières envoyée dans les colonies françaises par les Ministères de la guerre, de l'armement et des colonies*. Paris: É. Larose, 1920.

Froidevaux, Henri. *Une civilisation primitive disparue, les Caraïbes de la Guadloupe vers 1650*. Paris: Impr. nationale, 1953.

Gallois, L. *Les Andes de Patagonie*. Paris: A. Colin, 1901.

Guyon, Charles, and Rene Guyon. *A travers la forêt vierge, Aventures extraordinaires de deux jeunes français au Brésil*. Paris: Gédalge, 1907.

Kelehan, Martha. "French Colonial Perspectives on Latin America: Selections from the William J. Haggerty Collection of French Colonial History, Binghamton University Libraries." Binghamton University Libraries. http://library.lib.binghamton.edu/subjects/lacas/haggerty.html. Accessed June 30, 2008.

Patouillard, N. *Champignons de la Guadeloupe*. France: Société Mycologique de France, 1899.

Plane, Auguste. *À travers l'Amérique équatoriale: Le Pérou*. Paris: Plon-Nourrit et Cie., 1903.

9. The Lure of the Kekchi: A German Entrepreneur Becomes a Mayanist
Guillermo Náñez Falcón

Introduction

This paper is based on the Erwin P. Dieseldorff Collection in Tulane's Latin American Library. This is a massive archive of personal and business correspondence; account books; labor contracts; and research notes, manuscripts and drawings relating to Mayan studies and Guatemalan medicinal plants.

E. P. Dieseldorff (referred to as Dieseldorff in the remainder of this paper) was born in Hamburg in 1868 into a family of wealthy merchants. His father owned several ships that sailed the Baltic. One uncle, Charles William (referred to as "C.W." in the remainder of this paper), owned an import-export house in Belize from 1843-1862, and then moved to London to continue in the Central American trade. In 1865, H.R. Dieseldorff (referred to as "H.R." in the remainder of this paper), another uncle, was the first German to settle in the Alta Verapaz in northern Guatemala, where he established a general store in Cobán, the department capital, selling imported goods from England and Germany. Two of Erwin Dieseldorff's first cousins joined their uncle H.R. in 1880.

Thus, it was natural for Dieseldorff to have a driving entrepreneurial spirit. He envisioned a future in Central America in business and trade. After completing secondary studies in Hamburg in 1885, Dieseldorff worked for his uncle C.W. in London to gain experience in the Central American trade. His father's death in 1887 left Dieseldorff with a sizeable inheritance, which he was eager to use to build his own business and make a name for himself.

Although he was uncertain what exactly he wanted to do, in October 1888 at the age of 20, he sailed for Guatemala to join family members. The first few months he traveled about Guatemala testing investment opportunities, but finally settled in the Alta Verapaz, where he began to buy and sell properties and develop coffee plantations. By the time of his death in 1940, he was one of the largest private landowners in the country with a vertically integrated enterprise that included properties for coffee production, for seasonal labor, and for milpas for his agricultural workers.

Dieseldorff was primarily a businessman, yet from his earliest days in Guatemala he was attracted to the archaeology, language, religion and customs, and the medicinal knowledge of the Kekchi people of the Alta Verapaz. He made the study of these indigenous people a lifelong endeavor. His Mayan studies spanned the more than fifty years that he lived in Guatemala, and he made numerous contributions through excavations, publications, museum donations, and personal associations. This paper gives an overview of Dieseldorff's work, and concludes with some thoughts about his motivations and contributions.

A Budding Mayanist

When Dieseldorff arrived in the Verapaz in 1888, the exoticism of the highland tropics and its Kekchí inhabitants instantly captivated him. He was familiar with the travel accounts by Otto Stoll and William Brigham,[1] but could not have anticipated how the country would affect him. In letters to his mother in Hamburg, young Dieseldorff described in detail the topography, the climate, and the flora of the region and the customs and dress of the Kekchí Maya, who made up more than 95% of the population. He recognized the importance of knowing their language and began to learn it immediately. With a certain pride, in his second letter from Cobán he phonetically wrote the Kekchí numbers from 1 to 10.[2] He lamented the lack of textbooks with which to study.

The archaeological past of the area immediately captured his imagination. A few days after his arrival, he wrote to his mother that on a coffee farm he had visited, "I found many stone knives and arrowheads on a rock, where Indians of another age had thrown them…I also found some pretty clay shards, which look like Roman pottery, with Egyptian-style perspective of the figures."[3] Knowing little of the Maya at the time, he made comparisons with objects familiar to him.

Dieseldorff's arrival in the Alta Verapaz coincided with that of Dr. Karl Sapper, aged 22, and two years his senior. Sapper was a recent graduate of the University of Munich in Natural Sciences and brother of the Verapaz *finquero* (coffee planter), Richard Sapper. Together the two young men traveled to remote areas of the department to carry out a number of excavations. On one of their expeditions, Dieseldorff found "two idol heads, though not intact, and some pretty postsherds and stone knives."[4]

In mid-December, 1888, the two traveled to a site near Santa Cruz Verapaz, which was about seven hours' distance on horseback from Cobán, to excavate a burial mound. Dieseldorff reported, "We uncovered a few objects, but produced singular scientific results. We found pretty beads, some nice spear tips, vases in the form of human figures with heads as stoppers, a deep bowl painted red, and the tiny bones of a severed finger."[5] Of Dieseldorff's share, eight pottery pieces formed a complete pot with painted hieroglyphs, which he assembled. He made a drawing of this vessel and sent it to the British Museum, "for them to translate for me."[6]

In 1891, when he returned to Germany on a family visit and to tend to business, Dieseldorff carried with him some of the pieces that he and Sapper had uncovered, and donated them to the Royal Museum in Berlin.

There, Dieseldorff met the Director of the American Section of the Museum, the pioneer Mayanist scholar, Dr. Eduard Seler, who was to have a profound influence on Dieseldorff. They developed a close friendship, which lasted until Seler's death in 1922. After the visit, Seler published a report on Dieseldorff's donation in the *Zeitschrift für Ethnologie*. He called one of them a "particularly rare piece…a small vessel in the form of a human figure."[7]

Through Seler, Dieseldorff met the other two giants of Mayan studies in Germany: Dr. Ernst Förstemann and Dr. Paul Schellhas. The three men encouraged Dieseldorff to continue excavations and probably instructed him on surveying and recording techniques. It was on this trip that Dieseldorff began to form his personal research library in Cobán of the major works published at the time, including Förstemann's Dresden Codex facsimile and commentary, Brasseur de Bourbourg's studies of the Popul Vuh and the Rabinal Achi, works of Diego de Landa, Pío Pérez, John Lloyd Stephens, and others.

Upon returning from Germany, he undertook a solo excavation at Chamá, a property remotely situated in the far western Verapaz at the confluence of the Chixoy and Salbá Rivers. At the invitation of Ebenezer Cary,[8] the North American owner of the land, Dieseldorff began work in March of 1892, assisted by Carlos López, who had previous field experience under Alfred Maudslay. They surveyed, measured, and mapped the site, which consisted of two plazas. The men started excavation of a tumulus on the lower plaza and found five painted vessels, several unpainted pots, a skull, pieces of jadeite and beads. In a tomb on the banks of the Salbá, Dieseldorff made an extraordinary find: the famous Chamá vase on which is painted a vampire-headed deity, and a second vase depicting a procession of seven figures.[9]

The dig proved Dieseldorff a neophyte archaeologist. The first day's notes are thorough. The second day, heavy rain and a North American lady visitor interrupted work. Excavation notes became fragmentary after the third day, and Dieseldorff later reported that "no notes were taken at the time of the discovery of the grave" in which were found the two vases.[10]

Cary, convinced that the artifacts had great monetary value, forbade further exploration on his property. He kept a share of the findings, including the procession vase, which he sold. Dieseldorff made a colored drawing of the vase for publication, but he remarked with bitterness, "The original [vase] is now in the United States, where it most likely is the show piece in some drawing room." Dieseldorff's interest in the artifacts was scientific. He eventually donated his Chamá vase to the Royal Museum in Germany. Ironically, the Chamá vase disappeared in the bombing of Berlin during World War II; the Procession Vase now resides in the University Museum of Philadelphia. In making the drawings, Dieseldorff was the first person, according to Mary Ellen Miller, "to make 'roll-out' drawings of Maya pots, in which images from a cylinder vessel [are] extended onto a sheet of paper," a technique perfected with photographs by Justin Kerr.[11]

Dieseldorff quickly prepared reports on the excavation and submitted them, with his drawings, to the *Proceedings* of the Berlin Anthropological Society.[12] His footnotes cite extensively from the works in his library. Dieseldorff speculates on the ethnic origins of the makers of the pottery, as he saw similarities with carvings and glyphs from Copán and Quiriguá. Förstemann and Seler both commented on Dieseldorff's report, not entirely in agreement with his conclusions but generally favorably. Seler ended with encouraging words, "May Mr. Dieseldorff be enabled to continue his investigations and may equally active and equally successful workers come forward to other places to increase our knowledge."[13]

Dieseldorff, in March 1894, joined Alfred Maudslay and his wife on their expedition to Copán. Mrs. Maudslay remarked on his enthusiasm despite his near fatal accident with a poisonous snake.[14] In the process of digging under Stela 4, a broken monument of which only the feet remained, he discovered a stone block that had been used for structural support. It had hieroglyphs that dated it as being much older than the monument above. Maudslay thought the glyphs significant and included drawings of them in his *Biologia Centrali-Americana*.[15] Dieseldorff made other excavations on his own property Chajcar and, upon invitation of the President of Guatemala, General José María Reyna Barrios, at Acasaguastlán, always sent reports of his findings to the Berlin Anthropological Society in Germany.[16]

Concomitantly with his archaeological interests, Dieseldorff embarked on the study of Kekchí religious practices and their use of medicinal plants.[17] From 1890 to 1894 he mostly resided at Seacté, a property that he was developing as a coffee farm, situated a difficult eight- to ten-hour ride on horseback from Cobán.[18] Isolated from all Westerners in this remote spot, he lived with the Kekchí laborers and their families in a rude hut and shared their simple food of corn tortillas and black beans. By necessity, he learned to speak their language, and he began to record information about their rituals, customs, and beliefs.[19]

At Seacté, Dieseldorff developed a close relationship with the *curandero* on the property, Félix Cucul. Gradually he gained Cucul's confidence, and the two men often went on long walks around the property. Cucul spoke about the different plants that he used medicinally. Seacté in the lowlands of the Verapaz had a hot climate with particular flora. Later, when Dieseldorff owned estates in the cold regions of the department, he came to know the *curanderos* of these places, such as Tomás Caal of Chajcar and Martín Chub and Sebastián Maquín of Secac. Dieseldorff also worked with a fellow-German coffee planter, the Baron von Türkheim, who had compiled a herbarium of the plants of the department.[20] Dieseldorff noted that the *curanderos* lacked diagnostic skills, for they did not have medical knowledge or instruments. Dieseldorff acquired medical textbooks to educate himself and began to instruct the men. Dieseldorff found them willing to learn and experiment with different plants and new treatments.[21]

Dieseldorff was in the process of preparing for publication his compilation of medicinal uses of plants of the Verapaz when he made a discovery that interrupted his life for a number of years. He believed that *escobilla* had almost miraculous curative properties and became determined to introduce it to the medical world. Called *mesbé* by the Kekchí, it is a plant of the *Malvaceae* family, whose botanical name is *Sida rhombifolia*. In experiments on himself and his farm workers, he learned that an unguent of the leaves cured cases of chronic dermatitis, and that the inhalation of vapor from boiling the leaves alleviated bronchial congestion and, he came to believe, cured tuberculosis.

In 1912, he went to Berlin, where with his own funds he established a clinic, the "Mesbé Institute," for the treatment of tuberculosis and other maladies. He contracted doctors and other medical personnel. The clinic seemed on the verge of success when World War I began, and all physicians were inducted into military service. Dieseldorff was forced to close the clinic, and was unable to return to Guatemala until the end of the war.[22] In later years, Dieseldorff did not lose his faith in *mesbé* and approached doctors in the U.S. to make clinical tests, but with no success. He continued work on his pharmacopoeia of Kekchí medicinal plants and published it in the *Anales de la Sociedad de Geografía e Historia*.[23] The article gave the Kekchí, Spanish, and botanical names of 48 plants with medicinal uses made of them by the Kekchí, and included botanical drawings made by don Pablo Wirsing.

In the 1920s, at the culmination of decades of study of Mayan glyphs, calendar systems, religion and culture, Dieseldorff published at his expense in Germany what he considered his magnum opus, the 3 volume *Kunst und Religion der Mayavölker*.[24] The work was never for sale. He distributed copies to libraries and museums in Germany and the U.S. A translation of the work later appeared in Guatemala in the Anales.[25]

Reflections on Dieseldorff

Dieseldorff is not well known in the U.S., at least in part because most of his writings were published in Germany and Guatemala. Except for the two articles on the Chamá vase that appeared in Bowditch's *Mexican and Central American Antiquities*,[26] his major works are not available in English. Moreover, Dieseldorff was a self-taught scholar who worked outside the academic community. He regularly presented papers at the Congresses of Americanists and corresponded with the leading U.S. scholars of the day, yet did not find entry into the North American anthropology community, perhaps because he lacked an academic degree and a university or museum affiliation. His writings, however, were on a scholarly level and demonstrate knowledge of Mayan glyphs, iconography, cosmology, deities, and calendar systems, as well as a thorough understanding of the publications of German and North American Mayanists.

Dieseldorff's studies on Mayan religion, culture, and calendar systems were fundamental for his understanding of the psychology of the Kekchí. He had a strong affinity for the Kekchí, but consciously or unconsciously used this knowledge to benefit his enterprise. He understood that the life of the Kekchí was based on cycles of the planting and harvesting of their *milpa*, and that corn and *milpa* had a sacred significance for them. There were religious rituals for each time of the year that had been established by Kekchí traditions and beliefs. Recently, historian Wade Kit argued in his doctoral dissertation that Dieseldorff came to have an unwritten agreement with his farm workers that he would respect their customs, giving them days off for their rituals and religious festivals, in exchange for completion of their labor obligations during other times.[27] Dieseldorff admonished his administrators to respect the traditions of the workers, "Porque sin mozos no hay finca."[28]

In Guatemala, Dieseldorff was a corresponding member of the Academia de Geografía e Historia and published numerous articles in the *Anales* of the organization.[29] In the Spanish translation of *Kunst*, he singled out the contributions of Guatemalan Mayanists of his day, including J. Antonio Villacorta C., Virgilio Rodríguez Beteta, and Flavio Rodas.[30] He donated to the library of the institution the five-volume set of Seler's collected works.[31]

The final installment of *Religión* in the *Anales* ends with an admonition that Guatemala establish an anthropological museum in the capital to collect and preserve monuments and artifacts of the Mayan past. "Thus," he wrote, "Guatemala would fulfill its scientific mission as guardian of the remains of Maya science, an honor-bound obligation and a proud legacy to posterity."[32] The museum would be a tourist attraction and moneymaker as well, he argued. In time, the anthropology museum became a reality. In the early 1940s, after Dieseldorff's death, his son Willi donated his father's collection to the museum, which created a separate *sala* for its display.[33]

Conclusions

Dieseldorff was primarily a businessman, a coffee planter and exporter, a merchant. Yet, he had a passionate interest in the Maya throughout his life in Guatemala. His avocation afforded him psychological satisfaction and social prestige that he might not have otherwise had. When in Germany, or at international meetings of scholars, he was no mere man of business or a rich finquero, but a scholar, whom people addressed with respect as "Herr Doktor." Similarly, to his colleagues in the Academia, he was *"un Viejo Maya."*[34] The complexities of his personality are also reflected in the sobriquet that the *cobanero* made of his initials EPD. They referred to him as "El Puro Diablo."

NOTES

1. Otto Stoll, *Guatemala, Reisen und Schilderungen aus den Jahren 1878-1883* (Leipzig, 1886); William T. Brigham, A.M., *Guatemala, the Land of the Quetzal, a Sketch* (New York, 1887). Mentioned in E.F. Dieseldorff, San Francisco Miramar, to his mother in Hamburg, 4

February 1889; Ibid., Senahú, 4 May 1889. Dieseldorff Collection, Latin American Library, Tulane University. Hereinafter the abbreviation "DC" will appear for materials from this collection.

2. E.P. Dieseldorff, Cobán, to his mother in Hamburg, 22 November 1888, DC.

3. Ibid.

4. Ibid., 6 December 1888, DC.

5. Ibid., 27 December 1888, DC; unpublished typed manuscript with corrections in Dieseldorff's hand, "Excavación cerca de cueva de Santa Cruz Verapaz," DC, Box 154, Folder 3.

6. Ibid., 2 January 1889, DC.

7. Eduard Seler, "Alterthümer aus Coban, insbesondere abgeschittene Finger." *Zeitschrift für Ethnologie*, XXIII (1891), 828-29.

8. E[benezer] Cary, Chamá, [to Dieseldorff], Seacté, 4 March 1892, DC, Box 148, Folder 1.

9. Unpublished ms. In Dieseldorff's hand, [Chamá excavation notes, March 1892], DC, Box 154, Folder 32.

10. Erwin P. Dieseldorff, "Ein bemaltes Thongefäss mit figürlichen Darstellungen aus einem Grabe von Chamá," *Verhandlungen der Berliner anthropologischen Gesellschaft* (15 December 1894), 372-78.

11. Mary Ellen Miller, "The History of the Study of Maya Vase Painting," in Justin Kerr, *The Maya Vase Book, A Corpus of Rollout Photographs of Maya Vases*, I (New York, 1989), 129.

12. Erwin P. Dieseldorff, "Ein bemaltes Thongefäss von Guatemala," *Verhandlungen der Berliner anthropologischen Gesellschaft* (16 December 1893), 548-50; _____, "Ein bemaltes Thongefäss mit figürlichen Darstellungen aus einem Grave von Chamá" and "Ein Thongefäss mit Darstellung einer vampyrköpfigen Gottheit," Ibid. (15 December 1894), 372-78, 575-76; _____, "Das Gefäss von Chamá," Ibid. (21 December 1895), 770-76.

13. Ernst Förstemann, "Das Gefäss von Chamá," Ibid., (1894), 573ff.; Eduard Seler, "Das Gefäss von Chamá," *Zeitschrift für Ethnologie*, XXXVI (1895), 307-20; Erwin P. Dieseldorff, Eduard Seler, and Ernst Förstemann, "Two Vases from Chamá," in *Mexican and Central American Antiquities, Calendar Systems, and History*, translated and edited under the supervision of Charles Pickering Bowditch (Washington, D.C., 1904), 635-70.

14. Anne Cary Maudslay and Alfred P. Maudslay, *A Glimpse at Guatemala and Some Notes on Ancient Monuments of Central America* (London, 1899), 91-100, 119, 126.

15. Unpublished ms. In Dieseldorff's hand, "Descripción de las Ruinas de Copán por Don Erwin P. Dieseldorff," DC, Box 153, Folder 14; Alfred P. Maudslay, *Biologia Centrali-Americana; or Contributions to the Knowledge of the fauna and Flora of Mexico and Central America. Archaeology* (London, 18890 1902), Vol. 5, 66-67; Vol. 1, Plate CIV.

16. Erwin P. Diseldorff, "Neue Ausgrabungen des Hm. Dieseldorff in Chajcar, Guatemala," *Verhandlungen der Berliner anthropologischen Gesellschaft* (27 April 1895), 320-22; _____, "Religión y Arte de los Mayas," *Anales de la Sociedad de Geografía e Historia de Guatemala*, V, 4 (June 1929), 437-40, 448-51.

17. Unpublished ms. in Dieseldorff's hand, "Pharmakologie Kekchi," DC, Box 161, Folder 8.

18. Guillermo Náñez Falcón, "Erwin Paul Dieseldorff, German Entrepreneur in the Alta Verapaz of Guatemala, 1889-1937." Unpublished Ph.D. dissertation, Tulane University (New Orleans, 1970), 53.

19. Ibid.

20. Unpublished ms. in Dieseldorff's hand, "Hubarium des Herm Baron von Türckheim herin sind enthalten alle Pflanzen die in Coban & Ungegeng [sic] wachsen," DC, Box 161, Folder 11.

21. Erwin P. Dieseldorff, *Las Plantas Medicinales del Departamento de Alta Verapaz* (Guatemala, 1940), 5.

22. _____, *Heilung von Lungenleiden church Inhalation von Mesbé* (Belin, 1914); _____, *Mesbé bei chirurgischer Tuberkulose* (Berlin, 1914); Dr. Adolf Spangenberg, "Mesbé, ein neues

Heilmittel gegen Tuberkulose," *Reichs medizinal Anzeiger*, XXXVII, 18 (30 August 1912), 1-8; _____, *Mesbé bei Lungentuberkulose* (Berlin, 1914); _____, *Mesbé. Ueber das Tuberkulose-Heilmittel Mesbé* ([Berlin, 1914?]); Dr. Butzengeiger, "Erfahrungen mit Mesbé in der Behandlung chirurgischer Tuberkulosen," *Münchener medizinischen Wochenschrift*, 3 (1913), 1-4; Dr. V. Chlumsky, "Über Mesbébehandlung bei chirurgischer Tuberkulose und bei infizierten Wunden," *Zentralblatt für Chirurgie*, 9 (28 February 1914), 369-70; Dr. Neuber, "versuche mit Mesbé bei Lungentuberkulose ([Berlin, 1914?]); *Briefliche Mitteilungen von Patienten über Mesbé bei Lungentuberkulose* ([Berlin, 1914?]); Náñez Falcón, 74-78.

23. Erwin P. Dieseldorff, "Las Plantas medicinales del Departamento de Alta Verapaz," *Anales de la Sociedad de Geografía e Historia de Guatemala*, XVI, 2 (December 1939), 92-105; XVI, 3 (March 1940), 192-206. In recent years there has been renewed interest among Guatemalan scholars at the USAC in medicinal application of plants of the country, with Armando Cáceres as the leading researcher. See: Armando Cáceres, Blanca Samayoa, and Ligia Fletaes, "Actividad antibacteriana de plantas usadas en Guatemala para el tratamiento de incecciones." *Cuadernos de Investigación*, No. 4-90 (Guatemala, 1991); Armando Cáceres, *Plantas de uso medicinal en Guatemala* (Guatemala, 1996). Dieseldorff's interest in botany had practical, as well as medical, applications. He regarded agronomy as a valuable science for a coffee plantation owner. He conducted experiments with the use of natural and chemical fertilizers and pesticides, and he corresponded with agronomists in England and in the United States to seek their professional advice. In 1908, he published in Germany a manual on the cultivation of coffee, which gave practical advice. In 1908, he published in Germany a manual on the cultivation of coffee, which gave practical advice based on his own experiences. Erwin P. Dieseldorff, *Der Kaffeebaum. Praktische Erfahrungen über seine Behandlung im nördlichen Guatemala* (Berlin, [1908]); Erwin P. Dieseldorff, [Cobán], to Dr. L.O. Howard, Washington, D.C., 2 July and 1 September 1989, DC, Letterbook "Varias Cartas," 37-38, 209-10; _____ , to Walter T. Swingle, London, 8 August and 1 September 1898, DC, Ibid., 144-46, 208.

24. Erwin P. Dieseldorff, *Kunst und Religion der Mayavölker*, 3 vols. (Berlin, 1926, 1931; Hamburg, 1933).

25. See endnote 23.

26. See endnote 13.

27. Wade A. Kit, "*Costumbre*, Conflict, and Consensus: Kekchí-*Finquero* Discourse in the Alta Verapaz, Guatemala, 1880-1930." Unpublished Ph.D. dissertation, Tulane University (New Orleans, 1998).

28. Michael A. Polushin, "*Mozos, milpas y mojones*: E.P. Dieseldorff and Forms of Labour Control in the Alta Verapz, Guatemala." Unpublished conference paper presented at the Conference on Latin American History (CLAH) of the American Historical Association (San Francisco, December 1994).

29. Erwin P. Dieseldorff, "El Tuzltacá y el Mam, los dioses prominentes de la religión Maya," *Anales de la Sociedad de Geografía e Historia de Guatemala*, II, 4 (July 1926), 378-86; _____, "El Calendario Maya de Quiriguá," Ibid., XIII, 2 (December 1936); _____, "La Causa por la cual los Mayas de Quiriguá comenzaron su calendario en 22 de septiembre del año 3373 A.J.C.," Ibid., XVI, 4 (June 1940), 271-79.

30. _____, "Religión y arte de los Mayas," Ibid., V, 1 (September 1928), 66-86; V, 2 (December 1928), 184-203; V, 3 (March 1929), 317-35; V, 4 (June 1929), 432-53.

31. Carlos Schuchhart, "Oración conmemorativa en honor al Sr. Eduardo Seler," Ibid., XIII, 4 (June 1937), 393.

32. Dieseldorff, "Religión y arte," Ibid., 453.

33. Author's note: the *sala* disappeared in the remodeling of the museum, and most of the pieces from the Dieseldorff collection are in storage.

34. David Vela, "Dieseldorff: un viejo maya," *Anales de la Sociedad de Geografía e Historia de Guatemala*, XVII, 2 (June 1941), 90-100.

10. William E. Gates and the Collection of Mesoamericana

Mark L. Grover

The study of the Maya and affiliated indigenous groups in Mexico and Central America is a fascinating and ever-evolving field. Few disciplines have gone through as many changes as the study of the Maya during the past one hundred years. The recent deciphering of the ancient linguistic code has greatly expanded knowledge of this population and radically changed our understanding of who they were and of their role in the evolution of pre-Columbian civilizations in the New World.

Equally important to the history of the discipline is the presence of colorful and complex personalities. When thinking of just a few of the most prominent—Sylvanus Morley, J. Eric Thompson, and Frans Blom— one recognizes that their personalities, their experiences, and their frequent conflicts tell us a great deal about the intriguing history of the discipline. One of the earliest and most eccentric was William E. Gates. While Gates may have lacked the academic expertise of his colleagues, he possessed the passion and the capital that gave him an entrance into the discipline, helping him become a major participant in the early investigations of the Maya. He was not just a scholar but also an avid book and document collector who built the largest and most important private collection on Mesoamerica of the early twentieth century. For various reasons, the collection became separated and is now housed in the libraries of Tulane, Princeton, and Brigham Young University.[1]

Early History

Little in William E. Gates's background would suggest that he would spend much of his adult life studying Mesoamerican languages and culture. He came from a traditional American family. His ancestors lived in the Jamestown colony of early seventeenth-century Virginia and included Thomas Gates, the second governor. His family had a laudable history of political and social prominence in the United States.

Raised primarily in Philadelphia, Gates studied languages at Johns Hopkins University and graduated with an A.B. degree in 1886. He was admitted into the University of Virginia Law School but left during his first year due to problems with his eyes, deciding to move to Cleveland, Ohio to run a printing press. In the end, he did not enjoy the business, suggesting, "My fate was sealed, and my 'job' in this incarnation sealed upon me."[2] He was already interested in Mesoamerica, having purchased a copy of the Maya Codex Tro-Cortesianus (Madrid) in 1898, and printing *The Maya and Tzental Calendars* as a gift for his friends in 1900. In 1905, after receiving a family inheritance, Gates left Ohio and moved to California. He entered the Aryan Theosophical Society colony at Point Loma, outside San Diego, joined the faculty of their School of Antiquity, and became the manager of the small Aryan Theosophical Press. Within this academic and religious environment, he pursued what had become his passion—a full-time study of ancient America and the Maya.[3]

Early Maya Research

Gates's interest in Mesoamerica had its foundation in two episodes. Early in his adult life he became disenchanted with Christianity and the materialism of the world in which he lived. He was enamored with the writings of Helena P. Blavatsky, appreciating the inclusivity of the philosophy of the Theosophists that she expounded.[4] Blavatsky believed that ancient societies possessed wisdom and insight that far exceeded those of the modern world and that only the study of ancient language and thought brought one closer to the wisdom of the past. This idea fit with Gates's passion for languages: he eventually learned thirteen, most of them ancient. This strong belief in the importance of studying linguistics and archaeology was articulated in Gates's 1915 discussion of the importance of archaeology:

> Yet true Linguistics, united to true Archaeology, are the two sciences which have preserved, and hold for us when we can read them, the real past history of Man: how his thought has found forms for expression, and what he has done. Archaeology and Linguistics are the sciences of man's past social history; what he has done, and therefore, what he must be.[5]

His interest and publication on Mayan linguistics made him one of a small and select group of scholars.[6] Gareth Lowe suggests it was such an exclusive group that only fifteen prior to Gates had published on the topic, beginning with Lord Edward Kingsborough's reproduction of the Dresden Codex in his monumental work, *Antiquities of Mexico* (London, 1831-1848). Gates's most important American and British contemporaries were Charles P. Bowditch, Cyrus Thomas, and J. T. Goodman. There was also a small group of German scholars who were actively researching and publishing. All combined, it was a group of bright but often jealous and contentious scholars and Gates was probably the most controversial of them all. While Gates's publications were not particularly noteworthy or significant in comparison to the work of the others, his research did add to an understanding of the subject at that time. However, his eminence in the discipline came primarily from his insatiable passion and talent for collecting primary source material.[7]

Collecting Activities

Gates early recognized a critical dearth of published studies and printed primary source materials on Mesoamerica. His fascination with language led to a desire to examine all the documents available in the Mayan language. He began to carefully peruse auction and booksellers' catalogues in search of any documentation related to the Maya. He corresponded with librarians and museum directors worldwide in his quest to identify documents. He discovered a much larger universe of materials than first believed. He concluded there were probably over 100,000 pages of primary source documents written in Spanish or native languages about indigenous populations of Mesoamerica.[8] It became his goal to obtain a copy of all of the documents either by buying the original or copying the items. He worked with Eastman Kodak Company to develop a specialized photographic paper that would improve the quality of his reproductions.[9]

From 1911 to 1916, he spent most of his time collecting, spending thousands of dollars as he visited archives and libraries in the Americas and Europe to copy documents. He encountered significant challenges in this quixotic pursuit. As his collection expanded so did his pride, which grew to unappreciated heights. He occasionally offended those with whom he worked with his obsessive personality and his demands for complete compliance with what he wanted. He engendered almost universal suspicion or hard feelings toward him by archivists, scholars, and librarians on two different continents. His reputation preceded him: he was not allowed, for example, to see the very important Maya collection housed in the Archivo de las Indias in Seville, Spain. He had serious conflicts in Europe over copyright issues and problems of domain. But he was successful and, by 1914, he possessed copies of most available materials that existed in the United States and Europe.

Gates was financially stingy when it came to his own personal needs, but not in his pursuit of documents. For example, in 1915 he spent over $25,000 on books and manuscripts. He also purchased the most innovative and expensive copying machine that existed. When he discovered a new item, he almost always purchased it immediately, believing that to wait might be fatal. He was vindicated in this approach since he saw many documents he copied in Mexico were destroyed during the Mexican Revolution. He was able to state in 1916:

> When War broke out, I personally owned (then in California) had [sic] half of all known Middle American Indiana ms. material: and had just finished photographing 95% of everything in the world, know, (outside of Seville) which I did not own. That means some 75,000 pages of photos, of original mss or unprocurable imprints, mostly linguistic, but also all the early cultural records of penetration I could locate. Every great past collection found its way to my shelves.[10]

His focus moved south to Mexico and Central America beginning in 1914. He hired Frederick J. Smith to travel throughout Mexico and Guatemala for two years hunting for materials. Dissatisfied with Smith's results, Gates went to Mexico himself from 1917-1918. It was an eventful trip as he traversed between government-controlled areas and rebel-held parts of the country. Mexico was at the end of its revolution and in a challenging and dangerous condition. He described the intrigues of his experiences:

> On this trip of some 1500 miles on horseback, at times entirely alone, at times with escorts of Zapatistas or Oaxaca Serrano Indians as protection from the marauding Carranzistas, I set myself to penetrate to those places where no one else tried to go. I stopped in fully half of all the villages in Yucatan, out to the fringe of "civilization" and the "indio rebeldes."
> Everywhere I hunted manuscripts in the Maya languages, kept (by) friends with the official powers, and also gathered every scrap obtainable of print-ed material, books, pamphlets, newspapers, posters, election notices.[11]

His primary objective was to find indigenous language materials, but he also collected anti-Carranza materials. Never one to ignore issues, Gates became an ardent critic of both the Mexican and the U.S. governments and claimed the Carranza government characterized him as an "agent of the rebels."[12] He was particularly concerned with Mexican government policies related to the preservation of the indigenous past of Mexico. Though he may not have been appreciated by government officials, he seemed to have impressed some of the academic community with his knowledge and was named an "Honorary Professor" at the Museo Nacional de México.[13]

Guatemala

Gates did not return to California and the Theosophist School of Antiquity, but went east to pursue his research interests and become involved in lobbying activities related to the political situation in Mexico. For the next ten years, his focus was not on publishing.[14] In April of 1920, he participated in the organization of the Maya Society headquartered in Philadelphia, Pennsylvania. Gates was made president, due to his collection of materials, and Marshall Saville was named vice president. Unfortunately, Gates's controlling personality quickly doomed the organization. It functioned for a short time and sponsored no publications.[15]

Gates was given a position as an honorary research associate at the Carnegie Institution of Washington. In this position he became part of a research team headed by Sylvanus Morley that went to the highlands of Guatemala and Belize in 1921. This trip began a new and important phase in Gates's life. Because of the isolation from Spanish and Guatemalan cultural influences in many parts of Guatemala, Gates believed he would discover a linguistic structure among the indigenous population that closely approximated the ancient language of pre-Columbian civilizations. He hoped to find uncorrupted texts of the early Mayan languages unlike those he had already collected that had been influenced by contact with Spanish. He hoped that by spending more time with modern Mayan dialects he could better translate older documents that would then lead to a possible breakthrough in understanding the Mayan glyphs. He stated in a letter to George B. Gordon, director of the anthropological section of the Museum of the University of Pennsylvania, "I may not actually read the glyphs, but I will find out much, and will make future work on a wholly new and firm foundation."[16] After several months in Guatemala traveling, collecting, and studying local languages, he returned to the United States in August of 1921.

Gates became unhappy with Sylvanus Morley. While in Guatemala, he became concerned with what he considered were numerous unethical practices of Morley's, particularly related to taking artifacts out of the country without letting government officials know. Additional information gained on a return trip to Guatemala in 1922 convinced Gates that Morley could not be trusted and he broke with Morley and the Carnegie Institution.

On his trips to Guatemala, however, Gates had again impressed his hosts who named him the Director of Archaeology for the Republic of Guatemala. One of his goals was to build an archaeological museum in the country.[17] In this position, he turned his attention to protecting what he felt were the interests of Guatemala while, at the same time, enhancing his own activities. In 1922, he and others successfully lobbied the legislature of Guatemala to enact legislation meant to protect and safeguard Guatemala's archaeological riches. One provision restricted what foreign archaeological expeditions would be allowed to take out of the country. They could take away only half (as opposed to all, as had been allowed) of their excavated objects; the rest would remain in the country under control of the museum. All expeditions would be under the authority and control of the General Director (Gates) and the Museum Director (also Gates).[18]

The restrictiveness of the law offended Morley and others, and some regarded Gates's controlling role as unethical.[19] Even Gates' friend, George B. Gordon, after examining the law, questioned the numerous restrictions and chided Gates for his involvement: "This would appear to close Guatemala to scientific institutions both for archaeological work and ethnological work. Guatemala in this act goes further in this matter of exclusion than any other country. I presume that you are satisfied that this is for the general interest."[20] Gates began working actively to create a museum and to develop an exhibit in Guatemala for the four hundredth anniversary of the discovery of Guatemala in 1924. His personal battles with Morley, however, upset his plans. In the early summer of 1923, he learned that Morley had gone around him to the Minister of Foreign Relations, Roberto Lowenthal, and secured a license to work in the archaeological site at Petén.

Under that authorization, Morley expanded his work into Quiriguá and Copán and, without Gates's knowledge, took items from his dig and sent them to the United States. What this evolved into was a power struggle involving Guatemalan government officials, Morley and other scholars from the United States, and Gates. The final outcome of the dispute was that Gates lost the confidence and support of the Guatemalan government in 1923 and, under pressure, resigned from his positions and returned to the United States.[21]

Tulane

Gates returned to the United States struggling with serious financial difficulties. Earlier, he had purchased a hundred-acre farm in Auburn Hill, Virginia about 100 miles southwest of Washington D.C. near the city of Charlottesville.[22] He also bought land in Guatemala near Chichicastenango to be his residence while in the country. Realizing his predicament, in 1921 he sold those parts of his collection related to everything north of the Maya, which he called his "Mexicana." It also included most of the items related to the political situation in Mexico collected in 1917. He turned the collection over to the American Art Association to have it auctioned. He suggested its worth to be over $25,000 and was given a $20,000 advance by the Association, which he used on his activities in Guatemala. Getting the items ready for sale took time, so the sale was only finally announced in 1924 for April 9-11. A detailed and impressive catalogue of the collection was published and distributed across the country.[23]

The proposed sale of the collection created significant curiosity. Several potential buyers expressed interest and it looked to be an important event in the auction's history. However, sixteen days before the auction, Tulane University made an offer to purchase the entire collection as a unit and the auction was canceled. Considerable annoyance occurred in part because several potential buyers were already in New York in anticipation of the auction.[24]

The sale of the collection to Tulane was advantageous to Gates even beyond the $60,000 he received for the sale of the collection.[25] Tulane offered Gates a position to come to New Orleans to continue his research and collecting activities and also gave him the responsibility to organize and head a new academic unit called the Department of Middle American Research (now the Middle American Research Institute). The organization of the Department was abundantly supported by a generous grant of $300,000 by Sam Zemurray, head of the Cuyamel Fruit Company. Gates's responsibility was to head the Department, identify potential students from Central America, grant scholarships, and direct their research. Gates arrived at Tulane enthusiastic about his new position and challenge, in part because his assignment included not only all of Central America but also the Caribbean.[26]

Gates developed a grandiose vision for the Department and hoped Tulane would become for the geographical region from the United States to Panama what Alexandria had been to the Mediterranean world. For these grandiose ideas to become a reality, significant funding was required, and it was not long before Gates suggested (demanded) to Zemurray that his grant of $300,000 be augmented by an additional million dollars. In addition, Gates announced a program to encourage New Orleans businessmen to pay a five-year subscription of $100 in support of the Department and his expeditions to Latin America. Based on this financial agenda, Tulane advanced Gates $25,000 to be paid back by these funding activities. The funds supported an expedition to Mexico and Central America, two agricultural projects in Mexico and Honduras, and the purchase of books. Gates tried to hire established Mesoamerican scholars such as Thomas A. Joyce of the British Museum and Alfred V. Kidder of the Carnegie Institute. Unsuccessful in attracting established academics, he hired Frans Blom, a young archeologist from Harvard University, and an ethnologist, Oliver La Farge.[27]

The three were soon in Mexico and Central America. Blom and La Farge headed an exploratory trip in 1925 to the Mexican states of Veracruz, Tabasco, and Chiapas, and then went to Guatemala.[28] This expedition was important because it was one of the first by American scholars into areas considered marginally connected to the Maya. At the same time, Gates went to Tabasco with the New Orleans Commission, which was studying the economic value of plants in the region. He joined Blom and La Farge for a week to examine the Maya site at Comalcalco, and then went to Honduras to scout sites for future projects. Gates returned to Tulane with a proposal to establish a Tulane center for scientific research in Honduras that would produce detailed studies of the country in a variety of disciplines, with the ultimate goal of improving social and economic conditions in the country.[29]

The problems that plagued Gates throughout his life followed him to Tulane. His failures to obtain financing for his grandiose plans affected his credibility with the university. His program for subscriptions by businessmen never materialized. Pressure on Zemurray only antagonized the benefactor and resulted in no additional financial donations. The departmental budget was significantly depleted and university administrators found Gates's tactics to be dishonest and questionable. The fact that Gates spent most of his time at his farm in Virginia and in Mexico and Central America with little time in New Orleans did not help his cause. Because of these accusations, an angry Gates resigned as director of the Department on October 1, 1926 only to withdraw his resignation a few days later. Blom turned against Gates and requested he be put administratively directly under the University president, Dr. Albert B. Dinwiddie. His request was granted. Gates's library was removed and placed under the control of the Tulane University Committee. Gates instructed his attorney to begin a process against the university and planned to take his case to the American Association of University Professors. In the second week of March of 1927, the Tulane Board of Administrators voted to immediately end Gates's employment at the University. Gates was devastated and angry and wrote a fiery accusative pamphlet in defense of his activity at Tulane. Those feelings against Tulane went with him to his grave.[30]

He returned to his farm in Virginia without following through on his threatened suit.[31] But he was depressed and struggled for several months while contemplating his future. He told Edward E. Ayer, "I have decided to retire entirely from the field of American archaeological work and to put my collection for sale...I shall retain a small part of the materials, for my own shelves and reading."[32]

A significant element of his struggles was financial. The financial challenges of the next four years occupied his time. He was close to bankruptcy but was able to remain solvent through a variety of activities. He went through his remaining collection and selected 226 manuscripts, which he sold to Robert Garrett of Baltimore, Maryland. Garrett was an investment banker with a similar passion for collecting. In 1942, the collection was donated to Princeton University, Garrett's alma mater. Gates sold his Virginia farm in 1930 and moved to Baltimore.[33]

Second Maya Society

After a few months in Virginia, Gates turned away from the grandiose plans that occupied him at Tulane and decided to keep most of his collection. He still had much of the Maya part of his collection, which had grown some during his stay at Tulane. He stated to his friend C. T. Currelly, of the Royal Ontario Museum in Toronto, Canada, "Following the break-up of all my dreams for Central America, in the Tulane debacle, I am settling down to just what I can do with my studies—which I should perhaps have done long ago."[34] Gates focused the last ten years of his life on research and publication. His alma mater, Johns Hopkins University, made him a Research Associate. He had no teaching responsibility, though he did direct Ph.D. students. He organized the Second Maya Society at the university and established a publication series through which his research was published. Before Gates's death in 1940, the Society published twenty volumes, mostly his own works. He had help from Alan W. Payne who had been with him at Tulane and some students, one of whom was Elizabeth C. Steward, who received the first doctorate under Gates's tutelage in 1936.[35]

Gates turned his attention to the study of the language of the Maya in his first publication in 1931, *An Outline Dictionary of Maya Glyphs with a Concordance and Analysis of their Relationships*. It was beautifully published with handmade Italian paper and a gilded top. He hoped students would purchase it, but its high price of $35.00 was prohibitive for most. It was, despite its elegant appearance, an unfortunate publication because of serious errors. It was complicated in its presentation, poorly organized, lacked an index and table of contents, and was not actually a dictionary. As a result, it was essentially ignored by the Maya academic community with the exception of a thirty-three page glyph-by-glyph critique by Herman Beyer published in the *American Anthropologist*. Beyer stated, "When I commenced reading this costly publication I realized very soon that its author must have written it about twenty years ago, only adding a few phrases to modernize it...On the whole, the short treatise is faulty in method, full of errors regarding well-known facts, and abounds in mistakes in cross-references." He sarcastically did admit there were a few positive aspects of the book. "All these valuable little contributions to the advance of our science, however, could be comprised in a small paper, without the need of the costly and cumbersome apparatus of the Glyph Dictionary."[36] Though Beyer was a well-known expert on Mayan, the review was probably tainted with some antagonism because he had been at Tulane with Gates.

Gates did not write a response to the review and turned from analytical research on the glyphs to a focus on publishing the documents in his collection. Possibly his most important publication was the printing of the colored facsimile of the Dresden Codex in 1932. This publication was favorably received by the scholarly world. He also published volume one of a proposed *Maya Society Quarterly*, which he hoped would be a place that would make manuscript sources available in published form. The first volume was praised and Gates was pleased with what had been done.[37]

The second volume of the quarterly, however, was never published. Gates was beginning to experience health problems and unable to give attention to all he wanted, so he focused on publishing monographs in the Society series. In 1933, he published a complete photographic copy of the Madrid Maya Codex printed on linen with wooden end boards. He also printed a variety of smaller documents. One unfortunate publication was the 1935 printing of the Gomesta manuscript, which was purported to be a sixteenth-century key to Mayan glyphs but was proved to be a nineteenth-century fraud.[38] He also published with a limited commentary (probably fortunately), an English translation of fray Diego de Landa's sixteenth-century *Relación de las cosas de Yucatán*, entitled *Yucatan Before and After the Conquest*. It was the first English translation of the document but was to be superseded four years later by a translation of the same document by Alfred M. Tozzer, published by the Peabody Museum.[39] Gates then published *A Grammar of Maya* in 1938.[40]

It was fitting for the life story of Gates that his last publication created controversy and resulted in his leaving Johns Hopkins. In 1929, Charles Upson Clark, professor of history at Columbia, made Photostat copies of the Vatican document of an Aztec watercolor botanical picture book and, with the permission of Cardinal Eugène Tisserant, Librarian at the Vatican, deposited the photographs at the Smithsonian Institution with a public announcement of his discovery. A few years later, Gates contacted the Cardinal and received a copy of the photographs and a letter, which he contended gave him permission to publish them with an English translation—which he did in 1939 as *The De la Cruz-Badiano Aztec Herbal of 1552*. Johns Hopkins Press decided to print its own edition of the Aztec photographs edited by Emily Emmert for a third of the price of the Gates edition and Gates was furious. Gates left Johns Hopkins and moved into two study rooms at the Library of Congress where he continued his work on what he hoped would be a complete evaluation of Maya culture. The work was outlined and partially written by the time of his death in 1940.[41]

As Gates aged, his health continued to deteriorate and his research and writing activities decreased. As death approached, he renewed his interest in his earlier beliefs in theosophy. He traveled west in 1935, returning to San Diego for a visit to the Point Loma community. He also renewed his study and interest in Oriental religious thought. His life came to an end at the age of 76 on April 24, 1940 in the Union Memorial Hospital in Baltimore.[42]

Disposal of the Gates Collection

The management of the Maya Society and the disposal of his collection were left to the vice-president of the Society, his sister Edith McComas. She was able to distribute most of the publications of the Society and the organization ceased to exist. Gates's desire was that his collection remain as a unit and be placed in a library. McComas published an extensive catalog of the collection divided by type of materials.[43] Interest in the collection was limited among large research libraries because the valuable part of the collection—the original manuscripts—had been sold to Robert Garrett. Several Maya experts evaluated the collection. One who had particular interest was Dr. W. Wells Jakeman, a Professor of Archeology at Brigham Young University. At the time, Brigham Young University was a small regional teaching university owned by the Church of Jesus Christ of Latter-day Saints. Their library was small with few research collections. The University did, however, have a serious interest in Mesoamerica, based primarily on the Mormon belief that the indigenous populations of the Americas were descendants of religious immigrants who left Jerusalem in 600 B.C. The University had, in fact, sponsored a large scientific expedition from 1900-02 into Mexico, Central America, and Colombia. The president of the University, Benjamin Cluff, headed the expedition. It was a fact-gathering trip and they visited and photographed several of the ruins of Mexico and Central America.[44]

In the mid-1940s, the University began a small but important push to create centers of research. In part because of the presence of Dr. Jakeman, one of those areas was in Archeology/Anthropology. A separate department was established in 1946 under Jakeman and has continued to be an important part of the research component of the University. The connection between the religious belief and the department tainted its early development, but most of the research on Mesoamerica done by students and faculty has been valuable to the field.[45] Jakeman was able to convince his administrators that the Gates collection would be an important beginning step in developing the University's research component, and the administrators put up funding for the collection to come to the library. The overall library archaeological collection has been supported by additional purchases, but the Gates documents continue to be the foundation of the Mesoamerican collection at the University.

William E. Gates and Mesoamerica

Evaluating the contribution of Gates to the study of Mesoamerican research is problematic.[46] His contemporaries were strongly divided into two camps. His friends, including many in Mexico and Guatemala, had great praise for him as a collector and a person. One such friend was T. A. Willard who wrote the following to Gates's sister Edith, "In all my experience in the archaeological field there was no one else that I had regard for as I did for your brother...In fact I do not remember ever having an argument with your brother."[47] Gates was kind to young scholars and helpful in getting them started, particularly in providing them with copies of his documents. Eric Thompson, probably the leading expert on the Maya prior to the recent explosion of information on the topic, described him this way:

> Gates was a man with vision. His ideas on what should be done to set Maya research in a wide context of man and his environment were very sound and showed him years ahead of his fellows. The drawbacks were that men and money to carry them out were not available and Gates was no Aladdin to summon them to his service, although (alas!) he believed he had the knack of rubbing the lamp.[48]

The other group, many of whom had been the recipients of his wrath, characterized him as an arrogant, cranky, and insensitive scholar of average academic talent who had entirely too much energy, money, and time on his hands. Robert L. Brunhouse, Sylvanus Morley's biographer, stated that Morley believed Gates to be "brilliant, erratic, and bizarre, and declared that his unpredictable habits nullified whatever usefulness he might have." Continuing, Brunhouse stated, "Gates had a peculiar temperament that brought him into conflict with everyone with whom he worked. And at times he could be crude." And finally, "When Gates was unable to control other persons, especially persons he suspected of being stronger than himself, he made desperate charges based on half-truths at best and on mere suspicion at worst."[49]

To be sure, Gates was controversial, excitable, arrogant, and combative. Somehow that description fits well into the history of the profession, going back to John Lloyd Stephens, including Blom and Thompson and even extending somewhat to more recent times with Linda Schele. The discipline of Maya studies has historically attracted scholars with complicated personalities who often had serious disagreements that slowed creative research. One thing never lacking, however, was a passion for the subject. In that sense, Gates fits well into the history of the discipline.

To suggest that Gates merely had a passion for Mesoamerica might be considered an understatement. Consider this description by J. Eric S. Thompson of their first meeting. Thompson has just traveled all night and, after arriving in Baltimore, went straight to visit Gates. They talked (Gates talked) the entire day and into the night. "Gates was so full of his plans that he heeded neither contracting stomach or passing time. I, made of less stern stuff, got hungrier and hungrier." In order not to waste time, Gates suggested they not go out to eat but dine on flavorless hot chocolate and stale crackers. "I made a beeline for the nearest drugstore–eating places were closed–when I left late that evening."[50]

Part of the problem with Gates's scholarship was his energy and enthusiasm. Thompson again stated:

> This enthusiasm carried Gates to the heights whence he could see every aspect of the Kingdom of Maya research spread at his feet and–there was the trouble–waiting for him in person alone and unaided to explore. When it came to preparing his material for publication, that zeal was his undoing. It made him act like a town dog out for a country walk. The scents were so many that he never managed to pick out the important ones and follow them without distraction to the kill.[51]

Though Gates did not appreciate being characterized as just a great collector and transcriber of documents, that characterization is without question his legacy. But all academics learn quickly that fame is fleeting. For many, it is not long until perceived brilliant analysis and discovery are soon relegated to barely a paragraph — or even just a footnote — in the dissertation of some young Ph.D. who believes he/she is coming up with the latest innovative approach that will forever change and benefit the discipline. Gates's publications probably made it to the footnote stage sooner than most and now are seldom used. He was not even mentioned in the important history of the evolution of the Mayan language by Michael Coe. But his work as a collector of materials has greatly enriched scholars and the libraries of Princeton, Tulane, and Brigham Young University. His legacy as a collector is aptly stated by John M. Weeks in his introduction to a description of his collection:

> There can be little question of the value and significance of the Gates collection, and of its contribution to Middle American linguistic and historical research. Gates gathered into a central collection practically the entire corpus of extant primary source material for the region, and made much of it available to contemporary and future scholars through exchanges with several individuals and institutions. By collecting these documents Gates

saved much information from eventual loss or destruction. Finally, documents which may have remained little known and unused in private hands in the Americas and Europe were made available to researchers.[52]

What more can be said for those of us who have made it our life's work that same goal?

NOTES

1. Not all of the collection is in these three libraries. The San Diego Public Library received a gift from Gates in 1920 of several Oriental language volumes. The Library of Congress has his Theosophical materials. The Tozzer Library at Harvard includes over fifty thousand photo image copies from the Gates collection. Gates items have been identified in several other libraries. See John M. Weeks, *Mesoamerican Ethnohistory in United States Libraries: Reconstruction of the William E. Gates Collection of Historical and Linguistic Manuscripts* (Culver City, CA,: Labyrinthos, 1990), 10-20, and John M. Weeks, "Historical Notes on the Bowditch-Gates Middle American Indian Manuscript Collection at Tozzer Library, Harvard University," *Behavioral and Social Sciences Librarian* 11 no.1 (1991): 27-47.

2. William E. Gates to Alan Hazelton, July 26, 1938. William E. Gates Papers, MSS 279, LTPSC.

3. The most extensive biography of Gates is Gareth Lowe's, "Biography of William E. Gates" in MSS 279: Biography of William E. Gates: 20th & 21st Century Western & Mormon Americana, L. Tom Perry Special Collections, Harold B. Lee Library, Brigham Young University. See http://sc.lib.byu.edu. The following citations will be indicated as MSS 279, LTPSC. I used his history to guide me to sources within the letters and papers of Gates, which were then personally examined. A second biography is found in Robert L. Brunhouse, *Pursuit of the Ancient Maya: Some Archaeologists of Yesterday* (Albuquerque: University of New Mexico Press, 1975), 129-167. The Point Loma school was small and only became a college in 1914 and an accredited university in 1919. Emmett A. Greenwalt, *The Point Loma Community in California, 1897-1942: A Theosophical Experiment* (New York: AMS Press, 1979).

4. Helena Blavatsky, *The Key to Theosophy* (Pasadena, CA: Theosophical University Press, 1889). For a history of the movement, see Bruce F. Campbell, *Ancient Wisdom Revived: A History of the Theosophical Movement* (Berkeley: University of California Press, 1980).

5. William E. Gates, *The Spirit of the Hour in Archaeology* (Point Loma, CA: The Aryan Theosophical Press, 1915), 13-14.

6. For a history of the early study of Maya writing see, J. Eric S. Thompson, *Maya Hieroglyphic Writing: An Introduction* (Washington, DC: Carnegie Institution of Washington, 1950). See also Michael Coe, *Breaking the Maya Code* (New York: Thames and Hudson, 1992).

7. For a bibliography of his publications see, John M. Weeks, comp., *Mesoamerican Ethnohistory in United States Libraries* (Culver City, CA: Labyrinthos, 1990), 23-27.

8. William E. Gates, *The Maya Society and its Work* (Baltimore: Maya Society, 1937), 11.

9. Gareth Lowe, "Biography of William E. Gates," 17. William E. Gates Papers, MSS 279, LTPSC.

10. William E. Gates to Mortimer Graves, June 23, 1933. William E. Gates Papers, MSS 279, LTPSC. This letter was a long detailed response to a questionnaire from the American Council of Learned Societies.

11. William E. Gates, *The Maya Society and its Work*, 10-11.

12. William E. Gates, *The Maya Society and its Work*, 15. "William Gates Dies at Age of 76," *Baltimore Sun*, 25 April, 1940, sec. A, p. 5.

13. His antagonism towards Mexican officials can be seen in a talk given much later on November 5, 1934 at Johns Hopkins University. William Gates, *Rural Education in Mexico and the Indian Problem* (Mexico: [s.n.], 1935).

14. His only publication during this ten-year period was a short ten-page article in the appendix of a book by Sylvanus Morley, "The Distribution of the Several Branches of the Mayance Linguistic Stock," in Sylvanus Morley, *The Inscriptions at Copán* (Washington D.C.: The Carnegie Institution of Washington, 1920), 605-17.

15. Robert L. Brunhouse, *Sylvanus G. Morley and the World of the Ancient Mayas* (Norman: University of Oklahoma Press, 1971), 153.

16. Letter to George B. Gordon, March 5, 1921. William E. Gates Papers, MSS 279, LTPSC

17. "Museum Enriched by Gift of Works on Chinese Art," *San Diego Union*, August 14, 1921. Gates had stopped in San Diego on his way home from Guatemala where he gave a gift of Chinese linguistic books and documents to the San Diego Public Library.

18. For a discussion of Guatemalan laws related to the preservation of cultural patrimony, see Alfonso René Ortíz Sobalvarro, *La defensa jurídica del patrimonio cultural* (Guatemala: Procurador de los Derechos Humanos, 1994).

19. William B. Gates to George B. MacCurdy, January 27, 1923, William E. Gates Papers, MSS 279, LTPSC. The Carnegie Foundation was also concerned that items not be taken from the country and would fine researchers found involved in this practice. For the Guatemalan view, see J. Haroldo Rodas Estrada, *El Despojo cultural: la otra máscara de la conquista* (Nueva Guatemala de la Asunción (Guatemala): Caudal, 1998), 116.

20. George B. Gordon to William Gates, February 5, 1923. William E. Gates Papers, MSS 279, LTPSC.

21. For a history of this conflict taken from Gates' correspondence, see Gareth Lowe, "Biography of William E. Gates," 32-43. William E. Gates Papers, MSS 279, LTPSC. For a version from the Morley side see, Brunhouse, *Sylvanus G. Morley and the World of the Ancient Mayas*, 188-201.

22. The farm had at one time been part of Thomas Jefferson's Monticello. In 1922, he brought from Guatemala a Quiché native to help in his study of the language, who stayed only a short time and returned to Guatemala "homesick." See, William E. Gates to T. A. Willard, January 9, 1923.

23. *The William Gates Collection: Manuscripts, Documents, Printed Literature Relating to Mexico and Central America* (New York: American Art Association, 1924).

24. Robert L. Brunhouse, *Pursuit of the Ancient Maya*, 141-3. Philip Brooks, "Notes on Rare Books," *New York Times*, 18 Feb., 1934, BR23.

25. The value of the collection is questionable. The auctioneers felt they could bring in over $100,000 by selling the items separately; however, J. Eric S. Thompson, at the time a young Mesoamerican scholar, evaluated the collection and felt it was probably only worth $20,000. Thompson seriously questioned Tulane's purchase. "There was, of course, no one at Tulane with any idea of its coverage or of its worth. It would seem that Gates had gotten about three times the value of his collection and a job for life; Tulane had gotten a library lacking most of the standard works on the Maya and other peoples of Middle America and a director who would direct operations from his home in Virginia, for it had been agreed that Gates should spend as much or as little time in New Orleans as he wished. He spent little time in the department." J. Eric S. Thompson, "After the Smoke of Battle," 77, William E. Gates Papers, MSS 279, LTPSC. Robert L. Brunhouse, *Pursuit of the Ancient Maya*, 142.

26. William E. Gates, *A Gage of Honor: The Development and Disruption of the Department of Middle American Research of Tulane University at New Orleans* (Baltimore: Maya Society of Johns Hopkins, 1926), 3-4. This pamphlet is primarily a printing of the correspondence between Gates and Tulane. For information on Zemurray see, Lester D. Langley and Thomas

Schoonover, *The Banana Men: American Mercenaries and Entrepreneurs in Central America, 1880-1930* (Lexington, KY: University Press of Kentucky, 1995).

27. See Robert L. Brunhouse, *Frans Blom, Maya Explorer* (Albuquerque: University of New Mexico Press, 1976).

28. A description of the trip is found in Frans Blom and Oliver La Farge, *Tribes and Temples: A Record of the Expedition to Middle America Conducted by the Tulane University of Louisiana in 1925*, two vols. (New Orleans, LA: Tulane University of Louisiana, 1926-27).

29. Robert L. Brunhouse, *Pursuit of the Ancient Maya*, 145. Gareth Lowe, "Biography of William E. Gates," 17. William E. Gates Papers, MSS 279, LTPSC. He was approached by a representative of the Guatemalan government to establish a similar center in Guatemala.

30. Robert L. Brunhouse, *Pursuit of the Ancient Maya*, 148-51.

31. William E. Gates, *A Gage of Honor*, 6. For a description of the collection see http://lal.tulane.edu/gates2coll.html.

32. William E. Gates to Edward E. Ayer, January 10, 1927. William E. Gates Papers, MSS 279, LTPSC.

33. For a biography of Garrett see, *Robert Garrett & Sons, Incorporated: 1840-1965* (Baltimore, Press of Schneidereith and Sons, 1965). For a history of the collection see, Teresa T. Basler and David C. Wright, "The Making of a Collection: Mesoamerican Manuscripts at Princeton University," *Libraries and the Cultural Record* 43 no.1 (2008): 29-55. See the Gates' collection site at Princeton, http://libweb5.princeton.edu.

34. William E. Gates to C. T. Currelly, October 10, 1927. William E. Gates Papers, MSS 279, LTPSC.

35. For a small history of the Society, see William E. Gates, *The Maya Society and its Work*.

36. Herman Beyer, "A Discussion of the Gates Classification of Maya Hieroglyphs," *American Anthropologist*, New Series, 35 (Oct./Dec., 1933): 659, 694. See a discussion of Beyer in Michael Coe, *Breaking the Mayan Code*, 143-4.

37. William Gates and Agostino Aglio, *The Dresden Maya Codex: Reproduced from Tracings of the Original, Colorings finished by Hand* (Baltimore: Maya Society at the Johns Hopkins University, 1932).

38. William Gates, *The Gomesta Manuscripts, of Hieroglyphs and Customs: in facsimile* (Baltimore: The Maya Society, 1935). Franz Blom, "The Gomesta Manuscript: A Falsification," *Maya Research* 2 (1935), 234-47.

39. Diego de Landa, *Yucatan Before and After the Conquest* (Baltimore: The Maya Society, 1937). Diego de Landa, *Landa's Relación de las cosas de Yucatán: A Translation*, edited by Alfred M. Tozzer. Papers of the Peabody Museum of American Archaeology and Ethnology, Harvard University, Vol. 18 (Cambridge: The Museum, 1941).

40. William Gates, *A Grammar of Maya; Being a Complete Grammar of the Sixteenth Century Language, with an Introduction* (Baltimore: Maya Society, 1938). Like much of his writing, it was ignored by the profession, though it did sell enough to go through two editions.

41. He donated his religious literature on theosophy to the Library of Congress in 1939.

42. "William Gates Dies at Age of 76," *Baltimore Sun*, 25 April, 1940, sec. A, p.5.

43. *The William Gates Collection* (S. I.: s.n., n.d.).

44. For a history of the expedition, see Ernest L. Wilkinson, ed., *Brigham Young University: The First One Hundred Years*, vol. 1 (Provo, UT: Brigham Young University Press, 1975) 289-329.

45. Most of the research is published in the series, Publications, New World Archaeological Foundation. See Thomas A. Lee, *New World Archaeological Foundation obra, 1952-1980* (Provo, UT: New World Archaeological Foundation, 1981).

46. For a list of contributions, see Gareth Lowe, "Biography of William E. Gates," 51-3. William E. Gates Papers, MSS 279, LTPSC.

47. T. A. Willard to Edith McComas, October 1, 1941. William E. Gates Papers, MSS 279, LTPSC.

48. J. Eric Thompson, "After the Smoke of Battle," 81, William E. Gates Papers, MSS 279, LTPSC.

49. Robert L. Brunhouse, *Sylvanus G. Morley and the World of the Ancient Mayas* (Norman: University of Oklahoma Press, 1971), 188, 197-8, 153.

50. J. Eric Thompson, "After the Smoke of Battle," 74-5, William E. Gates Papers, MSS 279, LTPSC.

51. Ibid, 84.

52. John M. Weeks, compiler, *Mesoamerican Ethnohistory in United States Libraries*, 17. This publication is an important descriptive catalog of the entire collection and holding libraries.

11. Resources for the Study of Indian Languages in the Chicago Area
Gabrielle M. Toth

It would seem that this year's theme of indigenous peoples presents little possibility of a Midwestern, let alone Chicago, angle. When people think of the Midwest, the only Indians that come to mind may be those who run casinos or are namesakes of sports teams. In fact, the Chicago region has a substantial native history, including a native population today and, as our keynote speaker Alfred W. Crosby of the University of Texas reminded us, the remains of what many consider the most advanced native civilization north of the Rio Grande are in Illinois.

Now, I'd like to introduce you to two sources of material on one aspect of indigenous Latin American cultures that have found a home in Chicago: indigenous languages at the Newberry Library and the University of Chicago. The Newberry Library is a private, independent humanities research and reference institution in Chicago. While the Newberry is scholarly and prominent, it welcomes researchers aged sixteen and older into its reading rooms and offers a whole spectrum of exhibits, lectures, readings, symposia, classes, even music, some of which are free and are open to the entire community.[1] It is also home to more than 1.5 million books, 5 million manuscript pages, and 500,000 historic maps.

Among the four research centers at the Newberry is the D'Arcy McNickle Center for American Indian History. One of the collections held or housed by that particular center is the Edward E. Ayer Collection. This collection is considered one of the best of general Americana in the world and has been called by a former Yale University Library Curator "perhaps the finest gathering of materials on American Indians in the world."[2] In 1911, Edward F. Ayer (1841-1927) donated his collection of over 17,000 pieces documenting early contacts between Indians and Europeans to the Newberry Library. In fact, Ayer was the first donor of a major collection to the institution. He was also a member of its first Board of Trustees. In addition to this donation of items, the Ayer endowment fund has allowed the Newberry to collect over 130,000 volumes, over one million manuscript pages, 2,000 maps, 500 atlases, 11,000 photographs and 3,500 drawings and paintings on the Indians of the Americas.[3] These acquisitions are listed in both the Newberry's catalog and WorldCat.

One of the main subject areas of the collection is Native American archaeology, ethnology, art, and language. In these areas, many of the holdings focus on North American Indians. The language portion, however, offers some real gems of Latin American native languages. Among the most notable items in the collection are four Sahagún manuscripts including his Aztec-Spanish-Latin dictionary. How did this come to the Newberry? In 1903, Ayer acquired James Pilling's collection of North American Indian linguistics, which at the time was one of the largest Indian linguistics collections in the world.[4] Texts, grammars and dictionaries are all represented in the collection, as is at least one example of almost every North American native language.[5] Most of the books were tools of the missionaries.[6] Philippine and Hawaiian materials are also part of the collection. The Ayer collection holds over 50,000 volumes that relate to Latin America.[7] Holdings of Latin American materials are especially strong in Mayan and Mexican archaeological materials and linguistics. The collection includes printed and manuscript materials, manuscript reproductions and transcripts, and codices. Topically or thematically, the discovery, exploration, colonization, and early political and social development of Mexico and South American are high notes, with an especially strong collection of materials on 16th- to 18th-century colonial and Jesuit histories of Mexico, Peru, Brazil, Chile, Colombia, and Venezuela.

Edward Everett Ayer was born in what was then the wilderness of Wisconsin. One writer said Ayer had "only the advantages which normally come to frontier families of good standing, and his cultural opportunities and experiences were extremely limited, especially in regard to such artificialities as books." His academic training ended when he was twelve, when his family moved to Harvard, Illinois, and he went to work for his father. "At eighteen the narrowness of his immediate horizon became irksome and he sought adventure by means of the accustomed method of that time and region."[8]

Ayer followed the call to "Go West, Young Man." He hopped a covered wagon toward California, part of a wagon train often joined by Buffalo Bill, and the two became lifelong friends. Author Ruth Lapham Butler goes to great lengths to indicate that Ayer was not a gold rush speculator, though he did stop near Virginia City to earn money for the rest of his trip. When the Civil War broke out, he enlisted in the Union Army and was transferred southward, to Southern Arizona and the Mexican border. Here the story really begins. Ayer was put in command of men whose job was to protect the Cerro Colorado mine from various and sundry brigands, and the mine owner sent out a few books for the benefit of his workmen. Ayer had time on his hands, encountered Prescott's *The Conquest of Mexico*, and dug in. It was the first book he had ever read and "He had never experienced such pleasure. At home there had been only the Bible and the works of Josephus, and, as a matter of fact, there were few books accessible in the Illinois and Wisconsin of the frontier and fifties."[9]

In fact, he read it twice. In 1864, he resigned from the army, went home to partner with his father, purchased a small lumber interest, and, as soon as he could, bought his own set of Prescott's works on an installment plan.[10] Soon enough, Ayer's lumber business took off—he was making railroad ties in the 1860s!—and he spent half of his time traveling by train, which provided him with plenty of time to read. And plenty of time to buy, for by 1880 or so he had begun his collecting. His aim? To find out as much as he could about the natives of America and to gain that knowledge in as scientific a manner as possible. So he started collecting Indian paraphernalia from among the traders he met in his travels. These items now make up the Ayer Collection of the Field Museum in Chicago.

In the 1880s, Ayer was spending $40,000 to $50,000 per year on books, in London especially. Around 1900, Ayer decided to have a printed catalogue of his library, including critical notes crafted by specialists. He sent out works from his library, a few at a time, for just that purpose. He kept buying books, so the collection kept growing. In the end, Ruth Lapham Butler wrote, "Mr. Ayer's scheme proved idealistic, impractical, and expensive: the scholars were slow and Mr. Ayer grew impatient. In 1902 he gave it up entirely after expending $10,000, saying, 'If the scholars can get along without this work the lumber merchants will certainly try to.' "[11]

Until 1927, Ayer visited the Newberry daily when in Chicago and "He took the greatest satisfaction in having given students advantages which he himself had never had...[S]ometimes he gloated over an excessively fine bargain." But at the same time, Butler wrote, Ayer was modest about the great gifts he gave to the Newberry, the Field Museum, and the Art Institute of Chicago, speaking of his good fortune in having worked with those who allowed him to do as he wished.[12]

The *Popol Vuh* at the Newberry Library is currently, as of 2008, unavailable due to a major conservation and digitization project to make it more accessible to the public. The *Popol Vuh* is the Book of the Council or Book of the Community or Book of the People or Sacred Book. It is the creation account of the Quiché Maya people, held in deep reverence by them.

The Newberry's manuscript may be the oldest surviving copy. It is believed that Quiché nobility wrote the original manuscript of the *Popol Vuh* in the 16th century, using Latin orthography to render Quiché in a written form. That manuscript is not what the Newberry owns—it is lost. The Newberry's copy is believed to have been made from this original in 1701-03 by Dominican Father Francisco Ximenez. It was done in Chichicastenango, Guatemala, and is the Quiché text side-by-side with the Spanish translation. This manuscript also contains a Cakchikel-Quiché-Tzutuhil grammar, Christian materials, and some doctrinal "frequently asked questions" penned by Ximenez.

The Newberry notes that digital copies exist thanks to the work of Ohio State University-online and a DVD-Rom edition produced by Brigham Young

University's Neal A. Maxwell Institute for Religious Texts. In fall 2006, the Newberry mounted an exhibit, "The Aztecs and the Making of Colonial Mexico," which is available online at Newberry.org/aztecsexhibit.

The University of Chicago also has, in the words of Josh Beck, Associate Director of the school's Center for Latin American Studies, "a few different things that…would be directly relevant to scholars interested in studying indigenous populations in Latin America."[13] Most of these materials are linguistically oriented and are, with one exception, unique. The non-unique piece is the Chicago Archive of Indigenous Literatures of Latin America,[14] which will be described shortly.

The unique materials are linguistic surveys performed by University of Chicago linguists going back to the 1920s. They are unique not only because they go back to an earlier time period than typical, but also because they are linked to a set of audio recordings in the university's language archives. From the 1920s through the 1950s or so, but mostly in the '20s and '30s, the University of Chicago had a set of scholars—one scholar in the '20s and '30s, joined later by others—who would haul state-of-the-art recording devices deep into the jungles of Southern Mexico and Guatemala and record people speaking indigenous languages, then transcribe and translate those materials.

One key figure in all of this was Norman McQuown, Professor of Anthropology and Linguistics, who joined the university in 1946. Over the course of his 54-year career at the university, McQuown became an expert in the study of indigenous languages of Mexico and Central America. In the late 1940s, McQuown founded and organized the Collection of Manuscripts in Cultural Anthropology. This project actually accepted materials through the 1990s, and was primarily affiliated with University of Chicago scholars who saw value in archiving their field notes and transcriptions of their interviews. These field notes and transcriptions date back to the 1920s. All of this was microfilmed at the University of Chicago's library, with originals being returned to the scholars. The collection preserved materials that might otherwise have been lost, and provided a means of disseminating them. A guide to the collection is available online,[15] which, according to Beck, is just about the only way to access the collection. The university is now working on raising funds to digitize that microfilm and to develop a more robust guide.

What is currently in the guide, Beck noted, does not even constitute basic metadata, which is a problem. But basic, or typical, metadata standards would not really be sufficient to access these materials in the most scholarly productive way. They are now working on a system to catalog these individually rather than as a collection, and to develop a much more robust description of each item.

This collection holds, in microfilm, the equivalent of 200,000 pages of mostly typed material, primarily field notes and transcriptions. There are some photocopied materials, as well. But it gets better. These materials are directly linked to some 1,000 hours of audio recordings of indigenous voices taken from the 1920s through 1965. The University of Chicago has recently digitized these items as the 1950s-'60s materials were on deteriorating media.

Not long after McQuown set up the Collection of Manuscripts on Cultural Anthropology, he sought out laboratory space to provide for phonological analysis of the audio component of these materials and to make these important audio resources accessible to others. In 1954, he and Eric Hamp founded the Language Laboratories and Archives.[16] These 1,000 hours of audio recordings run from the 1920s through 1990s, and are almost exclusively Mesoamerican, with some Brazilian and other materials included, as well. Why Mesoamerica? Because a group of researchers, mostly anthropologists, were all there together, and were interested in various aspects of Mesoamerican indigenous people—anthropologists/sociologists like Robert Redfield, Sol Tax and linguists like Manuel Andrade. Redfield and Tax were engaged in questions of modernity and early pre-modern people engaging with the modern world. Andrade's work in linguistics and collection in the field helped the linguistics program become a leader in dialect study and the creation of orthographies, and helped form the foundation of phonological, morphological, and syntactic theory.

The other language represented in the collection is Aymara, which has been taught at the University of Chicago since the early 1990s. One professor, Allen Kolata, an anthropologist focused on archaeological work and reconstructing ancient agricultural practices for sustainability purposes, generated masses of graduate students. To serve them, the university developed an Aymara program. Materials in the collection include audio and video of native Aymara speakers onsite in Bolivia talking away, all for language pedagogy purposes. Aymara is one of four native languages regularly taught at the University of Chicago. The other three are K'iche' Maya, Yucatec Maya, and Nahuatl, which have all been taught since the 1960s. McQuown began teaching Mesoamerican indigenous language acquisition courses in the mid-1950s, and continued to offer them throughout his career. In the early 1960s, he obtained grant funding from an office of the U.S. Department of Health, Education and Welfare to develop the textbooks *Spoken Yucatec Maya* and *Spoken Quiché Maya*. In 2001-02, John Lucy (Human Development) taught the modern spoken Yucatec Maya year-long course sequence. Beginning in 2003-04, with support from a National Resource Center grant from the U.S. Department of Education, the Center for Latin American Studies reinstated a regular teaching schedule of year-long sequences in Modern Spoken Yucatec Maya, Modern Spoken K'iche' Maya and Modern Spoken Nahuatl under the direction of John Lucy.[17]

Thus, the audio archive had both a scholarly and a pedagogic purpose. Since the audio recordings have been digitized, the long-term solution to access is to donate these materials to the University of Chicago's Regenstein Library, making them available in their online catalog and via WorldCat. However, the Center for Latin American Studies will handle the detailing of the items. This goes back to the problem, as perceived by the Center for Latin American

Studies, with the typical metadata used. The typical metadata the library would apply is not sufficient for what scholars and speakers want and need to engage with these materials. So the plan is to create a front-end user database that offers more robust information, via a website, but which points to the library's catalog. The library retains the items and management of the digital repository; the Center for Latin American Studies just adds some value.

As for the types of metadata needed, Beck noted items like genre, format (as in single author or collection), and more specific details about language families. These examples he offered from the Chicago Archive of Indigenous Literatures of Latin America. With these books, they scan the cover, title page, and back page of every text so that users can see those before checking the link to see the full pdf. They have included individual chapter titles, with genre and language family information at the chapter title level. This archive is five or six years old, and is in the process of being built. It is in response largely to the fictional literature, primarily but not exclusively, that cropped up in the late 1970s and early 1980s as part of indigenous language revitalization movements.

Much of this literature was coming out of writing collectives, small co-ops and, occasionally, small publishing houses. Perhaps 500 copies of a collection of poetry would be published. These materials, Beck said, are not being archived elsewhere. The University of Chicago has about 450 items at the library, and they are using grant money to digitize the collection so that it is accessible to scholars and to the speaking communities as well. Thus far, efforts to reach out to Chicago-based speakers of these languages have not gone well, even though one would expect to find Nahuatl and Mayan speakers in Chicago. Beck said that colleague universities in Southern California are having success with this.

Another colleague institution whose work has been inspiring or helpful to that of the University of Chicago has been the University of Texas and their archive of the indigenous languages of Latin America.[18] They, too, digitize materials and then donate them to the Perry Castaneda Library, which manages the digitized objects. The website offers links, and if one agrees to the user conditions, they E-mail out a password for access.

According to Beck, the model is particularly appealing because the University of Texas has put a lot of care into describing how and why they have done what they have. So, for example, for the user, there is no mystery about why a certain type of metadata was applied. The University of Texas has been, in Beck's words, generous with advice and offers a wonderful model to follow.

NOTES

1.   Newberry brochure "Welcome to the Newberry Library". Chicago: Newberry Library.

2.   http://www.newberry.org/collections/ayer.html accessed 14 May 2008, "American Indian History at the Newberry Library."

3.   Newberry website, www.newberry.org/collections/ayer.html Accessed 14 May 2008.

4. http://www.newberry.org/collections/ayer1.html Accessed 14 May 2008.

5. http://www.newberry.org/collections/ayer1.html accessed 14 May 2008

6. http://www.newberry.org/collections.histling.html Accessed 14 May 2008.

7. http://www.newberry.org/collections/latinam.html Accessed 14 May 2008.

8. Butler, Ruth Lapham, "Edward E. Ayer's Quest for Hispano-Americana." *Inter-American Bibliographic Review* 1 (1941): 81-90.

9. Butler, p.82.

10. http://www.newberry.org/collections/Ayer_How_I.html Accessed 14 May 2008

11. Butler, p.88.

12. Butler, p.90.

13. Telephone interview of Josh Beck, 29 May 2008.

14. http://cailla.uchicago.edu/ Accessed 14 May 2008.

15. http://moca.lib.uchicago.edu Accessed 14 May 2008.

16. https://coral.uchicago.edu:8443/display/LA/Archives Accessed 14 May 2008.

17. http://clas.uchicago.edu/language_teaching/ Accessed 14 May 2008.

18. http://www.ailla.utexas.org/site/la_lands.html Accessed 14 May 2008.

Indigenous Languages, Books, and Writing

12. *In amoxtli, in amoxcalli*: el libro y la biblioteca prehispánica y su influencia en las bibliotecas coloniales en México

Saúl Armendáriz Sánchez

A manera de introducción

Los apasionados de la historia del libro y las bibliotecas vemos a los códices mexicanos como una verdadera fantasía que nos hace volar al pasado y proyectan un momento de la historia de Mesoamérica en donde el esplendor cultural alcanza niveles inimaginables.

Los códices (*amoxtli*) y las bibliotecas (*amoxcalli*) prehispánicas son en nuestros días materia de estudio constante donde no sólo los especialistas en antropología, arte e historia participan en su estudio, sino que su capacidad es tan amplia que permite que otros profesionistas como los bibliotecarios podamos involucrarnos con ellos y sobre todo contemplarlos como verdaderas fuentes de información que obligaron a los conquistadores a que las tomaran en cuenta para influir política, económica, religiosa y socialmente en un pueblo que buscó en todo momento conservar su cultura y tradiciones y que después de más de 500 años sigue con muchas de ellas.

La desaparición total de los *amoxcalli* y la destrucción indiscriminada de los *amoxtli*, lograron uno de los objetivos primordiales de los españoles, que era la implantación de su religión cultura y legislación, sin darse cuenta que la información contenida en estos locales y obras representaban no sólo la historia y religión de los pueblos vencidos, sino una forma bien estructurada de gobernar, manejarse económicamente y administrar el poder para el beneficio común.

Las bibliotecas prehispánicas y sus "escribanos-pintores" formaban parte importante de los recintos civiles y religiosos, los cuales almacenaban y creaban respectivamente las obras que detallaban los acontecimientos del momento, de acuerdo con las necesidades del gobernante en turno. Esto llevó a construir importantes bibliotecas en donde el almacenamiento de la información debía estar estrictamente organizado para su difusión y consulta, pero sobre todo protegido por conservar en gran medida la memoria de las naciones existentes en ese momento.

Con la llegada de los españoles y su proyección conquistadora, la tradición del *tlacuilo* (escribano-pintor) comenzó a desaparecer, sobre todo por la persecución que este recibió por ser considerado agente de influencia nociva para los grupos indígenas del momento, ya que podía leer, transmitir y conservar la cultura, pero sobre todo, asentar las ideas sublevistas que podría atentar contra la corona española, por ello su desaparición fue casi inmediata.

Bajo este régimen de gobierno, pero sobre todo religioso, los españoles comenzaron a fundar conventos y monasterios con miras a la evangelización de indígenas de la Nueva España y terminar así con sus "malos dioses" que provocaban un salvajismo comunal. Esto llevó como consecuencia a la creación de bibliotecas y al desarrollo de colecciones documentales que permitieran un desarrollo del clero, pero sobre todo que facilitaran el proceso evangélico de la nación conquistada, lo cual implicaba conocer la cultura, costumbres y religión indígena para realizar el proceso lo "menos doloroso posible".

Las bibliotecas conventuales y sus colecciones, sobre todo en los siglos XVI y XVII, estuvieron conformadas según la proyección europea, pero sin duda se sintieron influenciadas por la organización del conocimiento del México antiguo, en particular por los *amoxtli*, los *amoxcalli* y los *tlacuilos*, los cuales fueron desapareciendo de forma gradual pero que dejaron su huella en las bibliotecas de la época.

El objetivo del trabajo es presentar esta influencia y ahondar en aquellos puntos en donde los códices y sus creadores influenciaron la vida de las bibliotecas y de las colecciones de los religiosos que existían en ese momento.

Amoxtli, tlacuilo y amoxcalli

Para poder entender la influencia de los nativos de la Nueva España en los conquistadores de la corona española en el aspecto de las bibliotecas y las colecciones en los siglos XVI y XVII, es importante antes conocer la organización que tenían éstos, desde el personal que laboraba para el desarrollo de los códices, hasta su organización de contenido, conociendo de esta manera su influencia discreta pero directa con base a las necesidades de los españoles.

De manera general y sin hacer un estudio profundo, en el caso de los códices, estos pueden ser definidos como "los documentos pictóricos o de imágenes realizados como productos culturales de las grandes civilizaciones maya, azteca, mixteca, zapoteca, otomí, purepecha, etc., que surgieron y desarrollaron en Mesoamérica."[1] Por otra parte los códices son también definidos como "los manuscritos pintados o escritos dentro de la tradición indígena de manufactura."[2]

En su contenido se plasmaron los conocimientos de los sabios de la época en que se desarrollaron, mostrando sus logros y avances culturales y científicos; su desarrollo económico y administración tributaria; sus ceremonias, ritos y creencias religiosas; parte de su historia, geografía y genealogía; sus calendarios y eventos cronológicos, etc.

Se desconoce a ciencia cierta a partir de que fecha se comenzaron a elaborar en Mesoamérica, pero se tiene vestigios de códices mayas que fueron encontrados en tumbas de Guatemala y Belice que datan de los siglos 300 al 600 d.C. (periodo Clásico Temprano).[3] Lo que si se sabe es que estos se siguieron produciendo hasta el siglo XVIII, más de 200 años después de la conquista de Tenochtitlán, y se conocían para esta época como "testimonios pictóricos" o "joyas pictográficas", por representar imágenes y desconocer su contenido y su forma de lectura, debido en su gran mayoría a la desaparición total de los *tlacuilos* que pudieran dar sentido a la información inmersa en ellas. Así mismo, otro vestigio de la existencia de los códices es el que señala Jorge Angulo y que se encontró en un enterramiento maya en el Mirado en el estado de Chiapas y que data del año 250-500 d.C.[4]

Los formatos físicos o de presentación de los códices, al igual que los libros actuales, son muy variados y nos indican que existían *amoxtli* en forma de tira, la cual sí estaba escrita en forma vertical se le llamaba banda o si la posición es en forma horizontal se le denominaba tira y estas podían ser dobladas en forma de rollo o en forma de biombo. Así mismo se producían códices en forma de lienzos, de hojas sueltas o de paneles. Es importante hacer notar que muchas veces el formato se relacionaba directamente con su contenido, es decir los lienzos para la información cartográfica o genealógica, los biombos o tiras para las cuestiones religiosas o migratorias, así como para la historia de los pueblos, las hojas sueltas para los registros civiles o de tenencia, etc.

Por otra parte los materiales en que fueron elaboradas estas importantes fuentes de información son variados resaltando el papel indígena denominado amate el cual tenía una gran importancia ceremonial, social, económico y cultural dentro de los pueblos indígenas de Mesoamérica, demostrado esto en algunos códices, en donde este juega un elemento importante en los tributos que hacen los pueblos a la ciudad de Tenochtitlán. Existen además códices en cuero o pieles sobre todo de venado, textiles de algodón, palma o pita tejidas en telares de cintura y papel de maguey, empleando diversos utensilios para el grabado de la información en los mismos como "pinceles y plumones" hechos de madera, obsidiana, hueso, carrizo y piedra, algunos con pelo de venado u otro animal. Los colores empleados para plasmar la escritura eran tan variados que iban desde el blanco, pasando por el azul, escarlata, negro, añil, rojo o colorado, verde en distintas tonalidades, amarillo y ocre, pero en la época colonial el número de colores aumentó gracias a las pinturas para óleos y las tintas ferrosas.

Se desconoce si al momento de su confección llevaban un título, ni sabemos si contaban con una portada propia de identificación como las que actualmente se imprimen o las firmas de los autores. Por ello en la actualidad se les ha nombrado como códice o *amoxtli*, pero en nuestros días se les asocia con el lugar geográfico de origen o por el tema que tratan en su contenido, su formato o el material en que están elaborados, sus descubridores, los autores conocidos de los mismos, la biblioteca donde se encuentran actualmente, etc. Como ejemplo tenemos la Tira de la Peregrinación, el Rollo Selden, Plano de papel maguey, Lienzo de Tlaxcala, Códice Dresden, etc. Bajo estos elementos podemos dividir aún más a estos importantes documentos en prehispánicos y coloniales, siendo los de época temprana de la conquista confundidos por la hechura del momento y la influencia aún indígena de los *tlacuilos* que no habían desaparecido.

Los códices han sido tema de estudio a nivel mundial, arrojando infinidad de datos que han permitido reconstruir algunas partes de la historia de Mesoamérica, pero más aún, conocer la cultura y ciencia de un grupo importante de pobladores de América.

Los tlacuilos

Los *amoxtli* eran elaborados por expertos *"pintores-escribanos"* de amplios conocimientos en la plástica, las tradiciones orales, la cultura y la lengua indígena del pueblo al que pertenecía el documento. Estos personajes llamados *tlacuilos* (del verbo náhuatl *tlacuiloa* que significa escribir pintando) formaban parte de distintas clases sociales y podían ser tanto hombres como mujeres a quienes se les capacitaba de forma general en todas las ramas del conocimiento humano existente en ese momento. Posteriormente se les especializaba en algún tema en particular hasta lograr un conocimiento profundo basado en sus características y cualidades.

Una vez obteniendo el grado de *tlacuilo* y de recibir toda su preparación, pasaban a formar parte de una clase social mayor, por el hecho de que debían ocuparse a tiempo completo a esta actividad.

Las obras que realizaban (*amoxtli*) pasaban a fortalecer los acervos de los *amoxcalli* (bibliotecas), pero de manera anónima, debido a que su trabajo pertenecía a la comunidad a la cual servían. De igual forma y terminada su total preparación, eran enviados a centros especializados donde requerían sus servicios, es decir templos, mercados, palacios, tribunales, casas de tributos, escuelas, etc.

La experiencia para dar forma a los códices se la daba el tiempo y la destreza artística y cultural que cada uno poseía. Por ello los *amoxtli* rituales y calendáricos eran responsabilidad de los *tlacuilos* con mayor especialización, ya que sus conocimientos tendían a ser mayores lo que les permitía representar con exactitud los atavíos específicos que los dioses portaban.

Los primeros contactos que tienen los europeos con las *tlacuilos* es motivo de gran asombro por la forma de efectuar sus pinturas como lo señala Bernal Díaz del Castillo: "Traía consigo grandes pintores que los hay tales en México, y mandó pintar al natural rostros y cuerpos y facciones de Cortés y de todos los capitanes, soldados y navíos y velas y caballos y a Doña Marina y Aguilar y hasta los lebreles y tiros y pelotas y todo el ejercito que traíamos y los envió a su señor."[5]

Dos siglos después, los *tlacuilos* todavía son tema de estudio en las crónicas de los frailes pero bajo el nombre de "informantes". Esto lo demuestra Fray Francisco de Burgoa que señala en su obra cuando habla de los zapotecos y mixtecos: "entre las barbaridades de estas naciones se hallaron muchos libros a su modo, en hojas o telas de especiales cortezas de árboles que se hallaron en tierras calientes, y las curtían y aderezaban a modo de pergaminos, de una tercia poco más o menos de ancho, y una tras otra las zurcían y pegaban en una pieza tan larga como la habían menester, donde todas sus historias escribían... y para eso a los hijos de los señores y a los que escogían para su sacerdocio, enseñaban e instruían desde su niñez, y haciéndoles decorar aquellos caracteres y tomar de memoria las historias".[6]

Los amoxcalli

Los *amoxcalli* o bibliotecas prehispánicas, eran recintos construidos por los gobernantes de los distintos grupos étnicos que habitaban la región, con la finalidad de que en ellos se elaboraran y preservaran los códices que poseían el saber de la comunidad a la cual estaban dirigidos (sacerdotes, militares, gobernantes, civiles, comerciantes, etc.).

Su ubicación física se presenta principalmente en las grandes ciudades, en lugares conquistados por los grupos guerreros de gran arraigo o en regiones de amplio comercio. Dentro del poblado estas bibliotecas se establecían en mercados, templos, tribunales, palacios, área de recolección tributaria, etc.

Los encargados de custodiar las bibliotecas prehispánicas eran los ancianos, sacerdotes o maestros conocedores de la cultura y educadores de los *tlacuilos*. Los *amoxcalli* realizaban funciones semejantes a las bibliotecas de nuestros días, en ellos se agrupaban documentos de distintas temáticas que se encontraban a la disposición de aquellos individuos que tenían la capacidad de leer su contenido. Estos personajes, lectores de códices, por lo regular pertenecían a un extracto social alto, puesto que la cultura, al igual que en otras partes del mundo y en diversas épocas, no estaba dirigida a las masas, sino a grupos elitistas.

Los *amoxcalli* existían en un número importante de poblados y ciudades de gran trascendencia cultural. Gracias a las crónicas, se sabe que las cuidades en donde existían estos recintos prehispánicos son: Texcoco, Tenochtitlán, Mérida, Tula, Maní, Tlatelolco y Tlaxcala.

Los *amoxcalli* poseían entre sus principales funciones el acopio, el resguardo, la organización y la preservación de los libros pintados del México precortesiano. Entendiendo por el acopio, la recopilación de los *amoxtli* realizados por los *tlacuilos*; por resguardo, la actividad en la cual el *amoxcalli* protegía a los materiales de cualquier ataque físico o humano que pudiera afectar los códices; por la organización, el mecanismo que empleaban los cuidadores de libros (*amoxtlamalhuiani*) para la sistematización de sus colecciones; y por preservación, al sistema manejado por los *tlacuilos* para la reposición de los materiales deteriorados por el uso, así como la conservación física por medio de reestructuraciones de los mismos.[7]

La organización del conocimiento en la época prehispánica

La ciencia y la cultura, junto con diversos aspectos religiosos e históricos de la época prehispánica, fueron destruidos por los conquistadores al sentirlos una amenaza. Resulta muy difícil a esta altura hacer conjeturas de cuales eran los principales avances científicos y culturales que poseían los grupos indígenas de América antes de la llegada de sus conquistadores pues quedan pocos vestigios que documenten dichas actividades.

Sabemos que fueron excelentes arquitectos y urbanistas, además conocemos en gran medida sus importantes avances en la medicina natural o herbolaria, pero nos falta mucho más por conocer debido, en gran medida, a la tarea constante de la desaparición de una cultura realizada por los conquistadores de Mesoamérica.

Por ello, es relevante hacer notar la importancia de los códices para el conocimiento de los pueblos prehispánicos y sus culturas y ciencias desarrolladas, así como de su estructura política, económica y social, que sin duda fueron muy importantes y bien organizadas por la cantidad de décadas que perduraron.

Durante los estudios de los códices en las últimas décadas, se ha tratado de conocer cada día más de su contenido, descifrando su escritura y con ello la información que guardan a todos los niveles. La división temática de los *amoxtli* que se ha desarrollado desde el siglo XVIII, nos muestra una pequeña pero importante visión de los conocimientos y actividades científicas de lo que los grupos indígenas que existían en su momento, así como su pensamiento religioso y mítico que fue uno de los principales motivos de su destrucción.

Bajo estos elementos, el contenido temático de los códices se ha agrupado según el asunto más relevante del documento pictográfico, ya que por lo regular poseen varios, quedando esta estructura de la siguiente forma:

– Calendáricos-rituales
– Históricos, que se subdividen en históricos-cartográficos
– Genealógicos
– Etnológicos
– *Chilam Balam*
– Cartográficos
– Misceláneos (diversos o antológicos)
– Económicos, que a su vez son subdivididos en tributarios, censos y planos de propiedad
– *Techialoyan*
– No clasificados
– Inaccesibles[8]

- Almanaques y ruedas
- Litigios e historia natural
- Catecismos indígenas[9]

Como vemos, existe una gran variedad de temáticas dentro de los códices. Muchos de ellos no sólo tocan un tema o una parte histórica, sino que conjugan una serie de elementos que aumentan su valor y con ello podemos imaginar la gran influencia que tuvieron estas obras en las bibliotecas y en las colecciones conventuales de los conquistadores después de su llegada en 1519.

La división temática que mostramos se ha hecho de acuerdo con los documentos existentes en nuestros días, pero podemos imaginarnos que la riqueza temática fue aún mayor aunque desafortunadamente no se conoce por la merma sufrida por estos materiales prehispánicos durante el siglo XVI y parte del XVII. Si bien existen copias de algunos documentos originales que desaparecieron en las hogueras en los primeros años de la conquistas, estos no pueden mostrar en su totalidad el esplendor temático que guardaban los *amoxtli* creados por *tlacuilos* capacitados para el caso.

Dentro de las bibliotecas prehispánicas, la organización y acomodo físico de los códices se realizaba agrupándolos por especialidad (cronológicos, territoriales, tributarios, religiosos, astronómicos, genealógicos, etc.), ubicando a todos los pertenecientes en un área del conocimiento humano de aquella época en un solo lugar para su fácil consulta y manejo, separados por formato (tira, biombo, rollo, lienzo, etc.). Aunque se desconoce a ciencia cierta, debió haber existido en cada *amoxcalli* un registro de todos los códices que en allí se almacenaban, con la finalidad de su pronta ubicación y consulta. Lamentablemente no existe ninguno de estos registros y los códices han mermado tanto desde la llegada de los españoles que sólo existe menos de una veintena de los elaborados antes de la época precolombina.

Cómo se leen los códices

Debido a sus dimensiones y características de "imagen-escritura", los códices se leían colocándolos en el piso encima de unos "petates", ubicándolos para su lectura de izquierda a derecha y desplegándolos todos para su fácil lectura. Una vez colocados en esa posición, el *tlacuilo*, el lector y los oyentes se situaban alrededor del manuscrito, quedando a la vista de toda la información contenida, de esta manera el lector podía hincar su lectura al inicio, en la parte del medio o al final del documento según la necesidad.

La lectura ya propia del documento se hacía en forma de zigzag, es decir iniciando en la parte extrema inferior del lado derecho y continuando hacia arriba en cada una de las hojas por separado (cuadrantes) (un ejemplo clásico de ellos son los códices mixtecos prehispánicos).

Debido a que la escritura es por medio de imágenes, la lectura se inicia en la imagen principal del documento y de ahí hacia abajo y hacia delante.

Las figuras que contienen los documentos, parecen pinturas de personajes y objetos o lugares, pero en realidad son imágenes de un carácter simbólico, debido a que se trata realmente de representaciones de palabras y de ideas más que de cosas, se trataba realmente de una escritura "pictográfica" en donde los símbolos o glifos se dividen en dos: los fonéticos y los ideográficos.

La destrucción de los códices

El desconocimiento del valor cultural, histórico, religioso y científico de los códices y de sus "casa" fue motivo para que los españoles llevaran un proceso sistemático de destrucción de los mismos. Así mismo, la búsqueda de riquezas, la apropiación de tierras y el proceso evangelizador de los indígenas fueron motivos fundamentales para que estas importantes fuentes de información fueran destruidas en tan poco tiempo.

> Pronto desaparecieron las expresiones del arte oficial de los grupos prehispánicos en el poder y la práctica de los conocimientos a sus servicios... no obstante, la tradición de elaborar "libros pintados", iniciada siglos atrás en el México prehispánico, no se perdió con el triunfo de las huestes españolas, e incluso el lugar de procedencia de los códices coloniales coinciden, en su mayoría, con las áreas mesoamericanas...[10]

Un ejemplo lamentable de la destrucción de los códices y de sus recintos de resguardo y lectura son los que presentan en sus crónicas los frailes Pedro Mártir de Anglería, Pedro Sánchez de Aguilar, Antonio de Ciudad Real y Diego de Landa, quienes a pesar de su interés en estas obras y saber que podían ser leídas y que guardaban grandes conocimientos participaron en su destrucción o más bien dicho en su aniquilación.

Los códices coloniales y su influencia en la cultura novohispana

Aún después de la conquista los códices se siguieron produciendo en menor medida pero con un alto impacto en la cultura y en las tradiciones novohispanas. Aunque con otros fines se empleaban materiales prehispánicos pero con la influencia de otras novedades traídas del viejo continente, como las tintas ferrosas y el papel europeo de lino, cáñamo o algodón. A pesar de que algunos de los códices coloniales son copias de documentos más antiguos o nuevas versiones de otros ya desaparecidos, tuvieron especial influencia entre los frailes y científicos radicados en la Nueva España por la cantidad de información que en ellos se "leía".

En el aspecto económico, desde 1530 la Corona Española instruía a sus corregidores que pidieran a los indios los códices y que en ellos se marcaran los tributos recibidos para seguir con esta tradición, pero años más adelante el uso de los códices no sólo tuvo valor económico, sino además se utilizaron para darle legalidad a los litigios, a las tasaciones de tributos locales y generales, y a los trámites administrativos, etc.

Al darse cuenta los españoles del gran valor de los códices y de su complejidad temática y viéndolos como una excelente herramienta para "... conocer los aspectos de las culturas del México antiguo, como su historia y organización política, los sistemas tributarios, lo relativo a la tenencia y usufructo de la tierra, los recursos naturales y la producción, la religión y la cuenta del tiempo, con el objeto de fundamentar sus sistemas de dominio y evangelización"[11], permitieron y fomentaron la elaboración de estas fuentes y con ello una influencia directa en la cultura, economía y proceso de evangelización del momento.

La cultura y la ciencia traída de Europa se ven complementadas con los grandes descubrimientos que sobre la naturaleza y geografía se dan en la Nueva España por los estudiosos europeos y por los ya criollos nacidos en América, siendo los códices, sobre todo los coloniales, ya que los prehispánicos casi habían desaparecido o se encontraban fuera del país, grandes influencias a seguir o estudiar por su contenido y temática debido a que existían:

– Códices de carácter jurídico, principalmente los presentados por los indígenas durante un proceso civil, administrativo o penal generado entre los nativos y españoles.

– Calendárico-rituales, de carácter adivinatorio sobre todo y que se componían por lo regular de 260 días.

– Códices económicos, en donde se registraban los censos de la población, los tributos, los libros de cuentas, los registros financieros, catastros, registro de linderos y tenencia de la tierra.

– Mapas y planos, que incluían los elementos geográficos de un lugar o poblado, los caminos y su tipo (principales o veredas), los nombres de los lugares (toponimias), con base en su concepción del espacio y orientación de los *tlacuilos*.

– Códices históricos, que comprende el manejo genealógico de los grupos étnicos conquistados, la historia local de un señorío o de un conjunto de poblados, el registro de acontecimientos importantes, etc.

– Códices históricos-cartográficos,: que también influenciaron en la cultura y la ciencia de los conquistadores, sobre todo por la información de los poblados y eventos que en ellos se describen.

Como vemos la ciencia y cultura en los siglos XVI y XVII tienen influencia, no a todos los niveles pero si en la línea de información y evangelización, en los códices y aunque los *amoxcalli* ya no existen como tales, su impacto en los primeros contactos fue de asombro más no de estudio por el desconocimiento de los libros prehispánicos y de su contenido.

La influencia y el interés en las culturas prehispánicas en las novohispánicas por medio de los códices también se ven reflejadas en la trascripción con caracteres latinos y en papel europeo de distintas obras pictóricas, tal es el caso de los códices mayas que ahora conocemos como libros de *Chilam Balam*, en los que se consignaron diversos asuntos escritos en maya yucateco, así como el *Popol Vuh* que de acuerdo a los versados sobre el tema también es un códice trascrito.

Debido a que muchos códices coloniales se han considerado como pictografías "híbridas" de una importancia secundaria porque ya fueron elaborados bajo la influencia española, estos tuvieron una influencia también mayor entre la cultura y la visión que los conquistadores y evangelizadores tenían de nuestras culturas. Esto se muestra por las glosas en español o latín que presentan algunos documentos como concordancia y complemento del lenguaje glífico, por la influencia en la forma de pintar a los personajes y la visión de la lectura de los mismos.

Un ejemplo directo de la influencia de la cultura y la visión que se deja sentir por parte de los *tlacuilos* y de sus códices en la época colonial es el caso de la parte geográfica-histórica de las Relaciones Geográficas que fueron recopiladas entre 1579 y 1586 por órdenes de Felipe II, que pedía se compilara información del medio físico de distintas provincias de la Nueva España. En el caso de las ciencias tenemos el ejemplo del *Códice Martín de la Cruz o Badiano* de contenido botánico-medicinal, que cuenta con la tradición pictórica indígena, sobre todo náhuatl, y con glosas en español.

La influencia de los códices en la cultura novohispana se enfoca principalmente en la transmisión de información entre los conquistadores y los conquistados, siendo los documentos pictóricos coloniales "el resultado de diversos niveles de integración y asimilación de elementos indígenas e hispánicos".[12]

La edición de literatura religiosa y la evangelización

Un atributo de todas las culturas en la historia de la humanidad ha sido desarrollar los medios y soportes necesarios para almacenar y comunicar de forma masiva cuanto pertenece al universo del conocimiento del momento o de la época.

Por siglos, la tradición oral fue el principal mecanismo de comunicación en las culturas mesoamericanas, en donde la comunicación del conocimiento de padres a hijos pasaba por medio de la palabra y esta se repetía cuantas veces era necesaria para que permaneciera en la vida de la comunidad, hasta la aparición de los códices, en donde la similitud entre la aportación de la oralidad y la representación del códice es tal que prácticamente su unión hacen una sola estructura.

Durante el siglo XVI e iniciada plenamente la evangelización fueron los códices prehispánicos, que se salvaron de la destrucción, y los que se volvieron a pintar por órdenes de los frailes los que tuvieron una gran influencia en el proceso de conversión religiosa de los indígenas en el momento, todo ello aunado a la persecución religiosa que hacían los españoles en contra de los indígenas que no profesaran la religión católica.

Los códices, aún en los siglos XVI y XVII, contaron con una influencia importante, sobre todo para los intereses de los conquistadores y de los grupos religiosos que se encontraban en el proceso de evangelización de los nativos mesoamericanos. Este proceso, nada fácil, buscaba convertir a los indígenas en católicos, pero ¿cómo podría ser esto posible? Se afirma que "...los europeos debía aprender la lengua de los neófitos indígenas, y estos la nueva iconografía, el español y el latín. Además, no era tan fácil para unos enseñar y otros aprender ideas y conceptos provenientes de las religiones indígena y católica."[13]

Una de las principales herramientas y de las "primeras ediciones de literatura religiosa" empleadas para el proceso de evangelización, antes de que llegara la imprenta a América, fueron los códices o manuscritos testerianos, que sin duda abrieron un abanico de posibilidades a los frailes para hacer llegar sus creencias religiosas a una comunidad amplia apoyada con imágenes indígenas y glosas en latín que combinadas servían como medios directos de evangelización por ser los *tlacuilos* que acudían a las lecciones de catecismo sus inventores, empleando sus conocimientos directos y su tradición oral.

Podemos considerar estos códices parte de los libros de las incipientes bibliotecas que se comenzaban a formar en la Nueva España debido a sus características, que aunque no cuentan con los elementos de los libros europeos del momento, "...siguen el mismo sentido de lectura que se emplea cuando se escribe con caracteres latinos, las imágenes y las glosas–en náhuatl o latín–se dividen mediante líneas, a la manera de los códices mesoamericanos."[14]

El proceso evangelizador durante las primeras décadas después de la conquista fue un tema constante de los distintos grupos religiosos llegados a México durante ese periodo, todos ellos buscaban "la conquista espiritual del nuevo mundo" y además reformar el modelo de vida y cultura de los indígenas de la Nueva España por medio de la introducción y enseñanza de artesanías y artes, la instauración de conventos y colegios y la enseñanza de las formas de gobierno español a la élite indígena, empleando para ello la imprenta llegada a México en 1539 y la impresión con ella de libros que durante el siglo XVI alcanzó un número de 138 obras, cuya mayoría fueron redactadas por frailes franciscanos.

La evangelización, la imprenta, los libros de la época y su inclusión en las primeras colecciones de libros que años después se formaron como enormes bibliotecas conventuales, constituyeron verdaderas herramientas de conversión religiosa que dictaminó el tipo de material que se debía imprimir y el contenido de los mismos. Es así como los franciscanos, por ejemplo, requirieron para la evangelización dos elementos:

1. Un conocimiento preciso de las lenguas nativas y en particular una familiaridad con los conceptos y el vocabulario de las creencias religiosas y la moral indígena, pues de ninguna otra manera

podían encontrarse las palabras para llevar una expresión precisa y persuasiva de la doctrina y el culto cristiano.

2. Libros de texto que apoyaran la instrucción de los sacramentos, el latín y la literatura.[15]

La influencia de los grupos indígenas en las bibliotecas religiosas de México del siglo XVI se dio de forma directa por medio de la publicación de obras evangelizadoras en lenguas naturales como el náhuatl, el maya y el tarasco. Tal es el ejemplo, que de los 139 títulos que se editaron con imprenta en México, 80 de ellos fueron de autores franciscanos y de estos 66 se imprimieron en lengua náhuatl, principalmente leguaje del centro de México.[16]

Uno de los principales centros evangelizadores y educadores que surgió dos décadas después de la conquista y que contó con una de las bibliotecas conventuales más ricas y numerosa, fue el Colegio de Tlatelolco, abierto alrededor de 1542, siendo el lugar en donde se redactó la mayor cantidad de libros publicados en náhuatl y en el que maestros y estudiantes lucharon por la conservación del conocimiento y cultura indígena del momento y en donde las ciencias naturales contaron con un gran impacto, sobre todo en la medicina tradicional indígena y el uso de la herbolaria. Aquí mismo, la influencia indígena de los *tlacuilos* y de sus obras se vivió en carne propia, debido a que en este colegio se instruía a los jóvenes en diversas artes como pintura, música, encuadernación e impresión de libros y con ello le edición de obras evangelizadoras en lengua nativa y con una influencia indígena en su contenido y en su aplicación.

Doctrinas cristianas (29 títulos), confesionarios (12 títulos) y administración de sacramentos (8 títulos) fueron los principales temas de los títulos que se publicaron en este siglo XVI, debido a los objetivos y uso que se le daba a las obras y que quedan bien representadas en estos tres elementos. Así mismo, la influencia de la cultura indígena también se vio reflejada en el deseo de conocer el significado de las "imágenes-texto" de los códices y la forma del pensamiento de los nativos quedando plasmadas en los cinco vocabularios que se editaron durante este siglo y en los tres catecismos que se unieron a los códices testerianos.

Finalmente, la influencia indígena en la edición de libros en la imprenta llegada a América en 1539, se vio reflejada, a diferencia de algunos impresos europeos, en que las obras publicadas pasaron a ser libros de uso inmediato y prácticos, en vez de obras de consulta u objetos de arte como eran considerados algunos materiales de la época.

Las bibliotecas antiguas (conventuales y coloniales)

Como hemos visto en puntos anteriores del trabajo, tanto la impresión de libros, como el proceso de evangelización y la organización de colecciones en las bibliotecas se han visto influenciada por los *amoxcalli* y los *amoxtli*, buscando los conquistadores españoles conocer en mayor grado la cultura y forma de pensar de los pueblos indígenas para pasar de un proceso económico y territorial a una actividad de socialización y producción.

Las bibliotecas que mayor influencia tuvieron de los *tlacuilos* y de sus obras fueron las creadas en el siglo XVI y la primera mitad del siglo XVII, en donde aún existían "escribanos-pintores" originales sin una total influencia evangelizadora y civil por parte de los españoles, cuya aportación ayudó a entender la idiosincrasia de los conquistados.

La formación de las bibliotecas conventuales mexicanas se debe a los religiosos de las distintas órdenes que llegaron a México en los dos primeros siglos después de la conquista, quienes para realizar su trabajo evangelizador y educativo requirieron textos formativos, de esparcimiento y de meditación tanto impresos en América como en Europa, así como libros que pudieran cubrir las necesidades intelectuales, científicas y recreativas de particulares laicos.

Durante los primeros cien años después de la conquista de "México-Tenochtitlán" las bibliotecas que más abundaron las podemos dividir en tres partes: la de los conventos, las de los colegios y las de los particulares (un recuento completo de las mismas lo hace el autor Osorio Romero en su trabajo[17]). Entre las que podemos destacar se encuentran: Colegio de la Santa Cruz de Tlatelolco, Colegio Mayor de Santa María de Todos los Santos, Colegio de San Pablo; las particulares como de Juan de Zumárraga, de Vasco de Quiroga, de Bartolomé González, de Carlos de Sigüenza y Góngora, etc.; y de los conventos de los franciscanos como su Convento Grande de San Francisco, Santiago de Chalco, San Felipe de Tlaxcala, o de los carmelitas, mercedarios, dominicos y agustinos como son Casa Profesa, Colegio de Oaxaca, Colegio de Celaya, etc.

Para el siglo XVIII las bibliotecas conventuales son las más fuertes e importantes en colecciones y contenidos, existiendo tanto obras impresas en América y Europa, como manuscritos indígenas y obras publicadas en lenguas indígenas, no de tanto uso como las existentes en los dos siglos anteriores.

Las bibliotecas de los siglos XVIII y XIX ya no contaron con una influencia directa por parte de los *tlacuilos*, pero si sus obras formaban parte de sus colecciones como materiales históricos de gran valor económico por ser casi únicos y por la forma en que estaban escritos, sobre todo aquellos generados por *tlacuilos* pocos años antes y después de la conquista. Esto hacia que las bibliotecas no sólo tuvieran materiales de corte religioso de influencia europea, sino que además existieran obras indígenas de características particulares.

Las bibliotecas novohispanas se vieron influenciadas por las colecciones bilingües (lengua indígena y español) editadas en tierras mexicanas principalmente en los siglos XVI y XVII, en donde los códices empezaron a ser protegidos y a emplearse no sólo para fines económicos, censales y recaudatorios, sino además con un fin académico de enseñanza, ciencias y artes, en donde los hijos de los españoles ya nacidos en la Nueva España y los de los reyes y de alguna élite de los indígenas que había sobrevivido, debían contar con libros y fuentes de información que les permitiera estudiar y conocer la vida, naturaleza, geografía, ciencias, artes, historia, genealogía y medicina natural que les permitiera desarrollarse académicamente y entender el mundo que les rodeaba. Para ello, las bibliotecas representaban un excelente camino para lograr los objetivos no solo religiosos sino además académicos y científicos.

Los libros coloniales y su organización

Es cierto que las bibliotecas conventuales o novohispanas son consideradas unas verdaderas joyas de la historia del libro y las bibliotecas en México, por sus colecciones, contenidos y cantidad de obras que albergaban para la consulta, educación y evangelización de los indígenas, mestizos, españoles y ya mexicanos que habitaron nuestro país durante los siglos XVI al XVIII.

Debido a que los libros en las "librerías" conventuales formaban parte importante como obras de gran valor, se registraban en los "libros de joyas" de los conventos y se contaban con catálogos extensos, algunos ordenados conforme ingresaban a la propia biblioteca y otros de forma temática de acuerdo con la división de materias eclesiásticos existentes en ese momento. Estos primeros "catálogos" contenían solo el título y algunos el año de los materiales, dejando la mayor parte de la tarea de colocación, ubicación y préstamo al hermano bibliotecario, quién se consideraba un hombre culto y de amplios conocimientos.

La impresión americana de libros en los siglos XVI al XIX fue vasta, pero las bibliotecas conventuales fueron importantes consumidores de los mismos, contando además con una gran cantidad de libros europeos que apoyaban sus actividades.

La organización de las colecciones documentales en las bibliotecas coloniales variaba de orden religiosa, algunas acomodaban los libros por número en entrepaño y estantes es decir numeraban sus colecciones como el "Seminario de Morelia" anotando el número del libro, el número de entrepaño donde se encontraba y el número de estante en donde se ubicaba el libro, por ejemplo estante 5, entrepaño 4, libro 20, haciendo así una organización numérica progresiva conforme se incorporaba el material en la colección.

Otras órdenes lo hacían "a través de una catalogación temática y alfabética de autores. A diferencia de otras, las de México se distinguen, porque sus libros tienen una marca de propiedad o calcograma estampado a fuego con hierro candente en uno de los cantos que hoy en día se denomina marca de fuego. Pocas bibliotecas emplearon ex libris en estampa como la Turriana, la del Convento de San Francisco y el Seminario de Morelia, lo que si era de uso común es el ex libris manuscrito en español o en latín."[18]

Pero ¿cuál fue la influencia de los códices y los *amoxcalli* en la organización del conocimiento en las bibliotecas conventuales? Este es un tema que se debe de trabajar de forma especial y con mucho cuidado a falta de literatura que lo documento, y sobre todo por cinco importantes razones:

1. La mayoría de los *amoxtli* y de los *amoxcalli* como se conocían habían desaparecido por el proceso de conquista y evangelización que se dio en la primera década después de la caída del México Tenochtitlán.

2. Aunque existían *tlacuilos*, estos eran perseguidos y torturados para que ya no "escribieran" ni transmitieran sus conocimientos entre los demás pobladores, con la finalidad de erradicar todo rasgo indígena que evitara en primer lugar el saqueo de las riquezas y las tierras y en segundo que no se atentara contra "el proceso evangelizador de los indios sin alma".

3. Las primeras bibliotecas de los conventos y de los colegios se formaron con colecciones privadas de clérigos de alto rango en la iglesia católica, entre ellos Juan de Zumárraga, Alonso de la Veracruz, Vasco de Quiroga, etc., los cuales contaban con algunos códices.

4. Las incipientes bibliotecas conventuales se apoyaron en gran parte en la imprenta llegada a México en 1539, sobre todo para publicar diversos materiales que auxiliaran su labor evangelizadora, pero como ya hemos señalado la edición de material en lenguas nativas influenció directamente en la organización del conocimiento de estas bibliotecas.

Ahora bien, tomando en cuenta estos cuatro aspectos y desde un punto particular de vista, considero que la influencia en la organización de colecciones por parte de los *amoxtli y amoxcalli* en las bibliotecas conventuales se manifestó de las siguientes formas:

a) Debido a que la generación de nuevo conocimiento científico, civil y religioso se dio durante y después del proceso de conquista, con una línea temática distinta y una división social diferente, los documentos, códices y libros generados en este proceso, debían contar con una organización temática y documental distinta a la concepción que los europeos traían de sus tierra, por el proceso de adaptación y sincretización que se presentó, sobre todo la necesidad

de entender y conocer la forma de los nativos de pensar, estudiar,
trabaja y adorar a sus dioses para poder aplicar de forma más
rápida y conveniente la cultura española en todos sus aspectos.

b) Las incipientes bibliotecas conventuales que comenzaban a sur-
gir en la segunda mitad del siglo XVI, se alimentaron con libros y
manuscritos de origen mexicano, aparte de los libros que traían de
Europa, con líneas temáticas desconocidas muchas veces por los
conquistadores, por ello la temática manejada en esta parte de las
bibliotecas fue variada, según el interés de cada orden religiosa y
la idiosincrasia de la misma. Tal es el caso de obras como los códices testerianos, los manuscritos mayas, los códices geográficos y
de tipo religioso, los primeros vocabularios en lengua "mexicana",
abecedarios, doctrinas, confesionarios, cartillas, la concepción
en manuscritos y libros sobre el proceso de evangelización[19], los
primeros catecismos impresos y toda la documentación generada
por matrimonios, bautismos y demás actividades religiosas, obligaron a los frailes bibliotecarios a ordenar de forma especial las
colecciones para que pudieran ser consultadas lo más expeditas
posible. Esto sin duda afectó su organización temática y al mismo
tiempo la distribución y consulta de los materiales por parte de los
religiosos.

c) Durante el siglo XVII, el número de conventos y eventos religiosos y científicos proliferaron en la Nueva España, ampliando el
ámbito cultural, sacramental y territorial y con ello los temas de
los libros que se publican en América para cubrir las necesidades
de información de los religiosos en primera instancia y de los laicos científicos en segundo grado. La influencia de estos casos fue
directa, aunque en menor grado que en el siglo anterior, debido a
que la cultura española se encuentra más arraigada y su influencia
se da a todos los niveles. Con la cantidad de libros producidos
en México y aún existiendo un proceso final de evangelización y
combinación de culturas, la organización temática de las bibliotecas conventuales se vio influenciada, en un menor grado debido a
que ya habían entrado a nuestro continente un número importante
de libros y bibliotecas particulares organizadas con la técnica europea, desplazando por su número a la organización temática que
se estaba llevando en ese momento.

d) Finalmente, la organización temática en las bibliotecas novohispanas de los siglos XVI y XVII contó con una influencia en
el desarrollo de sus colecciones y por ende en su organización,

debido a que estaban enfocadas en tres aspectos fundamentales: la evangelización, la educación y el conocimiento de las lenguas indígenas. Por lo tanto, los materiales que adquirieron se enfocaron a estas áreas y su organización contó con una subdivisión temática amplia, no distante al 100% de la existente en Europa, pero si con características muy propias de los antiguos y nuevos pobladores de la Nueva España, tomado muy en cuenta que la bibliografía adquirida, ya sea local o de otro continente debía ser de uso y consulta inmediata por el proceso conquistador que se estaba dando en todos los niveles.

Como vemos, la influencia de los *tlacuilos*, *amoxtli* y los *amoxcalli* se da en distintos niveles y bajo diversas necesidades, tomando muy en cuenta los proyectos expansivos tanto civiles, militares y religiosos, que tenían los españoles en América, reflejando todo ello en las bibliotecas de los dos primeros siglos durante la conquista, la apertura ante las ideas locales y la aceptación por momentos los documentos indígenas como fuentes de información durante los procesos civiles y la evangelización.

La temática de los libros coloniales

Como sabemos, la organización de los libros en las bibliotecas novohispanas se realizaba durante el siglo XVI de forma temática principalmente y aunque existían en este periodo ya diez impresores laborando en la Ciudad de México la "temática general de esta primera producción bibliográfica mexicana, fue de carácter religioso ya que la imprenta se introdujo a la Nueva España con el fin de auxiliar a la evangelización de los indios"[20].

Por lo tanto, bajo esta dinámica "Los temas principales de estas bibliotecas conventuales respondieron a las necesidades de predicación y administración de los sacramentos; en cambio los de los colegios fueron de filosofía, derecho, teología y literatura; su lengua principal fue el latín, acompañado del español, francés e italiano"[21].

Esto lo podemos ver bien reflejado sobre todo en las bibliotecas del siglo XVI, por ejemplo la biblioteca del Colegio de San Nicolás en Pátzcuaro (que años más tarde se trasladó a la Ciudad de Valladolid), junto con otras de la misma orden religiosa, y que debían tener una bibliografía básica que consistía en "Los temas que recomiendan son, en primer lugar, la Biblia y sus comentarios; en segundo lugar los santos padres–Principalmente San Gregorio, San Bernardo y San Agustín-; en tercer lugar, libros de derecho canónico, especialmente las disposiciones del muy reciente Concilio de Trento; en cuarto lugar libros de teología–Pedro Lambardo y sus comentadores, San Buenaventura y santo Tomás-; en quinto lugar libros de predicación–en especial san Vicente Ferrer-; en séptimo, lugar las reglas y los prontuarios de la Orden; por último, en castellano se recomienda tener la Imitación de Cristo y la crónica de la Orden"[22].

Otra división por materia de los libros es la que muestra el autor Osorio, en la que señala que los libros se encuentran mayormente divididos así:

"Predicables
Expositivos
Moralistas
Duplicados
Escolásticos
Históricos
Varios
Místicos
Juristas
Gramáticos
Mexicanos
Manuscritos
Inútiles"[23]

En el caso de los de la división temática mexicanos no podemos dudar que sean vocabularios, gramáticas y seminarios en lengua indígena y quizá pudieron existir algunos catecismos o códices testerianos. Sabemos además que algunos códices y documentos en náhuatl pasaron a las bibliotecas conventuales donados por personajes importantes de la época, enriqueciendo los temas de las colecciones. Tal es el caso de la biblioteca particular de Sigüenza y Góngora, que legó una parte de su biblioteca al Colegio Máximo de San Pedro y San Pablo de los jesuitas, y que incluía mapas antiguos, códices, manuscritos en náhuatl, y un apartado denominado "cosas de Indios".

Como vemos, la división temática de los libros en las bibliotecas coloniales era muy variada, pero en la mayoría de los casos existía un apartado para los libros en lenguas nativas ya que el proceso evangelizador estaba en pleno apogeo.

Una forma más de influencia de los amoxtli y amoxcalli en las grandes bibliotecas coloniales

Como hemos visto, la influencia de forma directa e indirecta de los códices y de las "casas de libros" prehispánicos se ha dado en distintos niveles y bajo un esquema de destrucción y dominación total, debido a que al mostrar los indígenas sus códices a los españoles para reclamar sus derechos de tierras o mostrar sus territorios, costumbres o vida civil, estos eran considerados "obras del mal" y en su gran mayoría fueron destruidos en el momento y castigados o muertos los indígenas que los portaban.

La influencia de estas obras se ha dado en un nivel bajo pero que ha tenido de alguna forma impacto en las bibliotecas coloniales de los siglos

XVI y XVII, así como en la forma de conquista espiritual que emplearon los europeos utilizando a los *tlacuilos* y sus obras ya influenciadas por la cultura dominante para transmitir por medio de códices coloniales sus ideas.

Quizás una forma más de influencia de los códices en los recintos bibliotecarios del momento fue por medio de la tradición oral, que, si bien con un toque de cultura europea, contaba con un profundo arraigo entre los nativos y aun tiene impacto en nuestros días.

Cabe señalar que aunque la tradición pictórica de los códices desaparece durante el primer siglo después de la conquista cuando ya no existe rastro alguno de los *amoxcalli*, se utilizaron indígenas para hacer las pinturas y decoraciones en piedra de los templos. Estos recibieron la influencia de los pocos *tlacuilos* que existían e impregnaron en estos adornos algunos datos históricos, así como ciertas características de la escritura indígena tradicional.

A manera de conclusión

Como se ha visto a lo largo del trabajo, los *amoxtli* y *amoxcalli* representaron una parte fundamental en la vida cultural, académica económica y social de lo pueblos prehispánicos, sobre todo en la parte central de México donde la conquista se dio con mayor ímpetu, zona que constituyó el corazón del desarrollo de los conquistadores en la Nueva España.

Los códices, grandes obras maestras de los grupos indígenas del México antiguo y colonial, son sin duda alguna los precursores del libro en el país, independientemente de que su formato no contenga las características físicas de los libros que ahora conocemos y de que ya no se produzcan en la actualidad. Los pocos que quedan poseen los conocimientos, teorías, fechas, historias, descripciones, etc. de la mentalidad humana de una época fundamental en la historia de nuestro país. Con su información se puede detectar la ideología y la conceptualización de los acontecimientos vividos bajo una libertad completa y posteriormente una conquista cambiante y dominante.

Los grupos indígenas mexicanos que contaban con una escritura propia, papel de gran calidad y tintas, fueran capaces de impresionar, con el producto de estos materiales, a sus conquistadores, que de inmediato se interesaron en estos usándolos como trofeos o botines de la conquista y después como herramientas de evangelización y control económico.

La influencia dada por los *amoxcalli* y los *amoxtli* a las bibliotecas coloniales se acentuó sobre todo en los siglos XVI y XVII, en donde los primeros contactos con estas fuentes de información fue inicialmente de rechazo y destrucción y años más delante de herramientas de apoyo para comprender la forma de ver el universo por parte de los conquistados y someterlos a la nueva religión católica, completamente extraña para ellos por la cantidad de dioses a los que se les rendía tributo.

Así mismo, las colecciones documentales de las bibliotecas conventuales en estos siglos, se vieron afectadas en su desarrollo por el proceso evangelizador que se realizaba, en el que el idioma representaba un problema fundamental. Este proceso recurrió a los códices coloniales como fuentes de información que permitiera realizar el trabajo de forma más simplificada.

Las bibliotecas coloniales crecieron influenciadas por los acontecimientos históricos del momento, pero sobre todo de la cultura indígena de la época en donde la defensa de los indios por sus derechos, su educación y proceso religioso y la documentación generada de estos elementos conllevaron a un desarrollo sistemático de colecciones y a una organización temática que les permitiera a los españoles acceder de forma rápida a los datos necesarios para cubrir cualquier eventualidad en el proceso de conquista espiritual, económica y social.

La influencia de los *amoxtli* sobre las bibliotecas de los clérigos se manifestó en tres principales planos: la selección y adquisición de obras de apoyo para la evangelización, materiales de carácter artístico enfocado a la pintura para el uso de las habilidades de los grupos indígenas en la decoración de los templos y el desarrollo de la ciencias, sobre todo las naturales y geográficas, para la educación de los estudiantes criollos, indígenas y españoles en el nuevo continente con base en las necesidades existentes.

NOTAS

1. Joaquín Galarza, "Escribir pintando: los códices mexicanos," *Arqueología Mexicana* 4, no. 23 (1997): 7.

2. Carmen Aguilera, *Códices del México antiguo: una selección* (México: Instituto Nacional de Antropología e Historia, 1979), 15.

3. Laura E. Sotelo Santos, "Tradición milenaria: los códices mayas," *Arqueología Mexicana* 4, no. 23 (1997): 35.

4. Un posible códice de El Mirador, Chiapas (México: I.N.A.H., 1970), 5.

5. Bernal Díaz del Castillo, *Historia verdadera de la conquista de la Nueva España* (México: Porrúa, 1968), 151.

6. Francisco Burgos, *Palestra historial* (México: Archivo General de la Nación, 1934), v. 24, 288.

7. Saúl Armendáriz Sánchez y T. de Jesús Guevara, *Los "libros pintados" del México antiguo y colonial: Joyas pictográficas de la Biblioteca Nacional de Antropología e Historia* (México: el autor, 1990), 20.

8. Ibid., 4.

9. Galarza, "Escribir pintando," 9-10.

10. PerlaValle, "Códices coloniales: testimonio de una sociedad en conflicto," *Arqueología Mexicana* 4, no. 23 (1997): 65.

11. Ibid., p. 66.

12. Xavier Noguez, "Los códices Coloniales del centro de México," *Revista de la Universidad de México* 49, no. 525-526 (1994): 8.

13. Joaquín Galarza, "Códices o manuscritos testerianos," *Arqueología Mexicana* 7, no. 38 (1999): 35.

14. Ibid., 36.

15. Elvira Carreño Velázquez, "Las órdenes de San Francisco y la imprenta mexicana del siglo XVI," http://www.adabi-ac.org/investigacion_libro_ant/articulos/paginas/04art_ecv07.htm.

16. Ibid.

17. Ignacio Osorio Romero, *Historia de las bibliotecas novohispanas* (México: Secretaría de Educación Pública, Dirección General de Bibliotecas, 1987), 282.

18. Elvia Carreño Velázquez, "Las bibliotecas antiguas de México," http://www.adabi-ac.org/investigacion_libro_ant/articulos/paginas/04art_ecv01.htm.

19. *Cuatro siglos de la imprenta en México: una muestra tipográfica mexicana* (México: Universidad Nacional Autónoma de México, 1986), 5-6.

20. Ibid., 9-10.

21. Carreño Velázquez, "Las bibliotecas antiguas," http://www.adabi-ac.org/investigacion_libro_ant/articulos/paginas/04art_ecv01.htm.

22. Osorio Romero, *Historia*, 37.

23. Ibid., 116.

OBRAS CONSULTADAS

Aguilera, Carmen. *Códices del México antiguo: una selección*. México: Instituto Nacional de Antropología e Historia, 1979.

Armendáriz Sánchez, Saúl y T. de Jesús Guevara. *Los "libros pintados" del México antiguo y colonial: joyas pictográficas de la Biblioteca Nacional de Antropología e Historia. Estudio de presentación, historia, clasificación, conservación, etc., de los manuscritos (códices de la Sección de Testimonios Pictográficos de la BNAH)*. México: los autores, 1990. (Tesis de licenciatura de la Escuela Nacional de Biblioteconomía y Archivonomía).

Armendáriz Sánchez, Saúl. "El quinto centenario ¿y los libros de los antiguos mexicanos qué?: los códices, un panorama general." *Jornadas Mexicanas de Biblioteconomía* 23 (1992): 99-111.

Burgos, Francisco. *Palestra historial*. México: Archivo General de la Nación, 1934.

Carreño Velázquez, Elvia. "Las bibliotecas antiguas de México," http://www.adabi-ac.org/investigacion_libro_ant/articulos/paginas/04art_ecv01.htm.

Carreño Velázquez, Elvira. "Las órdenes de San Francisco y la imprenta mexicana del siglo XVI," http://www.adabi-ac.org/investigacion_libro_ant/articulos/paginas/04art_ecv07.htm.

Cuatro siglos de la imprenta en México: una muestra tipográfica mexicana. México: Universidad Nacional Autónoma de México, 1986.

Díaz del Castillo, Bernal. *Historia verdadera de la conquista de la Nueva España*. México: Porrúa, 1968.

Galarza, Joaquín. "Escribir pintando: los códices mexicanos." *Arqueología Mexicana* 4 no. 23 (1997): 6-13.

Galarza, Joaquín. "Códices o manuscritos testerianos." *Arqueología Mexicana*. 7, no. 38 (1999): 34-37.

Mejías, Hugo A. *Préstamos de lenguas indígenas en el español americano del siglo XVII*. México: Universidad Nacional Autónoma de México, 1980.

Noguez, Xavier. "Los códices coloniales del centro de México." *Revista de la Universidad de México* 49, no. 525-526 (1994): 5-9.

Osorio Romero, Ignacio. *Historia de las bibliotecas novohispanas*. México: Secretaría de Educación Pública, Dirección General de Bibliotecas, 1986.

Pompa y Pompa, Antonio. *450 años de la imprenta tipográfica en México*. México: Asociación Nacional de Libreros, 1988.

Sotelo Santos, Laura E. "Tradición milenaria: los códices mayas." *Arqueología Mexicana*. 4, no. 23 (1997): 34-43.

Un posible códice de El Mirador, Chiapas. México: Instituto Nacional de Antropología e Historia, 1970.

Valle, Perla. "Códices coloniales: testimonio de una sociedad en conflicto." *Arqueología Mexicana* 4, no. 23 (1997): 64-69.

ANEXOS

Algunos pasajes en donde se demuestra la importancia e influencia de los códices, los *tlacuilos* y los *amoxcalli* en el grupo invasor dominante:

...todo lo tenían escrito pintado en libros y largos papeles con cuentas de años y meses y días en que habían acontecido
...sus leyes y ordenanzas sus padrones todo con mucho orden y concierto...

Fray Diego Durán.

Historias de las Indias de la Nueva España e Islas de Tierra Firme.

...estos indios tienen por costumbre en cosas de comunidad y gobierno, que todos los que vienen tengan noticias de lo que se provee, Vuestra Señoría mandará, aunque se reciba alguna pena, que todos los que vienen sobre el tal negocio entren, y lo que así se proveyere el nahuatlato lo diga claro y recio, de manera que todos lo oigan, porque es gran contento para ellos, además que así conviene...

Relación de Antonio de Mendoza.

Y a tres sabios de Ehécatl (quetzalcóatl), de origen tezcocano, los comieron los perros. No más ellos vinieron a entregarse. Nadie los trajo. No más venían trayendo sus papeles con pinturas...

Manuscrito de Tlatelolco 1528.

...platicando con un indio viejo otomí, de más de setenta años, sobre las cosas de nuestra fe, le dijo aquel indio, como ellos en su antigüedad tenían un libro que venía sucesivamente de padres a hijos en las personas mayores que para lo guardar y enseñar tenían dedicados.

En este libro tenían escrita doctrina en dos columnas por todas las planas del libro [...] y preguntándole este religioso (Fr. Diego Mercado) al indio, de lo que contenía aquel libro en su doctrina, no le supo dar cuenta en particular, más de que le respondió, que si a el libro no se oviera perdido, viera como la doctrina que el les enseñaba y predicaba y la que allí se contenía era la misma, y que el libro se pudrió debajo de la tierra, donde lo enterraron los que lo guardaban cuando vinieron los españoles.

Fray Jerónimo de Mendieta.

Historia eclesiástica indiana.

Por los caracteres y escrituras de que usan, y por la relación de los viejos y de los que en tiempo de su infidelidad eran sacerdotes y papas, y por dicho de los señores y principales a quienes se enseñaba la ley y criaban en los templos para que la deprendiesen, juntados ante mí y traídos sus libros y pinturas que, según lo demostraban, eran antiguas.

Historia de los mexicanos por sus pinturas, 1533-1536.

Todas las cosas que conferimos me las dieron por pinturas, que aquella era la escritura que ellos antiguamente usaban...

Fray Bernardino de Sahagún.

Usaba esta gente de ciertos caracteres o letras con las cuales escribían en sus libros las cosas antiguas y sus ciencias, y con estas figuras y algunas señales de las mismas entendían sus cosas y las daban a entender y las enseñaba.

Fray Diego de Landa.

Se hallaron muchos libros a su modo, en hojas o telas de especiales cortezas de árboles que se hallaban en tierra caliente y las curtían y aderezaban a modo de pergaminos [...] donde todas sus historias escribían con unos caracteres tan abreviados que una solo plana expresaba el lugar, sitio, provincia, año, mes y día con todos los demás nombres de dioses, ceremonias, y sacrificios o victorias que habían celebrado y tenido. Y para esto a los hijos de los señores y a los que escogían para el sacerdocio, enseñaban e instruían desde su niñez, haciéndoles decorar [aprender] aquellos caracteres y tomar de memoria las historias, y estos mismos instrumentos he tenido en mis manos y oídolos explicar a algunos viejos con bastante admiración...

Fray Francisco de Burgoa.

*Yo canto las pinturas del libro,
lo voy desplegando,
yo papagayo florido
en el interior de la casa de las pinturas*

Cantares Mexicanos, (folio 51v)

..*de todo lo cual tenían grandes y hermosos libros de pinturas y caracteres de todas estas artes por donde enseñaban. También tenían libros de su ley y doctrina a su modo, por donde los enseñaban, donde hasta que doctos y hábiles no los dejasen salir sino ya hombres.*

Fray Diego Durán.

De los mapas de aquellas tierras hemos examinado uno de treinta pies de largo y poco menos de ancho, hecho de algodón blanco, en el cual estaba dibujada en detalle toda la llanura con los pueblos amigos y enemigos de Moctezuma.

Pedro Mártir.

En los libros de pinturas están vuestros cantos, los desplegáis junto a los atabales.

Cantares mexicanos (folio 15r.)

13. Las cartillas de alfabetización en lengua indígena: un intento por rescatar la riqueza lingüística de México

Micaela Chávez Villa
Víctor J. Cid Carmona

Antecedentes

A través de su historia, en México se han emprendido diversos esfuerzos para atender la educación de las más de 50 culturas indígenas que co-existen con los así llamados mestizos (mezcla entre los indígenas y los europeos), quienes constituyen la mayoría de la población. Los cálculos elaborados por el Consejo Nacional de Población (CONAPO), a partir de los datos censales recabados por el Instituto Nacional de Estadística, Geografía e Informática (INEGI), indica que la población indígena de México es de 12.7 millones de personas, lo que representa el 13% de la población nacional.[1] Aunque el español es el idioma oficial, "en México se hablan 62 lenguas indígenas, además de diversas variantes que en ocasiones son incluso ininteligibles entre sí y que son producto de culturas originarias de su territorio. Esta característica pluriétnica representa un importante patrimonio cultural, una variedad de saberes y sensibilidades desarrollados a lo largo del tiempo que se expresan en conocimiento y relación con la naturaleza, en historias, mitos y leyendas, en música, canto y danza, en hábitos de cocina y en objetos de arte, entre muchas otras expresiones culturales. Se trata de un enorme patrimonio de la nación: un acervo de la riqueza del México del siglo XXI."[2] El estado mexicano ha hecho esfuerzos e inversión para alfabetizar a la población en general y en particular a la de origen indígena. Con este propósito, en mayo de 1939 se celebró la Primera Asamblea de Filólogos y Lingüistas en la ciudad de México, en la que se acordó crear el Consejo de Lenguas Indígenas, en cuyos Estatutos[3] se expresan las siguientes finalidades:

1. Efectuar estudios estructurales y sociales de las lenguas indígenas

2. Contribuir a la solución de los problemas de la educación en tales lenguas

3. Entrenar investigadores[4]

Si bien fue posible emprender algunos trabajos en cumplimiento de sus finalidades, en julio de 1943 el subdirector, Wigberto Jiménez Moreno y el Secretario, Alfredo Barrera Vásquez, convocaron a los miembros del Comité del Patronato del Consejo a una sesión con el objeto de reanudar las actividades. En la sesión se acordó entre otros asuntos, invitar al Instituto Indigenista Interamericano (III) y al Instituto Lingüístico de Verano (ILV) a formar parte del Patronato del Consejo. Según se registra en el Boletín Indigenista de septiembre del mismo año, para aquél momento, tanto el III como el ILV habían aceptado ser instituciones patrocinadoras, nombrando como sus representantes al doctor Juan Comas y al profesor Richard Pittman[5], respectivamente.

En julio del siguiente año, 1944, la Secretaría de Educación Pública invitó a algunos miembros del Consejo de Lenguas Indígenas para que les explicaran las ventajas de la enseñanza de la lectura y la escritura en lenguas nativas como medio para que los hablantes de esas lenguas aprendieran rápidamente a leer y escribir en español. Los lingüistas refirieron los hechos que a continuación se resumen:

1. Numerosos grupos de indígenas desconocen absolutamente el español, para ellos, el aprendizaje de la lectura y escritura en español sin el uso previo de su lengua materna ha resultado en un fracaso, ya que se enfrentan abruptamente a un idioma totalmente ajeno al suyo.

2. Muchos de los hablantes de lenguas indígenas que hablan también español y por lo tanto, se han clasificado como "bilingües" en realidad poseen escaso dominio del español, lo que indica que su aprendizaje ha sido incorrecto y les resulta de poca utilidad.

3. Muchos indígenas han olvidado su lengua nativa y manejan escasa y deficientemente el español.

Refirieron también sus experiencias, métodos e instrumentos para la enseñanza de la lectura y escritura, primero en lengua indígena y luego en castellano, exhibieron las cartillas, periódicos murales y publicaciones hechas para tal efecto. En respuesta a lo anterior, el Secretario de Educación Pública solicitó a los miembros del Consejo la preparación de un plan para el cumplimiento de los fines de enseñanza de las lenguas. Adicionalmente, el 21 de agosto de 1944 se promulgo la *Ley que establece la Campaña Nacional contra el Analfabetismo*,[6] en cuyo artículo 14 se hace referencia puntual de la educación de las comunidades indígenas en los siguientes términos:

Articulo 14.- En vista de la importancia de cada uno de los grupos indígenas que habitan en el territorio nacional y del predominio que en ellos tiene su idioma nativo, la Secretaría de Educación Pública—de acuerdo con el Departamento de Asuntos Indígenas—determinará los procedimientos técnicos adecuados e imprimirá las cartillas bilingües que fueren necesarias para llevar a cabo, como complemento de la campaña contra el analfabetismo, una labor de enseñanza del español realizada en aquellos grupos por brigadas de instructores especiales, capacitados merced a cursos intensivos de adiestramiento.[7]

En atención de lo anterior y en cumplimiento de la solicitud del secretario de Educación, en septiembre de 1944, el Consejo de Lenguas Indígenas[8] propuso un Programa General, que contemplaba entre otros, los siguientes aspectos:

A) Plan

1. Selección de cuatro grupos indígenas para iniciar el trabajo de alfabetización: nahua, maya, otomí y tarasco (los tres primeros seleccionados en función de ser los que cuentan con mayor número de hablantes en lengua nativa, mayor índice de monolingües y por la gran extensión territorial que abarcan sus comunidades. Los tarascos en función de contar ya con experiencias previas en tareas de alfabetización).

2. Definición de tres etapas de trabajo:

Primera etapa:

a) Entrenamiento en la ciudad de México de cincuenta profesores, diez de cada una de las siguientes regiones: nahua del estado de Morelos, nahua del Estado de Puebla, maya del Estado de Yucatán, otomí del Estado de Hidalgo y tarasco de la Sierra del Estado de Michoacán.

b) Los profesores deben tener el grado de maestro normalista, ser nativos de la región respectiva y tener un conocimiento práctico de la lengua indígena correspondiente.

c) Los profesores deberán recibir los siguientes cursos de adiestramiento: lingüística, antropología, etnografía general de México y especial de la región a trabajar, pedagogía especial (incluyendo la técnica de la enseñanza de la lectura y la escritura de los idiomas indígenas y del español, con la colaboración de lingüistas y dibujantes para la elaboración de material didáctico).

Segunda etapa:

a) Al terminar los cursos de adiestramiento, los cincuenta profesores regresarán a sus regiones y se instalarán en la comunidad que se seleccione para trabajar.

b) Cada uno de los diez profesores se encargará de entrenar a otros diez profesores rurales, que cubran los siguientes requisitos: ser nativos de la región, tener al menos completa la educación primaria y dominar la lengua indígena de la región.

Tercera etapa:

a) Al concluir la segunda etapa se contará con quinientos profesores formados que trabajarán directamente con los indígenas analfabetos en las cinco regiones mencionadas.

3. Continuidad de la Campaña de alfabetización. Se propone aplicar el mismo programa para otras lenguas indígenas, aplicando las tres etapas ya descritas en otras comunidades.

B) Desarrollo

Para la ejecución de las tres etapas, el Consejo propone lo siguiente:

1. Constituir un Cuerpo Técnico, integrado por siete profesores lingüistas especializados en náhuatl, maya, otomí y tarasco; cinco ayudantes lingüistas, cuatro antropólogos especializados en cada uno de los grupos indígenas, cinco pedagogos y un dibujante.

2. El Cuerpo Técnico estará a las órdenes de un Director General que deberá ser un lingüista.

3. Los trabajos en cada una de las cinco regiones contarán también con un Director, que será el lingüista especializado en la lengua correspondiente.

4. Las funciones: El Director General coordinara los trabajos durante las tres etapas del Programa y será enlace entre los directores particulares y la Secretaría de Educación. Los Directores de sección vigilarán los trabajos de sus respectivas regiones. Los lingüistas se encargarán de impartir los cursos referentes a las lenguas particulares, enseñarán además la estructura, manejo y uso correcto de los alfabetos. Los ayudantes lingüistas auxiliarán en la dirección y vigilancia de los trabajos de cada región. Los antropólogos abordarán lo relacionado con las características raciales y culturales de las comunidades, particularmente de las suyas, con el objeto de aprovechar los factores positivos observados. Los pedagogos enseñaran la correcta aplicación de las normas pedagógicas en los trabajos de los maestros y trazarán los métodos para la formación de cartillas y textos, para ello contarán con la colaboración del dibujante, quienes además adiestrarán a los maestros en el trazado de dibujos adecuados al fin que se persigue.

De entre los maestros normalistas que recibirán el adiestramiento en la primera etapa, se seleccionarán aquellos que fungirán como inspectores del proceso de enseñanza en los pueblos indígenas (tercera etapa).

El Cuerpo Técnico, a través de sus directores, hará las pruebas de selección de los profesores para la primera y segunda etapas del Programa.

5. Se utilizará el Alfabeto del Consejo de Lenguas Indígenas,[9] tomando los signos necesarios para cada lengua indígena.

6. El método pedagógico que recomienda el Consejo para la elaboración de las cartillas del plan, es el denominado Global, por considerarlo el más apegado a la realidad lingüística y psicológica, además de ser el utilizado en el adiestramiento de los maestros.

A manera de corolario, cabe mencionar que tanto en la Primera Asamblea de Filólogos y Lingüistas como en la integración del Consejo de Lenguas Indígenas y la redacción del Programa para alfabetización, se contó con la participación de representantes del ILV, lo que permite observar el grado de influencia de dicha organización en los programas de alfabetización de comunidades indígenas de nuestro país.

El ILV y la alfabetización indígena en México

Los antecedentes de la llegada a nuestro país de William Cameron Townsend—fundador del ILV—se remontan a 1931, año en que el entonces Secretario de Educación Pública, Moisés Sáenz, lo conoció en Panajachel, Guatemala. Townsend mostró a Sáenz su escuela y le habló de las campañas de alfabetización emprendidas con el objeto de enseñar a leer a los indígenas la Biblia en su propia lengua. El misionero, había ideado un alfabeto para los cakchiqueles, analizado su sistema verbal, preparado una cartilla y había comenzado a enseñar a los niños a hablar, leer y escribir en español y en su propia lengua.[10] Moises Sáenz invitó a William Townsend para establecerse en México y hacer un trabajo semejante con los indígenas mexicanos.

Al momento de abandonar la comunidad, había alfabetizado a varios cientos de indígenas aplicando su método y tenía en sus manos un ejemplar impreso del Nuevo Testamento en la hasta entonces nunca escrita lengua cakchiquel.[11]

Para 1934 Townsend se había establecido en Tetelcingo, población de origen nahua en el Estado de Morelos.

Ese mismo año, el Presidente Lázaro Cárdenas visita la población donde encuentra a Townsend dedicado a la enseñanza de la lengua a niños y adultos de la localidad, y le ofrece su apoyo al lingüista para extender los trabajos a otros grupos étnicos. Preocupado por tal empresa, "Townsend funda el Summer Institute of Linguistics como estación de reclutamiento y formación de misioneros lingüistas y en el correr de los años establece a los egresados— por lo común, por parejas matrimoniales—en un centenar de grupos étnicos".[12]

En un informe sobre el ILV, preparado en 1944, Townsend refiere que las actividades comenzaron con dos estudiantes en una granja cerca de Oklahoma y puntualiza sobre la preparación de los estudiantes de la siguiente manera:

Los cursos en Oklahoma duran once semanas, comprendiendo...fonética, fonémica, morfología, sintaxis, así como la técnica del investigador;

también se dan lecturas respecto a cómo debe enseñarse a los pueblos primitivos a leer (recibe especial atención el método psicofonético), así como antropología, problemas de salubridad de los trópicos, etc.

Luego de concluir los cursos, el investigador es enviado a alguna comunidad cuyo lenguaje deba ser estudiado, se establece allí y en contacto con los habitantes, recopila, memoriza y analiza la lengua hasta ser capaz de conversar. A continuación el investigador abandona la comunidad y somete sus hallazgos a sus instructores, en las sesiones de verano en Oklahoma o en conferencias especiales en la ciudad de México.

Regresa a la comunidad luego de haber aclarado con sus instructores problemas sobre la lengua que estudia para trabajar más con sus informantes. Después de pasados cinco o diez años y haber catalogado sonidos, fonemas, morfemas, construcciones sintácticas y otros datos, el investigador competente es capaz de:

1. Escribir una gramática bastante completa

2. Integrar un diccionario de la lengua que está estudiando

3. Formular libros para enseñar a leer

Las gramáticas, diccionarios y vocabularios se ponen a disposición del gobierno correspondiente, en el caso de México, se presta especial atención en enseñar español a los indígenas.

Respecto de las motivaciones del fundador del ILV, es oportuno anotar ahora sus propias consideraciones:

> [El ILV] cree que los pueblos aborígenes son generalmente capaces de gran desarrollo, una vez que sean removidos la ignorancia, la superstición, el aislamiento y la inercia, pues han descubierto que tanto hombres como mujeres, han demostrado una gran habilidad, una vez que han sido ayudados intelectual, material y espiritualmente, por lo que es de creerse que la raza indígena es capaz de hacer lo que cualquiera otra raza.[14]

Es claro que desde su llegada a nuestro país, el fundador del ILV y su grupo de colaboradores tuvieron marcada ingerencia en los programas conducentes al estudio de las lenguas indígenas y en la alfabetización de las comunidades hablantes correspondientes. Independientemente de ello, no es hasta pasados quince años de actividad que, el 15 de agosto de 1951, se signa un Convenio de colaboración entre la Secretaría de Educación Pública de México, a través de su Dirección General de Asuntos Indígenas y el ILV, representado por su Director, Guillermo Townsend, con el objeto de desarrollar un programa de cooperación para la investigación de las lenguas indígenas de la República, además de estudiar las características culturales y biológicas de los distintos grupos indígenas.

Entre las finalidades y condiciones del Convenio se encontraban las siguientes:

Un programa de investigación, que comprendería:

1. Un estudio profundo de cada lengua, incluyendo el análisis de su sistema fonético y morfológico, así como una recopilación de su vocabulario.

2. Un estudio comparativo de las lenguas aborígenes entre sí y en relación con otros idiomas del mundo para su catalogación.

3. Un estudio antropológico integral de los diferentes grupos indígenas, consecuente con el estudio lingüístico.

4. Cooperación con otras organizaciones interesadas en la investigación científica de otros aspectos de la vida de los grupos indígenas.

Un programa de servicios prácticos, que incluiría:

1. La prestación de servicios de los investigadores del ILV como intérpretes y colaboradores, con las dependencias de la Dirección General de Asuntos Indígenas y con autoridades educacionales, sanitarias y otras que lleguen a las comunidades donde se encuentren los investigadores.

2. La organización de cursos de capacitación lingüística para grupos de maestros rurales que desempeñen sus labores educativas en comunidades indígenas y desconozcan las lenguas autóctonas.

3. La preparación de cartillas en los idiomas indígenas para facilitar a los hablantes de lenguas indígenas el aprendizaje de la lectura y la escritura.

4. La elaboración de cartillas bilingües (español-indígena) con el propósito de facilitar el aprendizaje del idioma oficial.

5. La traducción a lenguas indígenas de leyes, consejos sanitarios, labores agrícolas, curtido de pieles y otras manufacturas, así como de libros de un alto valor moral y patriótico.

6. El fomento del deporte, el civismo y el servicio cooperativo.

7. El desarraigamiento de los vicios por todos los medios posibles.

Además de lo anterior, el ILV:

1. Prestaría servicios gratuitos de algunos de sus profesores cuando la Secretaría de Educación organizara cursos para la capacitación de lingüistas mexicanos

2. Cooperaría con la Dirección General de Asuntos Indígenas en la publicación de una revista lingüística editada en México, así como en la preparación de exposiciones y conferencias filológicas indígenas organizadas por la Secretaría de Educación Pública[15]

Por su parte, la Secretaría de Educación Pública se comprometía a:

1. Gestionar ante la Secretaría de Relaciones Exteriores la permanencia de los investigadores del ILV, eximiéndoles del impuesto de extranjería.

2. Cooperar (con medicamentos) a la acción sanitaria de las enfermeras del ILV.

3. Facilitar la radicación en un lugar de la República, designado al efecto, de los profesores norteamericanos que el ILV contratar para la educación de los hijos de sus miembros.

4. Tramitar ante las autoridades la internación de técnicos norteamericanos en planeación y saneamiento, que fungirían como auxiliares del ILV.

5. Solicitar ante las autoridades competentes la autorización para que el ILV ocupe terrenos baldíos o federales por el tiempo que fuere necesario, en los sitios en que estableciera sus bases de investigación y sus servicios prácticos.

6. Gestionar ante la Secretaría de la Defensa Nacional los permisos para que el ILV adquiera y utilice aviones y helicópteros para trasladar a sus investigadores a las distintas regiones del país.

7. Gestionar ante la Secretaría de Comunicaciones y Obras Públicas los permisos para que el ILV adquiera y utilice equipos de radio-emisión y radio-recepción y otros que fueren necesarios, considerando que dichos equipos estarían al servicio del Gobierno Mexicano para su servicio.

8. Gestionar ante la Secretaría de Hacienda y Crédito Público los permisos para la legal importación, libre de derechos aduanales, del equipo, mercancías, maquinarias, aparatos, objetos y artículos que de común acuerdo se consideraran necesarios para el eficiente desarrollo de las actividades del ILV.

Se estipulaba en el convenio que podría ser reformado o ampliado en cualquier tiempo por acuerdo de ambas partes, su vigencia se establecía desde el momento en que se signaba hasta que concluyeran las investigaciones especificadas o hasta que el Gobierno Mexicano lo diera por finalizado, previa notificación con un año de anticipación.[16]

En virtud de los resultados, se confirma que varias de las finalidades y condiciones del Convenio se cumplieron, el ILV participó en la elaboración de

359 cartillas, de ellas, 72 (20.05%) las realizó de manera independiente, y 287 (79.94%) en forma conjunta con alguna dependencia nacional.[17] Además de este trabajo el ILV llevó a cabo la producción de diversos materiales bibliográficos relativos a los idiomas indígenas.[18] Como reconocimiento al apoyo recibido, el Gobierno de México, a solicitud de la Secretaría de Educación Pública, destinó al ILV—mediante la promulgación de un decreto de fecha 18 de mayo, 1960—un predio ubicado en el Distrito Federal, conocido como Rancho San Isidro para que el ILV construyera el *Centro de Investigación y Exposición de Culturas Indígenas en el País.*[19]

La colección de cartillas de la Biblioteca Daniel Cosío Villegas

La Biblioteca Daniel Cosío Villegas recibió la colección de cartillas de alfabetización como una donación de la Dra. Gloria Ruiz de Bravo Ahuja, profesora investigadora de El Colegio de México, quien ocupó también el cargo de Directora del Instituto de Investigación e Integración Social del Estado de Oaxaca. Las cartillas que conforman esta colección sirvieron de base para la elaboración del segundo volumen de su obra: *Los materiales didácticos para la enseñanza del español a los indígenas mexicanos.*[20] Consideramos importante la difusión de esta colección para que otros investigadores puedan beneficiarse con su consulta. En la obra de Ruiz de Bravo Ahuja se tomó una muestra de 88 cartillas para llevar a cabo el análisis formal del contenido. De manera crítica se hace la revisión para determinar:

> 1) si detrás de estos materiales puede advertirse una planeación lingüística congruente en lo relativo a la enseñanza del español a nuestras minorías étnicas, y 2) si desde un punto de vista lingüístico y pedagógico tales unidades didácticas pueden cumplir satisfactoriamente los objetivos que se proponen, a saber: la castellanización de los grupos indígenas de la República Mexicana, bien como tarea única y exclusiva, bien compartida con la alfabetización en lengua indígena o en español....[21]

La colección completa está integrada por 471 Cartillas y cuadernos de trabajo; 230 cuentos bilingües y 182 folletos bilingües, publicados entre los años 1935 y 1974, materiales que fueron reunidos de las siguientes instituciones: III, ILV, Instituto Nacional de Antropología e Historia, Instituto Nacional Indigenista y la Secretaría de Educación Pública, las cuales participaron en el proceso de elaboración de las cartillas. Entendemos que la colección que la BDCV posee es la más completa que existe ya que hicimos algunas búsquedas en catálogos de otras instituciones, incluido el Worldcat y notamos que faltan muchas de ellas.

En la elaboración de los materiales participaron instituciones nacionales y organismos internacionales, los textos de la colección están destinados a:

1. Alfabetización en lengua indígena: Pretenden enseñar a leer y escribir en lengua materna.

2. Alfabetización en lengua indígena y en español: Los materiales se inician con lecciones para alfabetizar en lengua indígena, posteriormente incluyen algunas lecciones en español.

3. Alfabetización en español y en lengua indígena: Pretenden alfabetizar primero en español y después en alguna lengua indígena

4. Alfabetización bilingüe: Se enseña a leer de manera simultánea en español y en lengua indígena.

5. Alfabetización trilingüe: Cartillas que pretenden alfabetizar en tres lenguas (p.e. mexicano, español e inglés)

6. Castellanización oral: Las cartillas y métodos pretenden enseñar oralmente el español.[22]

A partir de sus propósitos y características hemos integrado la siguiente tipología de las publicaciones que integran nuestra colección:

a) Pre-cartillas

Contenido: Incluyen palabras fundamentales del idioma que abordan, su propósito consiste en despertar el interés en leer y escribir entre los indígenas

Estructura: Divididas dos partes: 1) Se presentan palabras (esencialmente los nombres de animales) acompañadas de frases elementales, 2) Se incluyen los números con ejercicios para ejercitar su reconocimiento.

b) Cartillas

Contenido: Ofrecen elementos básicos para el aprendizaje de las lenguas nativas y el español, en caso de que se cuente con varias cartillas para una lengua específica, el contenido se complica paulatinamente y exige del estudiante mayor conocimiento de la lengua.

Estructura: En las cartillas se emplean cuatro tipos de materiales: 1) Cuadros fonéticos, para el repaso y ejercicios, 2) narraciones breves que tienen continuidad de pensamiento, con el propósito de estimular al alumno a leer comprensivamente, 3) figuras asociadas con palabras y frases con el propósito de introducir nuevas letras y nuevas combinaciones de letras, 4) Oraciones sin continuidad de pensamiento, para evaluar el grado de avance del alumno.

c) Cuadernos de trabajo

Contenido: Ofrecen ejercicios que complementan los que incluyen las cartillas.

Estructura: Los ejercicios están ordenados de acuerdo con una secuencia lógica en función de las lecciones de las cartillas.

d) Literatura: cuentos y relatos

Contenido: Narraciones y cuentos breves, relatados por hablantes nativos de las comunidades indígenas.

Estructura: Divididos en dos partes: 1) Texto en la lengua indígena, 2) texto en español.

e) Textos especiales

Contenido: Se refieren a asuntos específicos que los hablantes de lenguas indígenas deben conocer (p.e. los números, para reconocer las monedas y billetes, las unidades de peso y longitud—kilo, metro, vara, etc.—y ejercicios correspondientes).

f) Textos con fines informativos

Contenido: Textos que anuncian un acontecimiento específico que debe conocerse en el idioma nativo de alguna comunidad indígena (p.e. Campaña para la erradicación del paludismo).

Estructura: El texto se incluye en el idioma indígena y en español, se ofrece información específica sobre conceptos, procedimientos, fines y objetivos del tema en cuestión.

g) Manuales

Contenido: Ofrecen recomendaciones generales para mejorar las condiciones de los indígenas de diversas comunidades (p.e. mejoramiento de suelos de cultivo, prácticas de siembra y cultivo, etc.)

Estructura: El texto se incluye en el idioma indígena, se explican e ilustran las prácticas, procedimientos y técnicas del tema en cuestión.

h) Vocabularios

Contenido: Incluir únicamente las palabras más comunes que se encuentran en los idiomas a los que se refieren.

Estructura: Divididas en tres partes: 1) En orden alfabético las palabras en la lengua indígena y su correspondencia en español, 2) En orden alfabético las palabras en español y su correspondencia en la lengua indígena. 3) Apéndices: a) el alfabeto en la lengua indígena correspondiente, b) Notas sobre la gramática de la lengua en cuestión (pronombres, conjugación verbal, prefijos, etc.), c) Nombres de parentesco (mamá, papá, hermano, esposa, etc.).

A partir de lo anterior, se observa que los medios disponibles para la alfabetización son variados, se complementan y en varios casos permiten reconstruir imágenes de los grupos indígenas a que se refieren.

Consideraciones finales

1. La influencia que el ILV ha tenido a lo largo de su historia para el registro, sistematización, estudio y difusión de las lenguas indígenas de México es indudable.

2. La participación de los integrantes del ILV fue notable en el desarrollo de políticas públicas referentes a la alfabetización y castellanización de los grupos indígenas, particularmente entre 1940 y 1980.

3. En términos generales, se cuenta con estudios de prácticamente todas las lenguas indígenas habladas en nuestro país.

4. El ILV es la organización que ha desarrollado el más amplio programa relacionado con el estudio de las lenguas indígenas de nuestro país en todos los tiempos.

5. Además de los materiales para la alfabetización, el estudio de las lenguas indígenas se ha materializado en tesis doctorales, estudios comparativos entre las lenguas y artículos especializados.

6. Cabe destacar que el ILV tiene más de sesenta y cinco años ininterrumpidos de actividades en nuestro país, durante todo ese tiempo ha mantenido sus programas de investigación lingüística y publicación de resultados a través de diversos materiales.

7. Es posible acceder prácticamente a la totalidad de la producción bibliográfica del ILV a través de las Bibliografías que el propio organismo ha producido a lo largo de su historia, en total se cuenta con referencias de más de dos mil documentos.

NOTAS

1. Comisión Nacional para el Desarrollo de los Pueblos Indígenas, "Diversidad etnolingüística," Comisión Nacional para el Desarrollo de los Pueblos Indígenas, http://www.cdi.gob.mx/index.php?id_seccion=90 (consultado mayo 26, 2008).

2. Ibid.

3. Redactados por una comisión integrada para tal efecto por: Morris Swadesh, Wigberto Jiménez Moreno, Daniel F. Rubín de la Borbolla, Paul Kirchhoff, Ignacio M. del Castillo, William C Townsend (Fundador del Instituto Lingüístico de Verano, ILV), Juan Luna Cárdenas, Norman A. McQuown, Jorge A Vivó y Roberto J. Weitlaner.

4. Véase: *Memoria de la Primera Asamblea de Filólogos y Lingüistas* (México: Antigua Imprenta de E. Murguía, 1940), 83-84.

5. Cfr. "Consejo de lenguas Indígenas," *Boletín indigenista* 3, no. 3 (septiembre 1943): 184-186.

6. Publicada en: *Diario oficial de la federación*, agosto 23, 1944, segunda sección, 1-5.

7. *Diario oficial de la federación*, agosto 23, 1944, segunda sección, 3.

8. El texto completo del Programa se reproduce en: "El Instituto de Alfabetización en Lenguas Indígenas," *Boletín indigenista* 5, no. 2 (junio 1945): 172-180.

9. El alfabeto fue publicado en: *Memoria de la Primera Asamblea de Filólogos y Lingüistas*, 26.

10. Para tener una visión más amplia sobre la primera etapa de actividades del ILV en México, véase: Shirley Brice Heath, *La política del lenguaje en México* (México: Consejo Nacional para la Cultura y las Artes, Dirección General de Publicaciones: Instituto Nacional Indigenista, 1992) 151-180.

11. Jan Rus and Robert Wasserstrom, "Evangelización y control político: el Instituto Lingüístico de Verano en México," *Revista mexicana de ciencias políticas y sociales*, 25, no. 97 (julio-septiembre 1979): 143-144.

12. Gonzalo Aguirre Beltrán, "El Instituto lingüístico de Verano," *América indígena* 41, no. 3 (julio-septiembre 1981): 438-439.

13. Cfr. Cameron Townsend, "El Instituto Lingüístico de Verano," *Boletín indigenista* 4, no. 1 (marzo 1944): 46-52.

14. Ibid., 50.

15. Respecto de los trabajos de campo y la elaboración de las publicaciones se expresa en el convenio que serán gratuitos, por el contrario, los cursos especiales de capacitación lingüística para maestros rurales serán remunerados.

16. Para tener acceso al texto completo del Convenio véase: "El Instituto Lingüístico de Verano amplía sus actividades en México," *Boletín indigenista* 11, no. 4 (diciembre 1951): 332-339.

17. Cfr. Gloria Ruiz de Bravo Ahuja, Las cartillas, vol. 2 de Los materiales didácticos para la enseñanza del español a los indígenas mexicanos (México: Secretaría de Educación Pública, Dirección General de Divulgación, 1976), 25.

18. Para tener acceso a la producción bibliográfica del ILV véase: *Bibliografía del Instituto Lingüístico de Verano en México 1935-1984*, comp. María de Boe de Harris y Margarita H. de Daly (México: Instituto Lingüístico de Verano, 1985). *Bibliografía del Instituto Lingüístico de Verano en México 1985-1993*, comp. Kris Jones (Tucson: Instituto Lingüístico de Verano, 1995).

19. El decreto fue publicado en: *Diario oficial de la federación*, julio 28, 1960, 3. El plazo para la construcción del Centro fue de tres años, en virtud de no cumplirse la obra en dicho periodo, el 23 de abril de 1963, mediante otro decreto, el Gobierno ofreció una prorroga al Instituto para concluir la construcción, véase: *Diario oficial de la federación*, mayo 15, 1963, 5.

20. Gloria Ruiz de Bravo Ahuja, *Los materiales didácticos para la enseñanza del español a los indígenas mexicanos* (México: Secretaría de Educación Pública, Dirección General de Divulgación, 1976) 4 v. El contenido completo de la obra es el siguiente: v. 1. De la Conquista a la Revolución; v. 2. Las cartillas 1. Evaluación y crítica; v. 3. Las cartillas 2. Evaluación y crítica; v. 4. Propuesta de una planeación lingüística.

21. Gloria Ruiz de Bravo Ahuja, *Las cartillas*, vol. 2 de *Los materiales didácticos para la enseñanza del español a los indígenas mexicanos* (México: Secretaría de Educación Pública, Dirección General de Divulgación, 1976), 9.

22. Ibid., 16.

BIBLIOGRAFÍA

Aguirre Beltrán, Gonzalo. "El Instituto lingüístico de Verano." *América indígena* 41, no. 3 (julio-septiembre 1981): 438-439.

Bibliografía del Instituto Lingüístico de Verano en México 1935-1984. Compilado por María de Boe de Harris y Margarita H. de Daly. México: Instituto Lingüístico de Verano, 1985.

Bibliografía del Instituto Lingüístico de Verano en México 1985-1993. Compilado por Kris Jones. Tucson: Instituto Lingüístico de Verano, 1995.

Comisión Nacional para el Desarrollo de los Pueblos Indígenas. "Diversidad etnolingüística." Comisión Nacional para el Desarrollo de los Pueblos Indígenas. http://www.cdi.gob.mx/index.php?id_seccion=90 (consultado mayo 26, 2008).

"Consejo de lenguas Indígenas." *Boletín indigenista* 3, no. 3 (septiembre 1943): 184-186.

Diario oficial de la federación. Agosto 23, 1944.

Diario oficial de la federación. Julio 28, 1960.

Diario oficial de la federación. Mayo 15, 1963.

Heath, Shirley Brice. *La política del lenguaje en México.* México: Consejo Nacional para la Cultura y las Artes, Dirección General de Publicaciones: Instituto Nacional Indigenista, 1992.

"El Instituto de Alfabetización en Lenguas Indígenas." *Boletín indigenista* 5, no. 2 (junio 1945): 172-180.

"El Instituto Lingüístico de Verano amplía sus actividades en México." *Boletín indigenista* 11, no. 4 (diciembre 1951): 332-339.

Memoria de la Primera Asamblea de Filólogos y Lingüistas. México: Antigua Imprenta de E. Murguía, 1940.

Ochoa Zazueta, Jesús Angel. "El Instituto Lingüístico de Verano. Cuadernos de trabajo." *Estudios*, 11. México: Instituto Nacional de Antropología e Historia, Departamento de Etnología y Antropología Social, 1975.

Ruiz de Bravo Ahuja, Gloria. *Las cartillas.* Vol. 2 de *Los materiales didácticos para la enseñanza del español a los indígenas mexicanos.* México: Secretaría de Educación Pública, Dirección General de Divulgación, 1976.

Ruiz de Bravo Ahuja, Gloria. *Los materiales didácticos para la enseñanza del español a los indígenas mexicanos.* 4 vols. México: Secretaría de Educación Pública, Dirección General de Divulgación, 1976.

Rus, Jan and Robert Wasserstrom. "Evangelización y control político: el Instituto Lingüístico de Verano en México." *Revista mexicana de ciencias políticas y sociales* 25, no. 97 (julio-septiembre 1979): 143-144.

Townsend, Cameron. "El Instituto Lingüístico de Verano." *Boletín indigenista* 4, no. 1 (marzo 1944): 46-52.

14. A New World of Words: Amerindian Language Printing in the Colonial World

Daniel J. Slive

Introduction

This presentation is based on a gathering of approximately six hundred books from the colonial period in the Americas, containing Indian language material, held by the John Carter Brown (JCB) Library. The JCB Library is an outstanding collection of primary materials relating to virtually all aspects of the discovery, exploration, and colonization of the New World. From its beginnings in 1846, when the collector John Carter Brown began to focus on the early history of the Americas, the library has grown to include more than fifty thousand printed books, major holdings of maps and prints, and a large number of manuscript codices. While terminal collecting dates vary for different areas of the Western Hemisphere, the holdings range from the late fifteenth century to approximately 1825, when direct colonial European involvement in American affairs officially came to an end.

Reflecting the scope of the JCB, the majority of the Indian language material is printed (rather than in manuscript) and was published in both Europe and the Americas throughout the colonial period. The library's focus is concerned with the entire Western Hemisphere throughout this time period, and its Indian language holdings reflect this geographic and chronological range.

These works document the languages of some of the Amerindian populations in contact with Europeans during this era. The types of documentation include brief word lists, dictionaries, and grammars as well as texts translated into native languages found throughout the Americas. Not included are books that contain only single words mentioned in passing (such as "canoe" or "bar-b-q"). Works that contain only descriptions (but not documentation) of the languages (i.e., "the natives all speak sweetly") are not considered in this presentation either.

The difficulties of communicating across cultural, ideological, and linguistic boundaries played a role in relations between natives and Europeans throughout the colonial period. In addition to negotiating practical matters such as trade and the control of territory, Europeans also wished to communicate theological concepts for the purpose of converting Indians to Christianity. These various aspects of colonization contributed to the documentation and utilization of Indian languages in texts printed in both Europe and the Americas.

The early publication of Amerindian languages, often in the form of word lists and brief vocabularies, appeared in accounts of voyages and travels and other documents of colonial expansion. Initial word-gatherings were eventually expanded into more comprehensive vocabularies and dictionaries. Missionaries, who often spent years in a region learning the local language, collaborated with native speakers to create these dictionaries as well as grammars. These texts were intended to train others in the indigenous languages in which they would proselytize. In addition to language-learning tools, a variety of religious works were printed in Indian languages to assist in the conversion of indigenous peoples. A small number of secular texts, such as government documents, were also printed in selected native languages.

The creation, production, and utilization of these works represent a series of border-crossings and transformations as well as encounters, engagements, and exchanges. In addition to the primary geographic and linguistic borders between Europeans and natives, cultural, religious, and technological boundaries were also negotiated. The texts themselves represent a series of transliterations, translations, and transformations from oral, and previously non-alphabetic, language to written word in Roman alphabet to the printed page and the bound book created with European technology. The manner in which many of these works were utilized reflects yet another series of crossings as the printed texts were often read aloud to native speakers as part of the conversion process. Finally, the printing history of these books also reflects the transportation of European printing technology to the Americas as well as the movement of Amerindian languages back to Europe for press production there.

Note: The titles in the *citations* below are transcribed from the title pages of the original works, thus documenting the inconsistencies of the orthography and accentuation of the colonial period. However, typography and capitalization have been modernized. In the *descriptions* of the items, the spelling, accents, and capitals in the titles have been modernized.

I. First Impressions

The initial documentation of Amerindian Languages appeared in the form of brief word lists. These are most often found in various histories of the New World, descriptions of particular voyages, and chronicles by settlers, missionaries, and soldiers who spent time in the Americas.

1. Francisco de Xeréz. *Verdadera relacion de la conquista del Peru.* Seville, 1534.

Although not containing any word lists or other documentation of Amerindian languages, this book still serves as an appropriate introduction for this presentation. Its illustrated title page portrays the historic encounter between the Inca Atahualpa and the Spanish conquerors, led by Francisco

Pizarro. According to various chroniclers, the Inca Atahualpa was shown a copy of the Bible, with the explanation that it was the word of God. After examining the book but not "hearing" any words, the Inca summarily dismissed the book by throwing it on the ground in frustration. At that moment, the Spaniards attacked and captured Atahualpa, thus beginning the conquest of Peru. The image and the story symbolize the encounter, the conquest, and the multitude of cultural and linguistic misunderstandings that occured throughout the colonial period.

2. Pietro Martire d'Anghiera. *De orbe novo...decades*. Alcalá de Henares, 1516.

A member of the Council of the Indies and chronicler for the Spanish Crown, Pietro Martire d'Anghiera, known in English as Peter Martyr, produced the first official history of the New World. Appended to the 1516 edition, edited by the Renaissance humanist Antonio de Nebrija, is a five page "Vocabula Barbara" that includes words from the Antilles. (Nebrija also provided an appropriate quote for this presentation in his *Gramatica sobre la lengua castellana*, published in 1492, in which he wrote "language has always been the companion of empire.")

3. Antonio Pigafetta. *Le voyage et navigation, faict par les Espaignolz es Isles de Mollucques*. Paris, [ca. 1525].

Antonio Pigafetta's account of the Spanish expedition around the world from 1519 to 1522, under the command of Ferdinand Magellan, includes brief lists of words heard in Brazil and Patagonia.

4. Jean de Léry. *Histoire d'un voyage fait en la terre du Bresil, autrement dite Amerique*. La Rochelle, 1578.

French Calvinist minister Jean de Léry lived in the Rio de Janeiro area in 1556-1557 during an unsuccessful attempt at French colonization in Brazil. In his account of his experiences and observations is this colloquy between a Frenchman, newly arrived in Brazil, and a native. The dialogue serves as an introduction to the Tupi language, including basic grammatical rules and words and phrases useful for travelers. This is the first edition of his *Histoire*.

5. Alonso de Ercilla y Zúñiga. *Primera, segunda, y tercera partes de la Araucana*. Madrid, 1590.

Courtier and soldier Alonso de Ercilla y Zúñiga fought in the Spanish wars against the Araucanian Indians of Chile. His epic poem, *La Araucana*, records the history of these battles and the eventual defeat of the natives. In the preface to the first part, published in 1569, Ercilla explains particular terms "which because they are of Indian origin, are not well understood." In this Madrid 1590 edition, which incorporates all three parts of the poem, the poet expanded this small list into a glossary of "words and names, which although of indigenous origin, are heard and used so often in that region, that they have not been translated into Spanish."

6. Jacques Cartier. *Discours du voyage fait par le Capitaine Iaques Cartier aux Terres-neufues de Canadas, Norembergue, Hochelage, Labrador, & pays adiacens, dite nouuelle France, auec particulieres moeurs, langage, & ceremonies des habitans d'icelle.* Rouen, 1598.

This work includes a brief vocabulary of Iroquoian languages consisting of words for the numbers one through ten, human body parts, everyday objects, environmental phenomena, and practical phrases. It is appended to an account of Jacques Cartier's first voyage to New France in 1534, printed in Rouen in 1598. This French edition itself represents a series of translation processes, as the text was first published in Venice in 1556 as volume three of Ramusio's *Navigationi et viaggi.* That Italian translation had in turn been based on an unpublished French manuscript.

7. Pablo José de Arriaga. *Extirpacion de la idolatria del Piru.* Lima, 1621.

Pablo José de Arriaga, a Jesuit missionary, wrote about the eradication of idolatry in the Andes following his experiences as a *visitador*, investigating manifestations of indigenous worship. His manual, essentially a how-to book on finding and eradicating native religious activities, includes a glossary of sixty-four Quichua words with Spanish glosses, including terms and objects related to ritual practices.

8. William Wood. *New Englands prospect. A true, lively, and experimentall description of that part of America, commonly called New England.* London, 1634.

Intended to "enrich the knowledge of the mind-travelling Reader, or benefit the future Voyager," William Wood's *New Englands Prospect* was the first printed, detailed account of the geography and natives of Massachusetts. The five-page Massachuset vocabulary with English equivalents predates Roger Williams's *A Key into the Language of America* by nine years and John Eliot's "Indian Bible" by twenty-seven years, although both men may have assisted the author in the compilation of this "small nomenclator." Wood writes that "their language is hard to learn; few of the English being able to speak any of it, or capable of the right pronunciation, which is the chief grace of their tongue...They love any man that can utter his mind in their words, yet are they not a little proud that they can speake the English tongue, using it as much as their own, when they meet with such as can understand it, puzzling strange Indians, which sometimes visit them from more remote places, with an unheard language."

II. Dictionaries and Vocabularies

Expanding upon brief word lists, the next stage in the documentation of Amerindian languages was the creation of full-fledged dictionaries and vocabularies. These works were based on the collaboration of Europeans and Indians, although authorship is often given solely to the former. Such books were printed in the New World and in Europe.

9. Alonso de Molina. *Aqui comiença un vocabulario en la lengua castellana y mexicana*. Mexico, 1555.

The earliest printed dictionary of any Amerindian language, Alonso de Molina's vocabulary was printed in Mexico in 1555. Arranged alphabetically, it is translated from Spanish into "Mexicana" or Nahuatl, the language of the Aztecs. The author came to Mexico as a child soon after the Conquest and served as an interpreter between the first missionaries and the natives. In addition to this dictionary, he also wrote other works in Nahuatl, including a grammar, a *Confesionario breve*, a *Confessionario mayor*, and a *Doctrina christiana*.

10. Domingo de Santo Tomás. *Lexicon, o vocabulario de la lengua general del Peru*. Valladolid, 1560.

The earliest printed vocabulary for Quichua, the language of the Incas and the indigenous *lingua franca* of colonial Peru, was printed in Spain in 1560, as printing did not begin in Peru until 1584. Domingo de Santo Tomás was a Dominican priest and the first bishop of Charcas in Peru. The volume also contains his *Grammatica, o Arte de la lengua general de los Indios de los reynos del Perú*, the earliest published grammar of the Quichua language.

11. Gabriel Sagard. *Dictionaire de la langue huronne, necessaire à ceux qui n'ont l'intelligence d'icelle, & ont à traiter avec les sauvages du pays*. Paris, 1632.

The first printed Huron dictionary was issued as part of Gabriel Sagard's *Le grand voyage du pays des Hurons*, published in Paris in 1632. Sagard was a Recollect lay-brother who spent ten months in New France in 1624. His work is considered one of the most informative texts on the Huron language and a major source regarding the Recollect missions from 1615 to their expulsion from New France in 1629.

12. Roger Williams. *A key into the language of America: or, An help to the language of the natives in that part of America, called New-England*. London, 1643.

Roger Williams's *Key* is the earliest book devoted to an Amerindian language printed in English. It was also the first book published by Williams, the founder of Rhode Island. Dictionaries, vocabularies, grammars, and religious works had already been produced for the native languages of Spanish America and New France, but this was the first such book generated in the British colonies.

The phrase book is comprehensive in its treatment of Narragansett Indian life. Williams attempted to cover everything from the essentials of food, clothing, and shelter to customs, government, religion, commerce, and natural history. He observes in the section on travel that the Narragansetts "are joyfull in meeting of any in travell, and will strike fire either with stones or sticks, to take Tobacco, and discourse a little together."

13. Raymond Breton. *Dictionaire caraibe-françois, meslé de quantité de remarques historiques pour l'esclaircissement de la langue*. Auxerre, 1665.

14. Charles de Rochefort. *Histoire naturelle et morale des iles Antilles de l'Amerique . . . Avec un vocabulaire Caraïbe*. Rotterdam, 1658.

Raymond Breton, a French Dominican who served as a missionary on the island of Dominica, compiled this Carib-French dictionary, a small portion of which appeared earlier in a thirteen-page "Vocabulaire Caraïbe," published in Charles de Rochefort's *Histoire naturelle et morale des îles Antilles de l'Amérique . . . Avec un vocabulaire Caraïbe*. In the latter work, however, the words are arranged by subjects rather than alphabetically.

Bound with the JCB copy of Breton's Carib-French dictionary is his French-Carib dictionary of 1666. In addition, the Dominican wrote a catechism (1664) and a grammar (1667). All of these Carib language books were printed in Auxerre, France.

15. Antonio Ruiz de Montoya. *Vocabulario de la lengua guarani*. Santa María la Mayor, 1722.

This 1722 Guaraní vocabulary was printed by the Jesuits' mission press in Paraguay, which operated between 1700 and 1727. It was excerpted, with revisions, from the 1640 Madrid edition of Antonio Ruiz de Montoya's *Arte, y bocabulario de la lengua guaraní*. The mission press also published an edition of the author's *Arte de la lengua guaraní* in 1724. Here one can observe multiple instances of border crossings: the dictionary was created in the New World but the text was first printed in Europe. The actual books were transported to Paraguay, where they were reprinted on local presses using European technology that had also been shipped from the Old World to the New.

16. Johann Anderson. *Herrn Johann Anderson, I. V. D. und weyland ersten Bürgermeisters der Freyen Kayserlichen Reichsstadt Hamburg, Nachrichten von island, Grönland und der Strasse Davis*. Hamburg, 1746.

The appendix of this description of Iceland and Greenland consists of a brief vocabulary, a grammar, and some statements of Christian faith and prayers, all in Danish, German, and the Eskimo language (except for the grammar, which excludes Danish). The work was reprinted in German the following year and, by 1750, was also translated into Dutch, Danish, and French.

17. M. D. L. S. *Dictionnaire galibi, présenté sous deux formes: I. Commençant par le mot françois II. Par le mot Galibi. Precédé d'un essai de grammaire*. Paris, 1763.

Compiled chiefly from the manuscripts of the Jesuit Pierre Pelleprat, a missionary in Guiana, this 1763 Galibi dictionary is variously attributed to Simon Philibert de la Salle de L'Étang and Monsieur de la Sauvage. Earlier published Galibi vocabularies by Antoine Biet (1664) and Paul Boyer (1654) were also incorporated. It was issued as part of the Chevalier de Préfontaine's *Maison rustique*, a guide for successful emigration to Guiana, and also published as a separate work. The author expressed his confidence that the dictionary would be one of the "principal sources of success" for the colony. Note again that here the words are organized by subject ("Des Animaux") rather than in "purely alphabetical" order.

18. Jonathan Carver. *Travels through the interior parts of North America, in the years 1766, 1767, and 1768*. London, 1778.

In the chapter of Jonathan Carver's *Travels* entitled "Of their Language, Hieroglyphicks, &c," short vocabularies and numerical terms are given for the "Chipéway" and "Naudowessie" languages. The author, a British captain in the Seven Years War, claimed the former "appears to be the most prevailing [of the native languages of North America]; it being held in such esteem, that the chiefs of every tribe...speak this language alone in their councils, notwithstanding each has a peculiar one of their own." At least a dozen English editions—plus French, German, and Dutch translations—of Carver's *Travels* were published before 1800.

III. Grammars and Instructions

An additional element in the documentation and teaching of indigenous languages was the creation of grammars. These most often were produced in the style of Latin grammars then in use in Europe. Early on, many of the European authors expressed their awareness of the limits of this format for explaining such radically different, non-European, languages. However, the motivation to train missionaries in these languages as quickly as possible took precedence over their desire to explain the nuances of exotic languages. It should also be noted, however, that many of the authors, once reasonably fluent, were responsible for the creation of works in other genres, including dictionaries and doctrinal works.

19. Maturino Gilberti. *Arte de la le[n]gua de Michuaca[n]*. Mexico, 1558.

20. Maturino Gilberti. *Dialogo de doctrina christiana enla lengua d[e] Mechuaca[n]*. Mexico, 1559.

The first printed grammar of a Native American language was Maturino Gilberti's *Arte de la le[n]gua de Michuaca[n]*, published in Mexico in 1558. The author was born in France, ordained a Franciscan priest in 1531, and arrived in New Spain in 1542. In addition to this grammar, he also wrote a Spanish-Tarascan/Tarascan-Spanish dictionary and several doctrinal and devotional works in the same language, including his *Dialogo de doctrina christiana* printed in 1559. The language of Michuacan has been called "Tarascan" since the sixteenth century, but those who speak it today prefer to call it "Purepecha."

21. Luis de Valdivia. *Doctrina christiana y cathechismo en la lengua allentiac, que corre en la ciudad de S. Iuan de la Frontera, con un confessonario, arte, y bocabulario breves*. Lima, 1607.

In addition to publishing numerous works in Nahuatl and Quichua, printers in Mexico and Peru also published works for the conversion of natives who lived beyond the borders of the former Aztec and Inca empires. For the Allentiac language of the Cuyo region of Argentina, the Jesuit Luis de Valdivia wrote one of the few studies ever made of the language, accompanied by a short vocabulary, confession, catechism, and Christian doctrine.

22. Melchor Oyanguren de Santa Inés. *Arte de la lengua japona*. Mexico, 1738.

The publication of language-learning materials in Mexico extended beyond locally spoken dialects to include this 1738 grammar printed for missionaries preparing to work in Japan. Not having access to oriental typefaces, the authors and printers reproduced the Japanese words phonetically using Roman type.

23. Ildefonso José Flores. *Arte de la lengua metropolitana del reyno Cakchiquel o Guatemalico*. Antigua, 1753.

Authors of Amerindian grammars often remarked that the sounds of the native languages could not be adequately conveyed using standard Roman typefaces. In his Cakchikel grammar, printed in Guatemala in 1753, Flores attempted to introduce additional symbols to convey the proper pronunciation.

24. Horacio Carochi. *Compendio del arte de la lengua mexicana*. Mexico, 1759.

This second, abridged edition of Carochi's Nahuatl grammar includes additions by Ignacio de Paredes, a sometime superior of the Jesuit seminary at Tepotzotlán and rector of the college of San Andrés in Mexico. The copperplate engraving of St. Ignatius of Loyola instructing the peoples of the world also served as the frontispiece to Paredes's own 1759 *Promptuario manual mexicano*, a work containing fifty-two sermons and forty moral discussions in Nahuatl.

25. John Eliot. *The Indian grammar begun; or, An essay to bring the Indian language into rules: for the help of such as desire to learn the same, for the furtherance of the Gospel among them...* Cambridge, [Mass.], 1666.

With the assistance of a native interpreter, John Eliot wrote this introductory grammar to the Massachuset language for the officers of The Society or Company for the Propagation of the Gospel in New England and the Parts Adjacent in America. It was published in Cambridge, Massachusetts in 1666. The printer, Marmaduke Johnson, was also involved in the production of the New Testament (1661) and the Old Testament (1663) in the same native language. He was assisted by an Indian known as James Printer, whose knowledge of Massachuset clearly contributed to the production of these works.

26. David Zeisberger. *Essay of a Delaware-Indian and English spelling-book, for the use of the schools of the Christian Indians on Muskingum River*. Philadelphia, 1776.

Born in Moravia in 1721, Zeisberger served as a missionary in North America from 1740 until his death in 1808. In addition to this introduction to the Delaware language, he also produced a trilingual dictionary in German, English, and Delaware. Zeisberger expressed dissatisfaction with this publication of his work as four articles in his original manuscript (including reading lessons, conjugation examples, the Delaware numbers, and a short history of the Bible) were omitted and apparently replaced with the Lord's Prayer, the Ten Commandments, and a short litany, all in Delaware and English.

27. Daniel Claus. *A primer for the use of the Mohawk children*. London, 1786.

After introducing alphabets and vocabularies, the remainder of Claus's Mohawk primer is devoted to Christian doctrine and prayers, with the English and Mohawk languages on opposite pages. The engraved frontispiece depicting Indian children in a classroom represents the intention of the work as stated on the title page: "To acquire the spelling and reading of their own, as well as to get acquainted with the English tongue." This second edition was printed in London in 1786, five years after the first edition was published in Montreal. Claus, Deputy Superintendent of Indian Affairs in Canada for the British government, also translated *The Order for Morning and Evening Prayer, and Administration of the Sacraments, and some other Offices of the Church of England* into Mohawk.

IV. Sacred Texts and Doctrinal Works

For the missionaries, the goal of these linguistic labors was the translation of sacred texts and doctrinal works into the native languages and their dissemination in printed form. As with the grammars and dictionaries, it is important to recall the role that bilingual native translators played in the creation of these texts. It should also be noted that the transformation of these texts continued after publication as these books were often read aloud to others as part of the conversion effort, rather than silently to oneself.

28. Juan de la Cruz. *Doctrina christiana en la lengua guasteca co[n] la lengua castellana*. Mexico, 1571.

29. Pedro de Feria. *Doctrina christiana en lengua castellana y çapoteca*. Mexico, 1567.

Juan de la Cruz's 1571 *Doctrina christiana* is the most profusely illustrated book printed in Mexico in the sixteenth century. The text contains seventy-three separate woodcuts, some used multiple times to bring the total number of illustrations to 140. Nearly all of the illustrations had been used previously, either in Maturino Gilberti's 1558 *Thesoro* [sic] *spiritual en lengua de mechuaca[n]* or Pedro de Feria's 1567 *Doctrina christiana en lengua castellana y çapoteca*. Created expressly for this work, however, were the woodcuts of hands. The insertion of various type-printed labels on the fingers allowed this mnemonic device to be used throughout the book to assist the teaching of religious concepts such as the Sacraments, the Seven Deadly Sins, and the Ten Commandments.

30. Catholic Church. Province of Lima. Concilio Provincial (1583). *Confessionario para los curas de Indios*. Ciudad de los Reyes [Lima], 1585.

31. Catholic Church. Province of Lima. Concilio Provincial (1583). *Tercero cathecismo y exposicion de la doctrina christiana, por sermones*. Ciudad de los Reyes [Lima], 1585.

This 1585 trilingual *Confessionario*, written by order of the Provincial Council of Lima of 1583, was the second book printed in Lima. Written in Spanish, Quichua, and Aymara, it provided missionaries with texts enabling them to conduct confessions in two of the languages spoken in the Inca Empire. The JCB copy is bound with two other early trilingual religious works: *Tercero cathecismo y exposición de la doctrina christiana, por sermones* (Lima, 1585) and *Doctrina christiana* (Lima, 1584). Especially notable is the typographical layout involved in accommodating three languages on each page.

32. Bernardino de Sahagún. *Psalmodia christiana*. Mexico, 1583.

Four Nahua scholars assisted the Franciscan Bernardino de Sahagún in producing this hymnal. Printed in 1583, it is the only Nahuatl songbook printed in Mexico during the colonial period. The hymns were mostly derived from the liturgy and the lives of the saints. The native assistants' participation included translating texts from Spanish and Latin, refining the friar's Nahuatl, and typesetting. Here again one can appreciate the use of visual images, as well as language, to assist the missionaries' program of teaching and conversion.

33. Juan Pérez Bocanegra. *Ritual formulario, e institucion de curas, para administrar a los naturales de este reyno*. Lima, 1631.

Included in Pérez Bocanegra's *Ritual formulario* is an engraved kinship diagram of the Inca genealogical system indicating the general rules for both acceptable and prohibited marriages: relatives may marry only at the generation of great-great-grandchildren. While representing native Andean concepts and terms, the shape and form of this diagram (without the specific Quichua terminology) may also have been based on medieval European traditions for constructing genealogical models. This bilingual manual for priests administering to Indian populations in the Andes includes instructions on conducting baptisms, confirmations, the Eucharist, and confessions.

34. Lodovico Vincenzo Mamiani della Rovere. *Catecismo da doutrina christãa na lingua brasilica da nação kiriri*. Lisbon, 1698.

In addition to narrative texts, dramatic and musical performances were also found by the missionaries to be useful teaching tools. These songs in the Kariri language of Brazil were intended for native choirboys. This catechism also includes essential teachings and prayers such as the Ten Commandments, the Pater Noster, and the Ave Maria. The text, presented in Kariri and Portuguese in parallel columns, had to be printed in Lisbon, as printing was not established in Brazil until the early nineteenth century.

35. Bible. Massachuset. Eliot. 1663. *Mamusse wunneetupanatamwe Up-Biblum God*. Cambridge, [Mass.], 1663.

The Society for the Propagation of the Gospel amongst the Indians in New England was responsible for one of the landmarks of early printing in the British colonies. The "Eliot Indian Bible," completed in Cambridge in 1663, was the first Bible printed in the New World, and the first example of the translation and printing of the entire Bible into a new language (Massachuset) as a means of evangelism. Eliot had previously produced the New Testament in the Massachuset tongue, also printed in Cambridge in 1661. In all of these achievements he had the assistance of native translators.

36. Martin Luther. *Lutheri Catechismus, öfwersatt på American-Virginiske Språket*. Stockholm, 1696.

Martin Luther's *Der kleine Catechismus* was translated into the Delaware, or Lénni-Lenâpé, language by the Swedish missionary Johan

Campanius and edited by his grandson Thomas Campanius Holm, the first historian of New Sweden. The work was printed in Stockholm in 1696 at royal expense, expressly for the purpose of converting the Amerindian population. In addition to the religious teachings, the volume also includes a glossary of Delaware words.

37. José Agustín Aldama y Guevara. *Alabado en lengua mexicana*. Mexico, 1755.

While many major products of the colonial press have been discussed, other less imposing works were also printed in indigenous languages. One example is this broadside. Printed in Nahuatl in Mexico in 1755, it is a religious hymn that honors the Virgin of Guadalupe, the story of whose apparition aided friars throughout the colonial period in their attempts to convert the native populations. The author also compiled a synthesis of earlier Nahuatl grammars, entitled *Arte de la lengua mexicana*, published in Mexico in 1754.

38. Church of England. *The Book of Common Prayer, and administration of the sacraments...Translated into the Mohawk language*. London, 1787.

The first translation into Mohawk of *The Book of Common Prayer* was printed in New York in 1715, with later editions appearing in 1769 and 1780. This first illustrated edition, printed in parallel Mohawk and English, was revised by Daniel Claus, Deputy Superintendent of Indian Affairs in Canada for the British government, and printed in London in 1787 for the Society for the Propagation of the Gospel. In addition to the frontispiece of George III's reception of the Mohawk delegation to London, the volume contains eighteen engravings depicting biblical themes.

V. Secular Texts

While the great majority of religious texts, vocabularies, and grammars were produced with missionary motives in mind, some secular works in indigenous languages were also printed during the colonial period.

39. Provincias Unidas del Río de la Plata. Asamblea General Constituyente (1813-1815). *Decreto. La Asamblea general sanciona el decreto expedido por la Junta Provisional Gubernativa....*Buenos Aires, 1813.

This remarkable quadrilingual document of Argentina's General Assembly ratifies the September 1, 1811 decree of the Junta Provisional Gubernativa that freed the Indians from church-related tributes and *encomienda* and *mita* obligations. It is printed in double-column format on two sides in Spanish, Aymara, Quichua, and Guaraní.

40. Francisco Xavier Venégas. *Don Francisco Xavier Venégas de Saavedra... Ayamo moyolpachihuitia in Totlatocatzin rey D. Fernando VII....*Mexico, 1810.

In 1810, the government printed a broadside in Nahuatl declaring the cessation of tribute payments by the Indians of Mexico to the King of Spain. The decree was enacted in reaction to the Hidalgo revolt of 1810, which had wide support among the native population.

Conclusion

In this presentation, a wide variety of printed works that include Amerindian languages have been discussed. These range from the briefest of word lists to full-fledged dictionaries, grammars, Bibles, and doctrinal works. These printed works not only document—admittedly through a series of transliterations, translations, and inevitable transformations—indigenous languages as spoken centuries ago, but they also serve as evidence of the very real interaction and communication between Europeans, colonists, and the indigenous peoples throughout the Americas in the colonial period.

Finally, for more information on the Amerindian language sources at the John Carter Brown Library, please see the online database available at http://www.brown.edu/Facilities/John_Carter_Brown_Library/ildb/index.php (Website accessed November 11, 2011.)

Interpreters, Translators, and Collectors

15. Interpreting the Interpreters: Worlds Regarding One Another
Frances Karttunen

At the beginning of it all, Christopher Columbus wrote:

> I do not know the language, and the people of these lands do not under-
> stand me nor I them, nor does anyone on board. And these Indians whom
> I took along I often misunderstood, taking one thing for the opposite, and
> I don't trust them much, for many times they have tried to flee.

Coming up to 1992, as many nations, institutions, scholars, and non-
scholars were exploring ways to commemorate the 500th anniversary of
Columbus's first voyage, I began to write *Between Worlds: Interpreters,
Guides, and Survivors*. The book was my own assay in understanding the
motivation and the experience of individuals who have done the very first
knitting of seams between mutually uncomprehending groups of people.

The newcomers who burst on the scene were, most often, military men,
entrepreneurs, and missionaries—and often an amalgam of all these things.
Most were motivated by a desire to acquire something: material wealth or
souls. Some, against their better judgment, were intellectually voracious.
(Here I think of Fray Bernardino de Sahagún in particular, who late in life
found himself excommunicated because of the immense project he oversaw to
document Aztec culture.)

Rarely have newcomers benefited the peoples they have encountered.
(The descendants of those so "discovered" rightly protest that their ancestors
had been there all along, and they and their world were certainly not "new.")
Newcomers inevitably upset the local ecology, both biological and social.
They bring with them alien pathogens. Most bring violence. (Here I think not
only of pervasive sexual violence toward women, but also, specifically, of the
devastating psychological violence perpetrated against the Maya of Yucatan by
Fray [later Bishop] Diego de Landa—as just one egregious example.)

Yet newcomers—invaders, evangelists, investigators—inevitably, then
and now, find mediators: individuals who function as conduits of information
between themselves and the people with whom they want and need to
communicate.

Why would anyone assume such a role? Often the choice is not theirs.

191

In "Interpreters Snatched from the Shore," an essay I wrote for a conference at the John Carter Brown Library, I examined the experiences of individuals kidnapped into "total immersion" in European languages in order to be rendered bilingual and ultimately to serve as interpreters. Many shared the unfortunate experience of Pocahontas. After being presented in European royal courts and shown all about, they took sick and died before they could be returned across the Atlantic. And so the investment in them was lost.

Of the group of Tainos taken by Columbus all the way to Barcelona for presentation at court and baptism, only four made the return trip to Hispaniola. Three disappear from the records upon arrival, leaving just one to serve as an active interpreter.

Gaspar Corte-Real and Estevão Gomes shipped men and women from the northeast quadrant of North America to Lisbon, and Jacques Cartier took ten to France, where they all died. Of some sixty indigenes taken from the coast of what is now South Carolina to labor on the encomienda of don Lucas Vásquez de Ayllón on Hispaniola, one of them beat the odds with respect to disease and survived three years in Spain while serving as personal servant to don Lucas.

A young man from the coast of Virginia was taken first to Mexico City, where he received the viceroy's own name in baptism (Luis de Velasco), and then to Spain, and finally made it back home.

Tisquantum (whom we know as "Squanto," the helper of the Plymouth Rock Pilgrims) was a survivor returnee as well. An English captain, Thomas Hunt, had carried him off to be sold in Spain. When that scheme was thwarted, Tisquantum somehow made his way to London, where he lived for several years. Having acquired fluency in English, he embarked on a voyage back home only to find all his people dead of an epidemic that had spread, apparently, from European fishermen working the New England Coast.

Transported involuntarily across the Atlantic, these were the first Americans to have a look at Europe. They did not leave written accounts of their impressions, but for those who survived the experience, we do have some record of their behavior.

Squanto, finding himself utterly alone in his devastated land, attached himself to the Pilgrims soon after their arrival and put them in touch with Samoset, another English-speaking local. Tisquantum himself did not long survive his partnership with the germy Pilgrims.

Pocahontas, taken into custody by the Jamestown colonists, accepted conversion to Christianity, married an Englishman, bore him a son, and became a sort of Elizabethan trophy wife before she died waiting for her ship to clear the Thames on the way back to Virginia.

The servant of don Lucas Vásquez de Ayllón gained the trust of his master, was baptized with the name Francisco de Chicora, and gave every evidence of being a sincere Christian as well as an apt learner of Spanish.

Taken back to his native shore to serve as a trusted interpreter, he fled within days.

In Spain, Luis de Velasco (not the viceroy) testified fervently to the richness of his homeland and the spiritual hunger of his people. Taken at his word, he was attached to a group of Jesuit missionaries, and off they went. Greeted by his kin as one returned from the dead, Luis abandoned his duties to the Jesuits, returned to his own people, and ultimately—exasperated by the missionaries' importuning—led a party against the mission and did the Jesuits in. It is thought he may have been the same man as Opechancanough, an elder statesman of the Powhatans, who as a rather old man led two massacres of English would-be colonizers in Virginia.

Again and again in cases of coerced interpreters, we see individuals struggling to stay alive and to acquire the skills necessary to getting themselves back home. To some extent doña Marina ("la Malinche") falls into this pattern. Already involuntarily held by the Chontal Maya, she was given by the Chontales to Hernán Cortés in a group of women as part of a bribe to get Cortés to go after the Aztec ruler Moteuczomatzin (whom we know as Montezuma) and leave the Chontales alone. When Marina's valuable multilingualism was demonstrated a short time later, Cortés took her under his personal protection, and they became partners in negotiating what became the Conquest of Mexico.

From a Mexican post-colonial perspective, the issue became one of collusion of an indigenous woman with a male invader, and the whole concept of *malinchismo* took root. In both *Between Worlds* and in an essay "Rethinking Malinche" in the volume *Indian Women of Early Mexico*, I have explored the sources that might shed light on what happened in the 1520s and how the notion of Marina as *La Llorona*—a dangerous Lilith/Medea figure, as well as a sell-out—developed.

It seemed to me that everything that could be said about the topic had been said, but recently Camilla Townsend has added some sources I did not consult and has produced a book-length treatment of Marina with somewhat different interpretations of Marina's collusion.

The issue here is when interpreters apparently volunteer their services to outsiders, often to the real or perceived detriment to their own people. I have written of a number of such cases in *Between Worlds*, showing that often—as in the cases of Squanto in New England and Ishi of California, to name but two—the partnership has come about when there is little or nothing left of the interpreter's own community. It is a choice of a single desperately lonely individual finding an interested supporter.

Another factor driving individuals into the camp of outsiders is social marginality. Doña Marina may be a case in point. She was undoubtedly marginalized through having been handed on to the Chontales and then to the Spaniards, but toward the end of my essay in *Indian Women of Early Mexico*, I raise the possibility that already as a child, a temperamentally poor fit with uncompromising Nahua social roles for young noblewomen may have been the motivating factor in her initial abandonment. She may have been too gifted for her own good.

Another case in point is the Wampanoag preacher Hiacoomes, who served as interpreter for missionary Thomas Mayhew on Martha's Vineyard. Hiacoomes was also a notably gifted individual but of low social status in the island's native society. Mayhew and his associates, using John Elliot's primer for teaching reading and writing in the "Massachusett" language, discovered in Hiacoomes such an adept pupil that they put him in charge of teaching reading and writing to his fellow Wampanoag. Soon he became a powerful preacher and evangelist in his own right, a man who rose high above his station by virtue of his contact with the outsiders.

There was a price to be paid for such advancement. One was suspicion on the part of people like Columbus who were dependent on the interpreters. Writing of the suspicion with which the Spanish in Yucatan regarded men like their "interpreter general" Gaspar Antonio Chi, Nancy Farriss writes:

> If the Spanish were not prepared to grant full equality to talented Maya nobles…they were wise to see the risks in granting them the semblance of it. For if such men ceased to think of themselves fully as Indians, yet were not accepted as Spaniards, their equivocal social identity and sense of frustration would simply make them more likely to challenge the system, and their understanding of Spanish ways would make the challenge that much more dangerous.

When newly independent Mexico needed a scapegoat for centuries of colonization, who better than Marina, who had the "advantages" of being a woman, an Indian, and dead? And so in a wink she became sexualized and trivialized as a doxy who could not get enough of foreign men.

The notion of *malinchismo* continues unabated in literature, theater, and art. It has even raised its head, oddly enough, in a review of *Between Worlds*, in which the reviewer complained that I had devoted the first half of the book to a boringly minute examination of Marina's life and career. In fact, the chapter about Marina is just one of nine career biographies of interpreters in the book. These chapters average 25 pages apiece, and Marina's chapter is 22 pages long. And yet she was perceived as taking over the book, crowding out the other interpreters, women and men, who shared the pages with her.

One of my frustrations during the Columbian Quincentenary was the plethora of books and articles whose titles would lead one to expect that they were about indigenous peoples, but whose substance was in fact what Europeans thought about indigenous peoples. It is easy to see how this comes about. European written sources are very rich and accessible. Ethnohistorical sources for the Americas are truly challenging and require research skills beyond what have been part and parcel of training in history and literature.

Some of the indigenes the Europeans encountered had writing systems of their own, and soon after contact many of these peoples acquired alphabetic writing and used it to keep profuse records. Although there was a strong Mesoamerican and Andean tradition of record-keeping, however, there is no surviving evidence of a tradition of contemplative, self-reflective writing. Few are the journals—whether in indigenous languages or in Spanish, French, or English—recording what the interpreters thought of their experiences. (Guaman Poma de Ayala's sustained howl of anguish for the Andeans and for himself seems exceptional, but there is considerable uncertainty about who he actually was.)

In *Between Worlds*, through an understanding of their backgrounds, their behavior as far as we know about it, and how they were represented both by the Europeans and by their own peoples, I made my best effort to intuit what it must have been like for the interpreters of whom I wrote. Still, I am well aware that my effort was just one more interpretation, albeit the best I could synthesize from sources less exploited in the past.

Today there is a scholarly generation that has acquired heretofore unimagined skills in indigenous languages of the Americas. To them I wish to express my appreciation. Many of them are on the program of this meeting.

Yesterday was a rich day. There are two more rich days ahead. I wish I could be in two or three places at once to hear them all. We have a wonderful feast spread before us. Let us get on with it.

Thank you.

Note: By the way, after "Interpreters Snatched from the Shore" was published in the volume *The Language Encounter in the Americas, 1492 to 1800*, I received a message from my colleague, the late William Sturdevant of the Smithsonian Institution, that he had previously published a paper about these same individuals as the first New World tourists in Europe. Bill was very kind about my unwittingly following in his footsteps.

16. A Late Encounter: The Unusual Friendship between Percy Bigmouth and Martha Gene Neyland Revealed through Letters and Stories during the 1940s

Paulita Aguilar
Claire-Lise Bénaud

Seeking relief from the Texas heat, Martha Gene Neyland, like many Texans, spent her summers in Ruidoso. Nestled high in the mountains of Southern New Mexico, Ruidoso is surrounded by the Lincoln National Forest, providing opportunities for hiking, backpacking, horseback riding, and camping in terrain that ranges from the easily accessible to remote and rugged wilderness. It is there that Gene, as she is known, spent many summers during the late 1930s and early 1940s, with her mother and aunt who owned a cabin in the area.

During those summers, Gene's mother would rent her a horse from Wendell's Stable for the season and she rode almost every day. At least twice a week, Gene would ride to the top of Mount Baldy, also called Sierra Blanca. This mountain is 12,000 feet high and inside the Mescalero Apache Indian Reservation. All riders going to Baldy had to check in and out at the ranger station staffed by the Mescaleros. The forest ranger all those years was Percy Bigmouth. Since she had to sign in and out on each ride, Percy and Gene became well acquainted and this grew into a lasting friendship. Percy wrote her letters in the off season and sent her stories recounting Native American myths.

There is conflicting information about Percy's birth date. Various documents state that he was born either in 1891 or 1892, with one census record stating that he was born in Otero County, New Mexico, as late as 1897. He would have been 45 or 50 years old when he befriended Gene, who appears to be a young teenager in the photographs. These two unlikely people, with their vastly different backgrounds and age difference, struck a friendship that lasted for many years. The record of the friendship consists of several letters Percy wrote to Gene. They culminate with Percy's hand-written stories of Lipan legends and history in November 1948, after Gene's marriage to Jackson Harris, a physician.

Morris Opler, in his book *Myths and Legends of the Lipan Apache Indians*, published in 1940, writes that telling stories is not just about the telling of them, but is also a ceremony not to be taken lightly. He writes, "The narrating of myths was a vital and serious undertaking invading the boundaries of social organization and ceremonial life." So, why did Percy relate these stories to a non-Indian—and a young girl, for that matter? In one his letters, he writes that he is trying to preserve the stories of his people since the young people of his tribe have no interest in them. It is difficult to determine why Percy selected Gene, especially when some of the stories are sensitive, like the emergence of the Lipan people myth.

Percy Bigmouth, half Lipan, half Mescalero, lived on the Mescalero Apache Indian Reservation. This reservation was originally established on May 27, 1873 by Executive Order of President Ulysses S. Grant and was first located near Fort Stanton, New Mexico. It was relocated to Mescalero in 1883, and covers 463,000 acres between the White and Sacramento mountains. The Lipan Apaches from northwest Chihuahua, Mexico were brought to the United States around 1903 and placed on the Mescalero Reservation. In 1913, almost 200 members of the Chiricahua and Warm Springs bands of Apaches who had been held as military prisoners since the capture of Geronimo were moved from Fort Sill, Oklahoma to this reservation. The population at the time the reservation was established was about 400, but by now exceeds 3,300 enrolled members of the tribe. The Lipan and Chiricahua bands became members of the Mescalero Apache when the tribe was organized formally in 1936 under provisions of the Indian Reorganization Act.[1]

Percy's letters, along with four photographs and stories, were donated to the University of New Mexico Center for Southwest Research by Gene Neyland in 2006 (Percy Bigmouth Collection, MSS 779 BC).

Photographs

There are four photographs in the collection, all black and white.

The back of the one is inscribed in pencil with "Year 1940 by Percy BM" in Percy Bigmouth's handwriting. Inscribed in pen is "Ranger cabin, Gene on right, all wearing Percy's war bonnets, on left Travis Brown" in someone else's handwriting, perhaps Gene Neyland's. Percy took the group photograph and sent it to Gene. An unidentified woman may be Gene's mother or aunt. There is no mention of Travis Brown in Percy Bigmouth's letters. The three of them stand next to their horse and "play Indians." They wear Indian headdresses. The photograph is taken in front of the ranger cabin on a sunny day and has a dude ranch feel to it. Like many tourists visiting New Mexico, a state populated with several Indian tribes, the Neyland family participated in the myth of the West, dressed up as Indians, and rode Indian paint ponies. This was a popular era for western wear when children played "cowboys and Indians." Percy Bigmouth lent headdresses to tourists for photo opportunities.

Another photograph is inscribed with "Gene with Percy's war bonnet." It was taken the same day as the group picture in the summer of 1940.

The back of this photograph is inscribed with "Percy Bigmouth" and is not dated. Percy Bigmouth is wearing a war bonnet with modern pants, shirt, and cardigan. A third photograph is not inscribed. Percy stands in front of a tent (maybe a tepee) whose stakes show. His ornate shirt has rosettes on the shoulders, fringe, and white beadwork on the front.

Correspondence

The collection contains four letters written by Percy to Gene. Gene's letters are probably lost but we know that she wrote to him because he mentions it. These letters—it is not known if Percy wrote more letters and if Gene Neyland only kept these few—span nine years, from 1940 to 1949. Percy wrote with a pencil on lined Big Chief paper. The text is written as a single block, with no paragraphs, even when the letter is lengthy. The narrative takes the form of a spoken conversation. Percy signed his name Bigmouth, as one word. Despite his lack of schooling, Percy is a good writer. He brings up many topics, including his friendship with Gene, his life as a ranger, how he spent the holidays, his family, his hunting adventures, and his schooling.

Friendship

He writes about his friendship with Gene, which began when she was a young teenager and continued after she got married. He reminisces about the time they spent together and he tells her how he misses her.

"I didn't think I miss you, but I sure do." Letter dated Sept. 9, 1940

He signs his letters affectionately: "Yours truly compadre," "Yours truly friend," "Your Indian friend," and "Yours truly Indian friend." Because he writes during the off-season, he mentions how quiet things are at the ranger station and he shares his loneliness:

"And I had missing lot of my friends. Used to come up and visit me." Letter dated November 29, 1949

Life as a Ranger

It is evident that Percy enjoys the natural beauty of the land. He also enjoys hunting. This part of New Mexico has elk, mule deer, antelope, and sheep. He speaks of Indian boys having a grand time hunting for antelope, deer, and turkey. In a letter dated October 4, 1940, he describes the darting antelopes:

Right now they are out hunting antelope, on the Eastern part of the Indian Reservation. They have a grand time out there, they told me, the antelope running that way, some of them this way, just can't tell which way they going to shoot, though just for six days for the antelope season.

Schooling

He also discusses his education, gives advice to Gene, and tells her how he regrets not having enough schooling.

"Well Gene do your level best, while you are young, and study your hard good lesson, throw it on your strong shoulder, and reach for the top, push your class aside and be on ahead of them." Letter dated April 24, 1947

Percy is aware that he is writing a young girl who is still in school, and he encourages her to do well. He is able to adapt the level of his discourse to that of a school child. Maybe because he had no children of his own, Percy acted in a fatherly way. Even though his schooling was short, Percy's penmanship is beautiful. Gene Neyland says he learned it in Indian School—Percy says he went to school in Mescalero. And of course, Percy brings up a time-honored topic–the weather—in his letters.

"The days are getting cool, few people are around." Letter dated Sept. 9, 1940

"No rain, no thunder to scare, everything peaceful." Letter dated October 4, 1940

Lipan Mythology

Percy's stories, like his letters, are written in pencil on lined paper on Big Chief tablets. In his letter dated April 24, 1947, he mentions sending his stories to Gene.

"Your delightful letter had reach me, just two month ago, and happy to learn that you enjoyed my Indian story. Some of these fine days I'll try to add some more, if you say so. I'll be very happy to do that for you, since I know you for quiet [sic] a while." Letter dated April 24, 1947

Percy wrote these stories on three tablets over 2 years, from 1947 to 1949. The tablets are labeled: no. 1: Coyote Story; no. 2: Coyote Story; and, no. 3: Comanche and Lipan. The stories are quite lengthy, and range from 34 to 38 pages. Most Native American tribes do not have a written language; they passed on their histories orally from one generation to the next. Some non-Indians do not find the oral tradition credible. However, the oral tradition is as accurate as the written American history. Eve Ball,[2] who is known for her recording of Mescalero Apache oral history, noted that those who follow an oral tradition often had better memories than others who have a written tradition.[4] She also notes that Apache people were trained to memorize because lives often depended on accurately relating messages. Thrapp, in the preface to Ball's book, *Indeh*, also confirms that "it was through trained memories that the culture history of the People most frequently was passed from generation to generation."[4] Stories, myths, and legends are more than just stories; they are the history of a people and the truth as they know it.

Like the Jicarilla Apaches, the Lipan have a myth of emergence. In the beginning, the people—four-legged, two-legged, winged, rocks, and trees—lived in the underworld. A council was formed to determine where the people should move. Finally, they moved to the upper world, and "real humans" came after the animals, trees and plants. Lipan mythology includes a hero, called Killer-of-Enemies, who slays the enemies of the race and fights monsters, particularly the monster known as Big Owl.

Lipan mythology also includes the Coyote cycle. For practical instruction, Lipan stories teach the young and reinforce how a "good person" should behave. The stories give examples of the good as well as the bad. Examples of the bad are often about the tricks that Coyote plays on others and how the tables ultimately turn on him. These stories also explain why people act the way they do today. In Percy's own words in the introductory letter to the *Coyote 2* tablet:

> It's a night story you see, we don't have no written story like the white peoples have...The story will be more about coyote, when he visiting among his friends the animal and the owl...The coyote talk to the trees, even to the rock, and the water. But all the time he play a mean tricks on his friends. Though in return he always get the worse back on him. And today there are a lot of people that way, some tell big lie, and steal other wife, all these happen when coyote speaking like a human, as the old Indian used to tell their grand children. They too learn it from old grand parent.

Percy Bigmouth's Stories

Percy, aptly named Bigmouth, liked to tell stories. These range from "The Emergence" of the Lipan to stories about warfare between the Lipan and Comanche. According to several Opler informants, stories have a distinct order: "First comes the story of the emergence and Killer-of-Enemies, then the coyote stories, and then the stories of the people, of what been done lately."[5] Percy follows this order in relating his stories to Gene.

Often one story will run into the next story and it can be difficult to determine where one ends and another begins, but Percy does give an indication that he is onto a new story with phrases like: "Among us Lipans our story goes like this!"; "Well here, I'm going to write another story"; "It's the end of that story"; or, "Well let's have some fun with our friend the Coyote." His stories are also interspersed with historical information about his family, the different Apache tribes, or explanations of certain terms or events. Although Percy's stories are handwritten, reading his stories is like hearing Percy telling his story in person; he writes like he speaks. His skills as a storyteller are excellent because he keeps the reader involved in the story. One can almost hear him laugh as he explains the irony of Coyote's misfortunes. Percy's penmanship is good, while his grammar will be found lacking by experienced writers. However, this adds a sense of originality to the story. For example, he spells the word "insects" as "inspects" and a reader cannot mistake that he is referring bugs. Percy's first language was Lipan, even though his stories are written in English. One clearly gets the sense that he is spelling English words phonetically in a voice that has an Apache accent. The reader can almost hear how he talked.

It is important to note that not everyone, at least in Lipan culture, could be a storyteller: "The myths acted as a reservoir of information indispensable to the expert or the leader."[6] Before a person is considered a leader, he must know the stories about the emergence, coyote stories, and the history about the people. If a person does not have this knowledge, then he cannot lead. Although Percy did not have a leadership role within the tribe (i.e., he was not on the tribal council), he was still considered a leader because he possessed all the knowledge that was required of a leader or chief. Both people within his own tribe as well as the likes of Eve Ball and Morris Opler held him in high regard.

"Among us Lipans our story goes like this!"–Big Chief Tablet 1, Coyote no. 1

The first grouping starts with The Emergence story of the Lipan. Animals and plants are the main characters—"The People"—and they all speak the same language. Percy then tells about the birth of Killer-of-Enemies, who is the Lipan cultural hero, and his mother, Changing Woman. This grouping, labeled by Percy as "Coyote Story No. 1," includes the following stories: "The Emergence"; "The Birth of Killer-of-Enemies"; "Killer-of-Enemies Hunts with Raven Boy and Slays a Giant"; "Raven and the Origin of Death"; "Coyote Pursues the Insects Called Fat Skulls"; "Rabbit Plays Sick and Escapes from Coyote"; "Coyote Bites Rock Rabbit and Allows Real Rabbit to Escape"; "Wildcat Fools Coyote"; "The Turtles Go on a Raid"; and, "Coyote Dances with the Prairie Dogs including Wildcat Steals Coyote's Prairie-dog and Coyote Dives in the Water for Prairie-dog." These stories are comparable to the stories in Opler's text with the exception of "Killer-of-Enemies Hunts with Raven Boy and Slays a Giant."

"Well here goes the story about the coyote visiting the camp"–Big Chief Tablet 2, Coyote no. 2

The second grouping consists of six stories and is the only grouping with an introductory letter. In it, Percy writes about the content and purpose of the stories: Coyote visiting his animal friends, playing tricks on them, and also helping them at times. These are all stories about Coyote's exploits among the people: "Coyote Gets the Fat Away from Bear"; "Coyote Steals the Hawk Chiefs Wife and Is Made to Swallow Hot Rocks"; "The Shooting Contest for the Two Girls"; "Coyote is Stung by the Red Ants"; "Coyote Visits the Arrow

People and Hunts Buffaloes"; and "The Man Who Married a Dove." These stories explain why people act the way they do in certain situations and why animals have certain features. For example, the story about Coyote visiting the Prairie dogs includes an encounter with Bobcat where they each change the other's appearance. This explains why a bobcat has pointy ears and a coyote has a long snout.

Among Native American people, organ meat and fat is highly valued because it is considered delectable and nutritious. Coyote meets the Bear People who are forced by their Chief to relinquish all the fat from animals they kill. Coyote changes this and benefits all the people, and this is one story where he does not "get the worse back on him." In another similar story, Coyote gets back the tongue for the people, but he is punished for bringing about the death of a Chief and ill-treating his son and wife. Coyote is forced to swallow hot rocks and dies as a result. His accomplice in this story is the Bat, whose punishment is that he and his descendants must forever hang by their feet. Death practices are also explained: when the Chief dies, the wife and son are not allowed to reflect or look back on the Chief.

One theme common in Native American stories is prejudice, or the ill-treatment of people based on their looks. "The Shooting Contest for the Girls" is about a poor young man who is ill-treated by others. This man, named "Urinate on his Head," also has a big stomach and is considered slow. He comes into his own one day with the help of a relative, the Skunk, and wins the hand of a girl by shooting a bat out of a tree. He also proves that he has a strong arm and is an accurate shot with a bow and arrow. As the people prepare him for the wedding, they discover in his stomach all sorts of beautiful clothing. As a result, he is deemed wealthy, strong and a potential leader despite the ill-treatment he withstood. This story is analogous to European fairy tales, like Cinderella, where the one who starts out poor and ill-treated becomes rich and respected.

"Lipan Apache and Comanche Fighting Story of Old Days"–Big Chief Tablet 3, Comanche and Lipan

This last collection of stories is titled on the front of the Big Chief tablet as "No. 3: Comanche and Lipan!" Percy begins with an introduction of what he knows about the Comanche people. In this grouping are three stories about intertribal warfare between the Lipan Apaches and Comanche: "Comanche Captives are Returned to Avoid a Fight," "The Apache Defeat a Comanche Raiding Party," and "A Battle Between the Lipan and the Comanche." These stories reflect the difficult times and decisions that the leaders had to make. They also illustrate how people abducted during raids or battles were treated. According to Lipan Apache tradition, abducted people were taken care of like other family members and not treated harshly or enslaved. Interesting tidbits of information are also given. For example, the different tribes communicated by using American Indian Sign Language and some Lipan Apache could also speak the Comanche language.

The reader gets insight into the battles, the reasons for fighting, and how the battles ended. Lipan Apaches fought other tribes only to protect their families and herds of horses. They also took into consideration family ties. During one battle, the leader of the Lipan Apache warriors said that if he had relatives among the Comanche, he would declare a truce. Intermarriage among the Lipan Apaches and Comanche was somewhat common because the leader did find a relative among the Comanche, thus ending the battle. Personal vendettas were not a reason to go to war with other tribes. In one of the stories, one Comanche man did not want to end a battle because the Lipan Apaches had killed several of his relatives. The Comanche leader tells this man that if he pursued war against the Lipan Apache, tribe he would not receive any support from others because a treaty had been made. A treaty usually involved digging a hole and each leader spitting into the hole and then covering it with dirt. All bad feelings or reasons for wanting to go to war were buried and were not to be resurrected.

The role of women is also described. They were not passive figures; instead, they spurred men on to fight and served as messengers during battle. One Comanche woman who was about to be captured by the Lipan Apaches deliberately got down from her horse, removed all belongings, and shooed her horse away. This act was meant to roust the men into action. In another story, a Lipan Apache woman, stolen by a Comanche and raised among them, goes to the Lipan Apache men who are under siege to deliver a message from the Comanche leader. The woman in this story is completely calm and tells the Lipan Apaches that because she is with them they will not be harmed.

Conclusion

Percy Bigmouth played a significant role in preserving history. In the mid-1930s, he was an informant for Morris Opler; in the 1940s, he began his correspondence with Gene; and, in the mid-1950s, he was interviewed by Eve Ball and C. L. Sonnischsen. Both academics and Gene held him in high regard. Otherwise, why would she have saved the letters and the stories? Percy ventured outside traditional cultural boundaries by offering stories to a non-Indian girl. One can presume that Percy looked at Gene as an adopted child or grandchild in his tribe. This relatively small collection of four letters and three groups of stories is a rich memoir, not only of two people's unusual relationship, but also of a broader aspect of Lipan history that was woven into American life. It is a history that is not easily found in conventional history books and is a vivid first-person account by a Lipan Apache.

NOTES

1.   Phyllis Eileen Banks, "Bent and Mescalero, home of the Mescalero Apache." http://www.southernnewmexico.com

2.   In the 1940s and 1950s, Eve Ball (1890-1984) took down verbatim accounts of Apache elders who had survived the army's campaigns against them in the last century. These oral histories offer new versions—from Warm Springs, Chiricahua, Mescalero, and Lipan Apache—of events previously known only through descriptions left by non-Indians. A high school and college teacher, Ball moved to Ruidoso, New Mexico in 1942. After winning their confidence, Ball would ultimately interview sixty-seven Apache people.

3.   Eve Ball, *Indeh: An Apache Odyssey* (Provo, UT: Brigham Young University Press, 1980), p. xii.

4.   Ibid., p. xiv.

5.   Morris Edward Opler, *Myths and Legends of the Lipan Apache Indians* (New York: American Folk-lore Society, 1940), p. 8.

6.   Ibid.

17. Our Lady of Guadalupe: Influence of the Mestizo Icon on Mexico and the Catholic Church
Steven A. Kiczek

The icon and devotion of Our Lady of Guadalupe (*Nuestra Señora de Guadalupe*) is a good example of the influence of the indigenous peoples of Latin America on the rest of the world. This devotion to the Virgin of Guadalupe has exercised a strong influence on many people, especially Mexicans. At the heart of the devotion are the Nahua Indian "Juan Diego" and the message he brought to his people. This study is divided into four main topics: the material devotion, consisting of the icon itself and the devotional version of its history; the controversy over its origins; its influence on the history and culture of Mexico; and its influence on the Catholic Church. In this paper the phrases "Our Lady of Guadalupe" and "Virgin of Guadalupe" stand for the devotion in its widest sense, encompassing the image, the devotion and its message.

History of the Icon and its Devotion

There are three elements of Our Lady of Guadalupe that are separate yet interrelated: the image itself; the *cultus* or veneration rendered to the image; and the story of the appearance of the Virgin Mary to Juan Diego as depicted in various sources, especially the *Nican mopohua* (*Here Is Recounted*). The picture of the Virgin Mary is an icon. Since the Second Ecumenical Council of Nicaea (787), the Catholic Church has officially permitted the veneration, though not worship, of images of Jesus Christ, the Virgin Mary, and the angels and saints, since the images point to and direct the minds and hearts of the faithful to their prototypes. This is an important point in the history of the devotion to Our Lady of Guadalupe, since the first opposition to the devotion was raised by the first Franciscan missionaries in New Spain who were very worried that devotion to the image on the part of the new indigenous converts would lead to idolatry.

The image is a depiction of the Virgin Mary as a *mestiza* woman almost completely surrounded by a mandorla—that is, golden rays depicting sunshine. An angelic male figure at the bottom holds up a cloud with outstretched arms, behind which the Virgin Mary stands on a dark crescent moon. Her hands are folded in prayer, her head slightly inclined. Her outer robe is of a blue-green tint, upon which gold stars appear, and it has a gold border. The image contains a combination of Biblical, Catholic, and indigenous symbols. First, it evokes the woman described in the Apocalypse (12:1): "And a great sign appeared in heaven: a woman clothed with the sun, and the moon under her feet, and on her head a crown of twelve stars." In the Guadalupe icon the stars appear on her cloak, but otherwise the visual reference is clear. This is important because major Mexican theologians, since the 17th century (especially of criollo background) have interpreted this visual reference as a fulfillment of the Biblical text and as a sign of the special election of Mexico as a new Promised Land on the part of God. Regarding the stars, there was in the past a crown on the Virgin of Guadalupe's head, but it was removed. The icon also depicts traditional Catholic doctrines concerning Mary. Jeanette Favrot Peterson, points out some of these:

> In the end, as Levi d'Ancona notes, the most popular of these traditional themes, St. John's Apocalyptic woman and Mary surrounded by symbols of her purity, fused visually and symbolically with the Assumption of the Virgin to depict the Immaculate Conception. In all three types Mary is shown between heaven and earth, neither wholly earthbound nor remotely transcendental, as a bodily figure who mediates both spheres. It is a trio of overlapping Marian themes, the Mulier Amicta Sole [Woman clothed with the Sun], Assumption of the Virgin, and the Tota Pulchra [All Beautiful] that may have impacted the making of the Mexican Virgin of Guadalupe.[1]

Both Marian doctrines mentioned by Peterson are depicted in the icon, and in her article she discusses and reproduces a number of paintings from the late 15th and the 16th centuries that contain several features of the Guadalupe icon. She maintains that the Indian painter, Marcos de Aquino, consciously chose these features as themes in the mid-16th century.

Indigenous symbolism is also prominent in the icon. A good summary of the interpretation of indigenous symbolism can be found on the website of the Basílica de Santa María de Guadalupe (http://www.virgendeguadalupe.org.mx/estudios/interpretacion.htm; accessed on May 27, 2008). The traditional interpretation points out several features in the image that refer to Aztec culture: e.g., the stars on Mary's robe are said to match the constellations on the night of Dec. 12, 1531, when, the sources say, Mary appeared to Juan Diego; the Nahui Ollin, or Flower of Four Petals, an Aztec symbol of the divine presence, appears over the Virgin's womb, indicating the presence of Jesus Christ; Mary stands in front of the sun and on top of the moon, both indicating her relation to Aztec religion which she supersedes but does not destroy. According to these interpretations of the icon, it serves as a pictograph that reveals to the indigenous peoples the icon's meaning in a language they can understand.

The icon has existed since the 16th century, but the account of the apparition of the Virgin Mary to the Indian Juan Diego is separate from it. The famous story of the apparition first appears in two publications in the mid-17th century: Miguel Sánchez' *Imagen de la Virgen María, Madre de Dios de Guadalupe, milagrosamente aparecida en la ciudad de México*, in 1648, and Luis Lasso de la Vega's *Huei tlamahuiçoltica omonexiti in ilhuicac tlatocacihuapilli Santa Maria totlaçonantzin Guadalupe in nican huei altepenahuac Mexico itocayocan Tepeyacac*. The most important source is one section of Lasso de la Vega's work, entitled *Nican mopohua*, which tells the story of the Virgin Mary's appearance to an Indian man named Juan Diego. It is in this narrative where the strongest indigenous influence is present. The text is written in Nahuatl—either in well-written Nahuatl, with many "classical" features, according to Miguel León-Portilla, or in standard ecclesiastical Nahuatl, with a strong Spanish influence, according to Lisa Sousa, Stafford Poole and James Lockhart. León-Portilla is convinced that Antonio Valeriano, an Indian convert and scholar of the mid-16th century, was the true author or compiler of the *Nican mopohua*, relying heavily on oral tradition. Stafford Poole vigorously contests the idea of Valeriano's authorship of the text. Poole states categorically that Luis Lasso de la Vega is the only possible author.

In the narrative, the Virgin Mary appears to Juan Diego four times in early December, 1531. The first time he hears the singing of exotic birds and sees a brilliant scene of desert plants and rocks all resplendent in different colors. Mary appears to him and addresses him in a friendly and familiar manner. She tells him who she is, and that she wants to console his people. She also tells him to go to the bishop, the Franciscan Juan de Zumárraga, and tell him that she wants a temple built in her honor. Juan Diego addresses her in a familiar and humble manner. He does what he is told, but the bishop is not open to his message and Juan Diego is ill-treated by the bishop's servants. The next time that he sees Mary, he tells her that the meeting did not go well. He suggests that she send someone of high rank to the bishop. But she still wants Juan Diego. He then goes again to the bishop, who receives him, but is still not convinced. After this encounter, Juan Diego's uncle falls very ill. Juan Diego wants to avoid the Lady and go instead to find a priest for his uncle. Mary again appears to him, tells him not to worry about his uncle since she healed him, and asks him to pick various flowers that were made to miraculously bloom out of season and take them to the bishop as a sign. He does so, and after opening his *tilma*, or cloak, the flowers fall to the floor, blooming and full of sweet scents, and then her image appears on Juan Diego's cloak. Everyone is astounded, the bishop keeps Juan Diego's *tilma*, builds Mary a church and deposits the *tilma* there as a relic and an object of devotion. A detailed description of the image is also given at the end of the *Nican mopohua*.

A few indigenous elements of the story are very significant and have had a strong influence. The most important is Mary's initial address to Juan Diego:

> Know, rest assured, my youngest child, that I am the eternally consummate virgin Saint Mary, mother of the very true deity, God, the giver of life, the creator of people, the ever present, the lord of heaven and earth. I greatly wish and desire that they build my temple for me here, where I will manifest, make known, and give to people all my love, compassion, aid, and protection. For I am the compassionate mother of all you people here in this land, and of the other various peoples who love me, who cry out to me, who seek me, who trust in me. There I will listen to their weeping and their sorrows in order to remedy and heal all their various afflictions, miseries, and torments.[2]

What is significant here is the Nahua vocabulary used. The words used for God are very meaningful in Aztec religion. Miguel León-Portilla sheds light on some of the Aztec religious expressions:

> Tonantzin, Nuestra madre, Totahtzin, Nuestro padre, eran conceptos clave en el pensamiento nahua que así concebía a 'Aquel por quien se vive', supremo Dador de la vida, Ipalnemohuani. La noble doncella que habla a Juan Diego le da a entender su relación personal con él. En seguida pronunciará sus varios nombres o títulos, todos ellos tomados de la tradición religiosa prehispánica. Es inantzin, madrecita de Ipalnemohuani, 'el Dador de la vida', invocado así en muchos cantares y antiguas plegarias…La noble señora enumeró así algunos de los principales atributos del Dios que adoraban los nahuas y también los cristianos: él da la vida, está en todas partes y es creador de los humanos.[3]

In this narrative, the Virgin Mary uses words and names that resonate in the religious world in which Juan Diego was raised. A positive link is established with the native culture and system of beliefs, and they are thereby affirmed and validated within the context of the times. What they were taught in their own culture has value.

Another major element of native culture given prominence in the *Nican mopohua* is the theme of *flor y canto* (flower and song). As mentioned already, when Juan Diego first meets the heavenly woman, it is in connection with an atmosphere of exotic singing birds and very colorful plants and rocks; and the sign of proof of his mission is a batch of sweetly smelling brilliant flowers blooming during winter. Miguel Leon-Portilla explains the significance of these elements:

> Cantos al principio del relato y también del antiguo cantar [i.e. *Cuicapeuhcayotl*]; flores al final de uno y otro, son búsqueda o subconsciente

evocación de esa forma náhuatl de concebir lo que existe como "flor y canto," *in xochitl, in cuicatl*, palabras que, al unirse, connotan los conceptos de poesía y realidad preciosa. También, como lo dejó dicho el sabio Tecayehuatzin de Huexotzinco, cantos y flores son: "tal vez lo verdadero en la tierra," *aço tle nelli in tlalticpac*. Es así el Nican Mopohua expresión de flor y canto, símbolos que, como el poema de inspiración prehispánica, entretejen "la antigua sabiduría," in *huehueh tlamatiliztli*, con el mensaje evangélico que los frailes daban a conocer a los indios.[4]

"Flor y canto" evoke paradise, the divine realm, supreme happiness, the meaning of life and "the old wisdom" of their ancestors. It is not accidental or incidental that Mary's presence is connected with these elements, so full of meaning and close associations for the Aztec people. It is a sign of reaching out to them and of validation of their culture, including religion.

The icon and the *Nican mopohua*, though distinct, historically have been linked together. Without the narrative, the icon would be only one more depiction of the Virgin Mary and it probably would not have had such a great impact. The story without the icon would be just one more story of a Marian apparition. It is the combination of the two that has made the devotion of Our Lady of Guadalupe so powerful: Mary appearing as a mestiza maiden and speaking to a Nahua man in his own language.

The Controversy over the Origin of the Icon and the Devotion

The history of Our Lady of Guadalupe is both complex and controversial. Questions regarding its origin and historicity have been a longstanding battleground between traditional adherents ("apparitionists," *"aparicionistas"* in Spanish) and those who have fought against it for various reasons—religious, historical and scientific (anti-apparitionists, *"antiaparicionistas"*). The first controversy occurred in 1556 when the Archbishop of Mexico City, Alonso de Montúfar, preached a sermon on September 6th praising and promoting devotion to the Virgin of Guadalupe. He was a fervent promoter of popular devotion, including miracles, and he clearly believed that this devotion would attract the indigenous population. The Franciscan provincial, Fr. Francisco de Bustamante, responded on September 8th (the feast of the Nativity of Mary) by angrily denouncing the Archbishop. He was very worried that the Indian converts would get confused and lapse into idolatry. The Franciscans had carefully taught the indigenous converts that they should not adore images and that they needed to adhere to a spiritual worship of God that avoided idolatry. They also did not want the Indians to depend on miracles. They intensely disliked anything that was connected to the Guadalupan devotion, and believed that the confusion created in the Indians' minds would undo all their work. It is not clear that the image on the cloak that is known as "Our Lady of Guadalupe" was the center of the devotion at the ermita, or chapel, of Guadalupe at this time. Fr. Bustamante also stated that an Indian named "Marcos" created the painting very recently.[5]

This Franciscan opposition to the devotion of the Virgin of Guadalupe was strongly expressed again by the missionary and scholar of Nahuatl culture, Bernardo de Sahagún, in 1570. He wrote that the Indians at the church of Our Lady of Guadalupe were confusing the Virgin Mary, the "Mother of God," with a native goddess named Tonantzin, which means "our mother." The Franciscans were very worried that the Indians were worshiping "Tonantzin" under the cover of the Virgin of Guadalupe. Louise Burkhart, however, disputes this interpretation. She explains:

> In colonial records, indigenous myths are often adapted in response to Christian teachings: colonial Indians were adept at reinventing their preconquest culture in order to suit their colonial situation...There is no evidence that Tepeyacac held any special meaning for sixteenth-century Indians. Thus, the link between Our Lady of Guadalupe and any pre-Columbian goddess is, at best, tenuous. Tonantzin is Mary; Mary is Tonantzin. That Indians used this title for Mary indicates that they viewed her as a maternal figure personally connected to them. To understand what a figure like Our Lady of Guadalupe could mean to them, connections must be sought not to ancient goddesses but to the religious life of Christianized Nahua Indians in the Mexico City area during the second half of the sixteenth century. A rich Marian spirituality characterizes their devotional expressions, with Mary embodying traditional attitudes toward the sacred as well as new concerns derived from Christianity and colonial life.[6]

She maintains that Fr. Sahagún misinterpreted their use of the word "Tonantzin" when he believed that the Indians adored an Aztec goddess. The cultus at the shrine was the issue that caused him concern.

The other major controversies involve modern criticism. Some of the major anti-apparitionists are the following: Juan Bautista Muñoz (1794), Joaquín García Icazbalceta (a devout Catholic layman in the 19th century), Francisco de la Maza, Mauro Rodríguez, Edmundo O'Gorman, and Stafford Poole (a 20th-century Catholic priest). The main point that these historians make is that until the publication of Miguel Sánchez's *Imagen de la Virgen María...*, in 1648, and of Luis Lasso de la Vega's *Huei tlamahuiçoltica...*, in 1649, there is virtual silence regarding the apparitions of the Virgin Mary to Juan Diego. The now-famous image dates from the 16th century, but the famous story of the apparitions first "appeared" in these publications, and the historical critics have made this fact the foundation of their attacks on the traditional account of the apparitions and, by extension, on the devotion itself. The critics acknowledge the existence of the devotion, the cultus, the shrine, the pilgrimages, etc., but they maintain that these existed on their own without reference to any apparitions or to the figure of Juan Diego. Stafford Poole summarizes the critical stance regarding the apparitions thus:

> The years 1648 and 1649 are the crucial ones in the history of the Guadalupe apparitions. Miguel Sánchez made known to the criollos of New Spain a story that until that time was unknown or forgotten. Suddenly, as if out of nowhere, he gave them a story that he and they appropriated as divine witness to the legitimacy of criollismo. In the years that followed the predominantly criollo secular clergy would embrace the story wholeheartedly and spread it among the criollos. With Sánchez began the long process whereby Guadalupe was fused with Mexican identity. Laso de la Vega, in contrast, sought to bring the message of compassion and consolation to the Indians. If he had any success, it was limited, because it was not until the eighteenth century that the Indians began to seek refuge under the shadow of the Virgin of Tepeyac.[7]

The apparitionists have responded with a flood of apologetic literature in defense of the apparitions, Juan Diego, and the whole tradition, often relying on oral tradition among the Indians, scientific analyses of the tilma and its image, and the very existence and duration of the image itself.

Influence on the History and Culture of Mexico

Our Lady of Guadalupe's greatest impact has been on the history, people, and culture of Mexico. Probably no other person, movement, ideology, political party or entity has been more influential in Mexico's history and culture. This has certainly been the case since Miguel Sánchez and Luis Lasso de la Vega published their books in 1648 and 1649, respectively. Before that time, the cultus of Our Lady of Guadalupe at Tepeyac, just outside Mexico City, was gradually growing and gaining influence, but that influence was mainly local. Historical sources reveal that there was a significant level of devotion at the shrine at Tepeyac, among both the Spanish and the native populations. It is difficult to tell how widespread the devotion was among the Indian population. Certainly there were Indian converts who visited the shrine, since Bernardo de Sahagún complained about it. Also, apologists for Our Lady of Guadalupe point to oral tradition as the main source of natives' knowledge of the apparitions, since very little was recorded in writing.

The criollos in the mid-17th century were the main impetus for the growth of the devotion (Stafford Poole would say they were the sole impetus for it). Both Sánchez and Lasso de la Vega were criollos. As a group, they were looked down upon by Spaniards from the peninsula, since they were born in Mexico. The Spaniards, for one thing, had the original Virgin of Guadalupe in Extremadura after which the Mexican Virgin was named. The Spaniards, whom the criollos called *gachupines* as a label of contempt, also had another devotion to the Virgin Mary, along with an image, which they called the

"Virgen de Remedios." This was an artificial rivalry that reached well into the 19th century. The Virgin of Guadalupe provided the criollos with a heavenly patron, "born," so to speak, in Mexico. She was the Mexican Virgin Mary. She provided them with an identity of heavenly origin to which they could point and boast. They began to think of themselves as *mexicanos*, and to think of their land as "México" instead of just "Nueva España."

Beginning with the War of Independence in 1810, the Virgin of Guadalupe began to be invoked as a potent symbol of Mexican identity. Miguel Hidalgo y Costilla, a Catholic priest, led the war and had his followers invoke Our Lady of Guadalupe, employing her as both a visual symbol and a slogan. Our Lady of Guadalupe became the "criolla" Virgin and the Virgin of Los Remedios became the "gachupina," the Virgin of the Spaniards. Even though political rivals set these two devotions to the Virgin against each other, they were closely associated in the past, and Solange Alberro even goes so far as to state that they originally were the same. More indigenous people became involved in the War, and Our Lady of Guadalupe began to be used as a symbol of resistance, even a justification for rebellion. William B. Taylor recalls a powerful example of how the icon was used in this war:

> In December 1810, Father Hidalgo ordered the Indians of Juchipila...not to sack the estates of the local Spanish tax administrator. The Indians refused to obey, even after a direct order from their parish priest. They did it, they said, with the permission of the Virgin of Guadalupe. What had been forbidden only months before could now be accomplished under the higher authority of their protectress.[8]

Taylor remarks on the type of people who were attracted to the Virgin of Guadalupe as a political symbol during the War:

> The image of Guadalupe had a special appeal in places where people thought of themselves as Mexicans, or as members of a social category without privileges, or as members of a group whose privileges had been lost—notably creoles, the lower clergy, and landless farmworkers, including Indians who thought of themselves as Indians.[9]

After the War, the Virgin of Guadalupe continued to be politicized. As the Mexican State became more secularized and hostile to the Church, she became an inspiration to Catholics in their struggle to maintain a public role for the Church in Mexico. That situation continues to this day. She has continued to be an inspiration in armed struggles. In the Mexican Revolution of 1910-1920, the followers of Emiliano Zapata carried banners with the Virgin of Guadalupe. During the Cristero War (1926-1929), the rallying cry of the rebels was "¡Viva Cristo Rey! ¡Viva la Virgen de Guadalupe!" The Virgin of Guadalupe has a place even within the recent Zapatista movement. In an online article, Margarita Zires describes how the Zapatistas included the Virgin of Guadalupe in their cause. Subcomandante Marcos, in the mid-1990s, placed an image of the Virgin of Guadalupe in the midst of Zapatista assemblies and discussed issues and made decisions with her presence as a point of reference. Her image functioned as a sort of *escriba-oyente comunitario*, and was carried along. Zires describes the Virgin's role as follows:

> A través de la narración del proceso de deliberación, la Virgen se convierte en el símbolo de la solidaridad incondicional. Los pobladores de Guadalupe Tepeyac se convierten en el pueblo elegido, adonde la Virgen decide ir, subir y bajar montañas, cruzar selvas hasta encontrarlos...La gente la tiende a identificar con la comandante Ramona, una de las pocas mujeres guerrilleras de esa región que en la lucha zapatista ha sobresalido. La Virgen adquiere una identidad indígena y revolucionaria a la vez. Los rayos que la rodean muestran el carácter bendito y sobrenatural de esa imagen y, por lo tanto, de la lucha zapatista en la cual la Virgen se ve inserta en esa representación visual.[10]

Another example of the presence of the Virgin of Guadalupe in Mexican public life is the following:

> An enormous student strike was in progress at this time [1999] at the national university, and in this supposedly secular nation, a newsletter [Machetearte 50 (Dec. 7, 1999)] distributed by some of the strikers called on the Virgin of Guadalupe, 'Patrona de la Insurgencia' (Patroness of the Insurgency) to help them prevail. A huge picture of Guadalupe graced the fiftieth issue of this publication, and a double-page drawing in the center showed Guadalupe under an eagle (a strong national symbol drawn from the ancient symbol for Tenochtitlan), a pyramid, a church, a middle-class apartment house, a truck, an earth mover, an Aztec warrior, and a feathered serpent. The drawing evoked an enormous number of symbolic associations—the working and middle classes, the Aztec past, the Catholic heritage of the country, all centered on the Virgin Mother.[11]

This example shows how the figure of Our Lady of Guadalupe reaches beyond the sanctuary and the Catholic home and into the everyday affairs, even the public disputes, of general society.

The influence of Our Lady of Guadalupe reaches far beyond politics and national identity. One aspect of the Virgin of Guadalupe that has been emphasized by many writers is *mestizaje*. The Virgin of Guadalupe is often called *la morena*, and this feature of the icon has captured the hearts and imaginations of many people. This is an instance where the icon and the *Nican mopohua* work together, so to speak. The dark complexion of the original icon is very pronounced. The image on Juan Diego's tilma and the *Nican Mopohua* both emphasize Mary's dark face. She appears not as a Spaniard, nor completely as a native, but rather as a combination of the two.

In racially divided societies, such as Mexico and the United States, the mestizo features of the Virgin's appearance on the tilma/icon have served to spur pride in one's racial identity, as comfort in the struggles for just and equal treatment and respect, and as compassion in their suffering. Robert Goizueta, in an essay regarding Mexican identity, brings together various aspects of the Virgin's influence on these racial issues:

> To Western Christians accustomed to images of a blonde and blue-eyed Mary, this Lady must surely appear incongruous; her olive skin tells the indigenous people of Mexico that she, La Morenita, is one of them. It tells all Mexicans and, indeed, all Latinos that she is one of them…If Juan Diego is to be evangelized, it will be through a dark-skinned Lady on Tepeyac, the sacred place of the Nahuas, not through a Spanish bishop in his palace. Indeed, through Guadalupe, the very relationship between evangelizer and evangelized is reversed: the indigenous man, Juan Diego, is sent to evangelize the bishop.[12]

In general society, and to some extent even in the Church, "peoples of color" (to use the phrase sometimes in circulation) have been oppressed and been dealt second-class status. The radical nature of the Virgin of Guadalupe is that in this icon she is represented as a member of the lowest classes of society.

One such downtrodden group is the Indians themselves. Reference has already been made to how they played a role in the Mexican War of Independence, and how some of them appealed to the Virgin of Guadalupe in order to justify violent action. Nevertheless, it is somewhat difficult to find out what they themselves thought, in their own words, about the Virgin of Guadalupe. Almost all the available information concerns either mestizos and/or criollos, or was (and still is) written by them. If Antonio Valeriano were the original author of the *Nican Mopohua*, and if he drew upon indigenous legends, songs and other traditions in order to compose this foundational document, then it is a most valuable witness to indigenous thought. If, however, the document is only a *criollo* creation, as Stafford Poole maintains, then it serves only as a symbol and would not be an accurate reflection of indigenous belief. Linda Hall states,

> What seems evident to me is that following the Conquest, Marian devotion became widespread in central Mexico among the indigenous peoples and was conflated with the symbols and spaces of pre-Spanish religious belief. By the seventeenth century, her position as protector, miracle-worker, and active advocate for the Nahua and other indigenous peoples in the region was well established. Not just the Virgin of Guadalupe, but swarms of advocations and images of Mary were present and revered. Though by no means identical to or simply substituted for indigenous goddesses, she was often associated with indigenous sacred spaces. These connections, although they made the representatives of the Church nervous, were

nevertheless key in establishing Christian worship in forms that were intelligible to the native peoples and served their needs.[13]

The Virgin Mary, then, seems to have resonated with many Indians, since on religious, psychological and social levels she met many of their needs, or at least appealed to them. They had been decimated on many levels, and they needed to believe in someone or something that would help them cope with their new devastating reality. Richard Nebel gives an idea of where the Virgin of Guadalupe fits into the Nahua system of beliefs after the Conquest:

> ...la aparición de la Virgen a un representante de la raza indígena, Juan Diego, significaba un retorno a la Tonantzin, otorgándoles no solo la continuidad de su raza, sino sobre todo la continuidad de su fe en sus dioses propios. Por otro lado, la tradición de la aparición sirvió también como un testimonio simbólico para establecer que los indígenas eran tan capaces y dignos como los españoles de recibir la enseñanza de la fe Cristiana y de ser redimidos.[14]

In the 20th century, Indians participated in the Mexican Revolution and took part in social protest movements. As seen in the case of the Zapatistas, the Virgin of Guadalupe remains a strong symbol of inspiration for indigenous peoples. An incident from the early 1970s also reveals her influence. The Chinanteco Indians were protesting the building of the Cerro de Oro dam, which would have involved their displacement. A mysterious figure who called himself "Ingeniero el Gran Dios" claimed to speak for the Virgin of Guadalupe. He invoked the figures of Benito Juárez and Lázaro Cárdenas, and threatened serious consequences if the dam were built.[15]

The enigmatic figure of "Ingeniero el Gran Dios" gives a fleeting glimpse of this lasting influence, and his voice is a rare instance of Indians expressing, in their own words, their devotion to the Virgin of Guadalupe. Although there has been some syncretistic confusion in the devotion to the Virgin of Guadalupe, the Christian spirit of the devotion as expressed by Indians has been genuine. George L. Scheper looks negatively upon a tendency to misinterpret, or downplay, the Christian substance of Indian devotion. He states,

> the appropriation of Guadalupe that currently seems to have the most drawing power among intellectuals outside the strictly Catholic community is what might be called the indigenista interpretation: the interpretation that steps down from the universalizing reading of Guadalupe as Feminine Archetype and sees her instead as a specific mask or even disguise for a variety of Aztec fertility goddesses lumped together collectively as "Tonantzin," Our Little Mother...This is the old "idols behind altars" thesis most famously purveyed in the book of that title by Anita Brenner (1929), and now overwhelmingly pervasive in the neo-Aztec movement in Mexico and de rigeur generally in intellectual circles ever since the

Columbian Quincentennial became the occasion for privileging indigenous perspectives in revisionist readings of the New World encounters.[16]

Another way in which the devotion plays a positive role for native
peoples is in providing a space where their culture can be expressed in an
open and public manner. Konrad Tyrakowski describes how it is manifested in
public pilgrimages to the Basilica of Guadalupe:

> Grupos de la llamada "música azteca" tocan instrumentos indígenas an-
> tiguos como el *huéhuetl* o el *teponaxtli*, sacuden sonajas, acompañan con
> chirimías y tambores, y hacen sonar enormes caracoles. A veces se rep-
> resenta la 'Danza del Tigre'. Sin duda alguna estas actuaciones tienen un
> origen prehispánico.[17]

Chicanos provide another excellent example of how the Virgin of
Guadalupe's influence has expanded. These are Mexican-Americans who
strongly identify with their Mexican and mestizo identities. In many ways,
they have invigorated the devotion to Our Lady of Guadalupe, giving it new
life and varied expression. This icon and its particular devotion to the Virgin
Mary reinforce their Catholic identity and Mexican identity, both needed in
the exceedingly diverse and sometimes hostile social environment that is the
United States. Our Lady of Guadalupe provides a sense of stability and identity
and serves as a symbol of hope and compassion. The themes of liberation from
oppression, spiritual motherhood and ethnic identity often are connected with
the Virgin of Guadalupe in Chicano writings and culture. Andrés G. Guerrero
eloquently expresses what Our Lady of Guadalupe means for many Chicanos:

> Almost all Chicano Catholic homes in the barrios of the Southwest dis-
> play Guadalupe's picture. Pachucos sometimes tattoo her entire image on
> their backs. In the context of the Chicano experience of oppression Gua-
> dalupe is a strong symbolic spiritual mother who is always there to lend a
> helping hand to the poor...Hence, the concept of Guadalupe as a liberator
> and a mother of the oppressed is very real to us.[18]

On a different level—the domestic and the personal—the Virgin of
Guadalupe has been described as mother: mother of Jesus Christ, mother of
Indians, but also as a personal maternal figure. A Mexican woman who was
recently asked (April 2008) what the Virgin of Guadalupe means to Mexicans.
said, "Ella es mamá." This woman made the point that the Virgin Mary
(specifically as Guadalupe) is accessible. God the Father is considered as too
remote. Jesus Christ is the stern judge and thus is difficult to approach. And
many Mexicans approach the Virgin of Guadalupe as a personal mediatrix.
This is a cultural and social reality not in accord with Catholic doctrine, since
the New Testament reveals both God the Father and Jesus Christ as merciful

and approachable. But the social reality is that often in Mexican familial life, the father is a stern and fearsome figure. This is vividly described by John Bushnell, who wrote about the maternal role that the Virgin of Guadalupe played in the social life of the Ocuilteca Indian village of San Juan Atzingo:

> The Virgin of Guadalupe is a comforting, permissive figure who evokes a rather unique response among the villagers. I observed San Juan men, quite deep in their cups, make their way to the family altar, lift up the picture of the Virgin of Guadalupe, kiss and embrace the representation with an unashamed display of affection, and proclaim with tear-filled eyes, "Mamacita Linda!" Holding pottery cup or gourd bowl of pulque on high, they would exclaim with obviously deep feeling, "Pulque—the milk of the Virgin!" On occasions such as this, when San Juan men drop their normal reserve under the influence of alcohol, the differentiated role of the Virgin comes into focus. The eulogistic phrases and the emotionality suffusing such behavior indicate that this saint occupies the status of a mother-figure.[19]

The Virgin of Guadalupe also serves as a maternal figure on a larger scale. Octavio Paz, the Mexican novelist, comments on her maternal role:

> The Indian goddesses were goddesses of fecundity, linked to the cosmic rhythms, the vegetative processes and agrarian rites. The Catholic Virgin is also the Mother (some Indian pilgrims still call her Guadalupe-Tonantzin), but her principal attribute is not to watch over the fertility of the earth but to provide refuge for the unfortunate. The situation has changed: the worshipers do not try to make sure of their harvests but to find a mother's lap. The Virgin is the consolation of the poor, the shield of the weak, the help of the oppressed. In sum, she is the Mother of orphans.[10]

In San Antonio, Texas, the devotion to Our Lady of Guadalupe is called upon as an impetus to unite diverse peoples. In San Antonio, the Hispanic community is well settled. It was originally part of New Spain, and the Mexican population predates the English-speaking Anglo population. Nevertheless, ethnic tension persists and the Virgin of Guadalupe is enlisted, so to speak, as a bridge-builder. Timothy Matovina describes how this is put into action by one parish:

> Despite the limitations, inconsistencies, divergent views, and ambiguity that to some degree thwart Guadalupe's transformative influence, San Fernando leaders continue their plea for Guadalupe devotees to be ambassadors of the celestial mestiza and to promote their parish's penchant for dramatic public rituals. They also urge Guadalupe's faithful to provide a witness of faith, unity, and what Alejandro García-Rivera has called "subversive hospitality," a reversal of roles in which Mexican Americans are the Juan Diegos who welcome Anglo Americans and other San Antonians

to their parish and its traditions and provide a model for a new future of respectful pluralism.[21]

However, not every manifestation of the Virgin of Guadalupe's image is positive, or is interpreted in a positive way. Her image appears in many places in the American Southwest, some of them not very flattering: liquor stores, houses of prostitution, tattoos and clothing. The image has been appropriated even by Hispanic urban gangs as a badge of ethnic identity. This last situation occurred as a problem in 1998 in a Santa Fe, New Mexico, elementary school where some students were wearing the image of Our Lady of Guadalupe on their shirts. The principal considered the shirts to be "gang attire" and banned them from the school. This decision outraged the Catholic community and the Archbishop, who interpreted the decision as a denial of religious expression. The principal explained that the decision was made to protect the children of the school from the influence of gangs. The clash of interpretations was inevitable. In various venues, especially the media, members of the community debated the meaning of the Virgin of Guadalupe.[22]

Influence on the Catholic Church

The influence of the icon and devotion of Our Lady of Guadalupe has been very strong in the Catholic Church, especially in Mexico. The influence of the devotion has been both positive and negative. This section will first deal with the status of the devotion, and afterwards with its influence and meaning.

How has the devotion to the Virgin of Guadalupe fit into the missionary strategy, or doctrine, of the Catholic Church in Mexico and beyond? The first Franciscan missionaries, in the context of the Erasmian reform movement of the early 16th century, approached the "Indians" with a purist attitude and mentality, attempting to be faithful to the Bible and the doctrine of the Church in a way that could not accommodate indigenous practices and beliefs, especially human sacrifice. Another "strategy," or mentality, has its origin in the Apostle Paul's speech in the Areopagus in Athens (documented in the Acts of the Apostles), in which he appealed to their altar dedicated to the "unknown god," and thus to their ancestral practice, and this became a longstanding Christian approach to relating to the beliefs and practices of "pagan" peoples. Justin Martyr also expressed this in the 2nd century when he spoke of "logoi spermatikoi," or "seeds of truth," among the gentiles. Also, Pope Gregory I, advising Augustine, the first Archbishop of Canterbury, in England, told him to accept and integrate native practices even into the Liturgy to the extent that they did not contradict Christian doctrine. This advice was widely adopted in Europe through the centuries, resulting in many syncretistic practices regarding the "cultus" toward saints, the Virgin Mary, and sacred places. The icon and devotion of the Virgin of Guadalupe, along with the narration of the *Nican mopohua*, belong to this alternate missionary strategy, which consists of an attitude of acceptance of whatever good can be found in other cultures. This involves an attitude of loving respect and a willingness to listen to what the evangelized people have to say and offer. Clodomiro Siller neatly sums up this approach:

> El evento de Guadalupe, narrado en el *Nican mopohua*, visto en su estructura y simbolismo nahuas, restituye al indio su dignidad, recupera como cristiano el núcleo religioso indio, pone la evangelización como la acción liberadora de la Virgen con la colaboración del pobre, critica el esquema y metodología misionera de los religiosos españoles, y sitúa el lugar del culto y de la fe fuera de la dominación.[23]

In the last two centuries, and especially recently in the Church since the Second Vatican Council, much of the emphasis in missionary work, liturgy, theology and catechesis has been placed on inculturation, and the devotion to Our Lady of Guadalupe has played a strong role in orienting the Church in this direction. In this devotion, the emphasis is clearly placed on the native peoples of Mexico, and on the Spanish only through the mediation of the Indian Juan Diego, as the special recipients of God's care. In this case, the issues of both ethnic origin and social class are addressed, and the usual order is reversed. More than anything else, attitudes within the Church have been changed regarding ethnic and social relations and questions regarding social privileges. Certainly, the views of ecclesiastical leaders towards indigenous peoples have changed. Another benefit to Mexico and the Church is that the Guadalupe devotion has put Mexico on the Catholic map, so to speak, and it has enriched the Church's universality. This aspect has been brought out by Elio Masferrer Kan:

> Lo más importante del culto guadalupano es que representa un proceso social y colectivo mediante el cual la población mestiza construye una nueva versión del catolicismo, el catolicismo mexicano. Esto confiere al guadalupanismo un papel privilegiado en la construcción de la identidad nacional Mexicana. Pero aquí no termina la cuestión sino que de alguna manera marca el inicio del proceso. El culto a la Virgen de Guadalupe representa también la inserción de los mexicanos en un contexto universal y plural, donde se articulan manteniendo su propia *identidad*.[24]

Many theologians have addressed the issue of inculturation. One theologian on the popular level who has been a major proponent of the devotion and message of the Virgin of Guadalupe is Fr. Virgilio Elizondo, a priest from San Antonio, Texas, founder of the Mexican American Cultural Center, and now [2008] a professor of theology at the University of Notre Dame. He has written extensively on the Virgin of Guadalupe and *mestizaje* in a glowing and idealistic manner and, as a result, has drawn the attention of

Stafford Poole, who considers his treatment of history to be unrealistic and inaccurate. Nevertheless, Elizondo's interpretation of the *Nican mopohua* has been influential and needs to be treated here. It is an expression of liberation theology and an example of how the devotion to the Virgin of Guadalupe has exercised influence on the Church and society. Fr. Elizondo sees Juan Diego as a representative of a thoroughly oppressed people, the Nahuas. His culture and religion have been stolen from him. His people are demoralized, and the Virgin Mary appears and the tables are turned. Fr. Elizondo states,

> She appears as the Indian Mother of God and the abandoned mestizo child of the Indian people. Through her, God vindicates the downtrodden. In her, the Indians and their ancestors are vindicated. Through her, a new means of evangelization—purified of ethnocentric limitations—is suggested...In her we move from the radical opposition of the two religions to a new synthesis that will occur in the new life that she is about to give birth to—the new Christianity of the new humanity of the Americas. She will be the compassionate and listening mother of all who come to her.[25]

The devotion is fervently expressed as popular religion, especially in Mexico and the United States, but also in other Latin American countries, and even in Europe. The impact of the devotion is universal. Fr. Virgilio Elizondo advocates for the value of popular religion, since it is the spontaneous expression of the common people. In this way, the devotion to the Virgin of Guadalupe keeps alive a traditional manner of expressing faith for many people, and in the post-Vatican II era, with its de-emphasis of traditional devotions and Marian piety, that impact is very significant. As Jeanette Rodriguez states,

> To appreciate the significance of Our Lady of Guadalupe, it is crucial to understand the context in which she is recognized: popular religion... When I speak of Catholicism in relationship to the Mexican American culture, I am not referring to the institutionalized version of Catholicism, but to popular Catholicism, handed down through generations by the laity more than by the ordained clergy.[26]

Conclusion

The devotion to Our Lady of Guadalupe is one way in which the culture of the Aztecs has had a major impact on the world. It employs Aztec imagery and transmits a wholehearted sense of respect for the native peoples and their culture. It has functioned as a symbol and source of consolation and meaning for millions of people, especially in Mexico and the United States, but also for many people around the world. María Cristina Camacho de la Torre, in her book *Fiesta de Nuestra Señora de Guadalupe*, tells how the devotion to Our Lady of Guadalupe has found a home in various countries of Europe, Asia and Africa, including the Middle East. It was initially spread by missionaries, but has been adapted to various cultures over the years.[27] It has also served as the catalyst for a great change of attitude towards the native peoples and cultures of Mexico, and that is one of its lasting legacies.

NOTES

1. Jeanette Favrot Peterson, "Creating the Virgin of Guadalupe: The Cloth, the Artist, and Sources in Sixteenth-Century New Spain," *The Americas* 61:4 (April 2005): 591.

2. Lisa Sousa, Stafford Poole, and James Lockhart, eds. and trans. *The Story of Guadalupe: Luis Laso de la Vega's Huei tlamahuiçoltica of 1649*. UCLA Latin American Studies, vol. 84. (Stanford: Stanford University Press; Los Angeles, Latin American Center Publications, 1998): 65, 67.

3. Miguel León-Portilla, *Tonantzin Guadalupe: pensamiento náhuatl y mensaje cristiano en el "Nican mopohua"*. Sección de Obras de Antropología. (México, D.F.: El Colegio Nacional: Fondo de Cultura Económica, 2000): 59-60.

4. Ibid., p. 55-56.

5. See also Jeanette Favrot Peterson, "Creating the Virgin of Guadalupe: The Cloth, the Artist, and Sources in Sixteenth-Century New Spain": 585.

6. Louise M. Burkhart, "The Cult of the Virgin of Guadalupe in Mexico," in *South and Meso-American Native Spirituality: From the Cult of the Feathered Serpent to the Theology of Liberation*, ed. Gary H. Gossen in collaboration with Miguel León-Portilla. World Spirituality: An Encyclopedic History of the Religious Quest, vol. 4. (New York: Crossroad Publishing Company, 1993), 208-9.

7. Stafford Poole, *Our Lady of Guadalupe: The Origins of a Mexican National Symbol, 1531-1797*. (Tucson: The University of Arizona Press, 1995), 126.

8. William B. Taylor, *Magistrates of the Sacred: Priests and Parishioners in Eighteenth-Century Mexico*. (Stanford, CA: Stanford University Press, 1996), 294.

9. Ibid., 296.

10. Margarita Zires, "Nuevas imágenes guadalupanas: diferentes límites del decir guadalupano en México y Estados Unidos," *Comunicación y sociedad* (julio-diciembre, 2000) 38:7-8, http://www.allbusiness.com/sector-61-educational-services/723620-1.html (accessed May 1, 2008)

11. Linda B. Hall, Mary, *Mother and Warrior: The Virgin in Spain and the Americas*. (Austin, TX: University of Texas Press, 2004), 269.

12. Roberto S. Goizueta, "Our Lady of Guadalupe: The Heart of Mexican Identity," in *Religion and the Creation of Race and Ethnicity: An Introduction*. ed. Craig R. Prentiss. Race, Religion, and Ethnicity. (New York: New York University Press, 2003), 145.

13. Linda B. Hall, *Mary, Mother and Warrior: The Virgin in Spain and the Americas*, 133-4.

14. Richard Nebel, *Santa María Tonantzin, Virgen de Guadalupe: continuidad y transformación religiosa en México*, tr. del alemán por el Pbro. Dr. Carlos Warnholtz Bustillos, con la colaboración de la señora Irma Ochoa de Nebel. Sección de obras de historia. (México, D.F.: Fondo de Cultura Económica, 1995), 149.

15. Alicia Barabas, *Utopías indias*. Colección Enlace: Cultura y sociedad. (México, D.F.: Editorial Grijalbo, 1989), 248.

16. George L. Scheper, "Guadalupe: Image of Submission or Solidarity?" *Religion and the Arts*, 3:3/4 (1999): 352-3.

17. Konrad Tyranowski, "La Villa de Guadalupe: centro religioso y nacional: elementos del desarrollo geográfico del mayor santuario de México," in Giuriati, Paolo, and Elio Masferrer Kan, coordinadores. *No temas...yo soy tu madre: un estudio socioantropológico de los peregrinos*

a la Basílica de Guadalupe. (México, D.F.: Centro Ricerche Socio Religiose: Plaza y Valdés Editores, 1998), 71.

18. Andrés G. Guerrero, *A Chicano Theology*. (Maryknoll, N.Y.: Orbis Books, 1987), 104-5.

19. John Bushnell, "La Virgen de Guadalupe as Surrogate Mother in San Juan Atzingo." *American Anthropologist*, New ser. 60:2 (Apr. 1958): 261.

20. Octavio Paz, "The Sons of La Malinche," in *Goddess of the Americas = La Diosa de las Américas: Writings on the Virgin of Guadalupe*, ed. Ana Castillo. (New York: Riverhead Books, 1996), 207.

21. Timothy Matovina, *Guadalupe and Her Faithful: Latino Catholics in San Antonio from Colonial Origins to the Present*. Lived Religions. (Baltimore: The Johns Hopkins University Press, 2005), 171-2.

22. Deborah A. Boehm, "Our Lady of Resistance: The Virgin of Guadalupe and Contested Constructions of Community in Santa Fe, New Mexico," *Journal of the Southwest* 44:1 1 (Spring 2002): 97-98.

23. Clodomiro Siller, "La Iglesia en el medio indígena," in *Religión y política en México*. Coordinado por Martín de la Rosa y Charles A. Reilly. Sociología y política. (México, D.F.: Siglo Veintiuno Editores, 1985), 225.

24. Elio Masferrer Kan, "Peregrinos en la Basílica: una visión antropológica," in *No temas... yo soy tu madre: un estudio socioantropológico de los peregrinos a la Basílica de Guadalupe*. Coordinadores, Paolo Giuriati and Elio Masferrer Kan. (México, D.F.: Centro Ricerche Socio Religiose: Plaza y Valdés Editores, 1998), 148.

25. Virgilio Elizondo, *Guadalupe: Mother of the New Creation*. (Maryknoll, NY: Orbis Books, 1997), 66-67.

26. Jeanette Rodriguez, "The Common Womb of the Americas: Virgilio Elizondo's Theological Reflection on Our Lady of Guadalupe," in *Beyond Borders: Writings of Virgilio Elizondo and Friends*, ed. Timothy Matovina. (Maryknoll, N.Y.: Orbis Books, 2000), 113.

27. For an extended treatment, see Camacho de la Torre, María Cristina, *Fiesta de Nuestra Señora de Guadalupe*, 149-157.

BIBLIOGRAPHY

Alberro, Solange. *El águila y la cruz: orígenes religiosos de la conciencia criolla: México, siglos XVI-XVII*. Sección de Obras de Historia. Serie Ensayos. México, D.F.: El Colegio de México, Fideicomiso Historia de las Américas; Fondo de Cultura Económica, 1999.

Báez-Jorge, Félix. *Los oficios de las diosas: dialéctica da la religiosidad popular en los grupos indios de México*. 2a ed. Biblioteca. Xalapa, Ver., México: Universidad Veracruzana, 2000.

Barabas, Alicia. *Utopías indias*. Colección Enlace. Cultura y sociedad. México, D.F.: Editorial Grijalbo, 1989.

Benítez, J. J. *El misterio de la Virgen de Guadalupe: sensacionales descubrimientos en los ojos de la virgen mexicana*. Barcelona: Editorial Planeta, 2003.

Boehm, Deborah A. "Our Lady of Resistance: the Virgin of Guadalupe and Contested Constructions of Community in Santa Fe, New Mexico." *Journal of the Southwest* 44: 1 (Spring 2002): 95-104.

Brading, D. A. *Mexican Phoenix: Our Lady of Guadalupe: Image and Tradition across Five Centuries*. Cambridge: Cambridge University Press, 2001.

Bravo Arriaga, María. *La excepción y la regla: estudios sobre espiritualidad y cultura en la Nueva España*. Estudios de Cultura Literaria Novohispana 8. México, D.F.: Universidad Nacional Autónoma de México, 1997.

Burkhart, Louise M. *Before Guadalupe: The Virgin Mary in Early Colonial Nahuatl Literature*. IMS Monograph 13. Albany, N.Y.: Institute for Mesoamerican Studies, 2001.

-----. "The Cult of the Virgin of Guadalupe in Mexico." In *South and Meso-American Native Spirituality: From the Cult of the Feathered Serpent to the Theology of Liberation*, ed. Gary H. Gossen in collaboration with Miguel León-Portilla, 198-227. World Spirituality: An Encyclopedic History of the Religious Quest, vol. 4. New York: Crossroad Publishing Company, 1993.

Bushnell, John. "La Virgen de Guadalupe as Surrogate Mother in San Juan Atzingo." *American Anthropologist*, n.s., 60,: 2 (Apr. 1958): 261-265.

Camacho de la Torre, María Cristina. *Fiesta de Nuestra Señora de Guadalupe: celebración, historia y tradición mexicana*. Fiestas populares de México. México, D.F.: CONACULTA, 2001.

Campa Mendoza, Víctor. *San Juan Diego: el Ayate Códice, ícono sagrado*. México, D.F.: Consejo Nacional de Ciencia y Tecnología; Durango: Consejo de Ciencia y Tecnología del Estado de Durango, 2002.

Carrión, Jorge. *Mito y magia del mexicano*. 2a ed. Ensayos sobre el mexicano. México, D.F.: Editorial Nuestro Tiempo, 1970.

Castillo, Ana, ed. *La diosa de las Américas: escritos sobre la Virgen de Guadalupe*. Traducción de Mariela Dreyfus. New York: Vintage Español = Vintage Books, 2000.

Castillo, Ana, ed. *Goddess of the Americas = La Diosa de las Américas: Writings on the Virgin of Guadalupe*. New York: Riverhead Books, 1996.

Demarest, Donald, and Coley Taylor, eds. *The Dark Virgin: The Book of Our Lady of Guadalupe; A documentary anthology*. Freeport, Maine: Coley Taylor, Inc., 1956.

Ducey, Michael T. *A Nation of Villages: Riot and Rebellion in the Mexican Huasteca, 1750-1850*. Tucson: The University of Arizona Press, 2004.

Elizondo, Virgilio. *La Morenita: Evangelizer of the Americas = La Morenita: Evangelizadora de las Américas*. San Antonio, Texas: Mexican American Cultural Center, 1980.

-----. *Guadalupe, Mother of the New Creation*. Maryknoll, NY: Orbis Books, 1997.

Elizondo, Virgilio, and Timothy M. Matovina. *Mestizo Worship: A Pastoral Approach to Liturgical Ministry*. Collegeville, MN: The Liturgical Press, 1998.

Elizondo, Virgilio, Allan Figueroa Deck, and Timothy Matovina, eds. *The Treasure of Guadalupe*. Celebrating Faith. Lanham, Maryland: Rowman & Littlefield Publishers, 2006.

Flores y Escalante, Jesús, and Pablo Dueñas. *La guadalupana: patroncita de los mexicanos*. México, D.F.: Plaza & Janés, 2004.

Gallegos, Bernardo P. "Whose Lady of Guadalupe? Indigenous Performances, Latina/o Identities, and the Postcolonial Project." *Journal of Latinos and Education* 1:3 (2002): 177-191.

Gallo Reynoso, Joaquín. *Juan Diego Cuauhtlatoatzin, profeta-servidor: pistas para darlo a conocer y celebrarlo*. Ciudad de México: Obra Nacional de la Buena Prensa, 2002.

García Icazbalceta, J., Alonso de Montúfar, and P.F. Velázquez. *Investigación histórica y documental sobre la aparición de la Virgen de Guadalupe*. Nueva ed. revisada conforme a las originales. Colección "Del México eterno". (México, D.F.: Ediciones Fuente Cultural, 1952.

Giuriati, Paolo, and Elio Masferrer Kan, eds. *No temas...yo soy tu madre: un estudio socioantropológico de los peregrinos a la Basílica de Guadalupe*. México, D.F.: Centro Ricerche Socio Religiose; Plaza y Valdés Editores, 1998.

Goizueta, Roberto S., "Our Lady of Guadalupe: the Heart of Mexican Identity." In *Religion and the Creation of Race and Ethnicity: An Introduction*, ed. Craig R. Prentiss, 140-151. Race, Religion, and Ethnicity. New York: New York University Press, 2003.

González Fernández, Fidel, Eduardo Chávez Sánchez, and José Luis Guerrero Rosado. *El encuentro de la Virgen de Guadalupe y Juan Diego*. 2a edición. México, D.F.: Editorial Porrúa, 1999.

Grajales, Gloria, and Ernest J. Burrus. *Bibliografía Guadalupana (1531-1984) = Guadalupan Bibliography (1531-1984)*. (Washington, D.C.: Georgetown University Press, 1986.

"Guadalupe, Virgen de." In *Enciclopedia de México*. Ciudad de México: Compañía Editora de Enciclopedia de México, Secretaría de Educación Pública, 1987-1988: 6: 3542-3558.

Guerrero, Andrés G. *A Chicano Theology*. Maryknoll, N.Y.: Orbis Books, 1987.

Gutiérrez Zamora, Angel Camiro. *El origen del Guadalupanismo: fue Montúfar, y no Zumárraga, el Padre de la devoción a la Virgen de Guadalupe*. México, D.F.: EDAMEX, 1996.

Hall, Linda B. *Mary, Mother and Warrior: the Virgin in Spain and the Americas*. Theresa Eckmann, illustrations editor. Austin: University of Texas Press, 2004.

Ingham, John M. *Mary, Michael, and Lucifer: Folk Catholicism in Central Mexico*. Latin American monographs, no. 69. Austin: University of Texas Press, 1986.

Johnson, Harvey L., "The Virgin of Guadalupe in Mexican Culture." In *Religion in Latin American Life and Literature*, ed. Lyle C. Brown and William F. Cooper, 190-203. Waco, TX: Baylor University Press, Markham Press Fund, 1980.

Lafaye, Jacques. *Quetzalcóatl y Guadalupe: la formación de la conciencia nacional en México*. Traducción de Ida Vitale y Fulgencio López Vidarte. 2a ed. en español. Sección de obras de historia. México, D.F.: Fondo de Cultura Económica, 1991.

León-Portilla, Miguel. *Tonantzin Guadalupe: pensamiento náhuatl y mensaje cristiano en el "Nican Mopohua"*. Sección de Obras de Antropología. México, D.F.: El Colegio Nacional: Fondo de Cultura Económica, 2000.

Lozano-Díaz, Nora O., "Ignored Virgin or Unaware Woman: A Mexican-American Protestant Reflection on the Virgin of Guadalupe." In *A Reader in Latina Feminist Theology: Religion and Justice*, edited by María Pilar Aquino, Daisy L. Machado and Jeannette Rodríguez, 204-216. Austin, TX: University of Texas Press, 2002.

Matovina, Timothy, ed. *Beyond Borders: Writings of Virgilio Elizondo and Friends.* Maryknoll, NY: Orbis Books, 2000.

-----. *Guadalupe and Her Faithful: Latino Catholics in San Antonio from Colonial Origins to the Present.* Lived Religions. Baltimore: The Johns Hopkins University Press, 2005.

-----. "Our Lady of Guadalupe: Patroness of America." *America* 189:19 (Dec. 8, 2003): 8-12.

Maza, Francisco de la. *El guadalupanismo mexicano.* Tezontle. México, D.F.: Fondo de Cultura Económica, 1986.

Nebel, Richard. *Santa María Tonantzin, Virgen de Guadalupe: continuidad y transformación religiosa en México.* Traducción del alemán por el Pbro. Dr. Carlos Warnholtz Bustillos, con la colaboración de la señora Irma Ochoa de Nebel. Sección de Obras de Historia. México, D.F.: Fondo de Cultura Económica, 1995.

Nesvig, Martin Austin, ed. *Religious Culture in Modern Mexico.* Jaguar Books on Latin America Series. Lanham, MD: Rowman & Littlefield Publishers, 2007.

Noguez, Xavier. *Documentos guadalupanos: un estudio sobre las fuentes de información tempranas en torno a las mariofanías en el Tepeyac.* Sección de Sección de Obras de Historia. Toluca: El Colegio Mexiquense; México, D.F.: México, D.F.: Fondo de Cultura Económica, 1993.

O'Gorman, Edmundo. *Destierro de sombras: luz en eloOrigen de la imagen y culto de Nuestra Señora de Guadalupe del Tepeyac.* Serie Historia Novohispana 36. México, D.F.: Universidad Nacional Autónoma de México, 1986.

Peñalosa, Joaquín Antonio, comp., *Flor y canto de poesía guadalupana: siglo XX.* México, D.F.: Editorial Jus, 1984.

-----, comp., *Poesía Guadalupana: siglo XIX.* México, D.F.: Editorial Jus, 1985.

Peterson, Jeanette Favrot. "Creating the Virgin of Guadalupe: The Cloth, the Artist, and Sources in Sixteenth-Century New Spain." *The Americas* 61: 4 (April 2005): 571-610.

-----, "The Virgin of Guadalupe: Symbol of Conquest or Liberation?" *Art Journal* 51: 4 (Winter 1992): 39-47.

Petty, Leslie. "The 'Dual'-ing Images of La Malinche and La Virgen de Guadalupe in Cisnero's The House on Mango Street." *Melus* 25:2 (Summer 2000): 119-132.

Poole, Stafford. "Our Lady of Guadalupe: an ambiguous symbol." *Catholic Historical Review* 81: 4 (Oct. 1995): 588-99.

-----. *Our Lady of Guadalupe: the Origins of a Mexican National Symbol, 1531-1797.* Tucson: The University of Arizona Press, 1995.

Rodriguez, Jeanette. "Devotion to Our Lady of Guadalupe among Mexican Americans." In *Many Faces, One Church: Cultural Diversity and the American Catholic Experience,* edited by Peter C. Phan and Diana Hayes, 83-97. Catholic Studies Series. Lanham, Md.: Rowman & Littlefield, 2005.

-----. *Our Lady of Guadalupe: Faith and Empowerment among Mexican-American Women.* Austin: University of Texas Press, 1994.

Rodríguez, Mauro. *Guadalupe: ¿historia o símbolo?* México, D.F.: Editorial Edicol, 1980.

Scheper, George L. "Guadalupe: Image of Submission or Solidarity?" *Religion and the Arts* 3:3/4 (1999): 336-84.

Siller, Clodomiro. "La Iglesia en el medio indígena." In *Religión y política en México*, coordinado por Martín de la Rosa y Charles A. Reilly, 213-239. Sociología y política. México, D.F.: Siglo Veintiuno Editores, 1985.

Smith, Jody Brant. *The Image of Guadalupe*. 2nd and rev. ed. Macon, GA: Mercer University Press in association with Fowler Wright Books Ltd., 1994.

Sousa, Lisa, Stafford Poole and James Lockhart, eds. and trans. *The Story of Guadalupe: Luis Laso de la Vega's Huei tlamahuiçoltica of 1649*. UCLA Latin American Studies, vol. 84. Stanford, CA: Stanford University Press; Los Angeles: Latin American Center Publications, University of California, 1998.

Taylor, William B. *Magistrates of the Sacred: Priests and Parishioners in Eighteenth-Century Mexico*. Stanford, CA: Stanford University Press, 1996.

Testimonios históricos guadalupanos. Compilación, prólogo, notas bibliográficas e indices de Ernesto de la Torre Villar y Ramiro Navarro de Anda. Sección de Obras de Historia. México, D.F.: Fondo de Cultura Económica, 1999.

Villalpando, José Manuel. *La Virgen de Guadalupe: Una Biografía*. México, D.F.: Editorial Planeta Mexicana, 2004.

Wolf, Eric. "The Virgin of Guadalupe: A Mexican National Symbol." In *Reader in Comparative Religion: An Anthropological Approach*, [edited by] William A. Lessa and Evon Z. Vogt, 149-153. 3rd ed. New York: Harper & Row, 1972.

Zerón-Medina, Fausto. *Felicidad de México*. 2a ed. corr. y aum. México: Editorial Clío, 1997.

Zires, Margarita. "Nuevas imágenes guadalupanas: Diferentes límites del decir guadalupano en México y Estados Unidos." *Comunicación y sociedad* 38 (julio-diciembre, 2000): 59-76. Web. 2 May 2008. http://www.allbusiness.com/sector-61-educational-services/723620-1.html

Documenting Indigenous
and Human Rights

18. The Indigenous in Mariátegui
Richard F. Phillips

This paper is an effort to gain insights into the vast influence of José Carlos Mariátegui (JCM). Even prior to the initial issues of *Amauta* in 1926, and the 1928 appearance of his monumental *Siete ensayos de interpretación de la realidad peruana*, JCM's role as a proponent of the indigenous had swelled to amazing proportions. As the *Anuario Mariateguiano* stated in 1989, the work by JCM (and about JCM) is "virtualmente incontrolable."[1] The need to understand JCM is essential if one desires to comprehend the surging indigenous movements of today's Andes. This is in no way to overlook the influence of Manual González Prada's early anarchism, and certainly not meant to deny the major impact of Haya de la Torre in Pan-Indigenismo, but JCM is unique in giving a lead voice to Marxism, transcending the limits of the Marxism of those years, and maintaining a major, leading intellectual presence today.

When the April 16, 1930 special issue of *Amauta* put forward the news of JCM's death, he was only 36 years of age. The featured article lamented that the "más grande cerebro de América Latina ha dejado para siempre de pensar." Nevertheless, his influence persists.

His life, in spite of persistent physical ailments, was remarkably rich and full. When the dictatorial Leguía government placed him in Italy in 1920-1923 to sideline him and his critical voice,[2] JCM got exposure to a rapidly changing world as Europe emerged from World War I (the so-called war to end all wars). He came into contact with ideas on a broad scale. Mussolini and fascism were on the rise in Italy and elsewhere. In Russia, Marxism-Communism-Leninism-Trotskyism were working to weave the Soviet Union. And, of course, capitalism surged from the West, with British (and American) market penetration and consumerism digging roots into European and Latin American markets.

Peru was no exception. JCM returned to Lima in 1924 and found inspiration for his writings while the injustice from the legacies of colonialism continued to fester. Peru's landless indigenous masses, tied to archaic social structures of forced labor and poverty, ignited his inner strength to action. Western materialism encroached on native traditionalism, but rendered little gain to Peru's popular groups. The dogma and ideology of a highly charged Marxism dominated JCM's work, but at the same time a keen sense of the avant-garde warmed and enriched his output and editing. JCM was one who appreciated and defended creative personalities. In film, he found the mocking, social themes of Chaplin soothing to the pains of a mundane world. In music, he admired the freedom of Josephine Baker in the trials of racism. In the plastic arts, he embraced and promoted the use of indigenous images to humanize the struggles of the Andes.

It is striking to turn the pages of *Amauta* and to encounter the presentations of artists within JCM's intellectual circle. Much of the cover art throughout *Amauta*'s 32-issue run (1926-1930) was the work of José Sabogal. His stark images of the typical drew inspiration from native craft etchings visible on mates (household gourds). Sabogal's lead can be observed later in the poignant domestic scenes of the painter Camilo Blas. Julia Codecido is another artist that captured JCM's attention, and her portraits of the famous (such as Manuel González Prada) and the common (street scenes) add dignity and grace. Elena Izcue was a Peruvian who utilized pre-Columbian fabrics as a source for her paintings. In 1926, she did a book in Paris promoting indigenous art in Peru's school systems.[3] Also, the bold pencil stylings of Argentine artist Guillermo Buitrago were featured in the *Amauta* issue of June 1929. And JCM looked to Mexico for further material, highlighting Diego Rivera and Laura Rodrig.

Looking forward from today's perspective is a privilege. JCM and his influence are both mesmerizing and complex. Indeed, an essential place to start a contemporary review of JCM's contributions to the indigenous is the *Anuario Mariateguiano*—published from 1989 until 1999. One of its goals was to gather unedited and lesser known writings from various and sundry sources. Although JCM lived for only 36 brief years, he was an extremely prolific writer and correspondent. Volumes of the *Anuario* have collected letters from and to JCM involving César Vallejo, Unamuno, Waldo Frank, and other such notable intellectuals. The *Anuario* also pulled together essays from and about his works, as well as long-lost photos and images of JCM, his family and his associates, and compiled bibliographic guides to critical studies on JCM.

As stated, the *Anuario* was founded in 1989, and its original editorial lead was under JCM's sons, who remained involved throughout the *Anuario*'s 11-year run. Given access to inside-family confidential sources, the Anuario revealed, year after year, fascinating details on JCM's extraordinary intellect and life. At the same time, it captured the frustrations of his personal and political ambitions, framing them in both past settings and contemporary positions.

The initial 1989 volume of the *Anuario* looks at the classic figure that JCM has grown to be, one that is not "aséptico" and rigid, but rather one that is alive and inexhaustible.[4] This earliest volume of the *Anuario* sets the mold that other volumes would follow: re-editing unknown writings of JCM, offering transcribed letters with facsimiles of originals, and publishing critical essays. For example, *Anuario* volume 1 (1989) contained three "escritos olvidados" of JCM from the mid-1920s that were written for the Touring Club Italiano and its popular-market magazine *Le vie d'Italia e dell'America Latina*.

These are remarkable pieces as they give indications of the fire and rhetoric that would certainly mark JCM in later efforts, and thus certainly stand to add depth to JCM and his intellectual background and development. Indeed, the first of these articles for *Le vie d'Italia e dell'America Latina*, entitled "El desarrollo económico del Perú," would evolve to essentially become the text for the initial essay in his *Siete ensayos de interpretación de la realidad peruana* collection, with JCM's concluding paragraphs lashing out at Peru's feudalistic *latifundistas* for subjugating the indigenous majority.

Anuario volume 2 (1990) begins by pointing to the collapse of the Soviet Union, stating that these events reinforce the need to study JCM. Moving beyond these Marxist lines, this volume goes on to offer an essay on JCM by Rodrigo Montoya[5] that leads with a portion of two texts from JCM's hand that appeared in the journal *Mundial*. "Original sin" is the image that JCM invokes as he deplores Peru's marginalization of its indigenous majority.

Anuario volume 3 (1991) marked the 50th anniversary of JCM's death, and again makes reference to the crisis of world socialism. An insightful inclusion in this 3rd volume is the reprint of a short note from JCM in 1926 to a colleague in the highland city of Juliaca (Peru) concerning *Amauta* and how its "primer número está agotado."[6] Let it be noted that many libraries today are fortunate to hold facsimile runs of the important and scholarly *Amauta*.

Anuario volume 4 (1992) features an impressive image of JCM done in bronze. Editors comment on delivering "con mas punctualidad" this issue of the annual, and that makes an interesting connection to JCM's 1926 note on *Amauta*'s initial print run and distribution. This issue of the *Anuario* also picks up on the impact of JCM as seen in the eyes of contemporary critics in Japan and China.

Anuario volume 5 (1992) gives another color portrait, and lays out photos of JCM's youth and his early work in the Círculo de Periodistas. This *Anuario* gives revealing links to JCM as a commentator on the history of the New World, noting that JCM viewed Cristóbal Colón as one not to be scorned and castigated, but rather a man of vision. In his essay "Día de la raza," JCM celebrated latinidad—somewhat ironic given his role in indigenismo, much of which has grown to reject Western traditions. This also gives insights into JCM's rifts with Haya de la Torre.

Anuario volume 6 (1994) marked the centennial of JCM's birth, and featured a contribution by Cuba's Roberto Fernández Retamar of the Casa de las Américas cultural agency and publisher, which reissued JCM's *Siete ensayos* in 1963. Additionally, this issue of the *Anuario* culls a text from Roland Forgues (Mariátegui y la cuestión negra), which juxtaposes, in fascinating manner, the racial attitudes of the colonial era and the 1920s.

Anuario volume 7 (1995) offers impressive portraits of JCM by David Alfaro Siqueiros and the aforementioned Julia Codecido, as well as personal photos from his days in Rome. Also, there is an article by Nélida Flórez on the theme of women in JCM's work, and another by Rodrigo Montoya on ethnicity in JCM's times.

Anuario volume 8 (1996) reviews the Casa Museo José Carlos Mariátegui—a historic structure saved from demolition and declared a national historic monument by the government.

Anuario volume 9 (1997) is remarkable for its presentation of several never fully published speeches, probably from 1924, including JCM's first intervention on indigenous issues (with obvious influence by González Prada).

Anuario volume 10 (1998) focuses on Haya de la Torre and his break with JCM, with 20 pages of source documents related to APRA.

Anuario volume 11 (1999) is unfortunately the final issue; as is the case in most journals' ceasing, there is no notice of the termination.

In conclusion, there is value to the study of JCM and the indigenous-themed matter in his work. JCM's life and influence are important for Latin American Studies specialists to gain understanding of the fundamental changes in today's Andes. And, indeed, the Andes as a region is undergoing sweeping change. Be it separatist movements in Bolivia and Ecuador, environmental health issues in Peru, border tensions between Venezuela and Colombia, or feminist politics in Argentina and Chile, the Andes are breaking the structures of the traditional and reaching for reform. Librarians need to address information needs to facilitate user understanding of all of this. The influence of Mariátegui is one of the fundamentals to insights.

NOTES

1.   *Anuario Mariateguiano* (referred to subsequently as AM), v. 1, no. 1 (1989): 9.

2.   *Diccionario literario del Perú*, tomo 2, p. 61.

3.   Izcue, Elena. *El arte peruano en la escuela.* (Paris: Editorial Excelsior, 1926).

4.   *AM*, v. 1, no. 1 (1989): 9.

5.   *AM*, v. 2, no. 1 (1990): 45-68.

6.   *AM*, v. 3, no. 1 (1991): 15.

BIBLIOGRAPHY

Primary sources: by José Carlos Mariátegui

Amauta (Sociedad Editora Amauta, 1926-1930).
"En el día de la raza." In *La novela y la vida.* (Lima: Biblioteca Amauta, 1967).
7 ensayos de interpretación de la realidad peruana. (Lima: Biblioteca Amauta, 1928).

Secondary sources: on José Carlos Mariátegui

Anuario mariateguiano (Empresa Editora Amauta, 1989-1999).
Arriola Grande, Maurilio. *Diccionario literario del Perú* (Brasa, 1996).

Cuadernos americanos (UNAM, special issue no.48, 1994).

"Arte y arquitectura." In *Enciclopedia temática del Perú*. vol.15. (Lima: El Comercio, 2004).

"El fallecimineto del periodista Mariátegui." In *El Comercio*, April 17, 1930: p. 3.

Moore, Melisa. "Critical Junctures: Politics, Poetics and Female Presence in the Avant-Garde in Peru." In *Journal of Iberian and Latin American Studies*, v.12, no.1 (April 2006): 1-14.

"Sobre la captura de un grupo de comunistas" In *El Comercio*, June 10, 1927: p. 14

19. The Esther Chávez Cano Collection: An Archival Record of Violence against Women in the U.S.-Mexico Border and a Tool for Scholars and Activists

Charles Stanford

Molly Molloy

The Chávez collection is a unique representation of social justice and women's rights activism in Ciudad Juárez, a city whose notoriety for violence has greatly increased since the early 1990s when Esther Chávez Cano began keeping track of cases of murdered women. Her work became known to academics and activists on the U.S. side of the border in the late 1990s, and by that time she had already been working for nearly a decade to document the violent changes in Ciudad Juárez that often crept into the pages of Mexican newspapers with notices of young girls and women missing, or found dead, in the vacant lots of the sprawling desert city. It was late into the NAFTA decade before these events made it into the English-language press, and even as the real body count rose, those in power sought to diminish the significance, or even the reality, of the deaths of women and men in the border region. In addition to her work as a journalist and activist, in 1999, Chávez founded Casa Amiga Centro de Crisis, the only crisis center providing medical, psychological and legal services and shelter to women and families victimized by violence in Ciudad Juárez. Casa Amiga now provides treatment and services to more than 30,000 women every year.

Charles Bowden, a writer who has covered events in Juárez and other areas of the U.S.-Mexico border for more than 20 years, says something like this about what happens in Mexico: First, something happens (perhaps a crime, a murder, or another newsworthy event). Then, in the second stage, people create a lot of stories about what happened and theories circulate to try to explain it. In the third and final stage, the event disappears from the news, from the official accounts, even from the historical record...as if it never happened at all.[1]

Back in 1996, in the first article in the mainstream English-language press (*Harper's* December 1996) about the violence in Juárez, including the first real notice in our media of the murders of young women, Bowden wrote:

We have models in our heads about growth, development, and infrastructure. Juárez doesn't look like any of these images, and so our ability to see this city comes and goes, mainly goes. A nation that has never hosted a jury trial, that has been dominated by one party for most of this century, that is carpeted with corruption and poverty and pockmarked with billionaires is perceived as an emerging democracy marching toward First World standing. The snippets of fact that once in a while percolate up through the Mexican press are ignored by the U.S. government and its citizens.[2]

While researching a book about Juárez and the violence of the drug trade back in 1995, Charles Bowden went to the offices of *El Diario* looking for the negative of a photograph he had seen of a missing young woman. He met photojournalist Julián Cardona, and since that time they have collaborated on several books dealing with Juárez, the border, violence, and migration. Cardona wrote about the photo archive at the newspaper where he worked as a photographer and Esther worked as a columnist for some years:

> Archive is a pretentious word to describe the narrow room where our work ended up after an intense day on the street, days when some of us might have risked our lives for the perfect shot. In order to make room for new material, the guy in charge of the archive or one of his assistants would periodically destroy original negatives no longer considered necessary. As time passed, most of the new stuff would also end up in the garbage. I once searched for slides that had been taken of a case of anencephaly in a child born to a maquiladora worker—probably caused by inhaling toxic fumes on the job. I found that they had all been thrown away because "they were no longer of any use." In 1996, when "Los Rebeldes" (a gang accused of the murders of several women) were arrested, I photographed their mothers confronting the state governor after a public event. Since I was the only photographer there, I had doubts about turning them in, thinking that I should keep them—no one would know. It was a feeling I had at various times, not from fear of censorship or criticism—rather, negligence and incompetence were the more formidable rivals. In the end, these images were all lost.[3]

To most information professionals, the importance of archival records need not be stressed, and many know the difficulties of collecting materials from places like Juárez, and the added difficulties of dealing with sensitive materials that may threaten structures of power.

However, thanks to Esther Chávez Cano, the reality of the violent changes in her city cannot be denied. Journalists from all over the world began to visit Esther in the late 1990s and she would share with them her files and talk to them about the interlocking crises of uncontrolled growth with no economic and social infrastructure for the people living and working in the city that led to such violence. Her files document crimes that in many cases have never been solved and have essentially disappeared from the justice system as completely as the young lives disappeared from the streets of Juárez.

As time went on, Esther found that her files sometimes disappeared also, as she would generously loan things to reporters and researchers who might not always return them. In 2006, she contacted New Mexico State University Criminal Justice Professor Cynthia Bejarano who has worked with many families of victims and with activist groups in Mexico and the United States. Professor Bejarano contacted Molly Molloy at the New Mexico State University Library and we worked with the NMSU Rio Grande Historical Collections (RGHC) to secure Esther's documents. In late 2006, we brought seven large plastic file boxes from Esther's house to the Library, but it was not until Archivist Charles Stanford joined the faculty in the fall of 2007 that the collection was processed and made available to the public.

The newspaper clippings that make up the bulk of the Chávez collection trace the stories of individual victims, the growing public attention to murders of women over the years, arrests of suspects, government statements, and the activist groups that Sra. Chávez was involved in. Records from these activist groups give a glimpse into the workings of these groups, as well as the external challenges and internal struggles that they have faced in pursuing their missions.

Other documents show the efforts of international organizations and scholars to rally support and raise awareness of the murders of young women in Juárez and to increase understanding of the sociological factors caused by Juárez's unpleasant economic and social realities, and the efforts of journalists to bring the stories of the murders to the attention of more people.

The collection also touches on other matters like factory conditions; women's rights, including questions of sexual abuse and freedom and reproductive choice; and the politics of activist groups, including the controversies and rifts that occur.

Making these documents available on this side of the border opens them up to access by researchers and activists in the United States. Mexican activists have called for help from U.S. agents in investigating some of the murder cases and have sought to draw awareness to the Juárez murders throughout the whole world. A recently received modest grant will enable the digitization of the collection. Already several researchers have used it for various purposes, some coming from as far away as Yale University. A promotional spot on NMSU's KRWG-TV program *Aggie Almanac* has brought in at least one researcher, and it is expected that over time more researchers will come to use these records.

This collection is rather unusual in comparison to the others in the RGHC, which although it does already include some eyebrow-raising stuff, it still has historically focused on the normal course of late 19th- and 20th-century mainstream Anglo culture in New Mexico. The majority of the holdings in the RGHC are genteel and safe—safe if for no other reason than that so many of the people represented in them died a while ago, often of natural causes, or because so many of our holdings come from peaceful or common economic and cultural pursuits: ranching, mining, civic and service clubs, farming, and raising families. The Chávez collection comes into such an environment telling of unspeakable and ongoing tragedy.

Traditionally, the RGHC has been a historical repository. Even though people come to consult the material the organization holds on notorious incidents of violence like the Lincoln County War and criminals like Billy the Kid, there is that safe distance of time between the events represented by pieces of paper with picturesque old handwriting or type, and the present. The tragedy and violence that make for dramatic history can be enjoyed because the events represented by most of the holdings happened long enough ago. Having a collection like this disturbs the traditional concept of a place like the RGHC, introducing not only the unpleasant realities of recent murders but also the uncomfortable questions of current political power structures illustrated in the collection, including evidences of attempts to discredit and silence Esther Chávez and other activists and journalists, and in the very story of why this collection came here instead of staying in Juárez.

For whom is this collection held? Archives have been resources for academic historians for a long time now and that is all very well; this commercially-driven society greatly needs the clear eyes and level heads of responsible and well-trained historians. But one of the goals here has been to increase visibility and use throughout the entire public. Not everyone can be a specialized historian, but everyone can learn some basics about how to interpret and think about records and evidence. Everyone can be taught the importance of not shrinking from the problems of life and of recognizing the unpleasant things that may be going on close to their homes. But one of the most fruitful uses of collections that come from activist activity is as a resource for activists in plotting the course of their missions.

These documents not only help increase awareness of the violence in Juárez through the information contained in some of the material, but can facilitate scholarly study of an important activist project and serve as a resource for current and future activists in identifying problems they will face and strategies to use in carrying out their own missions. For this collection is principally the record of an activist project, reflecting the attitudes, ideals and purposes of Esther Chávez and her allies. It would be impossible for one person to put together an adequate archive of the violence in Juárez.

For activists to begin using the repository in greater numbers opens up questions that have the potential to disturb the quiet comfort that I think has been associated with this repository and others like it.

There is an attitude that archivists, especially those in academic institutions, must be neutral and impartial, whatever that is supposed to mean. To accept and house such a collection as this does seem more neutral at NMSU than it would in Juárez. Maybe that is a good reason for them to come here, so a semblance of neutrality is preserved, enough to keep everyone out of trouble.

Out of trouble beyond the troubling questions this collection has already opened, as do any records of political activism: once these records are taken, what other records of what kind of activism along the border is the organization willing to collect? How will it negotiate between the requests and expectations of cool, methodical scholars and passionate activists in appraisal, description and access?

Part of the hope for this collection has been to open up the door not only to more documentation of border problems, but also to the Hispanic culture of New Mexico and to provide greater access to Spanish-speaking researchers. It will not be possible to pursue this without confronting the history of power and dominance of culture and language in New Mexico since 1850. The RGHC has reflected this dominance, though not maliciously, naturally attracting the records of the powerful and influential. Facing up to this, and acting on intent to extend the scope beyond its historical core, will mean negotiating with that expectation of neutrality and re-investigating the philosophies and goals of the RGHC and repositories like it—challenging tasks that unfortunately do not tend to shine out in performance or use statistics.

So bringing in the Chávez collection does introduce some trouble into an institution—and a profession—that is not only expected to be neutral, but has often been seen as sedate, oriented towards antiquities, even dry and boring. But in going through any records people leave behind or consciously gather together, one catches glimpses of the range of human nature and experience. We see the complexity of life and are often brought face to face with things we would rather not think about. It is unpleasant to confront the countless newspaper articles telling of murders, abuse, oppression and violence that happen so close to home. But this collection is important precisely because so much of what it contains is unpleasant. And the trouble that such current records of such shocking events introduce is a stirring up that is greatly needed. Besides the increased number and wider scope of researchers it brings in, and in addition to the very important perpetual witness that it bears of violence and tragedy as well as grace, hope and dedication, it forces us to face up to questions of appraisal and documentation that defy easy answers, and for that we should be grateful, since archivists no longer have an excuse to avoid confronting these questions and holding their working answers under constant examination.

Despite the sporadic media attention to the sensational sexual aspects of some of the crimes occurring in Juárez throughout the 1990s and later, Esther Chávez has consistently maintained that the great majority of the 400-500 murders of women resulted from domestic violence or from the general situation of poverty and lack of social infrastructure in the city and the influence of the drug trade that has resulted in the deaths of at least ten times as many men as women during the same span of time. The Esther Chávez

Cano collection provides important documentation as to the true nature of this violence and has the potential to help establish this truth that may have been obscured by sensational press coverage.

The Chávez collection has already been used by at least one researcher who analyzed the various statistical sources on the murders of women in Juárez. Yale history student Erin Frey, in a paper not yet published, gathered information from this collection (in addition to numerous interviews with activists, reporters, scholars and others) to support her thesis that may prove quite controversial in the literature on "femicide." Her thesis is that attention in foreign media and from activists and some feminist scholars that emphasizes the more sensational "gendered" aspects of the killings (characteristics that at most apply to 70-80 out of 400-500 cases) has diverted attention from the real causes of murder and violence in Juárez: the lack of adequate living wages in the maquiladora sector, the lack of social infrastructure for those poor men and women who migrate to the border, the huge and violent influence of the drug trade in the city—not only the business aimed at crossing drugs into the United States, but also the explosion in the local domestic retail drug market. In Juárez, most men and women lack the economic means and social resources to maintain a stable and safe society. Exotic explanations are not needed to explain the murders of women. Both women and men face danger and mortality every day, as a byproduct of the social conditions in the border city.[4]

Beginning in the 1990s, statistics show that about 10 percent of the murders in Juárez were of women. On average, throughout the 1990s, nine men were killed for every one woman. However, during the wave of killings from January-September 2008, based on the statistics from the Subprocuraduría de Justicia del Estado (PGJE), the number of women killed was about 3 percent of the total. These current figures are by no means complete and rely on the data reported from the PGJE. Homicide investigations in Juárez are handled by two different offices: the Unidad Especializada para la Investigación de Delitos Contra la Vida-Special Unit for the Investigation of Crimes Against Life (UEIDCV) and the Fiscalía Especial para la Investigación de Homicidios de Mujeres-Special Prosecutor for the Investigation of Women's Homicides (FEIHM). As of September 16, 2008, the UEIDCV had undertaken the investigation of 939 victims; the FEIHM was investigating 22 cases.[5] A quick calculation shows that the women's murders under investigation from January-September this year made up about 2.4 % of the total. This in no way should minimize the horror of gender violence and domestic violence in Juárez—women are the great majority of victims in these cases. But attention must be focused on the totality of the violence—unprecedented in the history of the city and in the border region. As of October 30, 2008, the number of homicides in Juárez was already triple the number from the previous annual record of 309 in 2007.[6]

Since this paper's original presentation in June 2008, the death toll from homicide in Juárez has continued to climb. The monthly death tolls range from

45 in February to a high of 217 in August. On average, there were 4-5 murders per day in 2008. On August 13, eight people were shot to death at a drug rehabilitation center.[78] On November 13, the main crime reporter for *El Diario*, Armando Rodriguez, was assassinated in front of his home.[9] Other reporters have received death threats and the newspapers have replaced reporter bylines with the anonymous label "Staff" or "Redacción" on all crime stories.[10] On November 19, 2008, it was reported that murder would surpass diabetes as the major cause of death in the city.[11] On November 29, eight men who worked in a Juárez maquiladora were gunned down while dining in a restaurant together.[12] Another daily paper, *El Norte de Ciudad Juárez*, reported on November 29 that a total of 130 women had been killed violently thus far in 2008, raising the percentage of women to 9.2 percent of the total murder victims so far that year.[13] The murders of women include at least two U.S. citizens shot on Juárez streets in November and December. And the papers continue to report that almost none of these cases have been solved.[14] As of the end of November, *El Diario* reported a total of 1,407 homicides.[15] Nearly 40 more people were murdered during the first five days of December, including the assassination of the head of the Federal Prosecutor's office in Juárez. In all, 65 law enforcement officers have been murdered so far in 2008.[16]

On the Saturday morning after the events to honor Esther Chávez in November 2007, she was escorted to the archives stacks so that she could see her collection in its new secure location in Branson Hall. All of us who worked with Esther on this project have been inspired by her courage and her good humor. For the past several years, she has fought her own battle against cancer, while continuing to work at Casa Amiga and to tell all who will listen about the struggles of women, children and families in Juárez. As she said to those assembled to honor her on November 9, 2007,

> We have much work left to do, the road ahead is long and hard. There will come a time when my voice becomes silent so that new voices can be heard to carry on the struggle for the rights of women, which, as I have said, is also for the rights of men, because it is the struggle for a more just and democratic society for all.[17]

It is an honor to be trusted with this collection and to help keep the stories of these women of Juárez—the victims and their advocates, the dead and the living—from being silenced or fading into comfortable ignorance. In late November, it was also reported that Esther Chávez Cano would receive Mexico's National Human Rights Award for 2008 for her distinguished work over the past 16 years for the promotion and defense of women's rights and her continuing struggle to draw attention to violence against women in Mexico and the world.[18]

It is our hope that the Esther Chávez Cano Collection will be the seed to grow a more extensive archive of documentation of social justice organizations, public records, newspapers and other primary sources that will preserve the record of this violent and difficult time in the U.S.-Mexico border region.

NOTES

1. Carrier, S. (Writer) (2004). Juarez 5: Easy to Forget [Radio Broadcast]. In S. Carrier (Producer), *Juarez: city on the Edge*. USA: Hearing Voices; National Public Radio Day to Day. Retrieved December 2, 2008, from Hearing Voices: http://hearingvoices.com/transcript.php?fID125

2. Bowden, C. (Dec 1996). "While you were sleeping: in Juarez, Mexico, photographers expose the violent realities of free trade." *Harper's Magazine*, 293, 1759. P. 44. Retrieved December 02, 2008, from General OneFile via Gale: http://find.galegroup.com/itx/start.do?prodID=ITOF

3. Cardona, J. (2007). Carlos y mi ciudad. Unpublished manuscript. (Translation by Molly Molloy).

4. Frey, E. (2008). Femicide in Juarez, Mexico: The Hidden Transcript that No One Wants to Read. Unpublished manuscript, Branford College, Yale University, p. 39.

5. Rodriguez, S. (September 19, 2008). Sin resolver 97 de cada 100 delitos. *El Diario de Ciudad Juarez*. Retrieved from http://www.diario.com.mx/nota.php?notaid=30a44aa69e5be3ba0 0b41ab11a099595.

6. Chacon, A. (October 30, 2008). Van el triple de homicidios solosos que en el 2007. *El Norte de Ciudad Juarez*.

7. Quintero, A. (August 14, 2008). Asesina commando a 9. *El diario de Ciudad Juárez*. Retrieved from: http://www.diario.com.mex/nota.php?notaid=ab324c22c0e2e27046ecb05bab5e 2a39.

8. Molloy, M. (August 18, 2008). Massacre at CIAD #8 in Juárez. *Narco News Bulletin*. Retrieved from http://narconews.com/Issue54/article3181.html

9. Staff (November 13, 2008). Asesinan a reporter de El Diario. *El diario de Ciudad Juárez*. Retrieved from http://www.diario.com.mx/nota.php?notaid=295c9fb4d40adef540b837f7 3ede842d.

10. Staff (November 16, 2008). Crece el riesgo para reporteros. *El Diario de Ciudad Juarez*. Retrieved from http://www.diario.com.mx/nota.php?notaid=1bcf069b6deaac6b18b1165 a558caefe.

11. Staff (November 19, 2008). Prevén que homicidios serán principal causa de muerte aquí. *El Diario de Ciudad Juarez*. Retrieved from http://www.diario.com.mx/nota.php?notaid=05 8e498a48b89d27100ec3d24dcbb3a2.

12. Staff (November 29, 2008). Masacran a 8 en restaurante. *El Diario de Ciudad Juarez*. Retrieved from http://www.diario.com.mx/nota.php?notaid=6669d7209705a16045eacb69101 1b046.

13. Redaccion (November 29, 2008). Han matado a 130 mujeres. *El Norte de Ciudad Juarez*. Retrieved from http://www.nortedeciudadjuarez.com/paginas/seguridad/seg2.html.

14. Rodriguez, S. (September 19, 2008). Sin resolver 97 de cada 100 delitos. *El Diario de Ciudad Juarez*. Retrieved from http://www.diario.com.mx/nota.php?notaid=30a44aa69e5be3ba0 0b41ab11a099595.

15. Staff (December 1, 2008). Matan a otros tres; suman 1,407 homicidios. *El Diario de Ciudad Juarez*. Retrieved from http://www.diario.com.mx/nota.php?notaid=d065031226329505b 47fe220a11c54a8.

16. Staff (December 5, 2008). Van este año 65 oficiales asesinados de los 3 niveles. *El Diario de Ciudad Juárez*. Retrieved from http://www.diario.com.mx/nota.php?notaid=280ae81e 089f21f205d5e887dc4bb010.

242 CHARLES STANFORD AND MOLLY MOLLOY

17. Chavez Cano, E. (2007). Agradecimiento. Unpublished Speech. New Mexico State University. (Translation by Molly Molloy)

18. Barraza, N. (November 20, 2008). Esther Chavez Cano/Premio Nacional de Derechos Humanos "Contenta...aunque todavia no logramos lo que queremos". *El Norte de Ciudad Juarez.*

REFERENCES

Barraza, N. (November 20, 2008). Esther Chavez Cano / Premio Nacional de Derechos Humanos "Contenta...aunque todavia no logramos lo que queremos". *El Norte de Ciudad Juarez.*

Bowden, C. (Dec 1996). While you were sleeping: in Juarez, Mexico, photographers expose the violent realities of free trade. *Harper's Magazine*, 293, 1759. P. 44. Retrieved December 02, 2008, from General OneFile via Gale: http://find.galegroup.com/itx/start.do?prodId=ITOF.

Cardona, J. (2007). Carlos y mi ciudad. Unpublished manuscript. (Translation by Molly Molloy.)

Carrier, S. (Writer) (2004). Juarez 5: Easy to Forget [Radio Broadcast]. In S. Carrier (Producer), *Juarez: City on the Edge.* USA: Hearing Voices; National Public Radio Day to Day. Retrieved December 2, 2008, from Hearing Voices: http://hearingvoices.com/transcript.php?fID125.

Chacon, A. (October 30, 2008). Van el triple de homicidios dolosos que en el 2007. *El Norte de Ciudad Juarez.*

Chavez Cano, E. (2007). Agradecimiento. Unpublished Speech. New Mexico State University. (Translation by Molly Molloy)

Frey, E. (2008). Femicide in Juarez, Mexico: The Hidden Transcript that No One Wants to Read. Unpublished manuscript, Branford College, Yale University.

Molloy, M. (August 18, 2008). Massacre at CIAD #8 in Juárez. *Narco News Bulletin.* Retrieved from http://narconews.com/Issue54/article3181.html.

Quintero, A. (August 14, 2008). Asesina comando a 9. *El Diario de Ciudad Juarez.* Retrieved from http://www.diario.com.mx/nota.php?notaid=ab324c22c0e2e27046ecb05bab5e2a39.

Redaccion (November 29, 2008). Han matado a 130 mujeres. *El Norte de Ciudad Juarez.* Retrieved from http://www.nortedeciudadjuarez.com/paginas/seguridad/seg2.html.

Rodriguez, S. (September 19, 2008). Sin resolver 97 de cada 100 delitos. *El Diario de Ciudad Juarez.* Retrieved from http://www.diario.com.mx/nota.php?notaid=30a44aa69e5be3ba00b41ab11a099595.

Staff (November 13, 2008). Asesinan a reportero de El Diario. *El Diario de Ciudad Juarez.* Retrieved from http://www.diario.com.mx/nota.php?notaid=295c9fb4d40adef540b837f73ede842d.

Staff (November 16, 2008). Crece el riesgo para reporteros. *El Diario de Ciudad Juarez.* Retrieved from http://www.diario.com.mx/nota.php?notaid=1bcf069b6deaac6b18b1165a558caefe.

Staff (November 19, 2008). Prevén que homicidios serán principal causa de muerte aquí. *El Diario de Ciudad Juarez.* Retrieved from http://www.diario.com.mx/nota.php?notaid=058e498a48b89d27100ec3d24dcbb3a2.

Staff (November 29, 2008). Masacran a 8 en restaurante. *El Diario de Ciudad Juarez*. Retrieved from http://www.diario.com.mx/nota.php?notaid=6669d7209705a1 6045eacb691011b046.

Staff (December 1, 2008). Matan a otros tres; suman 1,407 homicidios. *El Diario de Ciudad Juarez*. Retrieved from http://www.diario.com.mx/nota.php?notaid=d0 65031226329505b47fe220a11c54a8.

Staff (December 5, 2008). Van este año 65 oficiales asesinados de los 3 niveles. *El Diario de Ciudad Juárez*. Retrieved from http://www.diario.com.mx/nota.php?not aid=280ae81e089f21f205d5e887dc4bb010.

Indigenous Influences in The Arts

20. The Pre-Conquest Aesthetic in Modern Mexican Silver

Penny C. Morrill

Modern Mexican silver is a renewed tradition, originating in the influence and application of diverse concepts and trends that has led to something entirely new. Based on the Arts and Crafts movement, pre-Columbian art, Modernism, and Art Deco, this art form has remained uniquely Mexican.

William Spratling, an architect from New Orleans, initiated the twentieth-century silver industry in Taxco, Mexico.

Figure 1: William Spratling. c. 1950. Spratling-Taxco Collection, Tulane University Latin American Library.

This paper will provide a brief history of Spratling's grand experiment, while shedding light on the elements of its success. It will discuss the development of a stylistic identity that contributed to and allowed for the continuous flow of new ideas.[1]

Spratling's arrival in Mexico was perfectly timed. An explosion of art and intellectual discourse in the late 1920s was drawing scholars, artists, and poets, all hopeful participants in a remarkable experiment. Mexicans were rewriting their country's history and placing art at the service of humanity. Spratling was teaching architecture at Tulane University in New Orleans when he was given a contract to write a book about Mexico. In 1929, he bought a house in Taxco and immersed himself in the life of this mountainside village south of the capital. *Little Mexico* debuted in 1932 to rave reviews. Almost simultaneously, the publisher went bankrupt and the author was forced to search for another way to make a living.[2]

247

"I decided to bring some goldsmiths up from Iguala, and put them to work in Taxco making silver...The first epoch, of say 15 years or so of making silver, was simply terrific. The thing increased with such leaps and bounds that we could hardly hold it down."[3]

In developing a modern industry in a remote mountain village, William Spratling can be viewed as a pragmatic visionary. His workshop, Taller de las Delicias, started modestly with a *maestro* and a half-dozen young men. Expansion took place at a rapid pace.

Figure 2: Façade of the Taller de Las Delicias. 1940. Postcard. Penny Morrill Collection

In less than ten years, Spratling had over 150 employees, producing tinware, woven rugs and blankets, furniture, silver jewelry and decorative objects. While silver had been mined for centuries in Taxco, the local people were now given the opportunity to benefit from the new industry.

The initial vision for Las Delicias was defined by several revolutionary concepts: an organizational hierarchy based on ability; a stylistic approach inspired by historical and regional art; the application of local traditional handicraft techniques; and the use of local, accessible, and inexpensive materials. Then Spratling added one final ingredient. This addition, as surprising as it may seem, was indispensable to the success he enjoyed. For the rest of his life, Spratling expended much energy in the creation of a marketplace.[4]

The workshop organized by Spratling was born out of the communal village *taller*, with its emphasis on shared participation.

Figure 3: Silversmiths in the Taller de Las Delicias. 1942-44. Spratling-Taxco Collection, Tulane University Latin American Library

Spratling merged this tradition with his experience as an instructor at the Arts and Crafts Club in the French Quarter. The artisans began as young men, working at simple tasks under the guidance of a *maestro*. Once a silversmith showed promise and an enthusiasm for learning, he was given increasingly complex work to perform. As the young man acquired technical skills, he gained greater responsibility in the workplace.

Spratling's designs expressed the mystical exoticism of remote times.

Figure 4: William Spratling. Quetzalcoatl brooch, 980 silver. c. 1940. Private Collection. Photograph by Luisa di Pietro

His work is reflective of his own life-long fascination with the pre-Conquest aesthetic: "I felt myself drawn with great force to pre-Columbian art. It is one of my passions."[5] Architectural aspects of pre-Columbian motifs predominate in Spratling's designs—the projections into space, pyramids and spirals, parallel lines, dynamic torques and twists, massive sculptural forms that become pins and pendants. For the young men who were employed in the workshop, the pre-Hispanic motifs originated in the art of their ancestors.

Figure 5: Temple of Quetzalcoatl, Teotihuacan. c. 1940. Postcard. Penny Morrill Collection

The images that influenced modern silverwork were the ancient representations of the gods their forebears had worshipped. The interpretation of natural phenomena was through the filter of Mexico's past.

Figure 6: William Spratling. Parrot brooch, 980 silver and amethyst quartz. c. 1940. Stella and Fred Krieger Collection. Photograph by Joel Lipton

William Spratling directed his stylistic vocabulary at those who thought the way he did, the "cultural pilgrims" who came to Mexico in those early years after the Revolution of 1910.[6] Many were intellectuals and among them were communists, all looking to discover the social and economic impact of the Revolution and to participate in change. They also brought with them a respect for the artisan.

In the early years, Spratling sold only on a retail basis in the store below the workshop. The late 1930s brought an expansion into the wholesale market. While Spratling's more commercial line of silver jewelry and hollowware was offered in the Montgomery Ward catalogue, his jewelry, tea sets, and sauce boats were available at Neiman Marcus in Dallas and at Gumps in San Francisco. In 1949, Spratling made the astonishing statement that, by 1945, he was selling to twenty-six outlets in Mexico and one hundred-forty in the United States.[7] It is possible that he may have also been selling his silver designs in commissaries on U.S. Army bases.[8]

Spratling's success bred more success as workshops sprouted up all over the little town just before the war. One of the earliest and the longest-lived was the Taller de Los Castillo. Since 1939, the four Castillo brothers—Antonio, Jorge (Chato), Justo (Coco), and Miguel—Antonio's wife Margot, cousin Salvador Terán, and now Antonio's children Emilia, Lily, and Wolmar have produced some of the most inventive and beautiful pieces that have come out of Mexico.

Figure 7: Los Castillo *Ce Acatl* necklace and cuff bracelet, 980 silver. c. 1940. Ron Belkin and Penny Morrill Collections. Photograph by Joel Lipton

From five-hundred craftsmen employed at the height of production during the war, Spratling, in 1948-49, relocated a much reduced workshop to his ranch in Taxco el Viejo. A commission from the U. S. government to create a handcraft industry in Alaska and a partnership with the silver company, Conquistador, were opportunities that enthralled and consumed him. Although the Alaska project was never implemented, the creative process of studying Alaskan indigenous art and responding to its inspiration were the catalysts that resulted in what many consider Spratling's best work.

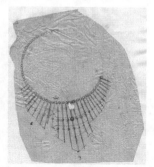

Figure 8: William Spratling design drawing for Needle Necklace. c. 1950. Spratling-Taxco Collection, Tulane University Latin American Library

The more successful silver designers in Taxco acknowledged and adopted another of Spratling's innovations—his insistence on the use of traditional materials. As in so many other choices he made, Spratling's emphasis on local materials originated in his sensitivity to indigenous cultural manifestations. Stones were chosen not for their preciousness, but for the contribution they made to the ultimate impact of the piece. For most of the silver *maestros*, the idea of incorporating common stones, tortoise-shell, rosewood, ebony, and copper was anything but limiting. Antonio Castillo recalled traveling to Oaxaca to view the gold that had been recovered from the Mixtec tomb at Monte Alban, with the intent of studying and replicating pre-Columbian techniques and use of materials.[9]

The decade of the fifties in Taxco was one of great experimentation and change. Margot van Voorhies Carr had her own workshop after 1948 and developed two lines, one in silver, the other in enamel on silver. She had come to Mexico from San Francisco, so it is not surprising to find influences from Japan and China in her work.

Figure 9: Margot Van Voorhies Carr design drawings for Chrysanthemum ensemble. c. 1950-55. Spratling-Taxco Collection, Tulane University Latin American Library

Margot used color expressively and imparted qualities of preciousness and femininity at a time when most designers were hammering out muscular, darkly oxidized, large-scale silver jewelry.

Figure 10: Margot Van Voorhies Carr design drawings for Spiraling Colors ensemble. c. 1950-55. Spratling-Taxco Collection, Tulane University Latin American Library

A number of Mexican designers looked to international trends in fine and decorative art for inspiration. Well known for his experimentation with the language of organic modernism, Sigi Pineda is thought to have broken away from Taxco's stylistic tradition. However, in retrospect, Sigi continued

along the path of the other great silver designers of Taxco, like Margot van
Voorhies Carr, Hubert Harmon, Valentín Vidaurreta, and Chato Castillo,
whose approach to form and use of materials has resulted in the unique and
unexpected qualities in their work that have made them so admired.[10] Whereas
William Spratling founded an industry and established a market for Mexican
silver, success would have been elusive had it not been for the continuous
flow of fine work from gifted Mexican designers. It is important to remember
that many of these artists were not followers of trends, but were talented and
enthusiastic innovators.

Figure 11: Sigi Pineda holding his design drawing. 2006. Photograph by Transluz Fotografía

The appeal of Mexican silver is in the quality of the interpretation of
indigenous pre-Columbian, colonial, and contemporary folk art. Spratling and
the others resisted slavish imitation and moved, instead, to subtle and suggestive
borrowings, all the while retaining symbolic references. The resonance of
these works reveals the fascination with indigenous culture, which was shared
by those who made the silver and by those who bought it. The best of the silver
designs are not cliché-ridden and, for this reason, they remain powerful in their
sensual impact and as artistic statements.

Figure 12: William Spratling. Petate pin and cuff bracelet. c. 1940. Ron Belkin Collection.
Photograph by Joel Lipton

What brought about this remarkable achievement? Spratling's organizational, marketing, and design experiments were prototypical, and easy for the silversmiths who had started out at Las Delicias and then set out on their own to replicate. Paramount was the insistence on the work of the hand and on experimentation, the beating heart of Mexican silver. Spratling's belief in the merits of a hand-wrought industry, based on good design and technical mastery, persisted in spite of high labor costs. This one aspect, the insistence on the touch of the hand, resulted in the employment over the years of incalculable numbers of artisans to meet demand for the product.

Today, there are almost 200,000 people living in Taxco. Few workshops exist and most of the silverwork is done at the behest of the wholesale market. The *mayoristas* [wholesalers] both in Taxco and outside of the city demand jewelry that is inexpensive and in a form that possesses already proven marketability. Therefore, tiny family workshops all over Taxco are given small amounts of silver to hammer into Mickey Mouse pendants, which then get attached to lightweight machine-made chains. Worse, this material is sold by the gram—as one silver designer commented, "like fish in the market."[11] An even more dangerous development is the importation of cheap jewelry from Thailand and China, sold as if produced in Taxco. This has led to joblessness and the lure of the drug market.

It is now essential to foster and bring great design to the marketplace. Over the last five years, this effort has been a priority for those who care about Mexican silver.

Figure 13: Agnes Seebass. Necklace and earrings. 2006. Photograph by Transluz Fotografía

Several bright new designers are getting attention in the marketplace, with the assistance of dealers and storeowners in the United States and Mexico. Agnes Seebass, whose workshop is in Taxco, and Martha Vargas of Michoacán are two talented contemporary designers.

Figure 14: Agnes Seebass. 2006. Photograph by Transluz Fotografía

In light of lower standards, negative market forces, the environmental impact of the industry, and the lack of governmental support for good design and technically superior handwork, the Spratling-Taxco Collection at Tulane University's Latin American Library takes on greater significance. The modern Mexican silver industry has become almost parenthetical, with a beginning and an end in sight. The collection will allow scholars to consider what went right and wrong in the development of this industry as they study these preserved materials, accessible now in a public collection. How wonderful it would be if these efforts could provide support and an incentive for great design and thus insure a bright future for Mexican silver!

NOTES

1. This paper borrows heavily from the author's essay in *Maestros de Plata: William Spratling and the Mexican Silver Renaissance*. Exhibition catalogue (New York: Harry N. Abrams, Inc., 2002): 12-69. For a fuller history, Penny Morrill and Carole Berk. *Mexican Silver: 20th Century Handwrought Jewelry and Metalwork* (Atglen, PA: Schiffer Publishing, Inc., 1994; 4th edition, 2007).

2. *File on Spratling: An Autobiography* (Boston, MA: Little Brown and Co., 1967). See the third chapter in Spratling's autobiography (ghost-written by Gerald R. Kelly) concerning his years in New Orleans, as well as the fourth and fifth chapters on the early years in Taxco. Spratling's *Little Mexico* (New York: Jonathan Cape and Harrison Smith, 1932), is a good read.

3. Robert David Duncan. "William Spratling's Mexican World." *Texas Quarterly*. Vol. IX, No. 1 (Spring 1966): 101.

4. Penny Morrill. "William Spratling and His Marketing Ways." *Silver Magazine*. XXXVI, 3 (May- June 2004): 2-9.

5. Beatriz Reyes Nevares. "Spratling Habla de un Arte Mas Humano que Divino el Cual Refleja la Cara Sonriente de México." *Suplemento de Novedades* (Jan. or Feb. 1961?): 1, 5. Translation by author.

6. Helen Delpar. *The Enormous Vogue of Things Mexican: Cultural Relations between the United States and Mexico, 1920-1935* (Tuscaloosa, AL and London: University of Alabama Press, 1992): 61.

7. "He's Teaching Eskimos in Mexico." The New Orleans *Times-Picayune, Dixie Roto* (June 1, 1949): 6. These numbers also appear in a 1951 document, reprinted in Morrill 2002, Appendix II, 258.

8.   Morrill 2004, 28-9.

9.   Author's interviews of Antonio Castillo, 1992-2000, Taxco-el-Viejo, Mexico.

10. Penny Morrill. "Hubert Harmon: Whimsy and Humor in Mexican Silver." *Jewelry.* Journal of the American Society of Jewelry Historians. 1 (1996-97): 64-77. For Valentín Vidaurreta, Chapter 2 in Penny Morrill's *Silver Masters of Mexico: Héctor Aguilar and the Taller Borda* (Atglen, PA: Schiffer Publishing, 1996): 72-95.

11. Author's interviews of Ana Brilanti, 1992-1999, Taxco, Mexico.

21. Spanish Pueblo Revival Architecture: Blending Native and New World Design in New Mexico
Audra Bellmore

The Spanish Pueblo Style, popular in the Southwest, merged two unique cultures: one native and one based on European settlement of the New World. When the Spanish arrived in what is now New Mexico in the 16th century, searching for gold, they instead encountered a highly developed Pueblo architecture, characterized by terraced houses built of stone and earth. However, the Spanish brought with them the rich building traditions of their own culture. And while the Spanish used these traditions in planning new structures, they were highly influenced by the climate, the availability of local materials, and the construction techniques of the native people. As a result, the Spanish and the Pueblo styles mingled together to form Spanish-Pueblo Style buildings, popular for over a period of approximately four centuries.

Characteristics of the original Spanish Pueblo structures influenced by the Pueblo culture included flat roofs, terraced levels producing a stepped effect, battered walls, blunt angles, projecting roof beams (later called *vigas* by the Spanish), and corner fireplaces. Spanish elements included rainwater gutters called *canales*, unpainted wood columns with wooden bracket capitals, porches or *portales*, walled courtyards, tile and brick floors. Building traditions shared by both the Spanish and Pueblo cultures were flat roofs and the use of adobe construction. The Spanish adobe is Moorish in heritage and comprised of sun-dried earthen bricks. The Pueblo adobe was based on larger sun-dried earthen forms or mounds covered in a stucco mixture made of mud and straw.

Figure 1: Photograph of Zuni Pueblo, New Mexico. Example of the historic Pueblo architecture. Date: 1879. Photographer: unknown.

Native American author Rina Swentzell, who grew up on the Santa Clara Pueblo explains, "In the Tewa language, the word for 'us' is *nung* and the word for 'earth' or 'dirt' is also *nung*. As we are synonymous with and born of the earth, so are we made of the same stuff as our houses."[1] This identification with the land is shared by both Native and non-Native inhabitants.

By the nineteenth century, Spanish Pueblo buildings were in danger of falling out of favor. With the emergence of the national railroad system, Anglo-American settlers and modern building materials arrived in New Mexico. Communities across the state were determined to conform to new American architectural standards and mimicked the latest fashions of the day, eschewing the traditional regional forms as outmoded. In particular, larger settlements with railroad stops such as Albuquerque, Santa Fe, and Las Vegas, NM, began to take on the appearance of a Midwestern town, with its typical eclectic mix of Italianate, Greek Revival, colonial, and bungalow styles.

An Archeological Revival

However, by the early twentieth century, a renewed interest in Spanish Pueblo architecture occurred, promulgating the design and construction of a unique new American style called the Spanish-Pueblo Revival. Although some of the earliest examples were built in California, the style became most popular in New Mexico, where the original prototypes survived. It is particularly common in Albuquerque and Santa Fe, New Mexico, where special design controls exist in the cities' historic districts.

The early Revival was primarily initiated by Anglo-American tourists and settlers, who traveled "out west" around the turn of the century, retreating from the hectic pace of Eastern urban life to picturesque towns, such as Santa Fe. And indeed, Santa Fe offered a dramatic visual change from the industrialized cities of the Northeast and Midwest. However, as Eastern products and architectural styles also reached west, Santa Fe started to lose its unique charm. Some local residents recognized the threat to tourism and the local economy. They advocated a return to the traditional regional style, which spawned an antiquarian fascination and interpretation of authentic Spanish Pueblo buildings.

Many of the educated, professional, and artistic settlers to Santa Fe were also drawn to the local climate, promoted as conducive to the recovery of tuberculosis infection. Indeed, one of the first converts to the regional style was Dr. Frank Mera, who contracted the local architectural firm of Rapp and Rapp to design his popular clinic, Sunmount Sanatorium, in the Spanish Pueblo Revival. Sunmount attracted well-off tuberculosis patients to Santa Fe to "take the cure." The picturesque environment delighted and inspired. Indeed, many patients stayed on in the area after their tenure at Sunmount and formed the roots of an arts community, which flourishes to this day.

Figure 2: Sunmount Sanatorium, Santa Fe, New Mexico. Architects: Rapp and Rapp. Date: c. 1920s. Photographer: John Gaw Meem.

Another early settler to Santa Fe who was instrumental in revitalizing the Spanish Pueblo Style was artist and photographer Carlos Vierra. His images of the local landscapes and indigenous architecture can be credited as one of the main inspirations to the rebirth of the Style. Vierra was a purist, intent upon preserving and recreating the original architecture of the area. Vierra's own home became a model and stimulus for other houses in the area.

However, many of these early examples of the Spanish Pueblo Revival, while highly charming, were so preoccupied with accuracy that they were almost archeological fantasies, lacking the organic nature of the original constructions. For instance, a significant example of the early Revival is the New Mexico Fine Arts Museum in Santa Fe, also designed by Rapp and Rapp. The exterior of this building is a conglomeration of elements drawn from the various pueblos and missions in the local area, including a general plan and south front reminiscent of the Acoma mission, an eastern entry resembling the Laguna mission church, and staggering walls mimicking the half porches of the Cochiti Pueblo. A strong influence on the archeological nature of the structure can be attributed to the Palace of the Governors in Santa Fe, an original Spanish Pueblo building and believed to be the oldest building in the United States, whose restoration was undertaken by the School of American Archeology in 1909.

John Gaw Meem: Popularizer and Modernizer

It was John Gaw Meem, a highly noted New Mexican architect and historic preservationist who practiced out of his Santa Fe office from 1924-1960, whose work inspired a new wave of Spanish Pueblo design. Meem began his career as a banker in New York City. However, after contracting tuberculosis, Meem was advised to move to a dryer western climate to recuperate. Drawn by an advertisement for the Santa Fe Railroad, Meem headed for New Mexico, where he developed an interest in the local indigenous architecture and the early examples of its revival, while recovering at Sunmount Sanatorium. After briefly studying classical architecture at the Design Atelier in Denver, Meem opened his first architectural office on the grounds of Sunmount in 1924.

Meem soon became the primary person responsible for the preservation and conservation of historic Spanish Pueblo buildings and in their revival during the first half of the 20th century. Unlike the early Spanish-Pueblo Revival buildings, with their quality of archeological reproduction, Meem's designs blended the forms of the traditional Spanish Pueblo buildings with all the requirements of modern living. Meem came from an engineering background and was interested in the application of the latest technologies and modern building methods, while remaining sympathetic to the look, feel and craftsmanship of the indigenous architecture. It was a happy marriage, resulting in some of the finest examples of the Spanish Pueblo Revival in New Mexico.

The Significance of the Spanish Pueblo Revival Style

Expressing Regionalism

The early 20th century was a period of great architectural eclecticism. Influenced by the World's Columbian Exposition in Chicago in 1893, which exhibited interpretations of primarily European styles, American architects created historical reproductions of Tudor, French, Dutch Colonial, Mediterranean etc. for their clients, regardless if they lived in Buffalo or Des Moines. However, a number of New Mexican architects, led by Meem, believed in expressing the "spirit of the region" in New Mexico by utilizing the traditional forms, materials, colors, and styles of the Southwest.

While Meem was not trying to imitate adobe architecture, he was, in his own words, trying "to recall by means of a conventionalized symbolic form the heritage of ancient buildings, or the characteristic shapes of the landscape."[2] Consequently, while Meem's Spanish-Pueblo creations do romantically recall another time, just as the popular period revivals of the day did, they also reflected the region, with a clear sense of place, rooted in historical tradition.

Figure 3: Amelia Hollenback House, Santa Fe, New Mexico. Architect: John Gaw Meem. Date: 1932. Courtesy of the University of New Mexico, Center for Southwest Research. Photographer: Ansel Adams

*Part of Larger National Movements: Picturesque and
Arts and Crafts Movements*

While Spanish Pueblo Revival architecture was rooted in expressing the spirit of the Southwest Region, the Style was also in–line with an earlier mid-nineteenth-century national movement toward "Picturesque" compositions. The Picturesque Movement looked to the romantic past for inspiration. Eastern styles such as Italianate and Gothic Revival stood as "picturesque" reactions to the formality of the classical ideals in art and architecture that had spawned the Georgian Colonial and Greek Revival styles, popular from colonization through to the early nineteenth century. Rambling, informal layouts and floor plans, asymmetrical placement of windows and doors, and lushly landscaped settings all characterized these homes. Although the Spanish Pueblo Revival took place several decades later, it may still be placed in this category for a number of reasons. Firstly, as a remote territory, all movements and fashions tended to reach the Southwest later than they arrived to the East. Secondly, many of the settlers to New Mexico came from Eastern and Midwestern towns and brought with them a knowledge and sensitivity to the romantic styles. Consequently, Spanish Pueblo Revival homes reflect the picturesque notion with their informal character, their romantic rendering of the historical past, and their conscious sympathy with the surrounding landscape of desert, mountain, blue sky and unique foliage. Turn-of-the-century travel writer and Santa Fe resident Charles Fletcher Lummis (sometimes referred to as the "first South Westerner") summed up New Mexico in 1926 with this romantic imagery: "There is no other state in the union of such centuried romance as New Mexico; nor other town so venerable as Santa Fe, nor other road with half the history, or a tenth the tragedy of the old Santa Fe Trail."[3]

The Spanish Pueblo Revival also reflects the broad movement toward Arts and Crafts art and architecture. The Arts and Crafts Movement in America occurred at the same general time period as the early revival of Spanish Pueblo. Both styles shared an adherence to informal layout and asymmetry, integration of house and landscape, simple ornamentation, and sound local craftsmanship. According to architectural historian Chris Wilson, Santa Fe builders also utilized the "ultimate Arts and Crafts symbol of the pre-industrial house, the ingle-nook, as the Spanish corner fireplace with built-in adobe benches."[4] It is also significant that many of the first supporters of the Spanish Pueblo Revival came from well-to-do Eastern professional and artistic backgrounds. It is likely that these settlers were familiar with the Arts and Crafts Movement's socialist philosophies toward art and architecture, which were thriving in America at the time. And certainly the disproportionate development of artistic organizations in small-town Santa Fe in the 1910s and 1920s, such as the School of American Research (1907), the Museum of New Mexico (1909), Committee for the Preservation and Restoration of New Mexico Churches (1924), and the

Laboratory of Anthropology (1927) illustrates the extreme interest in social, civic and artistic organization by the new settlers.

Creating Modern Buildings

As time progressed and tastes changed, the trend moved from historical recreations and period revivals to modernism in the 1930s. During this period, modernism generally advocated a straightforward approach to buildings and an honest use of materials, which did not hide away steel or concrete infrastructure. Historicism and the reproduction of historical styles were considered inauthentic, out of place, and out of touch. Consequently, the traditionalism of the Spanish Pueblo Style was in question. However, the idea of creating modern buildings is more complex than just stylization or the obvious use of industrial materials. Spanish Pueblo Revival Buildings were modern buildings in the sense that they combined old forms with modern technology, inspired by modern social/cultural needs. For instance, underneath the stucco, hollow bricks often replaced traditional adobe bricks, creating a much more structurally sound base. Traditional styling also disguised up-to-date electrical, plumbing and heating systems. Large open living areas flowed from one to another, in a manner advocated by early 20th-century English and American Arts and Crafts designers. Patios and terracing connected houses to the landscape and to the spectacular New Mexican vistas, the same way that Midwestern Prairie Style architects, such as Frank Lloyd Wright, rallied for. Additionally, windows and outdoor spaces were strategically placed to catch the intense sunlight and the desert breezes, in a way that pleased Progressive Era health and housing reformers. These up-to-date Spanish Pueblo residences also incorporated the same kitchens and bathrooms to be expected in the most modern bungalow. And ironically, the revival of the Spanish Pueblo architecture was in the right place at the right time. Even though these buildings expressed a regional tradition, they also shared many of the same elements and forms as the popular Art Deco and Art Modern Styles, including flat roofs, rectangular massing, smooth, fluid stucco covered exteriors, lacking superfluous ornamentation.

Indeed, one of the most significant visual examples of how the Spanish Pueblo Style harmonizes with the modernist is the campus of the University of New Mexico. Here, 1930s era Spanish Pueblo Revival buildings mix with 1960s and 1970s era modernist structures reminiscent of Pueblo design, with stepped back flat roofs, sparing ornamentation, and sand colored walls. A striking example of Spanish Pueblo Revival Style is the Zimmerman Library building, designed as a WPA project by John Gaw Meem in 1936. Underneath the smooth monolithic curves and blunt angles of structure lies lasting steel frame construction. The walls, while echoing the stucco covering found on early Spanish Pueblo buildings, are actually tinted Portland Cement, much more durable than the traditional mixtures of mud and straw.

Figure 4: Zimmerman Library, University of New Mexico, Albuquerque, NM. Architect: John Gaw Meem (1936). Southwest Postcard Collection, Center for Southwest Research, University of New Mexico.

Influencing the Vernacular

Commonly, successful high-style architect-designed buildings end up having a broader significance. These unique buildings inspire and become models for more modest, vernacular buildings. In this sense, Meem's much-admired Spanish Pueblo residences and public buildings influenced mass development of similar, more moderate homes. Indeed, Santa Fe and Albuquerque, both locations where Meem worked extensively, proliferate with neighborhoods of small-scale pueblos, built from the 1920s onward by local speculative developers, obviously using the grander residences designed for an elite clientele as models for middle and working class home owners. On a national scale, similar houses were also displayed in catalog house books and plan books in the 1920s and 1930s, such as Aladdin Company's Pueblo Style Bungalow.

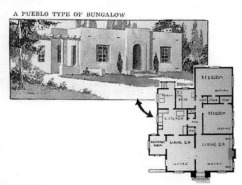

Figure 5: "Pueblo Style Bungalow" Aladdin Company, c. 1920s.

Selling the Romantic: Commercialism and the Spanish Pueblo Revival

While Spanish Pueblo Revival turned up in neighborhood housing, the style was also utilized in a wide variety of commercial structures. Initially, when the railroad brought commerce and tourism to New Mexico at the end of the nineteenth century, such enterprises inspired cheeky tourist destinations such as Wright's Trading Post in Albuquerque, which primarily sold Native American arts and crafts. Wright's sported an eye-catching, if inauthentic, mix of both Spanish and Pueblo elements, along with very non-Pueblo Northwest Coast-like totem poles. Such a hodge-podge is a good example of how exotic themes were used to entice tourists fascinated with anything "Indian." Similarly, the movie palace, the Kimo Theater (1927) on Route 66, in downtown Albuquerque displays a dizzying combination of Pueblo and Navajo symbols and motifs expressed in the geometrical patterning of the modernist Art Deco. Called Pueblo Deco, it was meant to pay homage to the Pueblos and other Native Americans, while still offering patrons and tourists the popular national Deco style.

Figure 6: Kimo Theater, postcard c. 1920s. Southwest Postcard Collection, Center for Southwest Research, University of New Mexico.

Kimo Architect Mary Colter also designed the Alvarado Hotel (1901-1904), part of the Fred Harvey chain of railroad hotels. Large tourist hotels, such as the Alvarado, catered to the whims of train travelers and appealed to their desire for the exotic.

Although the Alvarado was designed in full blown Spanish Mission Style, with buff colored walls, red tile roofs, stepped parapets and towers, Harvey realized the importance of packaging and included an "Indian Room," designed to look like the interior of a Pueblo adobe, complete with pottery, baskets, rugs, and jewelry, all available for purchase. Harvey provided an additional attraction by inviting women from the different pueblos, dressed in print dresses and shawls, to sell their pottery to tourists at the entrance of the hotel.

Figure 7: Alvarado Hotel, Albuquerque, New Mexico, c. 1930s. Southwest Postcard Collection, Center for Southwest Research, University of New Mexico.

Later, the development of the national highway system brought mass auto tourism to the area. Specifically, Route 66, the mythic "Mother Road," which ran from just outside Chicago all the way to California, cuts through central Albuquerque. From the 1920s-1950s, the New Mexico portion of Route 66 boomed with the construction of commercial tourist-oriented structures, such as gas stations, motels, and small entertainment venues (snake museums, rock museums, etc.). Many of these temptations displayed elements of the regional style, adapted for obviously modern functions and usages. A typical example might be a motel offering Streamline Moderne office with neon advertising sign, accompanied by rows of stuccoed motel rooms displaying projecting vigas, grouped around a Spanish Revival motor court, punctuated by a kidney shaped swimming pool. However disconcerting for the average architecture critic, it was a smart business move. While tourists desired all the comforts of the modern motel, they were also attracted to the elements of the regional style. They wanted to experience something different from what was available in their Eastern hometowns and even this mish-mash of styles must have seemed an exotic departure, exemplifying the myth of the Southwest.

Figure 8: Zuni Motor Lodge, Albuquerque, NM. Southwest Postcard Collection, Center for Southwest Research, University of New Mexico.

The Historic Preservation Movement and the Spanish Pueblo Revival Style

Preserving Spanish Pueblo/Spanish Pueblo Revival Buildings

In the 1920s, projects were developed to preserve, restore, revitalize and document historic buildings in New Mexico before it was a fashionable national movement. In the early 1920s, John Gaw Meem became an original member of the Committee for the Preservation and Restoration of New Mexico Churches, organized by a fellow Sunmount Sanitarium resident, Anne Evans, daughter of the Governor of Colorado. He was also a founding member in 1926 of the Old Santa Fe Association, whose mission it was to preserve the historic tradition of Santa Fe through a cohesive adherence to the Spanish-Pueblo and the related Territorial Style of design. Also in the 1920s, restoration projects were underway to repair ancient adobe buildings on several of the New Mexico Pueblos, including Acoma mission church. In the 1930s, a local architectural historian at the University of New Mexico named Bainbridge Bunting embarked upon a documentation project, which photographed and created measured drawings of historic New Mexico buildings for future research. In some instances, these materials remain the only testament to their existence. Presently in New Mexico, the State Historic Preservation Office leads an effort to declare the importance of Spanish Pueblo and Spanish Pueblo Revival buildings by nominating them to the State and National Registers of Historic Places. On a more local level, the designation of older neighborhoods into historic districts, where city ordinances prevail to preserve the character of older structures, has grown in places such as Santa Fe, Albuquerque, Roswell and Los Alamos.

Additionally, John Gaw Meem's family established, through a lasting endowment, an archive at the University of New Mexico with a mission to collect, preserve and provide accessibility to New Mexico's historical architectural records. Located in the Zimmerman Library on the University of New Mexico's main campus, the John Gaw Meem Archives of Southwestern Architecture houses the full collection of drawings and papers from not only the Meem firm, but from many of New Mexico's oldest architectural firms, designers, engineers, and preservationists. The archive documents the history of New Mexico's built environment. Everyday architects and historians request materials from the collections for the purposes of restoring and preserving buildings, writing state and national register nominations, or simply researching their own homes history. Through the activities of the Meem Archives, Meem's own passion for the study, design, preservation, restoration of regional buildings carries on.

In conclusion, the Spanish Pueblo Style of architecture possesses an interesting history, which merges the building techniques and characteristics of two distinct cultures: one Spanish and one Native American. The revival of the Spanish Pueblo Style in the late 19th- and early 20th-centuries in New Mexico also claims a unique background, which reflects a contemporary mindset toward commercialism and tourism. The Revival was also inspired by romanticism for a past way of life, jeopardized by the increased business and social pressures of late nineteenth century industrialized America. Similarly, related romantic movements such as Arts and Crafts, with references to pre-industrial life, reached west to New Mexico at this time through settlement and tourism and influenced the revival of the traditional style. And yet, even though Spanish Pueblo Revival buildings were reminiscent of local historic buildings, through the technical innovations of local architects, such as John Gaw Meem and others, they were also modern. Historic forms and local craftsmanship blended with up-to-date building methods and offered all the requirements for modern usage. As time progressed and tourism broadened to include road trips along Route 66, the fanciful, colorful highway vernacular including motels, gas stations, and entertainment and shopping venues, displayed ever-varying combinations of Spanish and Pueblo elements luring tourists mad for the "exotic." Today, Spanish Pueblo Revival buildings remain an important element of the Southwest cultural landscape. Indeed, Spanish Pueblo it is not a lost or outdated style, but one that persists throughout the region today.

NOTES

1. Rina Swentzell, "Remembering the Tewa Pueblo Houses and Spaces," in *The Multicultural Southwest*, ed. A. Gabriel Melendez, M. Jane Young, Patricia Moore, Patrick Pynes (Tucson: University of Arizona, 2001), pp. 86-90.

2. John Gaw Meem, speech delivered at the Annual Banquet of the University of New Mexico Chapter of Phi Kappa Phi, Albuquerque, New Mexico, 1953, John Gaw Meem Papers, Center for Southwest Research, University of New Mexico.

3. Charles Fletcher Lummis, "The Golden Key to Wonderland," in *The Multicultural Southwest*, ed. A. Gabriel Melendez, M. Jane Young, Patricia Moore, Patrick Pynes (Tucson: University of Arizona, 2001), pp. 7-10.

4. Chris Wilson, *The Myth of Santa Fe: Creating a Modern Regional Tradition* (Albuquerque: University of New Mexico Press, 1997), p. 145.

BIBLIOGRAPHY

"Albuquerque Tricentennial Pueblo Deco Tour." Albuquerque: Art Deco Society of New Mexico, 2005. 1-11.

Breeze, Carla. *Pueblo Deco*. New York: Rizzoli, 1990.

Bunting, Bainbridge. *Early Architecture in New Mexico*. Albuquerque: University of New Mexico Press, 1974.

Liebs, Chester. *From Main Street to Miracle Mile*.

McAlester, Virginia & Lee. *A Field Guide to American Houses*. New York: Alfred A. Knopf, 1984.

Meem, John Gaw. "Spanish Pueblo Architecture in Permanent Materials." *Explorations 1975*. Santa Fe, New Mexico: School of American Research, 1975, 2-5.

Melendez, A. Gabriel, M. Jane Young, Patricia Moore, and Patrick Pynes, eds. *The Multi-Cultural Southwest*. Tucson: University of Arizona Press, 2001.

Morang, Dorothy. "John Gaw Meem Receives Honorary Fellowship in Fine Arts." *El Palacio* 60 (July 1953): 275-278.

Mullin, Molly H. *Culture in the Marketplace: Gender Art and Value in the American Southwest*. Durham and London: Duke University Press, 2001.

"The "Santa Fe Style." *Sunset* (October 1989): 21-25.

Vierra, Carlos. "New Mexico Architecture." *Art and Archeology* 7 (January-February 1918): 37-49.

Wilson, Chris. *The Myth of Santa Fe: Creating a Modern Regional Tradition*. Albuquerque: University of New Mexico Press, 1997.

22. No Maya Libraries?: Representation in and Reception of Mel Gibson's *Apocalypto*

David C. Murray

Among their many intellectual achievements, the ancient Maya civilization invented, by 250 A.D. at the very latest—and likely hundreds of years earlier—a fully functional, phonetic writing system capable of expressing human speech. Scribes recorded sophisticated texts containing religious, astronomical, and almost certainly historical, literary, and even medical content—in other words, an entire system of human thought—in bark-paper books called codices. Of the many thousands of Maya codices that must once have existed, only four remain. Time, a humid climate, and the zealous, destructive tendencies of one 16th-century Spanish friar, Diego de Landa, conspired to ensure the destruction of the rest. As a librarian and longtime student of pre-Columbian Mesoamerica, I have often wondered about the nature of ancient Maya libraries. Were scribes, many of whom now appear to have been blood relatives of Maya royalty, responsible for safeguarding the codices, as seems likely? Or were a separate group of specialists—the librarians—responsible? Maya codices were not particularly fragile. If properly cared for, they could have lasted for decades, even centuries. It is intriguing, then, to think about where Maya codices might have been housed, and by what system cataloged and shelved.

It would be naive to expect these and other "burning" questions to be addressed in Mel Gibson's *Apocalypto*. After all, the film is a fictionalized Hollywood epic, not a PBS documentary. (For a good, recent example of the latter, I recommend Nova's *Cracking the Maya Code*.) Neither Gibson nor anyone else associated with the film claim *complete* historical accuracy.[1] According to the film's official website, *Apocalypto* tells the story of "young Jaguar Paw [who] is captured and taken to the great Mayan City, where he faces a harrowing end. Driven by his love for his wife and son, he makes an adrenaline-soaked, heart-racing escape to rescue them and ultimately save his way of life." *Apocalypto*'s simple narrative is divided into three sections of roughly equal length. The first third is set in and around Jaguar Paw's jungle village, which is brutally attacked by what can only be described as a bloodthirsty gang of warriors from a nearby Maya city. In the second third, Jaguar Paw and his remaining villagers are marched off to the decadent city to be subjected to all manner of unpleasantness. And in the final third, Jaguar Paw, who miraculously escapes his fate, is chased unceasingly back through the jungle to the site of his wrecked village, where his pregnant wife and young son await rescue.

I suspect that scholars—and here I am referring specifically to those who have devoted their entire academic careers to the subject—were secretly thrilled to find out that a major feature film about the ancient Maya would be made. Discounting *Kings of the Sun*, made in 1963 and starring Yul Brynner and George Chakiris, and *Royal Hunt of the Sun*, made in 1969 and starring Christopher Plummer as the Inca emperor Atahualpa, *Apocalypto* is the first Hollywood epic to treat any ancient New World civilization. (As an aside, it is hard to fathom why this should be the case, since the clash of worlds we call the Conquest makes Russell Crowe's tour of the Coliseum look like a walk in the park.) Certainly *Apocalypto*'s high production values, including especially its extraordinary yet somewhat flawed costuming, are a great enticement. For most in the academic community, however, it is fair to say that *Apocalypto* turned out to be an enticement with very little substance. The fundamental disappointment I have found in reading the academic reviews does not involve the film's numerous and rather egregious historical inaccuracies per se.[2] It is what those inaccuracies ostensibly convey about the nature of the ancient Maya that troubles many. I feel compelled, nonetheless, to take just a few minutes to look at some of the more troubling historical misses:

1. The film's first major historical error involves the absurd Yanomamo-like portrayal of the village Maya as hunter-gatherers, unaware of the presence of a grand city less than a day's march away. During the period under consideration, that is to say during the Late Classic Period, the primary-growth forest depicted in the film likely would not have existed due to deforestation. In addition, the Maya of this time were fully dedicated farmers, not hunters. At a mere day's march away from the urban center, such farmers would not have been sacrificial captives but rather peasants or citizens, if you will, of the state to which they are being led.

2. The second important way Gibson gets it wrong is the conflation, throughout the film, of Pre-Classic, Classic, and post-Classic imagery from widely varying geographical locations, particularly during the city sequences.

3. The third and perhaps most disturbing historical inaccuracy involves the highly problematic depiction of human bodies strewn Holocaust-like in an open pit as Jaguar Paw escapes the city. The problem? No archeological, art historical, or epigraphic evidence exists to support the belief that such an event occurred. As many academic reviewers have pointed out, would you dump dead bodies next to your maize fields?

4. The fourth, and in my view most bizarre (telling?), inaccuracy involves the anachronistic, *deus ex machina*-like appearance of Conquistadors at the end of the film. Recall that the events depicted in *Apocalypto* clearly reference the Classic Period, not the Post-Classic. The Spanish did not appear in Yucatan until 700 years after the Classic Period ended.

5. The fifth inaccuracy involves the fixation of the Maya elite on heart sacrifice. In reality, the heart extraction technique used so salaciously by Gibson in *Apocalypto* belongs to a cultural complex that likely originated in the Post-Classic Mexican Highlands—that is to say, with the progenitors of the Aztec Empire—not with the Lowland Maya. For those who might be unfamiliar with the historical sequence of ancient Mesoamerica, this would be somewhat like attributing the mass slaughter of gladiatorial combat to Classical Athens rather than Imperial Rome. It is beyond question that the Maya nobility were prone to violent displays. Indeed, such ritualized acts of violence are hallmarks of many states, ancient and modern, the world over.

The bottom line is that in Hollywood, historical half-truths can be and almost always are written off as "artistic license." Merely pointing out historical inaccuracies is therefore an insufficient critique. University of Miami anthropologist Traci Ardren, in a review for *Archaeology Online*, gets at the deeper problem with *Apocalypto*: "Gibson's efforts at authenticity of location and language might, for some viewers, mask his blatantly colonial message that the Maya needed saving because they were rotten at the core. Using the decline of Classic urbanism as his backdrop, Gibson communicates that there was absolutely nothing redeemable about Maya culture, especially elite culture which is depicted as a disgusting feast of blood and excess."[3] As Ardren points out, this message plays directly into a longstanding trope that has been used to subjugate the Maya for centuries. A corollary of this trope can be seen in the West's longstanding desire to explain away the inestimable cultural loss that resulted from the destruction of New World societies.[4] One need not fret too much about the passing of a people already decadent and, as depicted in the film, quite literally dying. Of course our contemporary understanding of Classic Maya civilization as revealed through a century of anthropology, art history, and epigraphy, and which has made tremendous strides in the last thirty years especially, provides an entirely different and far more nuanced picture than Gibson cared to promote in the film.

Evidence that the academic community's concerns are justified can be found in mainstream reviews of *Apocalypto*. To cite but two of many examples, Rebecca Murray on About.com pans the film for its "exploitative, over-the-top, and nauseatingly pointless display of bloodshed," yet later states, "apparently Gibson and company did their homework and by most accounts represent well that time in history and the culture of the Mayans." Or this from Sonny Bunch of the conservative *Weekly Standard*: "It is specious for professional historians and grievance groups alike to argue that *Apocalypto* is a wanton desecration of the memories of the Mayan people. While it may be an inconvenient fact that the Mayans were skilled at the art of human cruelty, it is, nevertheless, a fact." While Bunch may be stating a "fact," it is also beside the point. The ancient Maya civilization was one of the greatest and most accomplished in all antiquity. The Maya, as mentioned, invented a complete writing system recorded in books and maintained in libraries; the Maya invented positional numeration, including the concept of zero; they created high art whose aesthetic power continues to awe and inspire; they supported a population of millions in an environment ill-suited to traditional methods of agricultural intensification; and many other tremendous accomplishments besides. Perhaps Dr. Kathryn Lehman, a Latin American Studies scholar in New Zealand, has already asked the most important questions about *Apocalypto*: "All films are historically inaccurate. What we should ask [our] students is why now? What is happening to Maya and indigenous people today that prompts someone to represent them in this way? And most importantly: who benefits by this representation?" The answer to these questions will require more thought and discussion, but it is certainly worth exploring the relationship between the representation of indigenous peoples in films such as *Apocalypto*, on the one hand, and for example the contemporary Maya Renaissance in Guatemala, on the other. We might also profit by asking questions about our own role as academics and educators in informing popular representations of the Maya and other indigenous peoples of the Western Hemisphere.

NOTES

1. In an interview for *Variety* that appeared on 10/30/2005, well before the film was released, Gibson discussed the question of historical accuracy: "A lot of this, the storylines I just made up, and then oddly, when I checked it out with historians and archaeologists, it's not that far from wrong" ("The Flyin' Mayan: Gibson Talks About Upcoming '*Apocalypto*' ").

2. Besides Ardren, other academics who have commented on *Apocalypto* include Vanderbilt's art historian Annabeth Headrick; a team of three archaeologists from SUNY Albany; John Hawks, anthropologist at the University of Wisconsin, Madison; Zachary Hruby of U.C. Riverside; Gabriela Erandi Rico, at the time of the film's release a Mexican graduate student in Ethnic Studies at U.C. Berkeley; Annette Kolodny, professor emerita of American literature at the University of Arizona; and art historian Andrea Stone of the University of Wisconsin, Milwaukee.

3. Ardren, Traci. "Is *Apocalypto* Pornography?" *Archeology Online* (Dec. 5, 2006).

4. Benjamin Keen's 1971 *The Aztec Image in Western Thought* chronicles the West's 500-year on-again, off-again (fickle) fascination with the better-known Aztec civilization.

23. Native Americans as Portrayed on the Operatic Stage: An Introduction

Peter S. Bushnell

With the theme "Encounter, Engagement and Exchange: How Native Populations of the Americas Transformed the World," there are a number of options available relating to the world of music and the dramatic stage.

We are all familiar with how Native Americans (hereafter referred to as Indians) were historically portrayed on TV westerns and the various westerns from the U.S. movie industry. Many times, the Indians became caricatures and not characters. Since I have had a long-time love of opera, and knew of a few operas with Indian characters, I thought I would see what else I could find.

Opera as we know it began in Italy in the late 16th century. A prominent early topic was Greek mythology. Basically any topic was fair game, as long as it provided the opportunity for what could be considered spectacular stage effects.

By the late 17th century, Indians were beginning to appear as characters on the operatic stage. The Indian was considered an exotic character, which fit perfectly with the requirements for stage works. Henry Purcell's *Indian Queen* is one such example. It is one of Purcell's final works and is sometimes referred to as a semi-opera. This means that there is a lot of plain dialogue in addition to singing, dancing, and instrumental music as well as the opportunity for spectacular scenic effects. However, the plot of a semi-opera is of the type that gives opera a bad name in many circles because of its historically and geographically preposterous nature. The forces of the Mexican queen Zempoalla are struggling against the Peruvians, who are being led by Montezuma. Zempoalla has actually usurped the throne from the rightful queen, who happens to be Montezuma's long lost mother. Very few of the named Indians sing at all. Most of the music is concerned with Zempoalla's unspoken turmoil and guilt. In addition to the music by Henry Purcell, the masque music in Act 5 is by Daniel Purcell, Henry's younger brother. After listening to a recording and following along with a full score, one finds a good bit to enjoy. However, a performance of *Indian Queen* would not likely suit any venue larger than just a few hundred seats.

Crossing the channel to France, one finds a somewhat different type of stage work: the opéra-ballet. This is a stage presentation with the opportunity for both singing and dancing. Jean-Philippe Rameau's *Les indes galantes* (The Amourous Indies) of 1735 originally consisted of a prologue and two entrées (or acts), "Les incas du Pérou" and "Le turc généreux." "Les Fleurs" was added at the third performance. Finally, on March 10, 1736, a fourth entrée, "Les sauvages," was added. This became the final form. The prologue introduces the theme of aspects of love in far-flung lands. "Les incas du Pérou" takes place during a Sun Festival in the shadows of a Peruvian volcano. The Indian master of ceremonies, Huascar, is in love with Princess Phani, who loves the Spaniard Don Carlos. Huascar tries to convince Phani that the Sun God does not approve of her love for Don Carlos and caused the volcano to erupt. Don Carlos foils Huascar's attempt to kidnap Phani. Huascar then causes a further eruption of the volcano but is crushed by molten rocks. The setting for "Les sauvages" is North America. The Indian chief's daughter Zima has two European suitors, the Spaniard Don Alvar who Zima feels is jealous and loves her too much and the Frenchman Damon who she feels to be fickle and loves her too little. However, Zima chooses the Indian brave Adario in the end, and there is a great peace pipe ceremony with the shame-faced Europeans and the Indians. Here, it is the Spanish and French who appear as the caricatures rather than the Indians. "Le turc généreux" takes place on an island in the Indian Ocean while "Les fleurs" takes place during a flower festival, with one of the principal characters a Persian prince. I was able to listen to a recording of the two entrées while following a piano-vocal score. The Rameau is a later work than Purcell, and, Rameau is able to provide a more colorful score for the listener by using a larger orchestra. Les sauvages is the last entreé of the work, and its ending chaconne is of extra interest. By the 19th century, the chaconne is generally considered to be a variation form over a ground bass. Originally, however, the chaconne was a dance, often at a brisk tempo, and this is the basic form that Rameau uses. Musically, the most interesting aspect of the piece is that it starts in a minor key (D minor), switches to a major (D major), goes back to D minor, and returns to D major at the end. Because the trumpet of the Baroque period had no valves, and was normally constructed to sound in D, D major was considered the primary key for festive music.

One more Baroque opera worth mentioning is *Montezuma* by Carl Heinrich Graun, which deals principally with the Cortez-led Spanish conquest of Mexico. Overall, it is a tragedy where the Spanish are the bad guys, and Montezuma is led to his death and his intended kills herself, but the Indians are not necessarily portrayed as inferior to the white man.

For now I will skip the 19th century.

Giacomo Puccini's *La fanciulla del west* includes two Indians. Since the original setting is California at the beginning of the Gold Rush, having Indians on stage makes sense. Billy Jackrabbit is referred to as a Red Indian, along with Wowkle, his squaw. Both roles are small, but Wowkle is important as the only female voice in the whole opera besides the heroine, Minnie. In the

1930s, Howard Hanson wrote the opera *Merry Mount*. The one named Indian character is Samoset, with others in the chorus. The setting is 17th-century New England, featuring Puritans, Cavaliers, and Indians. The major roles are the Puritans and Cavaliers, with Samoset and his compatriots being accused of sorcery and causing the crops to fail. However, the Indian presence in the opera is a very minor part of the overall plot.

In the early 1960s, the Roger Sessions's opera *Montezuma* was premiered in Berlin. Sessions explores themes of cultural juxtaposition, conflict and assimilation, ethical ambiguities of military power and state versus religious authority. Before the end, Montezuma is assassinated by militant Aztecs. Sessions has the historian Bernal Díaz act as narrator and storyteller for the opera.

More recently, Thea Musgrave, in her opera *Bolívar*, includes no named Indians, but at the end of Act I, the hymn to the sun is sung in Quechua.

In the second half of the 20th century, there have been quite a few operas that include Indians in secondary roles as well as the major protagonists. *Opera News* is a good place to start if this is of interest.

And now, back to the 19th century.

One of the biggest names in all opera, of course, is Giuseppe Verdi, and there are two of his operas that merit discussion in relation to this topic. (Most of this material has come from a combination of sources, since a libretto or score does not always provide much information.) *La forza del destino* is based on *Don Álvaro, o la fuerza del sino* by Ángel de Saavedra, duque de Rivas. The lead tenor is Don Alvaro, the only son of a Viceroy of Peru who had gone against Spanish rule and then married the last Inca princess. In a class-conscious Spain, Alvaro being half Incan puts him in a lower position than that of the Vargas family. Alvaro is in love with Leonora di Vargas (the lead soprano) who is willing to run off with the one she loves. This, of course, does not happen (if it did, there would be no opera—or story to begin with). After the death of the Marchese di Calatrava (bass) in Act I, Leonora and Alvaro spend the rest of the opera running away from Don Carlos di Vargas, Leonora's brother (baritone), never to be reunited until the very end. When everything is over and done, Don Alvaro is the only one of the three leads still living after fatally stabbing Don Carlos, who in turn fatally stabs Leonora. If the action took place in a different geographical place and different time period, as long as Verdi kept the same music, *La forza del destino* would still keep its place in the standard repertory of opera houses around the world.

Over 15 years before *Forza*, Verdi premiered his opera *Alzira* at the Teatro San Carlo in Naples. The libretto was written by Salvatore Cammarano, and based on Voltaire's *Alzire*. The opera is set in Peru with more Indians than Spaniards as named characters. Even though Cammarano kept the basic plot, he eliminated most of the "Christian" vs. "barbarian" connotations of the original source.

The story itself concerns a love triangle typical in opera. Zamoro (a tenor) is the chief of a Peruvian tribe in love with Alzira (a soprano), the daughter of Ataliba (bass), chief of another Peruvian tribe. The third member of the triangle is Gusmano (baritone), the son of Alvaro, the Spanish governor of Peru. In the Prologue, subtitled "The prisoner," Alvaro, who has been captured by a band of Peruvians, is rescued from almost certain death by Zamoro. Alvaro is told to return to his people and tell them about the clemency of a savage. Finally, to get things moving, Zamoro learns that the Spanish have captured his intended Alzira and her father, so he prepares to go rescue them.

Act I, "A life for a life" finds Alvaro stepping down as governor in favor of his son Gusmano, who declares peace with the Incas and asks Ataliba for Alzira's hand in marriage. Even though part of him does not agree with what he has done, Gusmano has fallen in love with Alzira. However, Alzira does not return his love. Ataliba does his best to persuade his daughter to marry Gusmano. Alzira still refuses, even though it is believed that Zamoro is dead. Not until the next scene does Alzira learn that Zamoro is still alive. After the love duet between Zamoro and Alzira, Gusmano enters with Ataliba and others. Gusmano is ready to take his revenge when his father enters and recognizes Zamoro as the noble savage who saved his life. Alvaro tries to get his son to free Zamoro, but Gusmano refuses. Only when the Spanish captain Ovando brings news that the Incas are on the march demanding the release of their leader, Zamoro, does Gusmano do so, with the warning that they will meet again in battle.

The second and final act, "The vengeance of a savage" brings everything to a close: Zamoro is defeated; Alzira agrees to marry Gusmano to save Zamoro's life; Zamoro kills Gusmano on his wedding day; suddenly, Gusmano, knowing that he is going to die, pardons Zamoro and urges him to take care of Alzira. He bids his father farewell and then dies.

In the end all that remains is an opera that even Verdi did not like later in life. No attempt was made to make the music sound Indian (Verdi may never have heard music of the Americas). The whole story could easily have been relocated to almost any place else in the world and the music would have been the same. The Indians were treated like any other character in a Verdi opera of the time.

On March 19, 1870, at La Scala in Milan, Italy, a new opera by the Brazilian composer Antonio Carlos Gomes premiered. Since it was sung in Italian, the title was *Il Guarany*. (Because the premier and first scores were in Italian, the uniform title uses the Italian spelling.) The work was a major success and was performed over 20 times during the next two seasons. Even though Gomes was not an unknown composer, he was neither very well known. He was born in 1836 in Campinas, in São Paulo State (north and west of the city of São Paulo). Even though his family was musical, when he went to Rio de Janeiro to study at the conservatory, he did so against his father's wishes. At the conservatory, his composition teacher was the Italian Joaquim Giannini, who reinforced his predilection for opera. He eventually received a government scholarship to study at the conservatory in Milan. His principle teachers were Alberto Mazzucato and Lauro Rossi, both directors of the conservatory, with Mazzucato following Rossi. In 1866, Gomes graduated in composition and spent most of the rest of his life in Italy.

Il Guarany is based on the book *O Guaraní* by José Martiniano de Alencar. The action takes place in mid-16th century Brazil, and the general storyline could easily take place elsewhere. There are two different Indian tribes represented, the Guaraní led by Pery (the lead tenor) and the Aimorè, a more warlike tribe. The major Portuguese roles are Cecilia, her father Don Antonio de Mariz, and Don Alvaro, a Portuguese adventurer. Before the opera begins, Cecilia has been rescued from the Aimorè by members of the Guaraní, led by Pery. They of course fell in love, but Don Antonio wants Cecilia to marry Don Alvaro. By the end, Cecilia and Pery have been threatened to be eaten by the Aimorè, Don Alvaro gets killed, and Pery, having been baptized, obtains Don Antonio's blessing to marry Cecilia. Don Antonio helps the lovers escape by getting himself and the other adventurers blown up.

The music for *Il Guarany* was greatly admired by Verdi and is often compared to the elder composer's middle period, roughly 1848-1860. No works of Gomes have entered the basic repertory, but *Il Guarany* has enjoyed life both in Brazil (the Brazilian premier took place December 2, 1870, on the Emperor's birthday) and beyond. In 1994, a production was mounted in Bonn, Germany for Plácido Domingo. There is a 2-CD set of this production, which comes highly recommended, even if it is sung in Italian.

Looking at the big picture, there have not been many on-stage roles portraying Indians as the types of stock figures often found in some old TV westerns, or in the old cowboys and Indians movies of the mid-20th century. This is a trend that hopefully continues.

For most of the works mentioned, there are various recordings—full and piano-vocal scores and a few video recordings—the availability of which might be problematic depending on where one might live. As one example, the Naxos recording of the original cast for Howard Hanson's *Merry Mount* is not for sale in the United States, but can be obtained overseas. Local copyright law will determine what is available. Cost can also be a determining factor in what is purchased.

BIBLIOGRAPHY

Béhague, Gerard. *Music in Latin America: an introduction.* Englewood Cliffs, NJ: Prentice-Hall, 1979.

Berger, William. *Verdi with a Vengeance: an Energetic Guide to the Life and Complete Works of the King of Opera.* New York: Vintage Books, 2000.

Budden, Julian. *The Operas of Verdi: From Oberto to Rigoletto.* New York: Praeger Publishers, 1973.

Csampai, Attila. " 'Alzira': a Step Toward Mastery: the Genesis of Verdi's Operatic Style." Translated by Uta-Maria Steidle. Notes to recording of Verdi's *Alzira*. Orfeo, C 057 832 H, 1983.

Kimbell, David R. B. *Verdi in the Age of Italian Romanticism*. Cambridge: Cambridge University Press, 1981.

Marini, Mario. "The Girl of the Golden West": a Late Opera by Puccini. Translation by Enrica Mottley. Notes to recording of Puccini's *La Fanciulla del West*, Sony S2K 47 189, 1992.

The New Grove Dictionary of Opera. Edited by Stanley Sadie. London: Macmillan Press, 1998, c1997.

Scherle, Arthur. "Antônio Carlos Gomes: a Brazilian Opera Composer." Translated by Gwyn Morris. Notes and plot synopsis to a recording of Gomes' *Il Guarany*. Sony, S2K 66273, 1995.

Schillig, Rüdiger. Synopsis. Translated by Diana Loos. Notes to recording of Puccini's *La Fanciulla del West*, Sony S2K 47 189, 1992.

24. Incidents of Travel & Research into the Pre-Columbian Past

Daniel Peters

What this paper seeks to do, in a rather episodic fashion, is recount some of the experiences in writing what became a trilogy of historical novels about the major Pre-Columbian civilizations: the Aztecs, the Maya, and the Incas.

My story begins in the summer of 1978, after the publication of my first novel, *Border Crossings*, which was a love story set in the late 1960s about a draft-dodger. It was actually the third novel I had written, and I used up most of my stock of fascinating personal experiences in the process. As I cast about for where to go next, I got a call from my oldest friend, Dave Gregory, who was working on a graduate degree in archaeology at the University of Arizona. The ancient Maya were one of his specialties, and he suggested that I should write what he called a "prehistoric novel" about one of the major Pre-Columbian cultures. He had made this suggestion before, but this time I had a compelling reason to hear him.

My wife was then an Assistant Professor at the University of New Hampshire, so I took my faculty spouse card and headed over to the UNH library to see what they had in their card catalogue. Up in the stacks, by a process of elimination I can no longer recall, I decided to start with the Aztecs. There were more books on the Maya, but many of them seemed forbiddingly technical, and I think I sensed that the story of the Aztecs lay closer to the surface.

Among the books I took home with me that first time were Diego Duran's *History of the Indies of New Spain*, Miguel Leon-Portilla's *The Broken Spears*, and Burr Cartwright Brundage's *A Rain of Darts*. And what I discovered, as I went back and forth between them, reading about warriors, traveling merchants, shape-shifting sorcerers, and the composers of flower songs, was that this was a terrific story. There was no need to embellish the history and legend that had come down to us; if I could do that specific story justice, it would be enough.

My second response was to wonder why, in all my years of schooling, I had never been exposed to this story before. All I knew about the Aztecs was that they practiced human sacrifice and were conquered by Hernan Cortes, which was presented as a kind of cause-and-effect. Somehow, the full story never made it into the social studies curriculum, and even more astounding—given the possibilities for lurid exploitation—neither popular fiction nor Hollywood had ever given the Aztecs much play.

So now I had my subject, and I was so excited about it that I barely paused to consider if I was qualified to take it on. I had been an English major in college, with a total of one history course to my credit, and none in either Anthropology or Spanish. My one year as a graduate student had convinced me—I thought—that I was not cut out to be a scholar. I probably should have been more daunted by my deficiencies, but instead I set out to give myself a mini-doctorate in Aztec Studies. I pinned up a list of the Aztec gods on the bulletin board over my desk, and every day I'd try to memorize the next god's attributes, and learn how to pronounce the name: *Huitzilopochtli, Quetzalcoatl, Tezcatlipoca.* I also learned how to scour the bibliography at the end of a text, and as I read through the books in the New Hampshire Library, I started ordering more through Inter-Library Loan, university press catalogues, and remainder houses. It would not be too much of a stretch to say that at the age of thirty, as a student, I was born again.

In the spring of 1979, I fly to Tucson to join my friend Dave for a trip to Mexico. We take a train out of the border town of Nogales and spend the next two-and-a-half days getting to Mexico City. We have a sleeper compartment in the old Pullman car, but most of our daylight hours are spent standing on the platform between cars, staring out at the incredible, ever-changing landscape of Mexico. I had written a few, very tentative chapters of my novel prior to this trip, and after half a day on the train, I realize that it will all have to be rewritten, simply to include all the sensory detail. There was no way I could have smelled the dusty air or seen prickly pear silhouetted against adobe walls or vultures circling overhead while sitting at my desk in New Hampshire.

As soon as we check into our hotel in Mexico City, we head off to the Museum of Anthropology, and I swiftly make my way to the Aztec Hall and find a diorama of the temple precinct of Tenochtitlan, the Aztec capitol. It is big enough to walk around and I do so, looking for the key that identifies the various temple buildings. I am baffled when I cannot find one anywhere, in any language. Then I realize, as I stand next to the diorama and watch the tour groups come through, that the lack of a key is deliberate. The tour guides are being given an opportunity to earn their keep. I listen to the spiels being given in English, all of which turn their attention sooner or later to the *round* temple in the center of the precinct, the only round building in evidence.

This is, I know, the Temple of the Plumed Serpent, Quetzalcoatl. He was also known as Ehecatl, the God of the Wind, and the round shape of his temple was meant to facilitate the flow of the wind. Yet, as I stand eavesdropping, I hear the round building described as the Observatory, the boys' school, and the Temple of Tlaloc. None of the guides, in my hearing, gets it right; yet, the tourists all seem satisfied with what they have been told.

Part of the tentativeness of my writing, up to this point, has been due to the nagging sense that for all the books I have read, I still do not know enough. Now I am pretty sure I *do*, which is a liberating experience, though at the same time, paradoxically, it seems to impose an obligation upon me. Because I feel very strongly that I do not want to add to the general fund of disinformation about the Aztecs. I want my readers to walk away from *my* diorama knowing exactly which house the Plumed Serpent calls home.

A few days later, we book a tour out to the ruins of Teotihuacan. On the way, we stop at the Shrine of the Virgin of Guadalupe and, since it is Good Friday, there are modern-day penitents fulfilling their vows by crawling to the shrine on their knees. As we drive toward Teotihuacan, the first clouds we have seen in a week begin to gather ahead of us, above a range of steep brown hills. At a certain point, Dave points and says, "There it is."

Another moment passes before I realize that one of the hills is man-made. "The Temple of the Sun," Dave explains, and at that moment the radio begins to play Linda Ronstadt's version of the old rock-n-roll standard, "Just One Look." And that is probably all it took, back in 300 A.D., to convince people that a ruling elite who could raise a temple as high as the hills probably had the gods on their side.

We pile out of the van to find a thunderstorm in full progress over the Temple of the Sun. But there is no way I am not going to climb to the top, so up we go, ducking our heads at every fresh crack of thunder. Halfway up the steep flight of stairs, Dave tells me about a Mayanist named Dennis Puleston, who was recently killed by lightning at Chichen Itza. Apparently, the bolt of lightning came right through the walls of the Castillo to strike him. I thank Dave for sharing that, recognizing that he has truly become a social scientist— someone whose desire to observe the phenomenon is greater than his fear of being fried by it.

We make it to the top of the temple where, in addition to a tremendous view in all directions, we see bolts of lightning literally flash by horizontally, both above and below us. The booming of thunder is virtually continuous, and I have assumed a walking crouch, trying not to stand out above the crowd of other foolhardy tourists. And then I see, at the very summit of the temple, a Mexican gentleman and his two sons, and this gentleman is actually flying a kite. It is way, way up there, a speck against the thundering clouds, and he and his sons are laughing. I feel, simultaneously, proud of my prudence and utterly chickenshit. It occurs to me that I come from a culture that has long ago stopped trying to approach the gods where they live.

Back in New Hampshire, with visions of Mexico still dancing in my head, I make some critical decisions. The first and most critical is that I have to cover the whole ninety-year history of the Aztecs, from their rise in 1428 to their fall in 1519. I had originally been trying to write a novel of reasonable size that began just before the arrival of the Spanish and flashed back to all the legendary and historical events that went before. But there were too many of those great events, and I could not make them resonate for the reader until I had solidly established the cultural context, which was itself a formidable task. Since I could not count on the average reader to supply even the most mundane details of Aztec life—how they dressed, what they ate, where they lived—I would have to build my fictional world from the ground up. It made sense, then, to build my version of Aztec history in the same straightforward, step-by-step manner.

This decision gave rise to two rather contradictory impulses: to make a splash, and to get it right. The former came from the recognition that my modest novel had just turned into a multi-generational tale, with a huge cast of characters and a scale that was ninety years long and as far-flung as the Aztec Empire itself. Thinking small would not help me here, so my working title became *Towering Bestseller*, and I began to plot the novel out in blocks that were 100 pages long, rather than 25.

My second recognition was that in educating the reader, I was going to have to make a large number of educated guesses concerning the many gaps in our "factual" knowledge. Unlike the historians and anthropologists whose work I had read, I could not say, "We do not know what the Aztecs used for soap," or, "We do not have reliable data on how they buried their dead." My characters would certainly know every detail of their world, so if I could not find the desired fact in a book, I would have to weigh the possible alternatives and make an imaginative leap.

The question then became, "How educated do your guesses need to be?" Would I need to consult all the available sources, or should I just go ahead and fabricate? This is where the impulse to get it right reared its snooty little head. I remembered the diorama in the museum in Mexico City, and my unspoken vow not to mislead the tourists. I suspected that the readers of historical novels wanted to learn something while they were being entertained, and that they probably trusted the basic accuracy of the actual history they were getting in a fictional manner. So I decided that I would try to fabricate on the basis of the best information available to me—I would try to get myself out to the cutting edge of what was known, so that while the experts might quibble with my fabrications, they could not dismiss them out of hand.

Once I got going, the book seemed to have a momentum of its own, and the task of getting it right was made much easier by my discovery of Bernadino de Sahagún's twelve-volume *General History of the Things of New Spain*, aka *The Florentine Codex*. The UNH Library had only two of the volumes, but the rest were easily ordered from the University of Utah Press. I also corresponded with historian Burr Cartwright Brundage, who became a friend and mentor and did his best to answer my obtuse questions. The working title of my novel, coined by my wife in a nod to getting it right while making a splash, became *Moteczuma's Galoshes*.

When I completed what I thought was half of the novel, my agent sold it to an editor at Random House. Then I really had to go to work, in order to finish it and collect the second half of the advance, and toward the end I was turning out pages at a rate worthy of Thomas Wolfe. On my 32nd birthday, my wife and I met my editor for lunch in Manhattan, so I could turn over the final chapter. His first words to me, as he accepted the manuscript, were, "Have you heard about the other Aztec novel?"

I had not, but he filled me in: another historical novel about the Aztecs would come out in just a few months and had already sold to paperback and a book club. The publication of my novel was at least a year away. I had just been scooped, big time. At that point, I still had not come up with a real title for the novel, which was about an Aztec named Huemac. For unexamined fictional reasons, I had given Huemac sensationally bad luck, the "greatness of misfortune," as I called it. I had not thought I was writing an autobiographical novel, but as I staggered out of the restaurant, I had my title: *The Luck of Huemac*.

A year or so later, I sit outside the Peabody Museum in Cambridge, Massachusetts, waiting to meet an art historian named Clemency Coggins. Against the advice of my editor, I have decided to write another historical novel, this one on the Maya. He was concerned that I might be pigeonholed by reviewers and dismissed as a genre writer. But I had discovered several advantages in writing novels that had a subject. One was having sources of inspiration outside myself—texts and notes I could turn to when my creativity flagged. Another was the freedom to address truly large themes, like war and conquest, religion and magic, the florescence and decay of entire cultures. A third was the unexpected pleasure I derived from tracking down the facts and putting them in coherent order, the essential task of research.

I made my research task more challenging by focusing on the Maya of the Classic Period, which lasted from about 250 to 850 C.E. These are the Maya who built their great ceremonial centers in the rainforests of Mexico and Guatemala, who kept track of time and astronomical events with obsessive precision, and who left us the most beautiful and sophisticated pottery and sculpture in Mesoamerica. These are also the Maya who abandoned their ceremonial centers some 600 years before the arrival of the Spanish, in what has been called the "Classic Maya Collapse."

We may never know for certain what caused this collapse, and when I entered the field in 1980, not much progress was being made in unraveling the mystery. This was partially due to the fact that no one could fully decipher the elaborate hieroglyphic inscriptions the Maya had left behind. To a larger extent, though, it was due to a peculiarly ahistorical view of the Classic Maya that had been promulgated by two of the giants in the field, Sylvanus Morley and J. Eric Thompson. They had insisted that the Classic Mayan sites like Tikal and Copan should not be regarded as cities, in the sense of centers of urban activity. Instead, they were ceremonial centers whose only permanent inhabitants were a cadre of astronomer priests. The bulk of the population supposedly lived out in the hinterlands, practicing slash-and-burn agriculture and visiting the sites only on ritual occasions. According to the Morley/Thompson view, the Classic Maya, unlike those bloodthirsty Aztecs, lived in splendid and peaceful isolation, displaying little interest in wars of conquest or the glorification of kings.

This interpretation did not offer up much in the way of a real story, and I felt extremely frustrated until a new volume of recent scholarship entitled *Maya Archaeology and Ethnohistory* showed up in the UNH Library. I was immediately drawn to a pair of essays about Tikal that had been written by Dennis Puleston and Clemency Coggins, both of whom were making use of unpublished material from the Tikal Project. For the first time, I had a tentative dynastic genealogy, plus a cultural history that included the construction of pyramid complexes, long-distance trade in obsidian, cacao beans, and fine ceramics, and significant contact with the Central Mexican site of Teotihuacan. It was all enormously speculative, wrapped in a thick tissue of qualifications and scholarly disclaimers, but it was the closest I had come to a story in months.

So I sit down on a bench in the sun, outside a new library named for Alfred Tozzer, another famous Mayanist, and tell Clemency Coggins that I want to write a novel about Classic Period Tikal. Her immediate response is "It can't be done. We don't know enough." I have not had a lot of experience with archaeologists and scholars at this point, so I am temporarily crushed. I have not yet learned that most of them—the good ones—are totally dedicated to getting it right. That means walking a fine evidentiary line, where the worst thing you could be accused of is fabrication.

But then Clemency, true to her name, goes on to help me in any way she can, giving me references to pursue and the names of other scholars to contact. She also gives me my first sense of what might be called the Evolving Past, as opposed to the Established Past, the past according to Morley and Thompson. She makes clear that this nascent view of the Classic Maya exists largely in unpublished form: in dissertations, site reports, journal articles still in press, papers offered at conferences, and the personal communications between the people who are doing the most current digging and deciphering. In other words, it is time to get out of the library and talk to some of the experts in the field.

There is still snow on the ground as I drive westward across New Hampshire and then north into Vermont, heading for Burlington and the University of Vermont. I find my way to the office of William Haviland, an archaeologist and member of the Tikal Project. He knows what I want and immediately pulls out the unpublished manuscript of Dennis Puleston's settlement survey of the Tikal site, which would later appear as *Tikal Report 13*. Puleston had died in 1979, struck by lightning at Chichen Itza, but his survey shows clearly that the core area of Tikal had been densely populated in the Classic period. This means that Tikal was indeed a city, without the large tracts of uninhabited forest that would have been required for slash-and-burn agriculture. Instead, as Puleston suggested in his essay, the inhabitants must have been practicing some form of intensive agriculture, perhaps farming on raised fields in the seasonal swamps.

Having brought me fully into the world of the Evolving Past, Bill Haviland takes me home with him and gets out his data sheets on the palace group he had excavated at Tikal, giving me a short course in Classic Mayan building techniques. He also speaks about the geography of the site, the climate and growing season, the flora and fauna, the kinship structure, and the distribution of pottery and luxury goods. Most importantly, he speculates on the collapse, suggesting that the city was a highly centralized system in which many people had specialized occupations and were accustomed to having the necessities of life supplied to them—and were, therefore, unequipped to fend for themselves if the larger system failed to produce the goods. This also meant that a failure in one area—a shortage of food or firewood, for example—would have a ripple effect through all the others, as people turned from their assigned tasks to scavenge for what they needed. The final result might have been a chain-reaction breakdown of the entire system.

Later that evening, Bill shows his home movies of his first season at Tikal and regales me with stories of life in the field, planting the seeds for *Rising from the Ruins*, a novel that will not be written for another twelve years. The immediate result of this scholarly encounter, however, is a decision to tackle the mystery of the Classic Collapse head on—to recreate the city of Tikal as it might have been at its height, and to imagine how that chain-reaction breakdown might have occurred.

Some months later, after a trip to the Yucatan with my wife, I write a first chapter, setting it near the end of Katun 18 Ahau in the Mayan calendar, or around 790 C.E. In it, my character Balam Xoc, the religious leader of the Jaguar Paw clan, enters one of the temple shrines on Tikal's North Acropolis. After days of solitude, fasting, and ritual blood-letting, he has a vision in which he experiences the demise of his people, and he sees that the cause of their downfall lies in the distant past, when the foreigners from Teotihuacan came to Tikal. Balam Xoc emerges from isolation to utter a dire warning about the future, and to urge his people to defy the authority of the current ruler of Tikal.

Uncertain that I am on the right track, I send a copy of the chapter to Bill Haviland, hoping for a little reassurance. He writes back to say, with a certain astonishment, that I have described a perfect example of what the sociologist A.F.C. Wallace had defined as a "revitalization movement." The attribution sends me back to the library to find Wallace's article on the Iroquois, which in turn leads me to Max Weber's essay on *charisma*. With Wallace and Weber providing the intellectual underpinning, I proceed to write the story of Balam Xoc's attempt to revitalize his people, calling it, simply, *Tikal*.

The novel that followed the trilogy, *Rising from the Ruins*, was inspired by Bill Haviland's home movies and stories of camp life at Tikal, so naturally when I set out to create a fictional archaeological site, I made it a Mayan site.

Yet, when I went to the library to refresh my knowledge of the Maya, even though only ten or twelve years had passed since I first researched them, I found that the field of Maya Studies had undergone a remarkable transformation. The inscriptions the Maya had carved in stone and painted on pottery were now being read for more than just royal names and dates—now they gave dynastic records, historical events, and the details of religious rituals. The Evolving Past had taken over so completely that Mayanists were now writing narrative accounts of the wars between the major Classic sites, as if they were novelists, not scholars.

This transformation was due in large part to a singular achievement: the decipherment of the Maya hieroglyphs. Epigraphers had long suspected that the glyphs might function as parts of speech, but there was no agreement about which Mayan language was spoken or what kind of grammar was employed in the inscriptions. It was this agreement that had finally been reached, and while it seemed like a sudden breakthrough to me, it was actually the culmination of a long and arduous collaboration over many years, in which field archaeologists, iconographers, epigraphers, and art historians regularly crossed the boundaries of their disciplines to share their discoveries, hunches, and insights. Using colonial-era Mayan dictionaries as their language source, they were able to wring fresh meaning from artifacts that had been in our possession—as drawings or photographs—for many decades.

The decoding of the Mayan glyphic system demonstrates that it is still possible to advance our knowledge of human history and culture in meaningful ways. Given the slipperiness of the past—especially the ancient past—it is heartening to think that we can come to know it—and thus ourselves—better.

But the process of unraveling and re-evaluating the past is intrinsically slow and painstaking, and the requisite materials have to be kept intact and available, however long it takes. I remember how grateful I was to find the old Carnegie Institution volumes of Sylvanus Morley's *The Inscriptions of Peten* up in the stacks of the University of New Hampshire library. No one else had taken them out of the library in over thirty years, but at that point in my research I needed to examine the original source, and there it was.

This is where the members of an organization like SALALM come in—because the kind of scholarship I talk about cannot flourish without the resources provided by libraries, museums, archives, manuscript collections, and the purveyors and publishers of rare books and documents. These holdings are the ground and foundation, the reservoir of past and current knowledge that will nourish the scholarship of the future. So, clearly, this work is vital to the entire scholarly enterprise. You may even supply the inspiration for a novel or two, or perhaps a play, or a poem or a film or a folk song. And while you may find—as I have—that it is very hard to make a significant splash, I hope you'll take some solace and satisfaction in the knowledge that you have done your best to get it right.

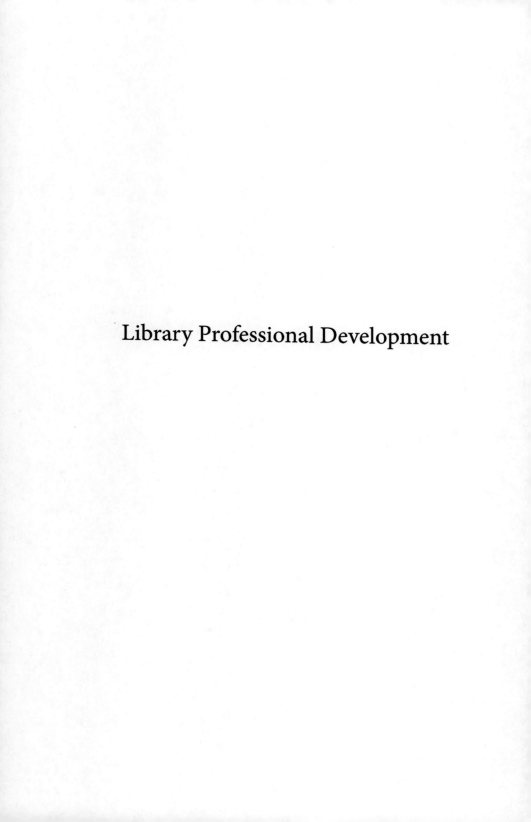

Library Professional Development

25. Searching for Professional Development Opportunities and Finding HAPIness

Marsha Forys

As today's panel illustrates, there are many ways to develop professionally. You can become active in organizations like SALALM. You can publish a book or an article, make a presentation at a conference, or perhaps be the editor of a journal. Something else you might consider doing is being a HAPI indexer. What does a HAPI indexer do and why would you want to be one?

HAPI, the *Hispanic American Periodicals Index*, relies on volunteer indexers to do much of the indexing of the over 300 journals it covers. Each volunteer selects a certain number of titles that his or her library subscribes to and agrees to look at and index each new issue when it comes out. Indexers are responsible for: (1) describing the physical characteristics of the articles, noting things like the page numbers and the presence of any illustrations, charts, statistics, etc.; (2) trying to verify the authors' names in a standard bibliographic source; and (3) assigning subject headings that best describe the content of the articles. Indexers are given the necessary tools to work with. They receive a template to fill in for each of the journals they index, a listing of authorized HAPI subject headings, and a detailed set of guidelines to follow. After indexing an issue of a journal, the indexer E-mails the filled-in templates to HAPI headquarters. That, in a nutshell, is what a HAPI indexer does.

Why would someone want to be a HAPI indexer? Rather than give only my own ideas, I decided to ask my fellow HAPI indexers about the benefits they see in being an indexer. To do that, I sent an E-mail message to forty current and former HAPI indexers. The message I sent was not a formal survey; rather, it was a way for other indexers to speak through me. Seventeen people out of forty replied, which was a response rate of approximately 42.5%. Fifteen of the respondents were current indexers and two were past indexers. The length of time the respondents had been indexers ranged from less than one year to over thirty years. About half the respondents had been indexers for ten years or less, and about half were indexers for more than ten years. What was impressive was how long some people had been indexers. One person reported indexing for fifteen years, one twenty-four years, and two for over thirty years. Clearly those indexers enjoy and derive some benefit from the activity.

I especially wanted to find out how HAPI indexing helps those librarians with their professional development. To do that, I asked them the following question: "At your institution, does the indexing you do for HAPI count as a professional development activity for your promotion and tenure process and/or during your annual performance review? Comments?" In looking at their answers, we need to remember that some academic librarians have faculty status and are concerned with fulfilling the requirements for promotion and tenure, which usually include professional activities like publication and being active in national organizations. Other academic librarians do not have faculty status but might still be held responsible for engaging in similar professional activities. Thirteen respondents said that HAPI indexing counts as a professional development activity and four said it did not.

When asked, "How has being a HAPI indexer helped you with your professional development?" respondents mentioned that it:

- Helps with collection development work.
- Makes one familiar with using the HAPI database which in turn helps them with their library instruction and with their reference work.
- Is a consistent, ongoing professional activity that can be high-lighted in one's annual performance review.
- Serves a continuing education function by keeping the indexers current with Latin American happenings and scholarship.
- Helps the indexers stay proficient in reading Spanish and Portuguese.
- Provides an excuse to take the time to read articles.

The final question was very open-ended, asking, "Do you have any additional thoughts or comments on indexing for HAPI?" Here are just some of their comments:

- HAPI indexing provides a respite from one's typical day-to-day work activities.
- It is a way for catalogers to be involved because they have skills that are easily transferable to HAPI indexing.
- Being associated with a high-quality independently-owned database makes the indexing experience enjoyable.
- Indexing is seen as a way to get involved in SALALM activities.
- HAPI indexing is a way to give back to the profession.

Two people addressed the issue of how much time it takes to index for HAPI. One said that the indexing is time consuming and that it is difficult to find time to do the indexing because of other job responsibilities. Yet someone else said that it is an intellectually demanding activity that does not take a lot of time to do and does not interfere with one's daily work schedule. So the question of time seems primarily to depend on an individual's circumstances. Speaking for myself, I have found that my job has busy times and slower times, and I do most of the indexing during the slower times of the semester.

It makes sense for librarians to be indexers. Indexing is a way for librarians to contribute to the world of knowledge by helping people find information while also providing them with a way to contribute to the profession. Nineteenth-century librarian William Poole realized this when he prepared an index to the periodicals in the society library where he worked. That index, when published, was the first general index to multiple periodicals.[1]

The goal of today's presentation was to get those in the audience who are not HAPI indexers to start thinking about including HAPI indexing among their professional development activities. Clearly the indexers who replied to my E-mail enjoy being HAPI indexers and see it as a means of professional development. Anyone searching for professional development opportunities and wanting to find HAPIness by being a volunteer indexer should contact the director of HAPI.

NOTES

1. William Landram Williamson, "Poole, William Frederick," vol. 23, *Encyclopedia of Library and Information Science* (New York: Marcel Dekker, 1968) 94-117.

26. You Can Do It All! But Do You Want To?: Identifying, Creating, and Enjoying Professional Development Activities

Anne C. Barnhart

Getting started as a new librarian can be challenging. One wants to get involved and knows that it is important to find professional development activities to gain experience and a bit of recognition. But when a librarian is just starting in the field, it can often be difficult to figure out which professional development opportunities are available. And new librarians often wonder if their lack of experience means that they cannot (or should not) pursue certain opportunities. Which avenues are appropriate and doable? And, how does one get started?

This paper is a summary of a conference presentation in which I addressed these issues and offered some advice based on personal experience. The examples come from the area of Latin American Studies librarianship; however, librarians in other areas will certainly find some of these comments to be applicable to their fields as well.

Identifying

New librarians do not really have a lot of librarian experience to talk about in a conference presentation, but this does not mean that they do not have areas of expertise that could be interesting and valuable for their colleagues. It can be very useful to begin presenting at conferences by using graduate school papers and projects as a base. Some of my papers had been written nearly a decade prior, so I needed to update them and re-familiarize myself with the material. These papers and projects became my first conference presentations and one of them became my first monograph. The papers I recycled were not just on "library" topics but also on Latin American Studies from my graduate work in that area. Reusing these class projects allowed me to have many topics to present on in conferences and, due to the varied nature of the topics, gave my *Curriculum Vitae* some variety.

Another simple way to build up a CV and to keep abreast of publications in the field is to review books. Reviewing for *Choice* is a great way to become familiar with reference books. This can be especially helpful to a collection development librarian because he or she can review the books before deciding if the library should purchase them. It also obligates one to become more intimately familiar with the holdings in one's own reference collection. Ideally, all librarians should spend time with reference books (or online reference sources) comparing them, looking for overlap and evaluating their content. But the reality is that most of us are simply putting out too many fires to have the luxury of that kind of time just for the sake of doing it. Reviewing reference books has helped me make that time. Through doing this, not only have I explored new reference books and made informed selection decisions, but I have also become better able to help my users with our reference collection.

I have also reviewed books for *Críticas*. *Críticas* is a publication (formerly in print and now online) of reviews in English of Spanish-language material. The editor sends me novels (I requested fiction) and I read them and write brief descriptions to help monolingual (primarily public library) librarians make selection decisions to serve their Spanish-speaking populations. In addition to helping the profession, reviewing for *Críticas* allows me an excuse for my guilty pleasure of reading heaps of fiction and offering my opinion about things without being asked. And since some of the books are reviewed before publication, I get to casually mention to graduate students and professors my familiarity with new works while I am benefiting from increasing my Spanish vocabulary.

There are other venues for writing reviews as well such as *Library Journal*, *Counterpoise*, *Reference Reviews Europe* and any number of academic journals in one's particular discipline. Often book reviewers get to keep the review copy for their personal collection, but typically they are not to be added to the library's collection; the publishers provided a free review copy but do not want to miss out on potential sales if the library wants one. I keep the review copy of useful reference books in my office because I am located far from the reference collection in my library and I find them to be helpful when meeting with researchers.

Another easy way to start getting involved professionally is to volunteer. Indexing is a good (and easy) way to do this. I have indexed for HAPI (*Hispanic American Periodicals Index*) since I was in library school. I believe it is one of the most rewarding ways to volunteer that there is. Indexing for HAPI has taught me how to better use the database for research. Since I understand the limits of its controlled vocabulary and the structure of its thesaurus, I am able to, fairly deftly, manipulate its search interface to tease out the information I want. Indexing for HAPI has helped me approach how to use other databases because I am intimately familiar with one. For this very reason, I have graduate students index articles as if they were putting them into a database as an information literacy assignment; it is a great pedagogic tool. Indexing also helps me keep up-to-date on the literature in specialized fields. Sometimes I see an article in a journal that hasn't been indexed yet and I know that the article would be interesting to a specific professor on my campus, so I photocopy it for that professor and send it in campus mail. This kind of personal contact with professors is invaluable for getting their support for other projects so, in this regard, indexing for HAPI helps me look good. And let us be honest—we all need to use indexes in our work, so by volunteering our time to help maintain one, we are significantly contributing to our profession.

Creating

Another very simple and straightforward way to volunteer is by joining one of the numerous committees in our professional organizations. SALALM is a small organization, and when it did not have the committees that did what I wanted and needed, I created new committees. I noticed that many of us in SALALM work with materials from Spain and Portugal, but there was no space for Iberianist discussions within the SALALM structure. I met with other SALALM members and we created ISiS (Iberian Studies in SALALM) to address these needs. Following that, I decided to create a space within SALALM for those of us who work with US Latina/o Studies as well, and thus ALZAR (Academic Latina/o Zone of Action and Research) was born. This strategy would not necessarily work well in a larger organization but, due to SALALM's size, I was able to create new committees where I could volunteer my time and get more out of it.

Another way in which I have created professional development opportunities is by taking advantage of a frustrating situation. Due to the economic reality of living in Santa Barbara, California, I started working part-time answering online reference questions for QuestionPoint (a division of OCLC). My experience with them allowed me to be an onsite trainer when the University of California decided to use the same chat software. It did not take any extra effort from me to take advantage of the knowledge that I had gained in my part-time job.

QuestionPoint answers reference questions for academic and public libraries in both English and Spanish. While this variety is often overwhelming, it still offers good experience in handling a mixture of patrons. Since I have experience that is not just limited to the realm of Latin American Studies, I have been invited to speak about the challenges of chat reference to librarians in Buenos Aires and Mexico. In addition to helping me out financially, my part-time adventures for QuestionPoint have allowed me to create professional development opportunities.

Another way to create opportunities is just by being observant. I sometimes step back and observe myself as I do my daily work and I wonder what would make my job easier. What would allow me to be more efficient? You might discover that there is a tutorial or a research guide that you could create that would be useful to you and your colleagues. Often there are projects, and not all of them have to be overwhelming, that are right in front of us that we could turn into professional development opportunities. This is how I started the specialized library research courses at the University of California Santa Barbara for Latin American & Iberian Studies and Religious Studies. I watched the graduate students struggle and I listened to their professors complain about the quality of their students' research and identified a few patterns. Then I looked at the internal structure of how the University of California Santa Barbara Libraries classes are established to see if it was possible to create something specialized. Developing the courses was not an extremely difficult task and having that experience is good for me professionally.

When I try something new, whether it is designing a tutorial, teaching a new class or working with a new technology, I take notes on my experiences. I write down the steps, make note of the obstacles, the successes and the disasters. Sometimes these notes have become presentations. It is important to remember that the failures, if told well, can be just as illustrative as (and often much more entertaining than) the successes.

A big hurdle many new librarians face is a lack of experience in writing and presenting. I practice by writing reports on my professional activities. When I return from SALALM, I write up a brief report of what I did at the conference. I often submit these reports to the library administration and then they can see what I am doing at SALALM and perhaps they can start to appreciate some of the more intangible work that we do. The reports would be useful even if I didn't share them because they help me remember any action items for which I am responsible and they are useful for me when I am up for review. By writing these reports, I am also practicing my skills of describing aspects of my job for others to read.

I also try to give an informal presentation in the library upon my return so I can practice talking in front of a group. Many libraries have a forum for sharing conference experiences, but if one's library does not already have an established space for this, it would not be very difficult to create a brown bag series. By creating a forum for this kind of discussion, a new librarian would have the added benefit of getting experience in organizing an informal lecture series.

Yes Happens

I have been thinking about this a great deal, and if I were a library administrator, I would start a campaign called "YES! Happens." "No" is not a very interesting word. It shuts things down. It closes roads. "Yes" is full of possibility. I would encourage my employees to act as if "yes" were the default answer. Unfortunately in the world of libraries, we are often faced with a lot of knee-jerk naysayers who say "no" and justify why it was a bad idea after rejecting it. This stifles creativity. I encourage all new librarians (and older ones) to think, "Yes."

When you have a new idea, pretend for a while that it is not just some crazy idea. Pretend that it is a mandate. Ask yourself *how* it can be done, not *if* it can be done. Pretend, just for a little while, pretend that "no" is not even an option.

Try this for a few months and I think you'll be pleasantly surprised by the ideas you come up with and the possibilities for seeing them through. Now, of course, there is always the reality check of a nay-saying administration looming over our heads. However, this exercise in thinking creatively will bear fruit. You will create professional development opportunities that you can accomplish.

Part of thinking "yes" is to be open to opportunities that present themselves. Sometimes I might stretch myself too thin and that is a valid concern, but saying "yes" has allowed me to experiment with new ideas, go new places and grow in new ways.

A personal example of this is the online course I teach through the University of Illinois at Urbana-Champaign (UIUC). Dumb luck, good timing, and a willingness to say "yes" is how I ended up creating and teaching that course. I was bored at work one day and was looking through the online courses taught at my alma mater to see if anything looked interesting to me. I saw that they had a theological librarianship course. I was surprised that they had such specific courses since I didn't remember anything like that from my days there. I sent my former advisor, Dean Linda Smith, an E-mail saying I saw that course and offered my services if they ever wanted an online Latin American Studies librarianship course taught. Linda wrote back telling me that UIUC and other library schools were in the final stages of putting together a grant proposal to develop specialized library courses and asked if I (and SALALM) would like to be part of the grant. Dumb luck, good timing, and a willingness to say "yes" are major keys to any success I might have.

Enjoying

Building up one's *Curriculum Vitae* is great, but only if one enjoys doing it. I have been lucky because I have found and created ways that I enjoy. Part of that for me has been because so often the professional is personal. I used the book review example of where a personal hobby (reading) of mine overlaps with a professional development opportunity (writing reviews). In your lives there are probably many intersections where your personal interests connect to this profession. Perhaps it is in volunteer work. Perhaps it will be a hobby. Perhaps it will come as a secondary job.

I have also gotten to know many SALALMistas over the years and I can say that some of my closest friends are members of this organization. This means that my work with them is also time spent with friends. With my colleagues and friends, I have purchased books in Chiapas and explored Buenos Aires. Right now this overlap makes a lot of what I do that much more enjoyable. And I also think the fact that we enjoy spending time together makes us better at what we do when we work together.

You need to be mindful about what you are doing and why you are doing it. Find your passion. Surprisingly, I discovered that I love teaching. I figured this out through watching my reactions to things and by being reflective.

Even my principal volunteer activity (coaching Team in Training) is a kind of teaching. It helps to have a passion. If a person does not feel passionate about this career, it becomes harder to enjoy opportunities because God knows we are not in it for the money.

It also helps to remind oneself that not all aspects of this job make the career. Developing the Library Science course helped me really appreciate that fact as I reflected on what my job is (telling kids how to print, rebooting computers, sitting through boring meetings) and what my career is (promoting Latin Americana and helping Latin American writers—both academic and popular—have their voices heard and legitimized in the U.S.). Often my day is bogged down by my job. Sometimes my job gets in the way of my career. But my job is also what allows me to explore this career. And when I look at it that way, it helps me have appreciation for it. At least on some days.

I also often think of Todd Sullivan. While I in the MA-PhD program at Indian University, Todd was a doctoral student in Religious Studies who bought a pick-up truck and, when asked why he needed a pick-up truck, said, "To help people move." He was studying for his qualifying examinations and would talk about his girlfriend and about how he had not been a good partner lately because he was so focused on his exams. "After my exams I'm going to make it all up to her. After my exams things will be better." At the time, I was not happy with my courses or the program. I kept thinking, "After this semester it will be better. After I'm done with the M.A. things will be smoother." And I was in a department where junior faculty said, "After I get tenure things will be better," and associate professors said, "Once I am full professor things will be better." See a pattern?

Five days after Todd finished his qualifying examinations, he was killed in a car accident. There was no "after my exams" for Todd. I often think of this when I am postponing satisfaction or happiness. I look at my present situation and think, "What if there is no after this?" If that thought is too depressing, I look for ways to change my present situation. Or I look for strategies to change my attitude about the present situation.

And sometimes that means I have to not do some things. And some of these things are things I enjoy. Some are things I am probably good at. This has been a struggle for me personally because I feel some bizarre work ethic that means my ability to do something also means I am somehow morally or ethically obligated to do it. I do not know where that comes from.

But, as Dr. Miranda Bailey said in a season finale of *Grey's Anatomy*, "I can't do everything and still have everything, so I have to let some pieces go." It is always better when people get to choose the pieces to let go before others make that decision for them.

Library Encounters, Engagements, and Exchanges

27. Where We Are, Where May We Be Going, and What Can We Do There?
David Block

Although this panel is well off the conference theme, I have thought for some time that SALALM needs to address the rapidly changing contours of research library collections and their implications for the kinds of information resources these changes require. A request by one of the *libreros* at the end of the New Mexico meeting convinced me to organize this paper. What my colleagues and I have to say is ominous. I am asking readers to consider the real possibility that in another five years neither librarians nor booksellers will be doing the work as it is now done. I want to stress from the outset that at least my portion is speculative and that the opinions expressed here have not been vetted by SALALM, its officers, or my paymaster. If I could make a wish, it would be to begin a discussion on how to ensure that the scholarship that treats Latin America will have smooth passage through the choppy weather that likely lies ahead.

Research libraries are all making the transition from analog to digital information, a theme awkwardly compressed into the title of this paper. In answer to the first of my questions, "Where are we?," I would argue that libraries are all in different places, but that all of them are somewhere on a continuum that leads from paper to electronic resources. Moreover, I would argue that all are moving in the same direction along the continuum, though at different speeds.

In the language used by librarians, this transition falls under the rubric of "access vs. ownership" or information acquired "just in time." As a way of responding to new models of information presentation, some have suggested that libraries re-conceptualize collection development altogether and have offered "knowledge management" as an appropriate substitute.[1] That is, the job of librarians is to provide the reader with "information objects"—sounds, images as well as texts—to interact with. There is always a lag between the formulation of an idea and its implementation. "Access vs. ownership" appeared in professional literature in the 1980s and was first discussed at SALALM in 1994,[2] but its implications are only now having a noticeable impact on research libraries. For several years, libraries have shed staff. Those who have survived have been redeployed and given additional duties, and as positions become available, they are assigned to the new growth sectors of computer applications

301

and public relations.[3] Many libraries, mine included, are no longer in a position to invest in paper collections as heavily as they have in the past, and very soon there will not be staff resources sufficient to process the quantities of paper that we currently acquire. Materials budgets have thus far lagged staff changes, but this will not last. The reasons are electronic (digital technologies enable us to do things differently) and economic (we do not have enough money not to).

This paper will lay out how I think these two forces, electronics and economics, are driving change and why I think there is no altering its trajectory. But first, a few words on the rationale behind library collections.

Background

Higher education in the United States is very competitive. In a way reminiscent of the Cold War arms race, universities have built larger and larger faculties, labs and football teams to insure their survival. Libraries are a part of the competitive behavior; they are often called upon to demonstrate their importance in attracting the "best faculty and students" to their institutions. Traditionally, libraries measured their strength through collection size and growth, the major statistics driving the Association of Research Library's canonical index. The movement of library resources from paper to digital has not changed the competitive behavior of the institutions, but it has shifted the indicators. Libraries now stress their importance as a place and as a provider of services wherever its readers may be and whenever they want to read.

I entered the profession just as the Research Libraries Group Conspectus wound down. This instrument, may it rest in peace, measured collections in excruciating detail on a scale of 1 to 5 and marked the high tide of assembling paper-based resources on individual campuses. Although undertaken in the name of building a "national" collection, the Conspectus put libraries' competitive behavior into stark relief. Rather than demonstrating complementarity, the Conspectus stressed local strength; a level 4 collection was better than a level 3, even if one was simply a larger version of the other. In addition, use of the materials was implied rather than specified. Now, one can no longer assume that collections justify themselves. To evoke, again, the phraseology of the Cold War, we must use it or lose it.

Use has always been and will always be the reason for collection development. For forty years, prevailing opinion held that bibliographers in close consultation with faculty would be in the best position to predict use, based on research and teaching at each institution. But bibliometrics has not supported this contention. The use of research library materials was first systematically documented in the late 1970s by Allen Kent, et. al, who found that 40% of the books in Hillman Library had never circulated and that the modal case for circulation in the collection was less than three. Books written in languages other than English showed particularly low use rates; Spanish-language items comprised only 2.52% of circulations recorded at

Hillman in 1979.[4] Despite the uproar that the "Pittsburgh Study" produced in the profession, its conclusions have stood for nearly thirty years without significant revision. With circulation as the most demonstrable test of value, and as automated systems compile these statistics as a matter of course, foreign language materials are demonstrably disadvantaged. As an indication of just how disadvantaged, one library administrator recently adopted the language that financiers employ to describe something that they want to dispose of, referring to foreign language books as "underperforming assets."

Electronics

A collection of electronic information offers many advantages over its paper counterpart, especially to those who do not read. It potentially allows simultaneous consultation by several users, the ability to search a text for the occurrence of key words or phrases, and access anytime and anyplace. Equally important to library managers, an electronic collection reduces processing costs and space needs. I will leave discussion of processing costs to my fellow panelists and briefly discuss space as a managerial consideration.

I have already pointed out that paper materials no longer receive top billing at research universities. Libraries throughout the United States are reconfiguring their insides, removing shelves and inserting a mélange of computers, meeting rooms, quiet spaces and decidedly unquiet coffee bars. Displaced books, like the lost boys of J.M. Barrie's play, have fled to bibliographic never-never lands off central campuses. Purchasing born-digital materials or converting existing texts to bit streams would disappear physical materials altogether and provide even greater spaces for reclamation.

If only the scholars would come onboard. Thus far digital journals, alone, have made their mark on scholarly communication. In Latin American studies, professors and their students now heavily consult JSTOR. And as a recent survey points out, the addition of OpenURL technology to traditional indexing tools has increased their use as well.[5] On the other hand, "electronic book" has proved something an oxymoron, as readers have not accepted them and publishers are reluctant to produce them. Latin American *editoriales* are beyond reluctant, unable as they are to invest in digital production equipment and lacking a mass readership capable of consuming the product. Nevertheless, for all the reasons cited above, the appeal of electronic books to libraries is irresistible, and, as Google, Microsoft and other enterprising technologists have shown, what is not digital already, can be readily made so.

Economics

One thing in this discussion is certain. Libraries will not be able to maintain their current hybrid existence. Simultaneous development of digital and paper-based collections and services will soon become unsustainable. Most libraries lack the resources to support what are essentially parallel programs, and the current status quo undermines both staff morale and users' confidence in emerging information policy. As libraries apportion their resources, digital collections are gaining larger and larger shares. The most recent statistical report from my institution shows that it now spends 39% of its materials budget on networked electronic resources, up from 16% five years before.[6] To date, the growth of electronic expenditures at Cornell has not come by reducing allocations assigned to library selectors, but it has reduced the total amount available for allocation and thus for the purchase of anything other than digital materials.

Economic constraints have increased administrators' characteristic impatience with redundancy, and they are now labeling multiple copies of paper materials as redundant. Many multi-library campuses currently operate under a "one copy" rule for books and subscriptions. The next step, already contemplated (though not widely instituted), is to extend the one copy rule to the acquisition of low-use materials by groups of libraries in the same region. Regional, electronically-linked collaborations are already taking shape, with the University of California system leading the way. For the past three years, Cornell has participated in a program of this sort, christened "Borrow Direct." It groups us with six other libraries in the Northeast and allows anyone with borrowing privileges at one institution to search a combined catalog and initiate unmediated borrowing requests for materials not available locally. Systems like these can provide remarkably quick service; Borrow Direct's turnaround averages 2.5 days.

Borrow Direct is currently only a discovery and delivery tool, but it enables participants to view the holdings of a seven-institution library that is almost as accessible to them as the ones on their own campuses. And if books seldom circulate on any of the campuses, one copy per region will satisfy readers' needs, or so the rationale goes. Libraries are gearing up for more extensive collaborations by employing computer programs to compare their holdings online. OCLC's WorldCat Collection Analysis tool allows groups of libraries to overlay their collections and determine where they duplicate, where they are unique, and where gaps exist.

While I am not aware of plans to deaccession books already on library shelves—that would be too expensive and violate state-supported libraries' covenants regarding curatorship of public property—there is growing interest in curtailing the duplication of current materials. The extent to which current acquisitions of Latin Americana duplicate is very difficult to measure. In fact, libreros are more qualified to quantify duplication than the library community. But one way to observe the issue is through the lens of the WorldCat Selection tool.

1 ☐	20080424	LC		2	Symposium on Comp...	[SBAC-PAD 2007]: 19th Inter...	IEEE Computer Soc...	2007	QA76.9.A73S93 2007
2 ☐	20080424	LC		11	Cangiano, Gustavo.	El pensamiento vivo de Artu...	Ediciones de la I...	2003	PQ7797.J32Z68 2003
3 ☐	20080424	LC	held	18	Oliveira, Valdeci...	Figurações da donzela- gue...	Annablume,	2005	PQ9697.O7L8355 2005
4 ☐	20080424	LC	held	29	Nolasco-Freire, Z...	Lima Barreto, imagem e ling...	Annablume,	2005	PQ9697 L54Z765 2005
5 ☐	20080424	LC		15	Berrini, Beatriz.	Utopia, utopias : visitando...	EDUC,	1997	PQ9697.D52C3633 1997
6 ☐	20080423	LC		40	Handal, Schafik J...	Una guerra para construir l...	Ocean Sur :	2006	F1488.3.H36 2006
7 ☐	20080423	LC	held	13	Balaguer, Alejand...	Pachacámac : develando el...	Andes y Mares,	2006	F3429.1.P2B35 2006
8 ☐	20080423	LC		34	Díaz Infante, Du...	Mañach o la República /	Letras Cubanas,	2003	F1760.M354D53 2003
9 ☐	20080422	LC	held	31	Bartet, Leyla.	Memorias de cedro y olivo :...	Fondo Editorial d...	2005	F3619.A73837 2005
10 ☐	20080421	LC	held	24	Machado Filho, Am...	Do português arcaico ao po...	EDUFBA,	2004	PC5045.D6 2004
11 ☐	20080421	LC	held	26	Cárdenas de Monn...	Juan Facundo Quiroga : otra...	Librería Histór...	2004	F2846.Q74C36 2004
12 ☐	20080421	LC	held	10	Taboada Terán, N...	Salvador Allende : mar para...	Plural Editores,	2004	F3097.3.T13 2004
13 ☐	20080421	LC		18	Muñoz Rivera, Luis.	Relatos políticos : la ép...	s.n.,	2003	F1975.R58M86 2003
14 ☐	20080421	LC	held	22	Urueña Cervera, ...	Bolívar republicano : fund...	Ediciones Aurora,	2004	F2235.3.U755 2004
15 ☐	20080421	LC	held	30	Camacho Navarro,	Siete vistas de Cuba : inte...	Universidad Nacio...	2002	F1776.S53 2002
16 ☐	20080420	LC		17	Cervantes Guerra,...	Félix Aceves Ortega /	Gobierno de Jalis...	2006	NA759.A25C47 2006

Fig. 1: Screen from WorldCat Selection Tool

What this single page demonstrates is that for several recently-published titles there are numerous copies housed in North American libraries. Should something like the one copy per region rule be instituted, the number of book sales to the U.S. market will drop. I cannot say by how much, nor can I say what it will mean to any of us — librarians or booksellers. But I must reluctantly predict that the days of librarians at multiple libraries selecting copies of the same items and of booksellers selling the same item to multiple clients are numbered.

Responses

My last question, "What can we do there?," asks us to consider how we can begin to plan for the fast-approaching, digital-dominated future. I will offer the following as a starter set:

1. It will be up to each library or group of libraries to redefine collecting profiles for paper materials. Some will see no need to change current practices. For others, the transition will mean maintaining traditional strengths and relying on regional partners for all but the most critical books and periodicals published in some countries or subjects.

2. Assuming that Latin American budgets escape rapine, libraries will expand coverage in their areas of strength. This is the intention of the Distributed Resources component in the Latin American

Research Resources Project and one that receives enthusiastic support from library administrators.[7] Scarce out-of-print materials, genres such as posters and music scores, regional newspapers, and grey literature are unevenly acquired by research libraries, and they are consistently mentioned by Latin Americanists as highly desirable for research.

3. As they expand their digital resources in Latin America, libraries will be in need of rights management—that is, the negotiation of the right to receive or digitize materials currently in copyright and to distribute them over a network. This is an area where I can only ask questions: are there periodicals and newspapers producing full-text editions in electronic format that could be licensed for use by students and faculty; would publishers in the region grant institutions the rights to convert their print backlist to digital formats? These are examples of areas that would allow libreros to market services in the way that they sell books and journals today.

I hope that this session will catalyze a conversation and perhaps spawn a working group to examine the issues raised at this panel. We really should not wait.

NOTES

1.   Joseph Branin, et. al, "The Changing Nature of Collection Management in Research Libraries." *Library Resources and Technical Services*, 44, no. 1 (January 2000): 23-31.

2.   An early summary of the access vs. ownership issue appears in Shirley S. Intner, "Differences between Access vs. Ownership." *Technicalities*, 9 (September 1989): 5-8. The SALALM panel, "Access vs. Ownership: Learning to Relate to the New Library Paradigm," appeared in two parts at SALALM XXXIX (1994).

3.   Earlier in the decade, Anne R. Kenney cited dramatic losses of positions in response to budgetary exigencies and suggested that libraries might actually be driven, kicking and screaming, to collaborate. Kenney, "Collections, Preservation and the Changing Resource Base," in *Access in the Future Tense*, 24- 27 (Washington, D.C.: Council on Library and Information Resources, 2004).

4.   Allen Kent, et. al, *Use of Library Materials* (New York and Basel: Marcel Dekker, Inc., 1979), 44 and passim.

5.   Orchid Mazurkiewicz and Claude H. Potts. "Researching Latin America: a survey of how the new generation is doing its research." *Latin American Research Review*, 42, no. 3 (2007): 161-182.

6.   Cornell University Library Annual Statistics Report 2006/2007 (full version) <http://ecommons.library.cornell.edu/bitstream/1813/10418/1/2007%20ASR%204%202%2008%20with%20links%202.pdf>. Graph S-9, 15.

7.   For a description of the Distributed Resources agreement, see http://www.crl.edu/grn/larrp/index.asp.

28. *Waquichastati?*: Aymara and Quechua in the Cataloging of Bolivian Materials
Tina Gross

I worked as a cataloger for the University of Pittsburgh library system's Eduardo Lozano Latin American Collection from 1998-2007. That collection has long had a focus on collecting books and other materials published in Bolivia, and so the catalogers working with its acquisitions frequently encountered texts in Aymara and Quechua. None of the catalogers on Pitt's Latin American Team had any background in these indigenous languages, which meant that cataloging them was often difficult and time-consuming. Fortunately, classes in both Quechua and Aymara were offered through the Linguistics Department's Less Commonly Taught Languages Center, and I was able to study Quechua for three semesters and Aymara for two in order to help with the cataloging of Bolivian materials in those languages.

In attempting to identify other catalogers who could discuss working with indigenous languages of other regions in Latin America, I was able to informally survey numerous other catalogers at Latin American collections at large U.S. research libraries. Some of what I learned about their experiences working with indigenous languages is reflected here.

I need to emphasize that I am not a linguist, and that my knowledge of Quechua and Aymara is very basic. These observations are based only on cataloging expertise, and the experience of performing bibliographic analysis on library materials from Bolivia over a period of several years.

Categories

There are four basic categories of works including Aymara and/or Quechua that catalogers at the University of Pittsburgh encountered when working on Bolivian materials:

- Complete works in Quechua or Aymara
- Parts of works (for example, a collection of essays chiefly in Spanish, but with one or two essays in Aymara)
- Works with "parallel text" (a cataloging term for the same text in more than one language) in Spanish and Aymara and/or Quechua
- Works in Spanish, with some text in Quechua and/or Aymara (quotations, chapter titles, etc.)

Pitt rarely acquired works entirely in Aymara or Quechua, but the latter three categories were common. The other catalogers I communicated with indicated that the majority of cases in which they encountered indigenous languages fell into the third category: works with the same text in both Spanish and in an indigenous language. The second and fourth categories were also common, but I was surprised that the SALALM catalogers I spoke with reported they encountered works entirely in indigenous languages rarely, or not at all. Catalogers at two very large research libraries (the Library of Congress and Harvard University) indicated that their institutions did collect indigenous-language materials, but that they were cataloged by units other than the general Latin American cataloging staff.

Cataloging Tasks

There are several kinds of tasks that might require particular attention when cataloging items in (or including text in) an indigenous language:

- Recording languages—All of the languages used in a multilingual work must be identified and the corresponding codes assigned to the bibliographic record, to enable searching by language. (This functionality is usually made available in online catalogs as a search limit.)
- Transcribing bibliographic data—The title, author, publisher and other bibliographic information must be identified and recorded. This is usually straightforward, but if the cataloger cannot read or understand the text, the different elements can be hard to identify—a series title could be confused with the publisher's name, or the typography could suggest that a phrase is a subtitle when it is really something else.
- Parallel titles—When a work has the same title in more than one language, both titles are recorded in fields that allow them to be searched or browsed. Like transcription, this is usually simple, but there are cases in which a cataloger may have difficulty determining whether a title in an indigenous language really is parallel to the Spanish (or Portuguese) title or not.
- Authority control—One of the functions of library cataloging is that when an author or institution has published under several different names or versions of their name, the user can find all of their works. This is accomplished by the creation of "authority records" which bring together all of the variations.
- Subject analysis—Cataloging guidelines indicate that if a topic represents 20% or more of an item's content, that topic should be represented in the subject headings assigned to the item.

Recording Languages

In our work with Bolivian materials at the University of Pittsburgh, the problem that we faced most frequently when cataloging a book with text in an indigenous language was difficulty in determining whether it was Quechua or Aymara. It may seem strange, but what language(s) a book is in is not always obvious. It is not common for this to be explicitly stated, since the intended readers would not need to have this information provided. The place of publication may be a significant clue, but there are many areas in Latin America in which more than one indigenous language is used. The Andes in Bolivia is a good example. Bolivian works related to Andean culture and history constituted the majority of cases in which it would have been plausible for the indigenous language present to be either Aymara or Quechua.

Because Quechua and Aymara co-existed for many centuries in overlapping geographic areas, mutual borrowing of words has meant that the two languages now share about 30% of their vocabulary. For the non-speaker, this means that determining a word is Aymara in no way means that it is not also a word in Quechua. Even terms that have a known origin in one language, and are generally considered to belong to that language, might still be used in the other. For example, *pachakuti* is a concept strongly associated with Quechua, but it is not uncommon to see it used in Aymara texts. Likewise, *mallku* is an Aymara word, but its presence in a text does not necessarily rule out the possibility that the language is Quechua.

While there is significant overlap in vocabulary, the suffixes used in each language are much more distinctive (although there are still some minor commonalities). Both Aymara and Quechua are agglutinating languages, and so words are constructed by appending suffixes. Dictionaries of agglutinating languages are particularly hard for non-speakers to use, because fully formed words as they appear in writing will not be found in a dictionary. Without some familiarity with common suffixes, a person does not know what to look up, and is not able to identify the different elements that make up words.

Because of these issues, identifying the language by using a dictionary, without having had any language instruction, was unreasonably difficult and time-consuming. It was largely this dilemma that prompted me to take advantage of the opportunity to study both languages, and being able to distinguish Quechua and Aymara from one another was the primary task that my very basic familiarity allowed me to perform.

Transcribing Bibliographic Data

Identifying the bibliographic elements is most challenging when they are not clearly indicated by the typography and layout of a book's cover and front matter, or when information that is usually found in a particular location is printed somewhere else (for example, the publisher's name is typically at the bottom of the title page, or on its verso).

Before I took Quechua and Aymara classes at Pitt, we had already gained some basic knowledge from experience that helped us to correctly identify different pieces of bibliographic information. For example, it was not uncommon to catalog books that gave their place of publication as "Chuquiago" or "Chukiyawu." This initially required consulting a reference work in order to determine that these are traditional names for La Paz, but it was not difficult to familiarize ourselves with such frequently-occurring terms.

Parallel Titles and Alternate Title Access

Works with "parallel text" in more than one language almost always have parallel titles. The persistent challenge was determining whether a title in Spanish and one in Quechua or Aymara really did say exactly the same thing. However, an error in this area would be less problematic than other kinds of mistakes. A catalog record should provide access to all significant titles of a work, and so even if an entirely different title in Quechua were erroneously coded as if it were a parallel title, users would still be able to find the work by searching for either title.

Variations in spelling and orthography presented an interesting question. Library cataloging attempts to anticipate ways in which searchers might look for an item, and to account for common spelling variations. When cataloging an item with an indigenous-language title based on older spelling conventions, it might be helpful to also include a version of the title using the current unified spelling system. For example, when a title includes the place name "Tiahuanaco," it could be useful to also provide access to the title with it spelled "Tiwanaku." We did not do this at Pitt, and it is not common practice in Latin American materials cataloging in the United States, but it could become a consideration when more indigenous-language materials are collected.

Authority Control

In order to provide access to all of the works by a particular author, catalogers must identify the authority record established for that person or institution and assign the correct name heading. Doing this for personal names can be difficult when the name is common, but the special challenges related to working with indigenous languages are mostly related to headings for institutions (or "corporate bodies," as they are called in cataloging). Assigning the heading for a different institution with a similar name would impede user access, since it would direct users to the works of the wrong institution.

When an authority record for a particular institution has not already been made, the cataloger may need to create one. This must be done with care, because an error in an authority record could affect many other records. At Pitt, situations in which we needed to create "corporate body" authority records for institutions were not common, but did occur. We saw very few names of institutions that were entirely in Quechua or Aymara, but names in Spanish including indigenous-language words were fairly common. For example, I contributed an authority record for the Wayna Tambo, a cultural center housing an important radio station, because several different permutations of its name appeared in different works (Centro Cultural Wayna Tambo, Casa Juvenil de las Culturas "Wayna Tambo").

Subject Analysis

In keeping with the 20% guideline, the subject analysis performed by a cataloger to determine the subject headings and classification number ought to include any sections in an indigenous language unless the proportion of it is very small. For example, say that a book consists of ten essays of roughly equal length, with eight essays in Spanish and two in Aymara, and that four of the Spanish essays are about the efforts to extradite Sánchez de Lozada, three are about the cocalero movement, and one is about the Asamblea Constituyente. In such a case, if neither of the essays in Aymara is about the Asamblea, then a subject heading for that topic might not be assigned because it only represents 10% of the work (of course, a cataloger might choose to provide more detailed subject analysis than the rules require, and at Pitt we often did so for Bolivian materials). But if either of the essays in Aymara was about it, then it would represent 20% or more of the work, and the subject heading would need to be assigned.

At the University of Pittsburgh, the materials that we encountered entirely in Aymara or Quechua tended to be mostly dictionaries and children's books, works with visual clues that helped us discern their subject content. Subject analysis is by far the most difficult task to perform on material in a language that one does not know well. Because of their descriptive nature, titles can be relatively easy to comprehend or translate, but when many pages of text need to be analyzed for subject content, a cataloger without what we call "bibliographic knowledge" of a language would need to spend much more time than is practical.

Conclusion

Given the growing prominence of indigenous culture and peoples in Bolivia and Latin America in general, it seems reasonable to expect that research libraries in the U.S. will collect more indigenous-language materials in coming years. Indeed, anticipating this was another factor that motivated me to take classes in Quechua and Aymara. The immediate need was moderate, but it seems poised to grow with an increase in the quantity of indigenous-language publications, and the numbers of them collected by U.S. research libraries. Indigenous-language Internet sites and resources are also growing in number and libraries with Latin American collections may consider cataloging them as one method to bring them to the attention of their users.

The profession of cataloging widely recognizes that functional familiarity with multiple languages is more useful than complete fluency in a small number. Since the need for catalogers to develop "bibliographic knowledge" of indigenous languages will probably increase, it is fortunate that such an increase in demand would be part of a larger groundswell of cultural output that will likely bring with it both increased academic interest and new opportunities to study indigenous languages.

Contributors

PAULITA AGUILAR, University of New Mexico

SAÚL ARMENDÁRIZ SÁNCHEZ, Universidad Nacional Autónoma de México

WILLIAM BALÉE, Tulane University

ANNE BARNHART, University of West Georgia

AUDRA BELLMORE, University of New Mexico

CLAIRE-LISE BÉNAUD, University of New Mexico

DAVID BLOCK, University of Texas at Austin

DEREK BURDETTE, Tulane University

PETER BUSHNELL, University of Florida

MICAELA CHÁVEZ VILLA, El Colegio de México

VÍCTOR CID CARMONA, El Colegio de México

RICHARD CONWAY, Montclair State University

ALFRED W. CROSBY, University of Texas

MARSHA FORYS, University of Iowa

TINA GROSS, St. Cloud State University

MARK L. GROVER, Brigham Young University

FRANCES KARTTUNEN, University of Texas

MARTHA DAISY KELEHAN, Tufts University

STEVEN KICZEK, San Diego State University

MARK LENTZ, University of Louisiana at Lafayette

MOLLY MOLLOY, New Mexico State University

PENNY C. MORRILL, Independent Scholar

DAVID C. MURRAY, Temple University

GUILLERMO NÁÑEZ-FALCÓN, Tulane University

DAN PETERS, University of Arizona

RICHARD PHILLIPS, University of Florida

KETTY RODRÍGUEZ CASILLAS, Universidad de Puerto Rico, Río Piedras

CHARLES STANFORD, New Mexico State University

DANIEL J. SLIVE, Southern Methodist University

PETER STERN, University of Massachusetts at Amherst

GABRIEL TOTH, Chicago State University

Conference Program

Friday, May 30, 2008

8:00 A.M. –5:00 P.M.	Registration
9:00–11:30 A.M.	Latin American Microforms Project (LAMP)
11:30 A.M.–1:00 P.M.	Lunch
1:00–3:00 P.M.	CALAFIA LANE LASER MOLLAS
3:00–4:00 P.M.	Ibero-American Studies in SALALM (ISiS)
4:00–5:00 P.M.	Academic Latino/a Zone of Action and Research (ALZAR)
5:00–6:00 P.M.	Nominating Medina Award Constitution & Bylaws
5:00–6:00 P.M.	New Members Orientation
6:00–7:00 P.M.	Welcome Happy Hour for New Members & ENLACE *becarios*
7:15–9:30 P.M.	ARL Latin American Research Resources Project (LARRP) Cataloging and Bibliographic Technologies

Saturday, May 31, 2008

8:00 A.M.–5:00 P.M.	Registration
9:00–10:00 A.M.	Marginalized Peoples & Ideas Hispanic American Periodicals Index (HAPI)
10:00–11:00 A.M.	Electronic Resources Cuban Bibliography Policy, Research & Investigation (PRI)
11:00 A.M.–1:00 P.M.	Joint Bibliographic Instruction/Reference Services Finance (I) *Libreros*
1:00–2:00 P.M.	Lunch
3:00–6:00 P.M.	*Libreros*/Librarians Consultations

2:00–3:00 P.M.	Audiovisual-Media
	Gifts & Exchange
	ENLACE
	Official Publications

3:00–4:00 P.M.	Editorial Board
	Membership
	Serials

| 4:00–4:15 P.M. | Coffee Break with *Libreros* |

| 4:00–6:00 P.M. | Executive Board #1 |

Sunday, June 1, 2008

| 8:00 A.M.– 5:00 P.M. | Registration |

8:00–9:00 A.M.	Acquisitions
	Access and Bibliography
	Library Operations and Services
	Interlibrary Cooperation

9:00–10:30 A.M. **Opening Session**
Rapporteur: *David Block*, Cornell University

Welcome Remarks *John B. Wright*, SALALM President, Brigham Young University

Lance D. Query, Dean of Libraries and Information Services, Tulane University

Thomas F. Reese, Executive Director, Stone Center for Latin American Studies, Tulane University

Hortensia Calvo, Director, The Latin American Library & Local Arrangements

Jose Toribio Medina Award Announcement

Keynote Address
Introduction: *John B. Wright*, Brigham Young University

Alfred W. Crosby, University of Texas
"The First Americans"

10:30–11:30 A.M. Book Exhibits Opening Reception

11:30 A.M.–1:15 P.M. **Panel 1: Demography, Ethno-Botany and the Environment**
Moderator: *Lynn Shirey*, Harvard University
Rapporteur: *Jean Dickson*, University at Buffalo, SUNY

William Balée, Tulane University
"A Review of Evidence for Pre-Columbian Banana Cultivation in South America"

Peter Stern, University of Massachusetts at Amherst
"The Berkeley School and the Great Mesoamerican Demographic Debate"

Ketty Rodríguez Casillas, Universidad de Puerto Rico, Río Piedras
"José Celestino Mutis Botanical Expedition: The Origins of Special Librarianship in Latin America?"

Panel 2: Professional Development: Opportunities and Strategies
Moderator: *Orchid Mazurkiewicz,* University of California, Los Angeles
Rapporteur: *Alison Hicks,* The Inter-American Development Bank

Adan Griego, Stanford University
"Opportunities within SALALM and with Other SALALM-like groups"

Marsha Forys, University of Iowa
"Searching for Professional Development Opportunities and Finding HAPIness"

Richard D. Hacken, Brigham Young University
"Publishing Instead of Perishing: Impetus and Ideas for Academic Publishing"

Anne Barnhart, University of California, Santa Barbara
"You can do it all! But Do You Want To?: Strategies for Identifying, Creating and Enjoying Professional Development Activities"

Panel 3: Documenting the Encounter and Exchange *CANCELLED*
Moderator: *Fernando Alvarez,* Library of Congress
Rapporteur: *Tracy North,* Library of Congress

Katherine D. McCann, Library of Congress
"Seeking Sources in HLAS on Ethnohistory and Ethnography"

Barbara Tenenbaum, Library of Congress
"Witnessing the Encounter: The Jay I. Kislak Collection at the Library of Congress"

Georgette M. Dorn, Library of Congress
"Spain's Presence on the 'frontera' and the U.S. War for Independence"

Tracy North, Library of Congress
"Commentary"

1:15–2:30 P.M.   Lunch

2:30–4:15 P.M.   **Panel 4: Gates to the Mayan World**
Moderator: *Margaret Rouse-Jones,* University of the West Indies
Rapporteur: *Elmelinda Lara,* University of the West Indies

Mark L. Grover, Brigham Young University
"William E. Gates and the Collection of Mesoamericana"

Hortensia Calvo, Tulane University
"Deciphering the Collector: The William E. Gates Collection at Tulane University "

Fernando Acosta-Rodríguez, Princeton University
"The Garrett-Gates Mesoamerican Manuscripts Collection at the Princeton University Library"

Russ Taylor, Brigham Young University
"The Last to the Table: BYU's William E. Gates Collection"

Panel 5: Indigenous Latin America in Special Collections: Codices, Chronicles, and Contemporary Rare Books
Moderator: *Martha Daisy Kelehan*, Binghamton University
Rapporteur: *Orchid Mazurkiewicz*, University of California, Los Angeles

Patricia Figueroa, Brown University
"A Stroll Through the Villa Imperial de Potosí"

Daniel J. Slive, University of California, San Diego
"A New World of Words: Amerindian Language Printing in the Colonial World"

Martha Daisy Kelehan, Binghamton University
"French Colonial Perspectives of Indigenous Latin America from the William J. Haggerty Collection of French Colonial History"

Marisol Ramos, University of Connecticut
"Indigenous Voices from Within: Aztec and Mayan Self-Depictions through Pre-Hispanic Codices at the Thomas J. Dodd Research Center"

Panel 6: Librarians and Students: Encounter, Engagement and Exchange
Moderator: *Anne Barnhart*, University of California, Santa Barbara
Rapporteur: *Melissa Gasparotto*, New York University

Jana Krentz, University of Kansas
"Integrating Information Fluency Theory into a Semester-Long Latin American Resources Course"

"LEEPin' Latinamericanistas!: Instructor-Student Reflections on the Online Latin Americanist Librarianship Course"
Participants:
Anne Barnhart, University of California, Santa Barbara
Gabrielle Toth, Chicago State University
Margie Baille, Clarion University
Chely Cantrell, Rosalind Fielder, Noah Lenstra, Tricia Leonard, Emily Shaw, Ricardo Szmetan, University of Illinois Urbana-Champaign
Laura Schmidli, University of Wisconsin

5:00–9:00 P.M.   Host Reception at Latin American Library, Tulane University

Monday, June 2, 2008

7:00–8:00 A.M.   Finance Committee (II)

8:00 A.M.–5:00 P.M.   Book Exhibits

8:00–9:00 A.M.   **General Session**
Introduction: *John B. Wright*, Brigham Young University
Rapporteur: *Sarah Buck Kachaluba*, Florida State University

Frances Karttunen, University of Texas
"Interpreting the Interpreters: Worlds Regarding One Another"

9:00–10:30 A.M.   **Panel 7: Interpreters and Translators**
Moderator: *Melinda Gottesman*, University of Central Florida
Rapporteur: *Philip S. MacLeod*, University of California, Davis

Claire-Lise Benaud and *Paulita Aguilar*, University of New Mexico
"A Late Encounter: The Unusual Friendship of Percy Bigmouth and Martha Gene Neyland Revealed through Their Letters and Stories during the 1940s"

John D. Charles, Tulane University
"Evangelization from Within: The Role of Native Intermediaries in the Making of Colonial Andean Catholicism"

Steven Kiczek, San Diego State University
"Our Lady of Guadalupe: Influence of the Mestizo Icon on Mexico and the Catholic Church"

Panel 8: Native Books and Writing
Moderator: *Ana María Cobos*, Saddleback College
Rapporteur: *Valentino Morales*, El Colegio de México

Víctor Manuel Aguilar Fernández and *Fidelio Quintal Martín*, Universidad Autónoma de Yucatán
"Las crónicas de Chacxulubchen y Yaxkukul: fuentes indígenas de los mayas de Yucatán para comprender la perspectiva del mundo actual"

Saúl Armendáriz Sánchez, Universidad Nacional Autónoma de México
"*In amoxtli, in amoxcalli*: el libro y la biblioteca prehispánica y su influencia en las bibliotecas coloniales en México"

Micaela Chávez Villa and *Víctor Cid Carmona*, El Colegio de México
"Las cartillas de alfabetización en lengua indígena: un intento por rescatar la riqueza lingüística de México"

Panel 9: Louisiana and Latin America: Manuscript and Archival Sources in New Orleans
Moderator: *Theresa Salazar*, University of California, Berkeley
Rapporteur: *Gayle Porter*, Chicago State University

David Dressing, Tulane University
"Indigenous Language Materials of Mesoamerica: The Latin American Library at Tulane"

Alfred Lemmon, The Historic New Orleans Collection
"Latin American Sources at The Historic New Orleans Collection"

Isabel Altamirano, New Orleans Notarial Archives
"Spanish Language Materials in the New Orleans Notarial Archives"

10:30–11:00 A.M.   Coffee Break

11:00 A.M.–12:30 P.M. **Panel 10: Material Aspects of Native Texts: Cataloging, Organization and Research**
Moderator: *Tina Gross*, St. Cloud State University
Rapporteur: *Nancy L. Hallock*, Harvard University

Gabrielle Toth, Chicago State University
"Resources for the Study of Indian Languages in the Chicago Area"

Tina Gross, St. Cloud State University
"*Waquichastati*?: Aymara and Quechua in the Cataloging of Bolivian Materials"

Panel 11: Music and Indigenous Populations
Moderator: *Peter Bushnell*, University of Florida
Rapporteur: *Marne Grinolds*, Ohio University

Alfred Lemmon, The Historic New Orleans Collection
"Latin American Colonial Music: Source for Indian Languages"

Jean Dickson, University at Buffalo, SUNY
"Carlos Curti—Italian, Mexican, American?"

Peter Bushnell, University of Florida
"Carlos Gomes and *O Guaraní*"

Panel 12: Communicative Encounters in Colonial Mexico
Moderator: *Teresa Miguel*, Yale University
Rapporteur: *Bridget Gazzo*, Dumbarton Oaks Research Library

Derek Burdette, Tulane University
"Crosses and the Communication of Catholic Doctrine in
Colonial Mexico"

Mark Lentz, Tulane University
"Colonial Literacy in Yucatec Maya: An Authentic Indigenous Voice, or
Regional Interethnic Lingua Franca?"

Richard Conway, Tulane University
"The Art of Economic Manuscripts: Nahuatl Writing in Land and Tribute
Documents from Central Mexico, 1540-1640"

12:30–1:30 P.M.   Lunch

1:30–3:00 P.M.   Librarian/Bookdealer/Publisher Meeting

3:00–4:15 P.M.   **Panel 13: Accommodation, Resistance and Indian Rights**
Moderator: *Paloma Celis Carbajal*, University of Wisconsin
Rapporteur: *Teresa Miguel*, Yale University

Richard Phillips, University of Florida
"Mariátegui and Indigenous Rights"

Philip Macleod, University of California, Irvine
"Native Accommodation and Resistance to Spanish Rule in Costa Rica,
1560-1750"

Federico Zeballos, Universidad Nacional de Córdoba
"Biblioteca y dictadura militar en Córdoba, 1976-1983"

Panel 14: Deciphering and Interpreting the Record: Texts of the Maya
Moderator: *Guillermo Náñez-Falcón*, Tulane University
Rapporteur: *Michael Scott*, Yale University

Victoria R. Bricker, Tulane University
"The Contributions of Indigenous Maya Documents to the History of
Writing and Languages"

Judith M. Maxwell, Tulane University
"Translating Colonial Kaqchikel Documents with De-Colonizing
Kaqchikel Speakers"

3:00–4:15 P.M.   **Panel 15: What Do Libraries Want Now?: Identifying Book Dealer Services to Support New Workflows and Staffing Models**
Moderator: *David Block*, Cornell University
Rapporteur: *Geoff West*, The British Library

David Block, Cornell University
"Where We Are; Where May We Be Going; and What Can We Do There?"

Edmundo Flores, Library of Congress
"How to Make the Most of Suppliers to Meet Changing Librarian and User Needs"

Scott Wicks, Cornell University
"From Pie in the Sky to the Tech Services Table: Services Academic Libraries Want from Their Vendors"

4:15–4:45 P.M.   Coffee Break

4:45–6:00 P.M.   **Panel 16: The Supplements to *The Handbook of Middle American Indians*: The New Guide to Ethnohistorical Sources**
Moderator: *Adán Benavides*, University of Texas at Austin
Rapporteur: *Cecilia Sercán*, Cornell University

Michel Oudijk, Universidad Nacional Autónoma de México
"Supplements to *The Handbook of Middle American Indians: The New Guide to Ethnohistorical Sources*"

Panel 17: Syncopating History: Jazz and Latin America
Moderator: *Laura D. Shedenhelm*, University of Georgia
Rapporteur: *Gabrielle Toth*, Chicago State University

Bruce Raeburn, Tulane University
"Beyond the 'Latin Tinge': Hispanics and Latinos in Early New Orleans Jazz"

Nicolás Rossi, Libros argentinos para todo el mundo
"Jazz in 1960s Buenos Aires: Remembrances of an *Aficionado*"

Panel 18: Outreach, Diversity and Services
Moderator: *Alma C. Ortega*, University of San Diego
Rapporteur: *Ellen Jaramillo*, Yale University

Molly Molloy and *Charles Stanford*, New Mexico State University
"The Esther Chávez Cano Collection: An Archival Record of Violence against Women in the U.S.-Mexico Border and a Tool for Scholars and Activists"

Alma C. Ortega, University of San Diego and *Marisol Ramos*, University of Connecticut
"Librarians Casting the Net: Outreach to Latin-American Students and Latino Students in Academia"

Margarita Vannini, Universidad Centroamericana-Managua
"El Tren Cultural de la Alfabetización"

7:00–10:00 P.M.   *Libreros'* Reception at the Louis XVI Restaurant

Tuesday, June 3, 2008

8:00 A.M.–3:00 P.M.   Book Exhibits

8:30–10:15 A.M.   **Panel 19: Inspiration & Agency: Native New World Contributions to the Arts**
Moderator: *Ellen Jaramillo*, Yale University
Rapporteur: *Katherine D. McCann*, Library of Congress

Penny C. Morrill, independent scholar
"The Pre-Conquest Aesthetic in Modern Mexican Silver"

Audra Bellmore, University of New Mexico
"The Spanish Pueblo Revival Style: Blending Native and New World Design in Early 20th Century New Mexico"

Maya Stanfield, Tulane University
"Agency and the Indigenous Art Collector in Colonial Peru"

Panel 20: Libraries and Library Services in the Post-Katrina Gulf Region
Moderator: *Peter T. Johnson*, Princeton University
Rapporteur: *Molly Molloy*, New Mexico State University

Lance Query, Tulane University
"Libraries in the Wake of Disaster: Lessons Learned from Katrina"

Andrew Corrigan, Tulane University
"In the Event of an Actual Disaster: Large-Scale Collections Recovery in New Orleans"

Sharman Bridges Smith, Mississippi Library Commission
"How the Past Affects the Future of Library Services in Post-Katrina Mississippi"

Panel 21: Indigenous Latin America in Film: Current and Historical Perspectives
Moderator: *Jesús Alonso-Regalado*, University at Albany, SUNY
Rapporteur: *Sócrates Silva*, University of California, Los Angeles

Gayle Williams, Florida International University
"The Indigenous Presence in Mexican Film"

Shana Higgins, University of Redlands
"Hollywood's Native Encounters: Representations of Latin America's Indigenous Peoples in U.S. Mainstream Cinema"

David C. Murray, Temple University
"No Maya Libraries?: Representation in and Reception of Mel Gibson's *Apocalypto*"

10:15–10:45 A.M.   Coffee Break

10:45 A.M.–12:30 P.M. **Panel 22: Early and Late Encounters: the Old World and the New**
Moderator: *Geoff West*, The British Library
Rapporteur: *Bridget Gazzo*, Dumbarton Oaks Research Library

Geoff West, The British Library
"Lost for Words: The Earliest Representations of the Americas in Spanish Sources"

Blanche T. Ebeling-Koning, Independent Scholar
"The Dutch West India Company in Brazil: Images and Maps from the Governor's History of His Eight-Years' Rule of the Colony"

Wilbur Meneray, Tulane University
"European and First Nations: Relations in the Southeast during the 18th Century"

Guillermo Náñez-Falcón, Tulane University
"The Lure of the Kekchí: A German Entrepreneur Becomes a Mayanist"

Panel 23: Archiving of Electronic Journals: Problems and Issues
Moderator: *Rhonda Neugebauer*, University of California, Riverside
Rapporteur: *Donna Canevari de Paredes*, University of Saskatchewan

Ken DiFiore, Portico
"Responding to the Digital Preservation Challenge: One Approach to Preserving E-Journals"

Vicky Reich, Stanford University and *Ruby Gutierrez*, University of California, Los Angeles
"It Takes a Community: Building and Preserving Important Hispanic Digital Collections"

Ruby Gutierrez, University of California, Los Angeles
"E-Journals and the Archival World: Perspectives from Latin America"

Panel 24: Latinos in New Orleans
Moderator: *Fernando Acosta-Rodríguez*, Princeton University
Rapporteur: *Holly Ackerman*, Duke University

James D. Huck, Jr. Tulane University
"Civic Engagement in New Orleans: Challenges for the Latino Community"

Martín Gutiérrez, Hispanic Apostolate, Archdiocese of New Orleans, New Orleans
"A Glance at the Hispanic Community Pre/Post Katrina and Its Most Pressing Challenges"

Cynthia M. Ceballos, Esq., Hispanic Chamber of Commerce of Louisiana
"Our Part in the Recovery: The Work of the HCCL on Behalf of the Hispanic Community"

12:30–1:30 P.M.	Lunch
1:30–2:30 P.M.	**General Session** Introduction: *John B. Wright*, Brigham Young University Rapporteur: *Sarah Yoder Leroy,* University of Pittsburgh *Dan Peters*, Novelist and Visiting Scholar, University of Arizona "Incidents of Travel & Research into the Pre-Columbian Past"
2:30–3:00 P.M.	**Town Hall Meeting & Announcement of New Officers**
3:00–4:00 P.M.	**Business Meeting and Closing Session**
3:00 P.M.	Book Exhibits Close
4:00–6:00 P.M.	Executive Board (II)